William F. Cody's Wyoming Empire

William F. Cody's Wyoming Empire

The Buffalo Bill Nobody Knows

Robert E. Bonner

University of Oklahoma Press : Norman

Library of Congress Cataloging-in-Publication Data

Bonner, Robert, 1938–
    William F. Cody's Wyoming empire : the Buffalo Bill nobody knows / Robert E.
Bonner. — 1st ed.
        p.   cm.
    Includes bibliographical references and index.
    ISBN 978-0-8061-3829-9 (hardcover : alk. paper) 1. Buffalo Bill, 1846–1917.
2. Pioneers—Bighorn Basin (Mont. and Wyo.)—Biography. 3. Pioneers—
Wyoming—Biography. 4. Frontier and pioneer life—Bighorn Basin (Mont. and
Wyo.) 5. Frontier and pioneer life—Wyoming. 6. Bighorn Basin (Mont. and
Wyo.)—History—19th century. 7. Bighorn Basin (Mont. and Wyo.)—Economic
conditions—19th century. I. Title.
    F594.B622B66   2007
    978'.02092—dc22
    [B]
                                                                    2007005381

The paper in this book meets the guidelines for permanence and durability of the
Committee on Production Guidelines for Book Longevity of the Council on
Library Resources, Inc. ∞

1 2 3 4 5 6 7 8 9 10

For Barbara

"The General . . . always insisted that, if you bring off adequate preservation of your personal myth, nothing much else in life matters. It is not what happens to people that is significant, but what they think happens to them."

Anthony Powell, *Books Do Furnish a Room*

Contents

Illustrations

PHOTOGRAPHS

MAPS

Acknowledgments

Since I first became aware that there would be a book at the end of this road, I have looked forward to thanking the people who have so generously helped me along the way. Historians may in some respects be the last of the preindustrial artisans, but we live and work among a scholarly culture of librarians, archivists, and other historians, and we always need a little help from our friends, scholarly or otherwise.

I began this book with a sabbatical year's research mostly in Wyoming, but also in Denver and Washington, D.C. My mother, Nancy Bonner, allowed her first-born son back into her home for a large part of that year, and then my sister, Barbara Luther, and her family sheltered me in Cheyenne. My brother, Dave Bonner, provided valuable assistance that year and in subsequent visits to the Big Horn Basin. Dear friends John and Marian Gruenfelder in Laramie, Bob and Judy Thompson in Denver, and Dick and Barbara Jorgensen in Washington, D.C., took care of me at various times in that year, enabling me to work productively as I learned this new field. Without their generosity I do not know how I could have done it.

My first and most enduring obligations are to the archivists and librarians who opened the mysteries of their collections to me. It began with Paul Fees and Frances Clymer at the Buffalo Bill Historical Center in Cody, and later Juti Winchester, Sarah Boehme, and especially Mary Robinson never failed to answer questions or to run down citations or photographs. Ann Marie Donoghue and Heidi Kennedy have worked hard getting photographs for me. Jeannie Cook, Lynn Houze (since moved to the BBHC), and Marylin Schulz at the Park County Archives in Cody, have provided me manuscripts and photographs and pursued all manner of telephone inquiries for me. At the Wyoming State Archives in Cheyenne, senior historian Cindy Brown has been the rock upon which this book was built, both when I have been there and when I have needed help at long distance. The staff of the American Heritage Center in Laramie, particularly John Waggener, Carol Bowers, Ginny Kilander, Leslie Shores, and Rick Ewig have been consistently helpful. Joan Howard and her successors at the Rocky Mountain Branch of the National Archives, and countless staff at the National Archives in Washington, D.C., the Newberry Library in Chicago, the Nebraska State Historical Scoiety, and the Western History Collection at the Denver Public Library have helped me find my way through the enormous collections they tend. Laura Foster at the Frederic Remington Art Museum in Ogdensburg, New York, Darlene Leonard at the St. Lawrence University Archives, Canton, New York, and Betsy Martinson and her staff at the Buffalo Bill Museum and Grave Archives, Golden, Colorado, gave me important assistance at critical points along the way, as did George Miles at the Beinecke Rare Book and Manuscript Library at Yale University, Bill Slaughter at the Latter-Day Saints Archives in Salt Lake City, Ellen Cone Busch at the Planting Fields Arboretum in Oyster Bay, New York (the ancestral home of W. R. Coe), and Steve Johnson at the Wildlife Conservation Society in New York City. Without the work of these people I would never have been able to start, let alone finish, a project like this.

Many who are not attached to libraries or archives have supported my research when I crossed into their territory. John Shields and Leah Bratton of the Wyoming State Engineer's office have given me important pieces of information on old water projects. Lee Ballinger and Jerry Bales, successive managers of the Cody Canal, helped me to understand the ditch and the country it runs through. Shawn Orbanick, currently the secretary of the Camp Fire Club in Chappaqua, New York, helped me with inquiries about Cody's connections to that organization. Bob Thompson took two days out of his life to work as apprentice researcher for me in the manuscripts at the Buffalo Bill Museum and Grave. Roger Hollander, current owner of Bill Cody's first ranch on Carter Mountain, gave me his time and assistance, including the loan of a four-wheeler, as

I set out to learn that site. Professor Michael Coe at Yale and Mrs. H. R. Coe of Cody, both members of the family founded by W. R. Coe, gave me time and important pieces of information. Former U.S. Senator Alan K. Simpson allowed me access to his family's papers at the American Heritage Center.

Carleton College has been a wonderful place to work for nearly forty years, and has been especially helpful to me with this project since I retired, providing an office and small grants for research and manuscript preparation. Neither the college nor the Department of History attempted to deflect me as I began the shift from English and European history to the American West; indeed, they found ways to encourage me and to turn my career change into a source of strength for all concerned. I consider myself very fortunate to have lived and worked here. In addition to support from Carleton, I have been privileged to receive two travel grants from the Fred C. Garlow Fund at the Buffalo Bill Historical Center and one from the American Heritage Center. In the fall of 2003 I held the Archibald Hanna, Jr., Fellowship at the Beinecke Rare Book and Manuscript Library at Yale University.

I have felt blessed by my new colleagues in the Western History Association. Coming into this work late in life, without any kind of track record, I was made to feel at home by Richard White, Patty Limerick, Don Worster, Don Pisani, Bill Rowley, Paul Hutton, Peter Iverson, and countless others. Conversations with fellow western historians like Dick Orsi, Mark Fiege, Judy Austin, Janet Ore, Laura Woodworth-Ney, Carroll Van West, Bill Lang, Bill Robbins, and John Faragher have helped me and this book take shape. Good friends Kirk Jeffrey, Peter Iverson, Michael Brodhead, Paul Fees, and T. J. Stiles read all or part of the manuscript, offering equal measures of encouragement and suggestions for improvement. Other good friends who know the West but pursue its literature instead of its history, Mike Kowalewski and Dan O'Brien, have talked with me far into many nights as I have shaped this book. I am rich in friends indeed.

Readers of this book will see immediately that I owe a particular debt to the work of my friend Louis Warren. His *Buffalo Bill's America*, published in 2005, established a new benchmark for work in this corner of the history of the American West. I have happily borrowed some of his ideas to support some of my own, and have offered in return some conclusions that differ from or extend some of his. I hope it is a fair trade.

Portions of several chapters have appeared previously. My article, "Buffalo Bill Cody and Wyoming Water Politics," published in the winter 2002 issue of the *Western Historical Quarterly*, 433–51, covered much of the same ground as chapter 10. The article is copyrighted by the Western History Association, and the material is used here by permission. Another article, "Elwood Mead, Buffalo Bill Cody, and the Carey Act in Wyoming," which was published in *Montana: The Magazine of Western History* in the spring 2005 issue, touches upon issues discussed in Chapters 2, 4, and 5. The journal has given me permission to publish.

The process of making a book out of what I wrote has brought me into contact with people of great talent and experience at the University of Oklahoma Press. Chuck Rankin took the manuscript in and helped me shape it in the early stages. Jay Dew, Jay Fultz, and Christi Madden have worked thoughtfully and carefully with me to get the book into a shape we could all be proud of. My friend and colleague, Tsegaye Nega, made a map of the Big Horn Basin, upon which the staff of the Press have built the map that appears here.

One debt is so great that a paragraph of acknowledgment can only begin to suggest it. Barbara and I have lived together now for forty-five years, through something more than the usual ups and downs of a long marriage. We have loved each other through many joys and repeated losses almost too painful to bear. She has helped me learn more than I probably wanted to know about living rightly. As a daughter of the West (Belle Fourche, South Dakota) she has welcomed my career shift, even when it has meant my being away for months at a time. And as a professional editor she has given my manuscript its most valuable reading. The dedication of this book to her is a small recompense for what she has meant to it and to me.

Introduction

This book took me by surprise. Although I grew up in the Big Horn Basin of Wyoming, surrounded on all sides by the legacy of Buffalo Bill Cody—perhaps, indeed, because of that experience—devoting any portion of my life to the study of this man was never part of my plan as a historian. In fact, I began my professional life as a student of British and European history, and worked more or less contentedly in those fields for twenty-five years. It was only in the early 1990s, when a major dislocation in my personal life led to a time of professional reassessment, that I first envisioned the journey that would lead to this book. Lying in bed just before sunrise on a summer morning in Belle Fourche, South Dakota, in the summer of 1990, in that state of liminal consciousness between sleep and wakefulness, I saw the opening sentence of Fernand Braudel's great book on the Mediterranean world in the age of Philip II unscroll inside my eyelids: "I have loved the Mediterranean with passion. . . ."[1] Before I fully awakened, I asked myself what it was I had loved as much as Braudel had loved the Mediterranean, and answered, "the land of the upper Yellowstone River basin." By breakfast time I had reorganized my life as a historian.

There remained an enormous stretch of ground to be covered, of course. I undertook a complete retraining, learning a new field and setting up a program of research. Having determined to return to the land I had known as a child and young man, I began to study the Big Horn Basin in the twentieth century. Buffalo Bill was not even on my horizon when I started out. I began with water, as life and history in a semiarid country must. In the course of learning something about water law and water development in Wyoming at the turn of the twentieth century, a strange and unexpected thing happened: wherever I turned, it seemed, I found myself face-to-face with William F. Cody. I found him where I would have expected to find him, but he also surprised me by showing up in different places, doing and saying things that seemed inconsistent with what I had read about him. I have fished and hunted, walked and driven the length and breadth of the ground Cody worked upon, and while that helped me in a myriad of ways with the details of this book, nothing prepared me for the totality of it. The common understanding of the work of Bill Cody as an actor away from the Wild West stage is no deeper among people who have grown up in Wyoming than it is in the country at large. I was meeting the Buffalo Bill nobody knows.

As I came to know this person and the world in which he worked, it became important to me to introduce others to him. Consequently, I set aside for a time my larger project of writing the environmental history of the rivers, mountains, and valleys of northwest Wyoming, and devoted myself to this new acquaintance. I thought it would be a short detour and a small book, but once again I was to be surprised. Four years and four hundred manuscript pages later, here we are. I no longer think of it as a detour. This work has brought me closer to knowing the interplay between nature and culture along the Shoshone River, which was always one of my goals. I have not reached the point where I could have answered my Braudel question by affirming great affection for Bill Cody, but nothing in this work has diluted or deflected my passion for the history I first embarked upon. I am as committed as I ever was to Braudel's identification of passion as the fountainhead of historical creativity. Everyone knows Buffalo Bill was a major figure in the cultural history of nineteenth-century America. A chance to look at him from the Wyoming point of view, with a Wyoming heart if you will, shows him to be a unique and meteoric figure in the history of the Big Horn Basin, but confused in his life and perplexing in the trail he left behind.

Although he has been the subject of hundreds of dime novels, countless stories and films, and dozens of more or less formal biographies, there remains a hole in the life of William F. Cody. That hole is the Big Horn Basin, the large corner of Wyoming that he called home for the last twenty years of his life, and where he poured out so much of his energy and worldly substance in pursuit of success in an entirely new line of work, that of empire-building in the undeveloped West. He talked constantly about Wyoming, by which he almost always meant the Big Horn Basin, as he traveled back and forth across America and Europe with his Wild West shows after 1895, but those who have undertaken to write the story of his life have often ignored Wyoming in assessing its meaning. Most biographers have understood very poorly just what Buffalo Bill did in Wyoming. Louis Warren, whose *Buffalo Bill's America* is the most recent account of Cody's life, pays more attention to the years and work that Cody devoted to Wyoming, and understands it better than any of his predecessors, but his fascination with the Wild West experience and Cody's life on the national stage ultimately prevents him from filling this hole. There still remains a need to understand Bill Cody on the ground in Wyoming, to come to know what he did and what he did not do there, and what it all might mean to our understanding of this man and the history of western America around the turn of the twentieth century.

In 1895, Buffalo Bill Cody was perhaps the most famous American alive, thanks to a lifetime of promotion that began when E. C. Z. Judson (Ned Buntline) wrote a book titled *Buffalo Bill, King of the Border Men*, in 1869. Three years later, when Cody was only twenty-six years old, the book was produced as a stage play in New York; Cody even appeared at a production of it. In 1871, when Cody was serving as chief of scouts for the Fifth Cavalry, General Phil Sheridan detailed him to guide a group of New York hunters who came west for some sport. He was already a famous personality as well as an experienced hunter, guide and scout, and a tall, handsome, engaging man into the bargain. Aware of the potential of his emerging fame, he founded a stage career of his own beginning in 1873, and for the next few years alternated between summer work with the army on the plains and winter tours of theaters in the East. By the end of that decade, the lure of show business overcame him: he published an autobiography and then turned full time to dramatic promotions. In partnership with Nate Salsbury after 1883 in the famous Wild West show, he made a name and a fortune that marked him as one of the great successes of the nineteenth century. He became the man who entertained (and, he would claim, educated) people of all classes, including royalty, all across America and Europe. Not bad for a fellow born in a cabin on the Iowa side of the Mississippi in 1846.[2]

When he first came to Wyoming with investment on his mind he
was in his prime: forty-seven years old, wealthy, the most famous avatar
of the Old West, yet still restless for accomplishment. In 1893, when the
Wild West was installed in Chicago, profiting from the traffic to the
Columbian Exhibition, he had taken in more money than in any previous year with his show. He was looking now to make a mark on the
New West. A nearly unbroken run of public success must have made him
feel invincible at whatever he chose to take on, or he would not have
chosen the course he did. He had already begun to think of irrigation
development and colonization in North Platte, Nebraska, where he had
ranched since the late 1870s. An attempt to build a canal there and attract
a colony of Quakers to cultivate the land did not succeed, although he
and his partner did manage to get about a third of the land on their
project irrigated. Whatever problems he encountered there were not sufficient to deter him, and he clearly did not take the time to investigate
the checkered history of private irrigation development in the West. The
fact that his wife, Louisa, was installed at his ranch near North Platte and
their relationship was breaking down added another reason, if one was
needed, to look west to new land for the next stage of his life.[3]

Don Russell titled his biography *The Lives and Legends of Buffalo Bill*
in implicit recognition of how difficult it is to pin down even the simple
facts of Bill Cody's life. So many people have spoken and written so
much about him, much of which is in conflict, that writing about him
is a constant process of sorting wheat from chaff. The surface of Russell's
text displays this sifting on every page. Famous as Buffalo Bill was, there
are parts of his life that remain obscure. The Wyoming phase is probably
better documented than many other areas, due to the determination of
his partner, George Beck, to file and keep virtually all the correspondence
that Cody and others wrote to him on the business of development and
colonization in Wyoming. Cody seems to have kept very few letters of
the thousands that were written to him; where Beck's determination to
keep the records does not touch we find many an empty space. Still, it
is frequently possible to pin him down long enough to glimpse the
man himself at work. This book sets out, through detailed examination
of Cody's work in Wyoming during the last two decades of his life, to
fill out the biographical record and to do it in such a way that his ordinary
human aspirations and activities shoulder aside the myths surrounding
him. In Wyoming we find this gigantic personality, in many ways a creation

of his own publicity, struggling to find a way to work with other men in the hard-edged world where success does not depend on acclaim. Neither the human nor the natural environment in which he set his mission proved particularly compliant, and his success was ultimately ambiguous, but those years furnish us with a story as good as anything told in the Wild West show.

The other men who worked with Bill Cody in Wyoming have remained for the most part unnamed, but it should go without saying that he never worked alone. He was brought into the Big Horn Basin by George Beck and Horace Alger, Sheridan businessmen who remained important partners in the company that built the Cody Canal and the town of Cody. When all is taken into account, one might even conclude that Beck was more important to the founding and growth of the town of Cody than was its namesake. Cody's Wild West partner Nate Salsbury, as well as George Bleistein and Bronson Rumsey, two businessmen in Buffalo, New York, were also of great importance in the story of the Big Horn Basin in those years. Elwood Mead, who ended his life and career as commissioner of the federal Bureau of Reclamation (and for whom Lake Mead is named), was Wyoming state engineer when Colonel Cody moved into the state. He and other leaders of the state engaged with Cody in many different ways as the celebrity morphed into the developer; their work shaped the outcomes as much as Cody's did. Buffalo Bill did a lot on his own to shape the economy and society of that corner of Wyoming, but his ability—or, too frequently, his inability—to work with others went a long way to determining his success.

When most Americans think of Buffalo Bill Cody, they see him through the lens of what Louis Warren calls his "frontier imposture." Warren invented this striking term to underline the element of theatrical self-presentation that Cody and others (less successfully) used to make a living at the end of the nineteenth century.[4] It is impossible to escape this element of Cody's life; by the time he came to Wyoming the character of "Buffalo Bill" was so thoroughly embedded in the identity of William F. Cody that separation was out of the question. The imposture was not just a role he played, it was part of his character. An attempt to look at Cody's life in Wyoming through some other lens, to see him, for instance as a corporation president intent on maximizing his business profit, can never succeed if the goal is to block out what we see through the first lens. He was a complex man, and his life should be approached with respect for that complexity. This means that we must necessarily look at him with both these lenses and perhaps some others.

William F. Cody brought a big package with him when he came to Wyoming. His immense success as Buffalo Bill had made him wealthy and famous in all corners of the nation. He had developed personal relationships with the elite of American political and economic life. There had also grown in him, however, a sense of his own ability and importance that was out of all proportion to his actual experience. The Big Horn Basin was not a stage or a show arena, and the development business in the West had left a lot of broken men scattered over the landscape. Constructing an irrigation system, attracting settlers to a new colony in the Far West, founding a town, and negotiating the thickets of government and politics required skills that Buffalo Bill had never needed to make his way in show business. His attempts to meet these challenges will show us a view of this conflicted giant of a man that can be found nowhere else, and open up as well the history of one of the last corners of the Old West.

William F. Cody's Wyoming Empire

CHAPTER ONE

Coming into the Basin

The Big Horn Basin is one of the dominant land forms in the northwest quadrant of Wyoming. Seen from above, it is a vast trough, roughly a hundred miles north to south and seventy east to west, lying between the Absaroka and Owl Creek mountain ranges on the west and the Big Horn Mountains on the east. The Big Horn Mountains are the eastern-most rampart of the Rocky Mountains; Yellowstone Park and Jackson Hole border the Basin on the west. The Basin derives its name from the Big Horn River running northward along its eastern edge, carrying all the water of the Basin off to join the Yellowstone River in southern Montana. The Big Horn actually begins as the Wind River, high up in the mountains of the same name, west and south of the Basin. It has cut two spectacular canyons, the Wind River Canyon at the southern end of the Basin (where the Wind loses that name and takes on the other) and the Big Horn Canyon on the north. People entering the Basin, however, rarely came through the canyons, following instead established trails over one or another of the mountain ranges or through the wide, easy pass at the north end. Two mountain rivers, the Shoshone (once the Stinking Water, so named for the sulphur hot springs near its own canyon on the western edge of the Basin) and the Greybull, drain west to east into the Big Horn, falling from above 5,000 feet altitude to below 4,000 in the fifty miles. The Basin is semiarid, with annual precipitation ranging from twelve or fourteen inches on the western slopes to six inches on the floor. Aboriginal human populations were never high in this environment,

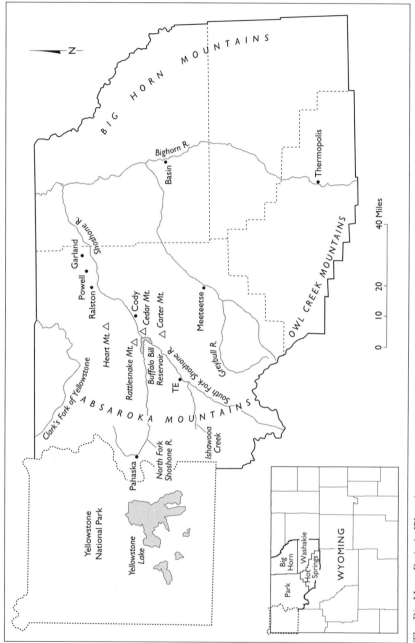

The Big Horn Basin in Wyoming.

although the first white explorers reported reasonably good populations of game along the rivers and up the valleys on the sides of the Basin.[1] Crow hunters would come down from the Yellowstone valley to hunt occasionally, and Shoshone and Bannock hunters would come east from their mountain homes to pursue the small buffalo herd, but none lived there routinely.

When and under what circumstances did Buffalo Bill first enter into the Big Horn Basin of Wyoming? It seems such a simple question, but in pursuit of an answer the historian must work through a bewildering variety of statements masquerading as answers. As a scout with the army in the decade after the Civil War, Cody no doubt learned the oral histories of the traders and trappers who had first described the interior West. John Colter, one of the first generation of mountain men, had been the first white American to enter the Basin, and he left a lot of stories behind.[2] Although Cody conducted his scouting mostly on the plains of Kansas and Nebraska until the Big Horn Expedition of 1874, he would have heard of the mountain trails; he probably knew, for instance, of the road Jim Bridger had marked into and through the Basin during the Red Cloud wars, as a safer route to the Montana gold fields than the Bozeman Trail had become.[3] Cody claimed in a newspaper interview in 1910 to have guided Yale paleontologist Othniel C. Marsh into the Basin in 1870, and consequently to have learned of its great agricultural potential. The fact is, however, that he was taken off that assignment just as it began and spent only one day with Marsh. He appears to have learned something about the geology of Wyoming around Marsh's campfire, but it was unlikely to have been specific to the Big Horn Basin, as Marsh probably never set foot in the Basin. They did form a friendship that endured at least a few years and probably included informal geological tutorials, including the idea that Wyoming's wide basins had once been the floor of an inland sea, a foundation idea of Cody's vision of agricultural development. The trail Cody claimed to remember taking into the Basin was Bridger's, which might mean he had planned to travel that way forty years earlier. It seems clear that he knew something and learned some more about the Basin in the early 1870s, but almost certainly he did not enter it at that time.[4]

Helen Cody Wetmore's adoring 1899 biography contains a pair of fables touching upon the question. The first is an account of how Bill heard of the Big Horn Basin, with its perfect weather, its healing waters, its abundance of game and grass, and all other creaturely comforts, from an Arapaho warrior in 1875. The Arapaho called the Basin "Eithity Tugala," the place on earth closest to heaven. She goes on to describe an 1882 trip Cody supposedly took over the Big Horns with an "exploring party." His eyes were inflamed and bandaged, so he rode with them while relying on another guide. At a point where they could see the Basin, Bill took off the bandages and drank in the unmatchable beauty of the place, with its distinctive landmarks, carpets of wildflowers, silver streams, and myriad of animals and birds.

This account is problematic from start to finish. Cody could have learned something from an Arapaho whom he met, although it does not seem likely. The Arapahos ranged generally south of the North Platte River, hundreds of miles to the south, and the Big Horn Basin was traditionally Crow hunting ground. A more telling objection is that the conversation, as related by sister Helen, reads more like a press agent's creation than a historical document, at once superlative in its adjectives and devoid of supportable facts. Her account of Cody's first vision of the Basin is even less believable. In the first place, the aspect of the Big Horn Basin most evident to a traveler on the crest of the Big Horns is its vastness and its aridity. Moreover, by 1882 his exploring days, such as they might have been, were far behind him. When we remember that this book, titled *Last of the Great Scouts*, was written for sale at Wild West performances, and that in 1899 Bill was actively promoting settlement in the Basin through his Wild West press agency, no reason remains to believe any particular thing in the book. It is part of that great cloud of make-believe that attended Buffalo Bill wherever he went in those days, until he himself was clearly confused about what he had done and where he had been.[5]

How much he might have seen of the Basin in 1874 we cannot say, but it is clear from the record of the Big Horn Expedition led by Captain Anson Mills in the autumn of that year that he crossed enough of the Big Horn Mountains to find the headwaters of the Nowood River, which joins the Big Horn River from the east in the central part of the Basin. Cody was scouting out a route by which the detachment hoped to surprise a group of Indians they were pursuing, but found that this stream was going to take them too far west, so they doubled back and found another way along the top of the mountains. This expedition crossed—and knew they crossed—Bridger's wagon road to Montana, so there can be little doubt that Cody had the Big Horn Basin on his mental map in 1874.[6]

Elwood Mead, Wyoming's first state engineer, who went on to serve as the first commissioner of the Bureau of Reclamation, appears to have been responsible for another bit of confusion on Cody's entry into the Basin. In their obituary published at Mead's death in 1936, two of his Reclamation associates credited him with intimate knowledge of the Wyoming backcountry, gained in part from a trip through the mountains with Buffalo Bill in 1888. In fact, Cody spent half of 1888 in Europe and did not even return as far west as Nebraska until mid-November. He did not see Wyoming at all that year. Careful collation of Mead's and Cody's known activities in those years leads to the conclusion that the commissioner's recollection in old age, expressed perhaps in conversation with his staff on one trip or another, must have been off by a few years. They were almost certainly not together in the Wyoming mountains until 1895.[7]

Buffalo Bill's life as a frontiersman came to an end after the Big Horn and Yellowstone Expedition of 1876, in which he stayed well to the east and north of the Big Horn Basin itself. For the next fifteen years he pursued his show business interests in the East and in Europe and his ranching interests in Nebraska. Home life with his wife, Louisa, seems to have deteriorated steadily during that time, and he began to think of alternative arrangements. It was probably inevitable that his eyes should have turned west. As the Burlington and Missouri River Railroad pushed its rails west and north from Nebraska, Cody's attention was pulled that way. His son-in-law, Horton Boal, having failed as the manager of Bill's North Platte ranch, took Cody's daughter, Arta, on the new train to Sheridan, Wyoming, in 1893. Tired of North Platte and always on the lookout for investment opportunities, Bill himself had already looked into Sheridan. Soon after the Burlington arrived there, in 1892, he had formed the W. F. Cody Hotel Co. His company furnished the new hotel the Burlington had constructed near its depot in Sheridan, and hired one of Cody's cronies from Omaha, George Canfield, to manage it. Cody also opened up a transportation company to take advantage of the railroad's presence.[8]

Sheridan in 1893 was a rough frontier town. Legend has it that Cody would sit on the porch of the Sheridan Inn and audition ropers and riders for the upcoming season of the Wild West. But Sheridan had also attracted a group of men who were interested in building up the country and making some money. Prominent among this group was the young son of a U.S. senator from Kentucky, George Washington Thornton Beck. Beck had come west initially in search of gold, but gave it up in deference to his father's wishes. Still determined to live in the West, he eventually made his way to the Big Horn Mountains, where a family friend, Colonel Nelson A. Miles, had suggested he might make a good living as a rancher. That was in 1879, when he was twenty-three years old. He set up with a friend as a sheep rancher, and soon ran the largest flocks in northern Wyoming. After ten years, he sold out in 1889 at a good profit. He had manipulated the public land laws to great profit, taking up as many homestead, timber culture, and desert land claims as he could manage in his own name and those of family and friends. He became a successful farmer as well as a sheep rancher, and even set up northern Wyoming's first flour mill at a town called Beckton. When he gave up ranching he began to invest in towns, first Buffalo and then Sheridan. His family's political tradition was deep and strong—in addition to his father the senator, he counted George Washington himself as a great-grand uncle. He was a member of Wyoming's last territorial legislature in 1889, where he was elected president of the Council. He was an unsuccessful candidate for Congress, running as a Democrat in Republican Wyoming, the first year of statehood. In 1902 he would be the Democratic candidate for governor; although he lost again, friends and associates commonly referred to him as "Governor" for the rest of his days. Beck was, then, a man of substance and wide experience, though only thirty-six years old, when he first made the acquaintance of William F. Cody.[9]

One of the interests that Beck turned to was mining. During the fateful year of 1893 he was looking into setting up a gold mine on Bald Mountain, atop the Big Horns, when he was approached by an old man who had walked up the mountain from the Basin side. This man, Labin Hillsberry, was himself a prospector, but in this case he was looking for financing for a water development. He described the Stinking Water country to Beck and sketched out the possibilities for irrigation from the South Fork of that river above Cedar Mountain, which was clearly visible from Bald Mountain on the Big Horns, although sixty miles away. Beck sent a friend, Jerry Ryan, with a wagon to take Hillsberry back and look at the country for him. When Ryan reported that autumn that it looked good to him, Beck began to prepare for a serious reconnaissance.[10]

Beck and Cody surely met in Sheridan, perhaps even at the Sheridan Inn, as early as 1893. There are stories of Cody taking hunting parties into the Big Horn Mountains and stopping at Beck's ranch on the way back to Sheridan to drink mint juleps made in water buckets. One of Cody's biographers hints at an earlier acquaintance, noting the presence of "the wife of George T. Beck of Wyoming" at Cody's North Platte ranch in the summer of 1888, when Arta was living there.[11] If Beck was married that early, no record of it shows up in Johnson or Sheridan counties; I have seen no evidence of his being married before 1896. There may, however, have been some prior connection between the Cody and Beck families, for the newly arrived Horton Boal was one of the party that Beck took into the Big Horn Basin in the summer of 1894 to look into irrigation development possibilities along the Stinking Water River. Beck's partner, Sheridan banker Horace Alger, had already agreed to pay Hillsberry $2,000 for the water right he had secured in 1893. The entire party consisted of eighteen men, including state engineer Elwood Mead and his assistant. They crossed the Big Horn Mountains south of Buffalo, crossed the Big Horn River and proceeded up the Stinking Water to Sage Creek, near the eventual site of the town of Cody. They spent the summer running survey lines over a territory roughly fifty miles long and twenty-five miles wide, extending from the mountains on the western side of the Basin all the way to the Big Horn River. Beck invested $2,700 in the trip, a considerable sum for a land speculation of this sort. Beck and Alger were obviously thinking big.[12]

When Buffalo Bill returned to Sheridan after his 1894 Wild West season, he learned from his son-in-law of the Big Horn Basin venture. Although 1894 had not been a good year for the show, he was nevertheless looking for investment opportunities. He was at the height of his powers as a man: not yet fifty years old, known from coast to coast, this very successful showman yearned to become a great capitalist as well, to convert the liquid capital of the Wild West show into a solid monument that would carry his name across time. Cody approached Beck and Alger and proposed to join their partnership. As Beck recalled, "Horace was quick to agree that by taking Cody in we would acquire probably the best advertised name in the world. That alone, we reasoned, would be advantageous and we thereupon made Cody president of the company we organized."[13] Cody had shown interest in irrigation as a way to build up the country around North Platte, and he had frequently expressed his hope to bring people to live in the great West he loved. The Big Horn Basin proposition, then, brought his interests and aspirations together at what seemed a very propitious time.[14]

Looking back, it was a fateful moment when Beck and Alger took Cody into their prospective plans for development. Their resources were limited compared to Cody's, and on their own they would surely have been forced to proceed cautiously. Bringing in Cody's name and wealth could have made it more possible for them to accomplish a modest irrigation project, if it had not come packaged with Buffalo Bill's grand conceit of himself and his unthinking, unmanageable drive to turn anything he did into a press agent's dream. Beck, in particular, can have had no idea what a life-changing step he was taking to enter into this relationship. He must have thought that, as the man who would be in charge on the ground, he would be able to maintain some kind of control. He was, after all, the scion of an important political family, with his own set of important friends and a habit of authority born of family privilege. Although in the long run it all worked out for him, in the next decade Beck often must have felt as if he had lassoed a whirlwind.

No doubt Beck and Alger showed Cody the extensive report Elwood Mead had prepared for them upon their return from the Basin. Mead eventually became one of the giant figures of western American history through his management of the Bureau of Reclamation in the 1920s and '30s. His first important professional position was that of territorial engineer for Wyoming, and he remained in that job for the first decade of Wyoming's statehood. Perhaps his most enduring claim to fame is the Wyoming water law, which became the model for many other western states as they faced the development pressures of the early twentieth century. Mead was a visionary thinker, a capable administrator, and a born promoter. On the evidence of the "Report on the South Side Canal" he prepared for Beck and Alger, however, it appears to be a good thing he did not have to make his reputation as a civil engineer.[15]

Mead's report referred to the "South Side" of the Stinking Water River. The north side of the river was already in the development process. Frank Mondell, a hard-charging young man from Newcastle, Wyoming, who would go on to a thirty-year career as Wyoming's congressman, had taken out a water right from the Stinking Water to develop 155,000 acres that lay north of the river.[16] Mondell had close ties with the Burlington Railroad, and was surely aware that they planned to run a line through the Big Horn Basin. His activity added to the sense of urgency with which the Sheridan group pursued their development. It must have looked to them as if the ground floor was about to be occupied if they did not move quickly.

In his report, Mead envisioned nothing less than an irrigation empire. Diverting water from the South Fork of the Stinking Water in the foothills of the Absaroka Mountains and bringing it around the west side of Cedar Mountain, he planned a canal that would carry water more than sixty miles, all the way to the Big Horn River on the east side of the Basin. He concluded from his survey that "considerably more than half" of this 400,000-acre tract was superior agricultural land. He noted in passing that the area was half the size of Rhode Island, and repeated this theme throughout the report, appealing implicitly to the imperial ambitions of those who would build "a canal large enough to water half a state." He described the construction difficulties that would be encountered, but minimized them. He calculated the size the main canal would have to be (fifty feet wide, ten feet deep) and the amount of water it would have to carry (2,700 cfs, or cubic feet per second), without any real sense of what such a construction project would entail. He estimated the cost at more than a million dollars. It was a colossal sum, more than had ever been spent on a water project in Wyoming, but Mead went on to paint his vision of the potential returns in such glowing colors that the readers must have found it hard to resist.

Mead asserted that the canal on the line he proposed would be secure and stable, with "less than 1000 feet of flume to leak and decay." Beyond that, he characterized the water supply from the South Fork as "exceptional in its volume and in the perennial character of its flow." He had measured it at 4,623 cfs on July 6, nearly double the maximum demand of the irrigation system. (He conveniently ignored early- and late-season flow estimates, which are usually less than 10 percent of the number he cited.) Operating on the conviction that a firm water right on good land was easily worth $10 per acre, he computed a return of two million dollars from land sales alone.

But potential returns were not to be limited to agriculture. He compared the Basin favorably with the Poudre valley of Colorado, home of the famous Greeley colony. There one could find towns with a total of 7,000 people with only 125,000 acres under cultivation and an inadequate water supply. He predicted that the land under this canal would one day support towns with 20,000 people, and more if manufacturing were established. Manufacturing would necessarily follow, he believed, because of the tremendous potential for hydroelectric power development at points along the canal. With generators at only one of the large drops along the canal, they could expect to produce electricity worth more than $300,000 per year. Electricity would "grind all the grain, propel all the cars and light all the houses within the borders of the irrigated territory."

Mead pulled back at the end of the report, noting that these returns he had sketched out were "ultimate, not immediate." He recommended that they proceed instead on a plan to develop only the upper part of the area, that around Sage Creek, building a canal just large enough to cover 25,000 acres. Staging the development in this way would enable them to build up the productive capabilities of the country so they would be in a position to undertake the larger work in two or three years. This canal would be only twenty feet wide and five feet deep, and the total cost would not exceed $150,000. It would follow the same line as the large canal but only for half the distance, and it could easily be enlarged when the time came. The smaller canal would have the virtue of securing to Beck and Alger's company the development of the entire area without incurring the full cost at the beginning. Selling the water rights for 25,000 acres would more than cover the costs, and this area would include the most desirable location for a townsite, along the river at the base of Cedar Mountain, where rail service already had been planned. He concluded by pointing out that sufficient power could be generated on this canal to provide a nice profit to the developers.

As Mead was preparing this report for his clients, the United States Congress changed the rules and prospects for western irrigation development with a single legislative stroke. At the instigation of Wyoming senator Joseph M. Carey, Congress passed the Arid Lands Act of 1894, which became known as the Carey Act. It was the first federal response to continued demands for assistance in developing western resources, intended to enable the construction of projects large enough that development of significant areas of land would ensue. The Act awarded a million acres of public land to any western state that would accept the terms of the law, on condition that the land would be passed to actual settlers on projects built by private developers under the supervision of the state. Developers would make their money by selling the water rights to settlers, who would ultimately take over and operate the canal systems. The theory was that essentially free land would provide an engine to drive development, and that state supervision would guarantee that the irrigation projects would perform to appropriate standards. In a postscript to his report, Mead drew Beck's and Alger's attention to this legislation. He promised that the State of Wyoming would soon provide a process by which developers could take advantage of the Carey Act: "Should the land under this canal be selected and secured by the Company on favorable terms it will add immensely to the value of the project and to the probable return to be derived therefrom."[17]

If this report sounds less like that of a neutral government employee than of a project booster, that is only to be expected. Beck had paid Mead to perform the survey, and the prospect of further employment with the company surely led him to paint the rosiest picture he could. Moreover, Mead interpreted his job as state engineer very broadly. He used his office, particularly his biennial public reports, to boost the state and its develop-ment prospects. A particularly good example of this promotional energy and initiative was his unilateral changing of the name of the Stinking Water River to the much more euphonious Shoshone. The new usage appeared first in 1892.[18] Mead advanced it tentatively, using the older name on his 1894 report to Beck and Alger, for instance. He did not appear troubled by the fact that the state engineer had no authority to do such a thing; the original name of the principal river could not be allowed to put off developers or settlers. Frank Mondell and Captain Hiram Chittenden of the Army Corps of Engineers both questioned him about the initiative, but once Bill Cody got into the irrigation busi-ness the new name was set. In 1901 the Wyoming Legislature ratified the fait accompli by exercising their authority to rename the river.[19]

The development company organized under the laws of Wyoming on March 20, 1895, was consequently called the Shoshone Land and Irrigation Company with William F. Cody as president. Cody, Beck, and Alger were joined by three others as shareholders, W. E. Hymer, Dennis Cunningham, and Jerry Ryan. Little is known about these last three men, except that Ryan was already working with Beck. Hymer, judging from events yet to come, must have been a crony of Buffalo

Bill's of some standing. Five days later the 1893 permit to divert water from the South Fork of the Shoshone to irrigate much of the land this new company was now going to develop was assigned by Labin Hillsberry and James Ryan to Buffalo Bill's new company. The state law implementing the Carey Act in Wyoming put the administration of it in the hands of the State Land Board, consisting of the governor, the secretary of state, and the superintendent of public instruction. They met to consider possible projects for the first time on April 2, 1895. The proposal for the Cody Canal, submitted under the date of March 27, was discussed over the summer and accepted September 14, 1895. The company stretched the process out by delaying its decision whether to undertake the entire South Side project or the smaller 26,000-acre plan. The directors finally decided on the latter plan, and the state engineer's permit to divert water from the South Fork for the Cody Canal, no. 1042, issued August 7, was for only the 350 cfs necessary to irrigate the smaller area. By the autumn of the first year the Cody project was ready to begin work.[20]

There is no doubt that Bill Cody himself conducted his own reconnaissance of the ground along the upper Shoshone in the late fall of 1894. Quite probably that was his first visit to the Basin; it is at least the first documented. George Beck conducted the tour. Beck tells an amusing story of that trip in his unpublished memoir. Cody wanted to meet several of the ranchers who were already installed along the Greybull River, and pay a visit to the wild little cowtown of Meeteetse. He and Beck took off in a new buggy Cody had brought out to the railhead at Red Lodge, Montana; they were going to meet old Colonel Pickett at the famous Four Bear ranch near Meeteetse. Along the way they encountered a herd of two hundred antelope, and Cody decided he would like to take one to Pickett. He leaped from the wagon and emptied the magazine of his favorite Winchester at them at relatively close range, but failed to hit even one. Beck was flabbergasted, and laughed so hard he nearly fell out of the buggy. "Damn you, Beck," Cody said, "if you ever tell this on me, I'll shoot you." "I don't think I'm in any danger," Beck replied. "If you couldn't hit two hundred antelope right in front of you, you couldn't hit me!"[21] Beck was careful to follow this story with other accounts of Cody's genuine prowess with a rifle; he did not care to damage Buffalo Bill's reputation, for the humor in his own story depended upon it.

The Stinking Water had carved an impassable canyon between Cedar and Rattlesnake mountains, the first battlements of the high Absarokas. Above the canyon the river branched; the North Fork descended from the eastern edge of Yellowstone National Park, and the South Fork headed up just outside the southeast corner of the Park. Cody and Beck journeyed around Cedar Mountain and up the South Fork above the canyon, to see the place where Mead proposed to locate the diversion works for their canal, and Cody scouted around the area. He was obviously thinking of land for a ranch. He found some that he liked along the north slope of Carter Mountain, overlooking the South Fork. The land had several small lakes on it, which Cody named after members of his family (Irma, Arta, Orra, Lulu, Kitty, Clara, and Cody). In the spring of 1895 Cody applied to the state engineer to appropriate the water in those lakes "for domestic purposes and watering live stock and to begin the propagation of game and food fishes."[22] There may be some confusion as to just when he first entered the Big Horn Basin, but it is not hard to see when he considered himself ready to make it his own.

As we set out on the trail of Buffalo Bill's life and work in Wyoming, it will help to keep in mind where it was he thought he was going and what he expected to be doing. In the early months, before his project was officially authorized, well before the first dirt had been moved on the canal, he wrote to his old friend in Deadwood, Mike Russell. Hoping to get Russell and some big players from Nebraska to join with him, he presented a very persuasive picture of the future of the Big Horn Basin. It was a great thing to have a chance to be in "on the ground floor" of an enterprise like this. Greeley, Colorado, "ain't a potato patch to ours . . . its an empire of itself." All of Utah only cultivated 240,000 acres, but along the Shoshone they were looking at 300,000 acres in all. It was to be "the greates[t] land deal ever . . . undertaken." He ended by tossing his friend a big chunk of bait: "We will all have a big farm of our own that will if anything should happen . . . support us in our old age and we can lay under the trees and swap lies."[23]

Let's see how that all played out.

CHAPTER TWO

"Christopher Columbus" Digs a Ditch

"Chaos" would be only slightly too strong a term to describe the first year and a half of work on the Cody Canal. A changing cast of actors took upon themselves the task of building an irrigation system in land that none of them knew, with an uncertain plan of construction and an even less certain idea of how to finance the work. They set to work within the legal and bureaucratic framework of a new and untried land law, the Carey Act, and in political circumstances that none of them could have anticipated. The company that began the work was inadequate to sustain it; the company that took the job over once it was begun was a stronger group but the directors were dispersed over thousands of miles of America and were essentially strangers to each other. As they came to know each other and the size of the job they had taken on, all manner of troubles threatened to overwhelm this project they had so blithely undertaken. Not the least of these troubles was the personality of the president of the these companies. In a nutshell, Buffalo Bill had allowed his tremendous success as a showman to go to his head; he had convinced himself by the time he came to Wyoming that he was an *homme d'affaires*, a great capitalist who deserved to be at the head of big business enterprises. The pursuit of this illusion wore hard on him and on those who went with him.

Bill Cody was not a patient man. His way of doing business was to project a rosy vision of what a scheme might accomplish, then employ others whom he could press to do the painstaking work of construction.

In the Wild West show, he never stopped troubling Nate Salsbury in the management of the business, even though Salsbury—surely the managing partner—liked to picture him as a figurehead.[1] Along with his impatience, Cody carried unquestioning confidence in his personal ability to make things happen and an inflated notion of his own importance. Consider this example, one among many. Before the State Land Board had even met to consider the Shoshone Land and Irrigation Company proposal, Cody wrote Elwood Mead that he was waiting upon word from President Grover Cleveland, which he was sure would come soon. "Be sure and get everything else ready with State Land Board so there will be nothing in the way there to prevent our locating settlers at once."[2] When the ditch had yet to be approved, let alone started, a letter talking about bringing in people "at once" reveals with striking clarity the gap between vision and execution that would bedevil the company's affairs from beginning to end. And, as usual, he had to remind Mead that he knew the president.

As it happened, the Company did not wait for final approval before beginning work. George Beck, who played a role in the canal company roughly equivalent to Salsbury's with the Wild West, took charge of the construction effort. In the summer of 1895 he purchased supplies, hired men, and set up camp at Marquette, a little town near the forks of the Shoshone. He hired an engineer to recheck the survey and to estimate the amounts of material that would need to be moved. Elwood Mead remained on the payroll as consulting engineer, at an annual salary of $1,000, but he stayed in Cheyenne; the actual engineering work on the ground was done by men Beck employed. When the Land Board issued their approval in September, Beck was ready to move immediately into construction. He had brought in a good-sized crew: as many as eighty-four men were on the payroll in November, and this in a spot fifty miles from the railhead (at Red Lodge, Montana) and two days' ride from a town. It was a mild autumn, and this was a promising beginning, whatever Colonel Cody may have thought.[3]

The plan of the canal that Beck started to work with had not been completely stabilized. Mead had suggested different ideas at different times: the location of the headgate moved after the first survey, and the line of the canal in his first report had been revised at least once after the company had been formed but before work had begun.[4] The basic plan was to take water from the South Fork at an approximate elevation of 5,700 feet, high enough to enable a gravity flow that would cross the divide between the South Fork and the valley where they would plant the town. It would also allow them to irrigate a few thousand acres in the South Fork valley, the area that would come to be known as "Irma Flat." After roughly twelve miles tending generally east and north, the canal would be dropped into a natural streambed, Sulphur Creek, flowing north toward the Shoshone River along the base of Cedar Mountain. Then, after approximately half a mile, the canal would leave Sulphur Creek and flow north and east around a formation they called Red Bluffs, from there into a small regulating reservoir on the bench above the townsite, and then on to Sage Creek east of the town. The elevation of the bench above town was about 5,100 feet; the 600-foot drop in elevation from the headgate was what led Mead to talk up the hydroelectric possibilities of the canal.

Any parallel between the Wild West show and the business of the Cody Canal does not go far. Buffalo Bill never was away from his show, and he never was present during the construction season on the ditch. This situation made him profoundly anxious, and the consequences of that anxiety fell most heavily on Beck. On his way east in March 1895, Cody worried about financing, and asked Beck if he had spoken to Bronson Rumsey (a Buffalo, New York, acquaintance of Salsbury's) and his brother about investing. From the outset, he seemed almost desperate to have information from Beck; it was obviously hard for him to have his fortunes in the hands of others. In May he urged Beck not to let anyone get ahead of them on either side of the river: "I fear you don't appreciate that enterprize as much as I do . . . We must get to work and do something and that right away. Will you put your shoulder to the wheel and hoop things up[?]"[5]

Cody was concerned about his new company's financial credibility. In June 1895, he was temporarily elated when he thought W. A. Paxton, an Omaha merchant of considerable financial heft, would be coming in with them, and he had convinced Nate Salsbury to join in. As it happened, Paxton did not come on board, and Cody's spirits fell as fast as they had risen. As he traveled from Boston to Newport he promoted the project with eastern financiers. Horace Alger traveled with him some of the way, hoping to take some well-heeled men west. Cody had serious doubts about the long-term viability of the original syndicate: "If this is to commence this summer," he wrote Beck, "you and Alger will have to

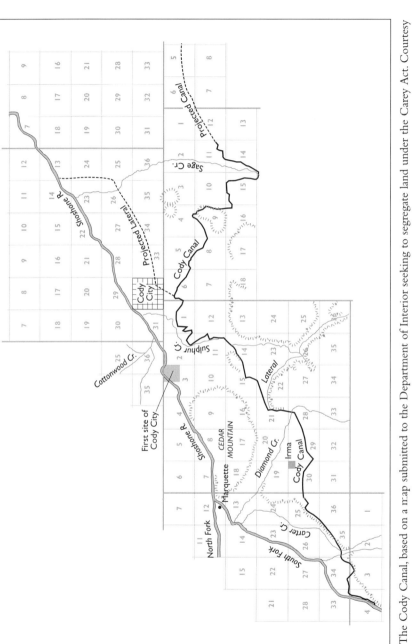

The Cody Canal, based on a map submitted to the Department of Interior seeking to segregate land under the Carey Act. Courtesy of Wyoming State Archives, Department of State Parks and Cultural Resources, Cheyenne, Wyo.

put your shoulder to the wheel and call a meeting & reorganize. Those who cant ante drop out."[6]

No detail was too small for Buffalo Bill to worry over. Did Beck have the right people doing the right jobs, was Beck doing a decent job of supervising them, and so forth. He bombarded Beck with exhortations like "Lets get to work no more nonsense." Despite the fact that their project had yet to receive official approval, he wrote Beck every week or two all summer long in that tone, promising to do his part and urging Beck harder and harder. In July he conceived the idea of printing up a folder to be given out at Wild West shows, which required Beck to produce pictures, maps, and the like immediately. He closed that letter saying, "We must now push things, we *must get there*. You sleep just 4 hours a day no more till that is a success."[7]

Buffalo Bill's energy was prodigious, and his outlook generally optimistic. He seems to have set out to will the world to do his bidding. But his mercurial temperament took some dips as well. He was particularly up and down in August of 1895. Writing to Mead, he was full steam ahead, in spite of any problems that might arise. "And I want no men in the co. but responsible men and will stand no more nonsense. If they don't put up and I have the contract for the land in my name I will put the ditch through myself." In the same vein, he continued, "It's a great scheme. And I will do it alone if I cannot connect my self with responsible men. It's a great enterprize I know, but rather than be connected with unreliable men I will do it alone."[8] A few days later, however, after digesting reports of a company meeting in Sheridan, which he had, of course, missed, he complained to Beck, "I cannot make out if anyone put up any money. And if there is any likelihood of any one going to put up— If no one is going to put up what is to be done[?] Shall we throw up this deal [?] . . . if work cannot be commenced in Sep.—we had better quit."[9]

The longer they were forced to wait before beginning work the more, it seemed, Bill Cody found to worry about. "For K Christ hire someone to write me!" he ended one letter to Beck. Did Beck think they should try to get anyone in on the ground floor? Salsbury believed that if Beck could get the canal built all the way to Sulphur Creek he would be able to borrow all the money they needed, and that might be better than having more investors in the game. At the same time, in a lighter mood, Cody started planning the first of what would become annual hunting parties up the South Fork of the Shoshone. He wanted to know what the living conditions were like, and what weather they could expect. Would they have to bring their own whiskey? Life could not be all work, even for the heavily burdened capitalist.[10]

Early in October, having started construction at last, Beck wrote to Cody that he was cutting the canal to a width of fifteen feet. In reply he got an explosion. The Colonel claimed to have written twenty-five letters insisting on a big ditch. "I came near falling dead & I did some tall cussing when I read your letter. . . . If it cant be 20 feet on the bottom call me out. I will quit."[11] Cody was surely right about the size of the canal, and Beck immediately acknowledged that; he reported to Mead that "the ditch has been widened by Mr. W. F. Cody's request to twenty-one feet (21 ft) on the bottom."[12] Nevertheless, George Beck must have felt he had been yoked to one of the Wild West bucking broncos as he picked up his mail each week.

Buffalo Bill seemed to be everywhere in the fall of 1895. Early in October he was in Washington, where he saw Senator Francis E. Warren and Secretary of the Interior Hoke Smith. Warren thought him "much bothered" about the Big Horn Basin work.[13] He was also involved in serious negotiations with a potential colony of immigrant Germans. He needed to know from Beck how many acres they might be able to irrigate next year if they could dig the canal all the way to Sulphur Creek before winter. Would it be possible to deliver water by June 1? The colonization scheme Cody was working on apparently depended upon the crew being able to finish up enough canal in the spring to supply water for the Germans, a hopelessly unrealistic approach to a difficult and complex operation. And Cody was determined to get his advertising going. He again urged Beck to send photos and write-ups to his sister Helen's newspaper, the *Duluth Press*, so they could be printed and he could start advertising at Atlanta. Unsurprisingly, he wanted Beck to get it done right away.[14]

Worried as he was about difficulties with the Wild West, the Colonel was never too busy to exercise detailed supervision of the work in Wyoming. He complained that he saw too many people listed as foremen on the expense statements Beck sent. He was bringing investors out in a few weeks, and "we must make a showing when the men get there or our gig is up. Now George. Make every man jump to his work & *stick to it*."[15] Cody was not, in fact, as confident as he tried to appear.

In a rare confessional moment, he admitted to Beck that things made him uneasy, and that he worried about spending other people's money. "I will feel awful if money is uselessly squandered there. . . . I want them to feel that we are working on business principles. And doing our level best." Calling Beck "My Dear Friend," he closed with a standard exhortation, "For God's sake hoop them up."[16]

By the end of October, Cody was in despair. His examination of the accounts Beck sent indicated that it was costing too much to move dirt—he was sure he could get it done for half what Beck was paying—and the men were making too much in wages. He had no idea, of course, of the difficulties of digging a canal through what Beck called "cemented rock," and Elwood Mead's blithe underestimates of cost provided his only standard of judgment. It was not hard to see that actual costs were outrunning estimates even at this early date. He wrote that he could not carry the unexpected raise in estimates, and directed Beck to shut work down, saying as he did so, "George, you bet I am half sick."[17] Yet, in another letter the same day, he went on at some length about the need to construct a substantial building there that could serve as a hotel and as an office building, and urged Beck to stick to the job. It is true that he ended this letter with a wail, "All is ruined," but the force of it was to stir Beck and Hymer to work.[18]

A week later he once again commanded Beck to cancel orders for winter groceries and stop work. Out of money, and suddenly aware of the uncertainties of the Carey Act ("Salsbury writes me no business man will now touch it"), Cody asked Beck to let him down easily and quietly as possible. "I am blue all over," he wrote as he signed off.[19] When Buffalo Bill and his party came west that fall, arriving in Red Lodge, Montana, November 18, they were only six in number. They did some prospecting for gold and looked over the canal work, which Beck had managed to continue in spite of the order to stop. The canal was more or less finished for close to eleven miles when they quit. Beck reported blandly to Mead that everyone who came out loved the country and seemed satisfied with the work.[20]

For his part, Elwood Mead was working to earn his retainer. He tried to keep the directors aware, primarily through correspondence with Horace Alger, of what they would have to do to take maximum advantage of their situation. His 1894 report had included a suggestion that they could consider fluming a ditch across the river and irrigating another

15,000 acres north of their planned town. This idea remained alive in the mind of one or another director for several years, although the company never officially took a step in that direction. Mead urged the directors to make up their minds and act before someone else did; Bill Cody took his advice to heart, but none of the others did. He also asked them to come see him about planning the canal from Sulphur Creek around the Red Bluffs. This, he knew, would be expensive and difficult work, and he thought it would be worth their while to consult with him early on. Mead had even suggested in his first plan for the 25,000-acre option that they avoid that patch altogether, but he had apparently accepted the company's decision to go around Red Bluffs without argument. Beck did meet with him, but those few miles were to prove over the next few years more than a match for the two of them and for many others.[21]

Cody's remark about the Carey Act reveals his discomfort in the world of politics. He was taken completely by surprise when opposition arose to the Carey Act in Wyoming, led by Johnson County state senator Robert Foote. Johnson County, site of the famous conflict between the Wyoming Stockgrowers Association and a collection of struggling small ranchers known as the Johnson County War, was a stronghold of Wyoming populism; Foote was its voice. In a long letter to the secretary of the Interior in August 1895, Foote laid out the "crimes" committed, mostly by Elwood Mead, in the name of the Carey Act. They amounted to parceling out the land of the Basin to a "Land Ring" based in Cheyenne, to the detriment of real people who wanted to occupy the land in question. Buffalo Bill Cody was mentioned by name as one of the malefactors in question. Mead had been telling Cody that his and Wyoming's interests were one and the same, and now here was someone accusing him of subverting the interests of the State. Cody learned of Foote when he was in Washington in the fall: "I seen Hoke Smith. Also Senator Warren—and told them that if they believed him [Foote] and did not want the ditches built for my part I would quit."[22]

Obviously, Cody's frequent promises to quit must be treated as skeptically as his claims to gargantuan achievement. He was aware, of course, that the people he knew and liked wanted him to keep at it. His way of responding was typical. A few days after his first conversations about Senator Foote, Cody was using him as a goad. "Let's begin to advertise before Foote knocks us out," he said to Beck.[23] A good public relations offensive would put the right light on things, and people would see that coming to farm under the Cody Canal was the way to make Wyoming's future. Perhaps only a man with Cody's particular experience would think to start an advertising blitz before he had actually built anything. Of course, as he was himself a product of promotion, he naturally applied it to this new venture. At least he knew now he had to deal with the uncertainties of politics as well as those of land development.

After the Land Board had accepted the Shoshone Land and Irrigation Company's request to segregate 26,000 acres of land along the Shoshone River, there remained some difficult bureaucratic terrain to be crossed. The Cody Canal project was of great importance to the leaders of the state of Wyoming. Senator Francis E. Warren had long pushed for cession of public lands to the states; he had to make the Carey Act work or risk losing important political ground. Elwood Mead, a client of Warren's, stood to attract considerable attention to himself as well as growth to the state if he could make the Carey Act work. But the Carey Act, as noted above, was not popular with everyone. In addition to the ire of populists on the land, Mead perceived considerable hostility within the byzantine bureaucracy of the General Land Office, as they in effect lost control of millions of acres of their domain. Offering as their excuse a lack of clear guidance from Washington, Wyoming local land offices rejected all Carey Act applications in that first year. The State then forwarded them to Washington, where the Interior Department had to figure out how the law would be administered. Mead and Warren saw a chance to manipulate the celebrity of Buffalo Bill to help shape the processes of the Carey Act administration in ways that were congenial to the states, and in the process cement their own positions within state and federal government.[24]

In that busy fall of 1895, Buffalo Bill wrote Mead from New York that he was willing to call on Hoke Smith, secretary of the Interior, to try to move things along. Mead replied that he and Warren had been talking about the best way to do that. Mead gently put him off, promising to get all the papers together and take them to Washington, where Senator Warren could lean on the Interior Department. He wanted to use the Cody project to make the fight with Interior because it was such a great project, and they had already got a start.[25] The company had, of course, just begun work on the ditch, but Mead's foremost reason would certainly have had more to do with Cody's fame than with any other consideration. Buffalo Bill was Wyoming's first celebrity as well as a great hope for development. Mead and Warren were quite as willing as Beck and Alger had been to ride Cody's fringed coattails to success, but the stakes were too high to leave matters in Buffalo Bill's personal charge.

Cody tried to keep in touch with Mead as he did with Beck, but it was, of course, a rather different relationship. As state engineer, Mead held a position of power and prestige and could help or hurt a man like Buffalo Bill considerably. Compared to his correspondence with Beck, that with Mead is more careful and considered, less expressive of the mercurial temperament of the Old Scout. The two of them appeared to be taking each other's measure by mail. It was not an easy correspondence to keep up. Letters would miss Cody unless Mead knew his advance route well enough to send them ahead. Mead was also a busy man, but through Horace Alger in Sheridan he kept in touch with the crew building the canal. Early in September 1895, Mead met the assistant surveyor in Sheridan and prepared final plans for the upper portion of the canal. Although less experienced in the field than many, Mead had an intuitive sense of development work. He wrote Cody to be sure to have a substantial headgate installed, for that was the "show piece" of the canal, and a good headgate would "give tone to the work."[26] Cody, of course, agreed: who knew more than he about showpieces? The two men were well matched. Both of them were more comfortable dealing with the big picture than with details, and both instinctively looked for the public relations angle on any enterprise they undertook. Any irrigator would want a good headgate; perhaps only these two would be concerned first of all about the "tone" it would communicate.

Cody continued to push immediate colonization as he had in the spring. "I am red hot after a big colony of Germans all with some money," he wrote Mead in September. The representative of this putative colony had, however, asked him some questions he could not answer, questions about title, cash payment for water rights, etc. He needed Mead's help to know how to reply, and of course he needed it at once. Despite the fact that he had signed the Carey Act application, and presumably read the engineer's reports, he also wanted to know how many acres the company had applied for. "I must know soon as I want to continue the

The headgate of the Cody Canal, along the South Fork of the Shoshone River. Courtesy of Park County Archives, Cody, Wyo.

ditch all winter, and want to know how big to build it." He concluded, "Keep me posted on all points without fail," and finally, almost plaintively, asked, "Can I do any good by calling on Hoke Smith?"[27]

As his Wild West tour dragged to its end, Cody loaded some of the anxiety Beck usually received on Mead's back. He learned toward the end of October that the segregation for lands under the Cody Canal had not yet been filed at the U.S. Land Office in Lander. He also heard that others were filing on the land, and started to panic: they needed to start work immediately, for "no one I can get will help protect me."[28] Mead attempted to calm him. He reported that besides William E. Hymer's own filing for 320 acres near the hot springs (of which more below) there was only one 160-acre filing under the ditch, and now all the land in their project had been reserved from further filing, although the application had not yet been approved. The Land Office was insisting on regulations that kept the State's maps from being approved. Mead was at some pains to make clear that the State was doing everything possible to move it along.[29]

After his November trip to hunt and to view the work along the South Fork, the Colonel went back to North Platte to rest and recover. His mood took another upswing, and he began to make plans. One of these involved stocking his Wyoming ranch and providing horsepower for the ditch work. On his way back to Nebraska, he stopped in both Red Lodge and Billings, Montana, and bought up every scraper in both towns for shipment to Beck. During the winter he purchased a herd of horses from his friend Mike Russell at Deadwood, and moved them on into the Big Horn Basin. Russell's South Dakota brand, TE, became Cody's Wyoming brand. He also shipped in another, larger herd from Nebraska and a pack of blooded greyhounds for hunting deer. He was preparing seriously for both work and play in Wyoming.[30]

Nor was state engineer Mead idle during the winter. In December he sent Cody a draft copy of an article he had written for *Irrigation Age*, George Maxwell's periodical that boomed ceaselessly for western water development. This piece described the Cody Canal project in the most glowing terms, advancing claims that were possibly more extravagant than Mead's 1894 report. He wrote of the project as if both north and south sides of the river were already incorporated into the survey. It was no longer the modest 26,000-acre version of the 1894 report. He now envisioned the canal watering land on both sides of the Shoshone, up

Elwood Mead, Wyoming state engineer, 1890–1899. Courtesy of Wyoming State Archives, Cheyenne, Wyo.

to 150,000 acres in all. The magnitude of the project overshadowed all past development efforts in Wyoming, and was "destined to exercise a decisive influence on the future of the state."[31]

The publication presented Mead an opportunity to attack his enemies and to praise his friends. Near the end he injected a quote from Cody

that purported to explain the origins and purpose of the great irrigation work: "I propose to leave a monument of my work for the west by
founding a colony in the Big Horn Basin which shall be to Wyoming
what the Greeley Colony is to Colorado." This project, said Mead, was
a different kind of water development, one in which "philanthropy is to
share with profit in all its transactions." It was not a speculation, and the
goal was to have a self-supporting population of settlers in possession of
the canal when all was done. A plan operated on these terms could not
but succeed.[32] Buffalo Bill must have loved it. Not only did it shine the
light of philanthropy on his actions, Mead's article effectively and publicly
merged the self-interest of Bill Cody with the long-term interests of the
state of Wyoming. This melding suited the purposes of both Elwood
Mead and Buffalo Bill, each for his own reasons. It became a recurring
theme of Cody's development activities for the rest of his life.

After resting up at home, the Colonel found time to journey to the
east in January, to pursue at last his plan to convince the secretary of Interior to sign the papers for the Cody Canal. Beck traveled independently
to Washington, where Buffalo Bill ordered him to see both the president
and the vice-president; "if nothing can be done we must close down on
work at once."[33] Cody thought a delegation of "Warren, Mondell, Mead,
and other Wyoming men" should descend upon Secretary Smith en masse
to find out whether he was going to do anything; "if not I propose to stop
all work in basin."[34] It was reported that Smith was waiting upon proof of
the arid character of the lands applied for. Senator Foote had protested
that timber grew on the Big Horn Basin lands included in Carey Act
segregations, and the Department of Interior was compelled to investigate. Congressman Frank Mondell, who watched affairs closely on the
company's behalf, thought the problem lay with Department legal staff,
who were not satisfied with the maps. There was no timber on the Cody
Canal segregation, however, and soon after Cody himself went down to
Washington Secretary Smith signed the contracts.[35]

Mead invited Cody and Beck to Cheyenne in February for a conference, after which the two of them went back to the Basin to test placer
gold locations along the Shoshone and prospect for coal (which they
found) at a site convenient to their prospective town. Cody's negotiations
with the German colonists seemed also to be succeeding, as he claimed
to have located fifty German families and sold them five thousand acres
of land. They were to arrive in the Basin early in April, and he was sure

he had another colony of fifty families that would commit in the spring. Reminding Mead that this would mean work for him in getting contracts ready, Cody concluded, "You will appreciate that I have worked hard to make this a success, and a failure just at this stage would not only be damageing to me but also to the state of Wyo."[36]

(Those colonists, of course, never materialized. It would have been a miserable year for them if they had, since the crew had managed only seven miles of canal construction in the 1895 season. Nor did the next fifty families arrive that summer. In addition to a few German priests who visited the canal and townsite in 1896, seven families came out, and one stayed; all the big talk came to no more than that. This affair introduces the reader to one of the continuing problems of Cody's—and of historians trying to follow him. No expression of numbers from Bill Cody, be it acres, dollars, colonists, or whatever, can be believed simply on his own authority. His active imagination and energy seemed to produce numbers out of thin air to support whatever project he had in mind at the time. This is not to say that he was always wrong, only that one needs some corroboration before going very far along this kind of trail with the Old Scout.)

Mead sent Cody a copy of the February 1896 issue of *Irrigation Age* containing the Cody Canal article. Obviously proud of his public relations coup, he boasted, "You are becoming more noted as a builder of canals than you ever have been in your previous enterprises no matter how great their success." This kind of hyperbole was equal in its own way to Cody's, but he was obviously proud of himself. He closed his letter jocularly, saying, "A letter from Senator Warren a few days ago said that the President had not yet signed the contract for the Cody Canal. What is the trouble between you and Grover?"[37] He followed that with one in the same vein to Senator Warren, pointing out that the senator would have to start watching the German vote if Buffalo Bill carried through. "It looks as though we would have to send Cody and his Wild West show down to jar Grover loose from the contract in his possession."[38] For his part, Buffalo Bill claimed to be "sweating blood trying to get President to sign contract."[39]

The contract in question in Washington was the one giving over to Wyoming the authority to segregate the land for the Cody Canal project. Mead kept in touch with Cody, reporting that he had been urging the Wyoming delegation in Washington to get the president to sign. He was obviously unhappy that the State had done its work but the federal government was letting them down. Mead and J. A. Van Orsdel, attorney for the Shoshone Land and Irrigation Company, had been working hard to prepare the form for water right contracts between the State and the company and the settlers and the company. He was sure the contracts would satisfy Cody and his company. Seeking perhaps to flatter Buffalo Bill, the state engineer noted that, when finished, "it will probably be the form adopted by the state for all enterprises under this law."[40]

Forming a company that could handle this job was not a simple task. Of the original six, only Cody commanded real capital; Beck and Alger brought managerial and financial skills, but had little in the way of resources after their original stock purchase. Cunningham and Ryan contributed very little, and Hymer was a small-time operator who brought them more trouble than support. Virtually as soon as the Shoshone Land and Irrigation Company came together, they began to look for major investors to join them. In the summer of 1895 Cody convinced his Wild West partner, Nate Salsbury, to invest with them. He then turned his energies on a group of Omaha investors headed by W. A. Paxton. Paxton kept the company in suspense much of the early summer of 1895. He objected to the presence of Hymer, but Cody was loath to cut him loose. At the same time, Cody began to agitate with Beck to get the little guys of the original company out of the way. This uncertainty on the part of the president of the company was becoming a significant source of difficulty for the enterprise. One day he agreed that Hymer must be cleared off, then two days later he wrote Hymer directly with orders to undertake organization of the townsite. For this and other reasons, Paxton finally decided against joining them.[41]

As soon as he signed on, Salsbury began to counsel caution where his partner was pushing full steam ahead; in particular, he advised his new partners to hold off pushing the ditch work until they had secured sufficient financial backing to carry it to completion.[42] Later that summer Cody and Salsbury persuaded George Bleistein, a printing magnate from Buffalo, New York, who did business with the Wild West, to become a principal investor. Although the new company, to be known as the Shoshone Irrigation Company, would not be incorporated in Wyoming until June of 1896, it was in effect running the operation from September of 1895.[43] There were some potential legal problems in compensating the

The board of directors of the Shoshone Irrigation Company. Seated, William F. Cody and George T. Beck. Standing, left to right, George Bleistein, Henry M. Gerrans, and Bronson Rumsey. Neither Horace Alger nor Nate Salsbury, both founding members of the company, appear. This may be a late photograph: Alger had retired and Salsbury had died by the end of 1902. Courtesy of George T. Beck Papers, American Heritage Center, University of Wyoming.

three who were to be dropped, and, of course, Cody worried about that. He felt vulnerable unless things were taken care of, and, having brought them aboard, he began to express concern about his new partners. He told Beck, "We have got our friends into this and *we must protect them.* Our everlasting reputation is at stake. All our energy & what brains *we possess* must be brought into action. Nothing must be left undone— George, I look to you to attend to this until I can get there to help you."[44]

Another possible investor was Russell Higbie of Deadwood, South Dakota. Alger knew him and talked to him, but Higbie would not sign on to any enterprise that included W. E. Hymer. Alger himself suspected Hymer of using his connection with Buffalo Bill to gain credit for a townsite scheme of his own in Red Lodge, Montana. Higbie, who had visited the ditch site that summer, also had other, more substantial reasons for declining to join them. He was uncertain about the company plans, but he could see that they were larger than the present capital could expect to carry through. Of course, the company itself was uncertain about its plans, which caused no end of difficulty in organizing. Mead had recommended that they take the 26,000 acres at the head of the canal and develop it first, including a townsite, but Cody continually talked about crossing the river and expanding the project. They had federal authorization under the terms of the Carey Act to irrigate only 26,000 acres, but Hymer was writing up estimates for 121,000 more acres on the north side. Cody and his friends, then, while in the familiar bind of being turned down by big investors because so few big money men were on board, also discouraged potential investors by the obvious lack of certainty in their own planning.[45]

George Bleistein was an avid hunter, and he fell in love with the Big Horn Basin when he visited there in the summer of 1895. He was one of the party Cody brought out for a hunt in November, and he brought along another Buffalo man, Bronson Rumsey. After that trip Rumsey also pledged $5,000 for a full partnership. These two, with Cody and Salsbury, Beck and Alger, made up the original board of directors for the new company. Rumsey and Bleistein set about trying to attract other investors, but found themselves hampered by the ramshackle nature of the company's plans. Rumsey pleaded with Beck in January 1896 to provide firm estimates of cost so they would know how much stock they were going to issue, a key point with any potential investor. Without better organization from the top, however, they all remained confused and the prospects of the company remained too murky to attract capital.[46]

Cody worried about the quality of his company even as he worked to get President Cleveland to sign the papers to segregate the land. "I appreciate the fact but I dont presume another member of the Co. does, that there is several things that have to be rushed." He asked Beck if Rumsey's brother was going to join them, and then in a fit of ill temper he asked, "or are you checking out and giving no one any warning until checks go to protest?"[47] Protesting that he had no idea what the expenses were, he again urged Beck to have someone write him. He was pulled in several directions, feeding money into the ill-fated Black America show while Salsbury was ill, claiming he would have sent $3000 for the canal if all the other things had not been draining him. A nervous micromanager like Buffalo Bill could not help but feel the strain of his position.[48]

The original company had been formed more or less on the fly in order to take advantage of the Carey Act. But the working of that Act, as seen earlier, was excruciatingly slow. Investors balked at joining an enterprise as uncertain as the Carey Act seemed to be that winter. In addition to the slow pace of bureaucratic action, a variety of motives cut across the activities of those who did invest, causing confusion as to which of them supported which company goals. For instance, Cody, Beck, and Alger formed a separate Shoshone Power Company, which was intended to develop the hydroelectric potential of the canal of which Elwood Mead had written so much. Every contract with a settler under the canal contained a provision acknowledging the right of the Power Company to use water in the canal and stipulating what the company would pay in the way of operation and maintenance of the canal. The investors were interested also in a number of placer gold claims staked out by Beck and friends upriver on the South Fork and downriver on Alkali Creek. Although placer claims were separate from the water project, they clearly figured largely in decisions to join or stay with the company. A telegram from Cody to Beck in April 1896 is emblematic of the hurried and confused character of the Shoshone Land and Irrigation Company affairs: "Arranging funds have you filed placer claims where is Mead answer quick leaving for New York."[49] What kind of business, Beck might have wondered, can be conducted under these conditions?

Before leaving for the East, Buffalo Bill had let loose some steam at George Beck. He had returned to ditch camp at Marquette after Beck left and found "nothing was being done on business principles." There was no order to the equipment or supplies; everything was "laying around loose." It was, apparently, not hard for him to see disorder in the work of others. He intended to take charge and get things straight with Beck as soon as they could meet.[50] Two weeks later, he was on his way to Chicago to start the summer season. Cheered briefly by the news that President Cleveland had signed the contracts, he nevertheless remained depressed by what he had seen in Wyoming. "With all my work and worry I have got to go rehearsing and jump into a hard summers work a tired man. But I wont care if I don't have to bear the brunt of bad management on that ditch. So for Gods sake George keep things straight there."[51]

These repeated complaints about George Beck could not have been entirely without foundation. Although Cody's ability to manage even simple enterprises was ridiculed by Nate Salsbury, and he was clearly more a part of the problem here than of the solution, Beck did not make it easy for his partners. For one thing, he famously enjoyed his whiskey, and may well have found himself unfit for duty many a morning, as Cody alleged. For another, he was, in 1896, courting a young woman whom he had hired to work for the Company, Daisy Sorrenson, and they would soon be married. More to the point, however, was his go-along, get-along personality. He was not a driver, as Cody was, and people seem to have taken advantage of him. He relied on subordinates like Charles Hayden to manage construction work. He did not like delivering bad news, and frequently chose to send no news at all rather than stir things up. Having worked most of his life alone or in simple partnership, it took him quite a long time to recognize just how important communication was to the operation of something as complex as what they had in hand. It is not clear that any of the others could have managed the work on-site any better than Beck did, but there is no doubt that he could have been a better corporation man.[52]

Discouraged as he apparently was, Cody forged ahead. He asked Mead to prepare a write-up of the lands under the canal and send maps of the canal to Chicago. He was preparing to merge the publicity of the Wild West with the publicity for the Cody Canal, and obviously hoped that this would encourage colonization. Apparently, the similar requests he had repeatedly made to Beck the previous fall had produced nothing, and he hoped for better from Mead. In March he talked to Mead of a thousand people coming to take up farms by the first of June! Cody wanted Mead to hurry up to the Basin and push the work so they could finish the 25,000 acres in time for this year's crops, and also to prepare estimates for the North Side work that Cody still thought they could do. "A great deal depends on you," he said in closing.[53] There is no record of what Mead thought when he received this colossal misapprehension of the work they had in hand.

The spring of 1896 was difficult for everyone connected with the Cody Canal, but it was surely harder on Bill Cody and George Beck than the others. Cody's personality, which had overpowered whatever plans Beck and Alger might have had, precipitating them all into this big development without sufficient thought or preparation, was a major part of the problem both for himself and for his colleagues. It cannot have been easy for Cody to feel himself fully extended in the ditch business and yet have so little control over the actual work. He rode Beck mercilessly from March on into the summer, demanding performance even as he made Beck's life miserable through his own scatter-gun approach to the company's affairs. Other directors of the company were clearly sympathetic to Beck in his role as Cody's whipping boy. Salsbury respected Beck and wrote him frequently. He knew better than anyone what it was like to work with Buffalo Bill. When Cody was talking about a colony of two hundred going out to the Shoshone, Salsbury said, "This is good news if true. I am only afraid that it is a hope on his part, not backed by contracts."[54]

Salsbury tried to counsel Beck on the best way to manage. He urged caution about assuming responsibilities in "the Basin scheme." He did not blame Beck for the situation they were in, but he obviously thought the manager needed to apply a brake when money was not in the bank. He promised to come out to Wyoming, not because he thought he could help Beck much in the management, but because he might be able to help "shift the load a little," no doubt referring to Beck's lonely position as the object of Buffalo Bill's anxiety and fits of high dudgeon.[55]

Elwood Mead, as Cody had directed, prepared for a spring trip to the Big Horn Basin. He needed to know from Buffalo Bill how much money the company had ready to spend in the next three months, so he could make judgments on how best to do the work. It is not clear whether he thought it was feasible to complete the irrigation works for the first 26,000 acres in that season, nor whether he believed that Cody would send a thousand people out by June, but he was as publicly committed to the success of this enterprise as anyone else. He and Buffalo Bill were embarked upon a dangerous game, in which their public protestations about the project's glowing future obviously served to reinforce each other's determination to pursue it. Cody had convinced himself that if Mead got up to the Basin and prepared the surveys for the north side of the river, his partners would go along: "As we will have a big outfit all organized I believe the co. will say push ahead and take chances."[56] He was to learn that others did not always see these things as he did. And, although Mead started for the Basin in April, he learned when he got to Sheridan that Beck was in Omaha, and consequently he called off his trip and returned to Cheyenne.[57]

The revised vision of the Cody Canal that Mead unveiled in *Irrigation Age* would have required more survey work, since they had only completed the survey work for the south side of the river. George Beck himself decided in March 1896 that they did not have the time to make a survey and to file an application for segregation of lands on the north side while they tried to complete the canal they had under contract. It was a wholly practical decision, especially if the company intended to have actual colonists for whom to provide water in 1896. At that early date Beck might have begun to appreciate the size and difficulty of the operation he had in hand, even without the prospect of running the ditch across the mouth of Shoshone Canyon in a giant flume to irrigate thousands of acres north of the river. Neither Bill Cody nor state engineer Mead had a comparable understanding. Beck was the man who had to get the work done, and he had good instincts in such matters. The Cody Canal remained a south side proposition. Bill Cody would keep the idea of watering the north side alive for another fifteen years, but never as part of the Cody Canal.[58]

The second season of construction on the canal began in March 1896, with more confusion and less energy than had been the case in the fall. It appears that Beck delegated construction supervision to other men, and his fellow directors were consumed with anxiety over the project. Having failed to get Mead up to Marquette to look things over, Buffalo Bill was reduced to hectoring Beck to get things done. He complained about money matters and what seemed to him to be inefficiency in construction. He was particularly hard on Beck's work habits. He blamed Beck's mismanagement for the fact that camp was still at Marquette in April.[59] Throughout that month Cody kept at Beck on that subject. He thought Beck was hurting the company by being away from the work frequently, and failing to keep investors apprised of what was being done and how long it would take.[60] At the end of the month, sending him $5000, he confessed he did not know where the rest of the next payroll was going to come from. He was incensed that the canal was still not to Sulphur Creek, for which he blamed the manager. He concluded, "Although Rumsey says this is not a one man company I have to personally endorse for everything and I get the blame for everything—and no one even tells me whats going on. I am most heartily discouraged."[61]

The Buffalo men were obviously clamping down on their wallets as the costs rose at the ditch camp. Early in May, Buffalo Bill realized that he and Salsbury were going to have to bankroll the project, and he turned his thoughts to making sure they got their share of company stock for it. At the same time, Alger, tired of wiring people for funds that would not come, put the company's fiscal situation in a nutshell: "I will keep calling for money and undoubtedly the Col. will in some way provide."[62] In May some letters from Beck calmed the Colonel considerably and opened up the other side of his personality; one of them "made me ten years younger. I am fond of you, I allways did like you. There now—you see I was getting it from all sides & I got nervous and feared you were not pushing fast enough." He sent another $5,000 to cover the next payroll, and urged his manager to put on full force. The canal having reached Sulphur Creek, it was "the Red Bluffs and let's go for it!" On the back side of the letter he scrawled, "Without a Christopher Columbus where in hell would America have been. Also the Basin!"[63]

Only a week later "Christopher Columbus" was yelling at the crew again. He had received bills from merchants in Red Lodge that Beck had not told him about, and he was hopping mad. "George, these letters settle it. I cant stand being treated this way any longer. Its not justice or even friendship." He accused Beck of not caring or of being drunk all the time, and directed him to trim the work force to reduce expenses, saying "there is no one now to protect your bills but myself. . . . George, its not right. Still your discouraged friend, Cody."[64] A couple of days later he demanded "a business reply" from Beck, speaking "as President of the Co." Beck's reply it still did not satisfy him. Cody and the investors wanted an account of money spent and debts contracted that Beck seemed reluctant to provide. They wanted to know his plans. As far as they could tell Beck kept no records of land sales, and "everything at that end is run like a widow woman farm. No system at all."[65] He ended the letter with another threat to drop the whole business if things did not shape up.

Bronson Rumsey did his best to keep Beck's spirits up in those difficult months. He told Beck that he had had to correct several misconceptions that George Bleistein had picked up from conversations with the Colonel, and even alluded to the possibility that Cody was not entirely stable: "They say everyone is crazy on some one subject; I wonder if I am or somebody else."[66] And two weeks later: "I suppose you are so busy answering the Col's telegrams & letters that you cant find time to relieve the mind of your humble servant."[67] Rumsey himself had received many hasty, worried telegrams from Cody, and had sufficient understanding of Buffalo Bill's temperament that he even warned Beck to burn letters in which he spoke candidly of the Colonel. All those who worked with him recognized that Bill Cody himself was the source of a great deal of the difficulty and disorganization of which he constantly complained.

Faced with cash shortages and uncertainty about the state of construction in Wyoming, Nate Salsbury and the Buffalo directors got together in May 1896 and produced a plan for refinancing and reorganization. They asked Buffalo Bill to use his influence in Omaha to place some $10,000 to $15,000 worth of bonds to provide construction cash, and they recommended adoption of a plan put forward earlier that spring by Alger to close down the Shoshone Land and Irrigation Company in favor of a new company to be called the Shoshone Irrigation Company. The major investors had finally concluded that the legal organization of the original company, in which each major partner held four hundred shares of stock with a par value of $100 per share, opened each of them to $40,000 liability for company debts. This was an untenable situation. They had to reorganize to establish limited liability and to give them the kind of footing they needed to issue bonds.[68]

Placing bonds was really only a hope at that moment, and not a very strong one. Cody could attract no interest from Omaha banks. The need for money, on the other hand, was real and immediate. Salsbury spelled things out to Cody with his customary clarity and candor. He had promised earlier at a meeting in Philadelphia to put up another $5,000, and Beck was begging him for it. He told Cody he would not send any more until the affairs of the company were straightened out, and he advised him to pull back as well. The Buffalo men were not putting in any money, as they heard Cody promise at that meeting to cover the May payroll, "a foolish promise, but one I will assist you to carry out." The group's recommended reorganization included important changes in the conduct of daily business "so that we may not be managing this matter from the various parts of the continent." He clearly did not see this as only a problem with George Beck. The company needed to provide a secretary for Beck to manage the correspondence, and he could not be asked to run all over the country to meet with investors, immigrants, and all other kinds of people and still manage construction on the canal. This should simply be a matter of company policy, which would not require Cody personally to do anything. "I take it for granted that you on your part will agree that this should be done."[69]

Salsbury's letter started the move toward fundamental reorganization, from which emerged the Shoshone Irrigation Company as successor to the Shoshone Land and Irrigation Co. A Sheridan attorney drew up the articles, which were ready for signature by May 21. The financial crunch continued, however. Alger reported that even after Cody had paid in $5,000 and another investor $2,000 they were still over $5,500 behind in current obligations. Ominously, they had taken in only $160 on water right contracts that spring but construction expenses continued in spite of letters from everyone urging Beck to go slow. Others besides Cody were starting to grow upset with Beck's failure to keep them posted on work in the Basin.[70]

At the end of May 1896, there was a genuine crisis in relations among the leaders of the company. Cody wrote to Beck that they would meet in Chicago in early June. The Buffalo men had insisted on the meeting to put the company on a better business footing. Cody blamed Beck for all the troubles, although his conclusion that "its been a go as you please outfit with no business head to it" could as easily have been turned back on him.[71] Beck came out of Wyoming to attend the Chicago meeting, where President Cody berated him again for failing to get out of bed and help him negotiate with potential settlers. "George, you are supposed to draw a salary from our company and do you think you deserve it?"[72]

This entire set of letters from Cody to Beck in April and May of 1896 reveals not only Buffalo Bill's mercurial temperament but his fundamental incapacity as a manager. Nate Salsbury knew these things well: "A partnership with W. F. Cody certainly is a picnic, as it is viewed in Hell." Salsbury had extensive experience of Buffalo Bill's credulity, his inability to sort good information from bad, his impatience, and his need to surround himself with people who played up to him. "It would not be so bad," he said, "if he had the common intelligence of a child, or if he could remember from one day to another the experience he has already passed through."[73] These are peevish words; Cody was quite intelligent enough and was not senile. Still, the failure of discipline with which he so often taxed Beck was clearly a fault in his own way of working, and the man who knew him best had his finger on it. If Cody had not also brought great amounts of compensating good humor, energy, and determination, to say nothing of money, to the enterprise, things would have fallen completely apart in 1896 or 1897.

In Beck's defense, the ditch business was much more complicated in 1896 than it had been the previous fall. The crews were working in much more difficult terrain, where they had to manage not only drops

The long flume around the Red Bluffs, under construction in 1896. Courtesy of George T. Beck Papers, American Heritage Center, University of Wyoming.

in elevation but the kind of soils that did not hold ditch walls very well. The soil was particularly difficult to manage where the canal took a wide turn around the Red Bluffs. Breaks were frequent occurrences, and not only in the first year. A great deal of time and money had to be devoted to rebuilding sections of the canal that would not stay built. They eventually had to install a 1500-foot flume to get water past the Bluffs. What could look like carelessness to worried investors two thousand miles away was simply the reality of the gypsum and gravel the Cody Canal had to traverse on its way to decent farmland. The meeting Cody called in June in Chicago gave Beck an opportunity to talk with the assembled directors and seemed to clear the air. Beck at least had an opportunity to explain what the problems were and how the money was being spent. Tempers cooled for a while.[74]

But as the summer wore on, relations among the partners remained difficult. Men who worked for Buffalo Bill in the Basin apparently tried to curry favor with him by attacking Beck. Early in July, having heard from others in the Basin, Cody wrote to Beck, "That climate out there must be very productive in regard to liars if I am to believe one sentence in your letter." He had heard "ten thousand . . . things from people you little suspect," and was getting ready to fight back, "for its not my nature to lay down and quit, when I am not in the wrong. No one will apologize quicker when I am wrong."[75] He then proceeded, in a friendly sort of way, to let Beck know that he was satisfied for the most part with what Beck had done but was not happy with things he had left undone. He told Beck he was not careful enough in detail to manage such a work. (Since Buffalo Bill himself was not known for his detail-management skills, this lecture may have been a kind of exercise in psychological projection.) On the other hand, there seemed to be cause for criticism. In the month since their Chicago meeting, Cody had learned of more than $1,000 worth of bills that Beck had not mentioned then. He pleaded again for the manager to improve his business habits. "Its your carelessness thats giving our co. such a bad name. You don't mean to do it, but its been your way of doing business all your life." In conclusion, remembering that Nate Salsbury was visiting the ditch camp, he "hope[d] to God Salsbury wont catch the disease of carelessness & neglect that is prevalent in that country".[76]

The company decided at its Chicago meeting that it needed to issue $50,000 in bonds to finish the construction of the canal. Salsbury and Bleistein undertook to sell the bonds. Elwood Mead, who had not been to see the work since the previous summer, spent almost half of July working on the canal and extending the survey on the north side of the river. Cody professed himself pleased with the reports from Salsbury and Mead, but continued to try to drag construction information out of Beck.[77] "I feel my name and honor is at stake in that enterprise. Warn me of any danger to our credit, don't leave me in darkness," he wrote in August.[78] But the bonds did not sell, "for the reason of you blooming free silver Democrats" (among their other differences, Buffalo Bill was a thoroughgoing Republican and Beck was the son of a Democratic senator and an organizer of the Wyoming Democratic Party). He thought they could only place the bonds after the election, and not then if the Democrats won. If they could hang on until November, he could go to New York and raise some money.[79]

Nate Salsbury thought there might be reasons closer to home why the bonds were not selling: "Why in the name of ____!! ____!! don't you send Bleistein a copy of the reports?" he asked Beck late in July. Men trying to sell company bonds needed good information to be able to negotiate effectively with potential buyers. Of course, Salsbury shared Bill Cody's opinion of "the blatherskite" Bryan and his effect on the money market. Organizationally, the company was taking small steps. Beck seems to have been preparing reports, although not distributing them as all would have liked. But the bond sale that summer fell flat.[80]

The company prepared a statement of the "Resources of the Shoshone Irrigation Company" to support the sale of the bonds. The statement emphasized the value of the company's franchise from the State: 24,600 acres under the ditch, for which they could charge $10 per acre, gave a gross value to their land of $246,000, against which $50,000 bonding looked rather small. The statement emphasized the money ($60,000) they had already spent and the miles of ditch they had completed, and noted that the state engineer had recently complimented the company on "a fine piece of work." They claimed (by some extraordinarily imaginative accounting) to have sold $21,600 worth of water contracts before midsummer of 1896. With this kind of security, they expected to be able to repay any bonds sold within five years. Beyond their land and their ditch, they noted the likelihood of the railroad coming into the Basin and the wide variety of other natural resources, including abundant water; they went so far as to claim that the Shoshone, their ordinary mountain river, would "furnish more power than either Great Falls, Mont., or Minneapolis, Minn.!"[81] Clearly, they hoped to attract people who might be interested in full-scale development of the country.

Beck had received $6,000 after the Chicago meeting, and it had come with a forceful directive from the Buffalo men that it be used "for payment of men and Mr. Mead, and for nothing else whatever."[82] Buffalo Bill continued to supply chunks of money, amounting in all to more than $10,000 over the course of the summer, but construction costs consumed it all.[83] That meant there was nothing with which to pay creditors, and that led in turn to predictable difficulties. Near the end of July, a merchant in Billings succeeded in getting an attachment on some of Buffalo Bill's teams as satisfaction for some debts. Instantly, every person the company owed sent in a statement asking for settlement. Beck was afraid to show his face in Red Lodge. He put the creditors off with more promises that money would flow when the bonds sold, but his hands were pretty well tied.[84]

Beck did not think that Salsbury and Bleistein were sufficiently energetic in pushing the bonds; in fact, he did not think them very

enthusiastic about the whole enterprise of the canal. He did not, apparently, convey those sentiments to Buffalo Bill, but he confided in Alger,
the only other Wyoming man in the group. He felt the lack of the
bond money on any number of accounts, but most particularly because
the fall of 1896 was the moment of the formation of Big Horn County,
and there was a contest to see which town would be named county
seat. Although there were older towns in the Basin, Beck believed that
the fledgling town of Cody had a chance to achieve that distinction. He
began campaigning in August, driving fifty miles a day across the Basin.
He urged Salsbury to lend some energy to the cause, but of the directors
only the president took to the idea.[85]

By the end of August, most of the directors were ready to call an end
to the work for the year. Only Buffalo Bill was continuing to put money
into the canal, and he could not supply enough to keep crews on. He
sent another $5000 in September that was entirely consumed by mer-
cantile and construction debt, and even then more debts remained. Beck
wanted desperately to push ahead with the work, mostly for the sake of
winning the county seat fight. He thought there was no chance at all if
people around the Basin knew the company could not finish their ditch.
He also knew, from experience around Sheridan, that the value of their
town lots would double or triple if Cody were the county seat, which
made it hard to give up the fight. He even was willing to travel east himself
to try to push the bonds.[86]

Salsbury offered Buffalo Bill and Beck cautionary advice in August
and September. He had traveled to the Basin in July to look matters
over for himself, and upon return had urged his fellow directors to get
together enough money to finish work on the ditch. That had not happened, and Salsbury felt it was his duty to warn his active partners
against continuing. To Beck he protested the impossibility of financing
by bonds and warned against the folly of spending any money on the
county seat race unless he could be sure they would have water to the
town in the fall. He intimated that it might be wise to get out and cut
their losses. "I have learned to discard my hand pretty well and am now
struggling with some of my habits. . . . How would it do for you to
follow my suit?"[87] He reminded Buffalo Bill that Ed Goodman, Cody's
nephew, had recently written that it would take four more months to
get water to the townsite. If they kept at the task in dribs and drabs, it
would bleed them dry. Salsbury refused to ask the Buffalo men to do

anything more, and he urged Cody to call off work until they had money in the bank to complete it. "You know how that scheme eats up money, and if you don't stop it somewhere we will be in the hole with it on our hands and nothing to meet the liabilities with."[88]

As the others fell away, Cody and Beck seemed to become more determined to push work on the canal. Cody wrote several times a week begging for information; at one point, Beck pulled him up short and pointed out that he had actually written nine pages in the last two weeks and did not deserve to be hounded in that way. Cody asked for specific construction estimates, which Beck supplied as soon as they could be put together. Cody wanted to know who was pushing them the hardest for money, and tried to scrape together what he could so Beck could keep some of them satisfied. For his part, Beck tried to clean up the financial and legal mess left behind by the failure of Cody's first colonization scheme, and protect Buffalo Bill's interests as well as those of the Company. Cody, ever the optimist, had not given up entirely on his Buffalo colleagues even then. He urged Beck to send some pictures to Buffalo: "*pictures* sometimes make people *put up*—its true in the show biz." But the whole load fell on these two in that difficult fall, and they carried it with a will, hoping—as Cody said, echoing Mr. Micawber—that "something may turn up."[89]

At the end of 1896, Beck submitted a summary report to the directors covering all the work on the ditch since the beginning. The canal was finished most of the way to the townsite, sixteen miles from the headgate. There was a good-sized dam in the Sulphur Creek gulch, about twelve miles from the headgate. From that reservoir a ditch ran to a 1500-foot flume around the troublesome Red Bluff structure, which enabled them to fill a regulating reservoir on the bench land above the town. They were prepared to bring irrigation water into the town. Beck appeared to think the main construction work was done, and that extension of the canal could wait until there were settlers who needed water on the lower benches near town. He considered the Red Bluff flume a temporary structure, to be replaced with a permanent cut through the rock when water contracts demanded it and when they had sufficient income to pay for it. He reported that he had spent $77,598, and that the company had an inventory valued at $12,243 and outstanding liabilities of $4,297.[90]

The $77,598 did not represent total cost to the end of 1896; they had spent more than $88,000 on the project. And it is impossible to know precisely where the money came from. There survive only scattered and occasional attempts to sum up or suggest how much any of the investors had contributed. Alger, Beck, and Cody, the three continuing members of the original company, received credit for work done before the Shoshone Irrigation Company was organized; Cody got $4,000, the others $2,500 apiece. All the directors of the new company put up $5,000 initially, as did some other investors who held stock but no office; one note of Buffalo Bill's indicates that there were a total of ten men who subscribed that price. There were also notes of subsequent contributions from some of them—notably Rumsey and Salsbury—of a few thousand at a time. Buffalo Bill estimated in May 1896 that he had put in another $13,500 and it is known that he subsequently provided $5,000 to cover the May payroll. He continued to supply money to meet emergency needs into the autumn when all others had pulled back. The nature of the records defeats precise calculation, as both Cody and Salsbury appear to have invested money on their own as well as jointly. From one viewpoint, the operation might justly have been named the "Wild West Canal," since the two of them put up $50,647 through 1896. But Buffalo Bill's total contributions in the first two years probably amounted to over $30,000, significantly more than a third of the total committed to the project. He surely paid enough to have the canal named after him.[91]

Bill Cody's support of the ditch work extended beyond his subscriptions to pay men and buy supplies. After he moved his horses to his new ranch on the South Fork he made both horses and men available for work on the canal in return for stock credit. For a company chronically short of cash, this was a matter of great importance. Records do not allow us to know for certain just how valuable these in-kind contributions were to the canal effort, but some idea of it may be inferred from the single record that does survive. Between July 1 and November 24, 1896, Buffalo Bill devoted his own men, teams, and materials to the canal in return for $1,581 worth of company stock. Making matters worse for Cody, but better for the company, he then turned around and allowed $1,338 of that to be charged to him at the company store to support the work of the men he loaned to the ditch, leaving him at the end of the year entitled to only $243 worth of stock. If in subsequent years of construction he made similar deals with his crews, he should be credited with at least $5,000 more of the cost of the work than the regular accounts show.[92] No one has ever questioned Bill Cody's generosity.

Beck clearly believed that the construction work was nearly done. They had the machines and men in place to complete in the spring what they would need to get water to whatever lands they could sell over the winter. He urged that the directors turn their attention to attracting good settlers. But the reports of the men who were actually doing the work reveal how much Beck's wish was father to his thought where the ditch was concerned. In particular the flume at Red Bluff was already a considerable source of difficulty, and the ditch leading to it leaked so badly that it was not always possible to get water into the flume. They had run the ditch through a prairie dog town, and had to enter into a kind of hand-to-hand combat to keep all the water from draining away. That ditch and flume would bedevil the canal for years, but Beck chose to ignore these signs of possible trouble. Failure to heed them would come back to haunt the company in years to come.[93]

They had been at work on the canal for a little over a year when Beck made his report. In that year they had learned—or should have learned—what an immense and complicated job they had on their hands. The environment through which they were running the canal had proved to be much more resistant in practice than it had looked on paper in Elwood Mead's survey. Operating a major construction project in essentially a wilderness environment, with an uncertain work force and an inexperienced manager, made for problems that inevitably cost more than the easy estimates made at a desk in Cheyenne. The ordinary problems at the ditch were complicated by the complexity of the personalities who were undertaking the project. Investors spread across the East needed good information from the Basin, which was seldom forthcoming. Beck unaccountably resisted repeated demands for reports from the field. Bill Cody blew hot and cold, but always loud, stirring up his partners and making life all but impossible for George Beck. Elwood Mead collected his retainer but provided very little concrete assistance in the field work, although we should note that Beck rarely asked for it. It would have taken an organizational genius to handle this set of problems, and all the Shoshone Irrigation Company had to offer was a set of flawed human beings.

It is striking that at the end of 1896 the two who had spent most of the year in vexed antagonism were the ones who were most determined to carry on. Their personal and working styles were still at odds with each other, and would remain that way, but they needed each other. Bill Cody, who began by treating George Beck more as a menial worker than as a partner, joined with him in the push for the county seat and came to see his work as essential to the company. For his part, Beck learned that Cody was going to be the reliable member of the financing syndicate, and he chose to fall into step with him rather than follow the more cautious advice of Nate Salsbury. Beck and Cody had determined to push ahead, not only with the canal but with the building of a town. Their relationship would be tested again as they pursued that goal. There was stress and strain enough along the Cody Canal to test everyone who was caught up in it.

CHAPTER THREE

A Town in the Wilderness

The founding of the town of Cody was probably the company's major achievement of 1896, but, like everything else involved in this enterprise, it was completed in fits and starts and not without bruised egos and intrigue. Here again, it was Buffalo Bill's nature—quick to act, slow to consider the consequences, and loyal to a fault to old companions— that made what could have been a relatively simple process chaotic. This was not his first attempt to start up a town on the frontier, but his brief experience with the ill-fated Rome, Kansas, when he was only twenty-one years old and not yet famous offered few guidelines for what he encountered along the Shoshone in the 1890s. William F. Cody in 1896 was a far different man from the Bill Cody of the 1860s, and the world he lived in had changed beyond recognition.[1]

Buffalo Bill was quite taken with the mineral springs that empty into the Shoshone River as it flows through a shallow canyon just east of the mountains. The springs had been responsible for the name given to the river by local Indians and early settlers, "Stinking Water." He was aware that the Crows had considered the springs healing water, and he envisioned a spa of European splendor built around them. In company with Charles DeMaris, an early settler who had land near the springs, W. E. Hymer, one of the partners in the Shoshone Land and Irrigation Company, and a trader from Red Lodge named H. P. Arnold, Cody was persuaded to set up a town near the springs even before the canal construction began in the fall of 1895. The surveyor the company had hired to check Mead's original lines before they started digging platted the town for them, and the plat was filed in October 1895. As these men conceived it, Cody City (the name they chose) would have straddled the river, and the springs would have been part of the town, overlooked by parks on both sides of the river.[2]

By the fall of 1895, Hymer had effectively been eliminated from the Shoshone Land and Irrigation Company. But earlier that year he had filed a homestead claim on the quarter-section where they wanted to locate Cody City. There is evidence that Buffalo Bill had been unhappy to see Hymer left out as the Company reorganized. Hymer had been a friend from earlier days in Nebraska and Cody apparently saw nothing wrong with getting into the townsite business with him. Cody really wanted a place along the river where he could make use of the springs, and Hymer wanted to make his own fortune by attaching himself to his famous friend. In March 1896, Cody and Hymer applied to the state engineer for a permit to take water from the springs and pipe it half a mile across the river to bathhouses and residences on the south side, where most of the town was planned. It was, however, a hasty application, and Elwood Mead felt obligated to reject it as insufficiently definite as to the means of diversion and amount of water to be diverted.[3]

Buffalo Bill had kept Beck engaged in correspondence about the townsite, as well as everything else, from the time they began work. He obviously expected Beck to be part of the townsite operation. He told Beck he had directed Hymer to include the sulphur springs in the townsite and find out the best way to get title. He and Beck even joked about making sure there was a "gin mill" in the town; Cody was afraid it "would keep me full all the time." In September, Cody wrote to Beck, "I know you don't like Hymer, but he is a pusher. And that's the kind of men we want with this big job."[4] A week later, thinking about the town again, he reported that the manager of the Sheridan Inn, George Canfield, was trying to get him to build a cheap hotel at the springs that he could operate. "But I think the Co. should be interested and the Hotel built in town & pipe water." He also reported that Salsbury and Bleistein wanted to name the streets of the town after leading Union and Confederate generals, and have "wide streets & high license [fees] to keep out cheap gin mills."[5] A week later he even sent Beck a list of his own favorite Union generals, leaving it to George to select the Southerners and to decide the number of streets. Buffalo Bill's list had no fewer than eighteen, some of them fairly obscure; the plat used only six of them.[6]

Colonel Cody and a party, including his wife, Louisa (seated in front of him), in the canyon above Cody where the sulphur springs enter the river. If Cody's first plat had been the basis for the town, this spot would have been in its center. Courtesy of Park County Archives, Cody, Wyo.

Nate Salsbury, a genuine promoter, was keen to see the town get going. He and Bill Cody talked about it in the fall of 1895, especially about the prospects of the railroad coming into the Basin and the possibilities of developing the springs. Salsbury was quite serious about forming a stock company just to push the mineral water from the springs. He thought they could sell stock to prominent physicians all across the country, using their influence to build up the reputation of the water, "and reputation is all that is wanted to coin a fortune out of hot water."[7] He had some ideas about handling the visitors that would go far to popularize the place, but he did not want to talk about them for fear someone would let them escape into common conversation. He did say he thought it would be folly to put up cheap buildings at the springs. They should do it right and build nothing they would have to pull down and throw away. Streets should be at least eighty feet wide, maybe wider. The success of Colorado Springs owed something to giving the public breathing room, and with a whole state to spread out in, "it would be a fatal oversight to neglect this important point."[8] These recommendations on wide streets would not prove hard to follow, and overall it is easy to see the advantage that the vision and experience of men like Salsbury brought to the group. Unfortunately, developing the springs on a European or even Colorado model would remain no more than a dream.

In late October, after the Cody City plat had been filed, the Colonel asked Beck what he knew about the title to the land the townsite occupied. He had heard that Hymer had gone to Lander to file, but wanted to know what Beck knew. "Wish you and Hymer could work together then you would know what he is doing, & . . . you would have an even brake [sic] with him. You are there to guard interest of our Co, so you ought to keep posted on all points. And don't let us get run up against a brace game, if there is any dainger [sic] of it."[9] A week later he learned that Hymer had filed on the site in his own name and he was hopping mad. "I would not have lost that Town site for $25,000 in cash. Oh why did you not do as I asked you to. That was to take up the land. Hymer now claims it all. I would like to know what you propose to do." Cody clearly thought Hymer was outmaneuvering Beck on townsite matters. Forgetting for the moment his own ambiguous dealings with the man, he asked Beck, "Why did you give him our surveyors to survey a town site for himself, when we wanted the town for ourselves? I hope you can fix it up."[10]

Clearly, Buffalo Bill had been uncertain of Hymer and had needed Beck's help to see the situation clearly. But his own actions obviously sent contradictory signals to the men with whom he worked. In the event, he felt betrayed, and Beck got the brunt of it, as usual. But after that outburst he nevertheless filed jointly for the water right at the springs with Hymer. He seems to have had a difficult time sorting out his own goals, and his reluctance to part with his old friend only confused matters for himself and his new partners. He wanted desperately to find a way to keep control of the springs, as they were an essential part of his vision of the future of the town. He might also have been flattered by Hymer, who not only named the town after him but noted on the plat that he did so "in honor of Col. Wm. F. Cody."[11]

In the spring of 1896, George Beck and Charles Hayden, the surveyor-assistant manager of the Shoshone Irrigation Company, drove a stake in the center of section 32, township 53 N., Range 101 W., and began to lay out streets for a new town. This site was about two miles east of Cody City, along the river, on the second of three terraces that stepped up from the canyon. In Beck's account, written decades later, it was his decision to set up this town, and it was in opposition to Buffalo Bill that he did it: "Inasmuch as he had not asked any of our company to come in on [his] new project, I objected. I decided to lay out another. . . . After all, if Bill Cody could lay out a town, so could George Beck."[12] He went on to say that they tried to name the town Shoshone, but it was rejected by the U.S. Post Office. He submitted three other names—"of which Cody was definitely *not* one"—and when Buffalo Bill found out about it he sent a man to Washington to have the Post Office name it Cody, and to cancel the application for the first town. "It was not long after that," Beck wrote, "that I received formal notification from Washington that we had a post office and that its name was Cody. That's how one town got to be named after one man. As it pleased Buffalo Bill tremendously and did the rest of us no harm, I let it go at that."[13]

However, Beck's account of the founding of the town is not the only one to survive. Charles Hayden left a detailed memoir of those days, and there are interesting differences from Beck's. In the first place, he recalls that Colonel Cody rode with him and Beck from Marquette in February 1896 to the site of the new town, and together they determined how it would be set up. Moreover, Bronson Rumsey was along and he sketched out the plat. Hayden says Cody and Hymer had had a falling out over townsite matters at Cody City, after which "the Col. paid all bills and dropped out at the new townsite." They started surveying their new town on March 1. On this telling, Buffalo Bill was actively involved in the making of the present town, and Beck gives up center stage.[14]

Beck's account betrays, at a distance of more than thirty years, the animus of a man who felt overshadowed by the great Buffalo Bill, and may therefore be suspect in some degree. It could simply be the revenge of the living on the dead, for the years of chiding Beck had to endure from the Colonel. (The chiding was particularly severe, as already seen, in the spring and summer of 1896.) Cody certainy was not guilty of failing to consult with Beck or others. We have seen how Cody urged Beck to look out for the interests of the company in townsite matters. None of this explains Cody's application for water rights in partnership with Hymer. However, that could have been an artifact of earlier plans, perhaps actually mailed in by Hymer after Cody had decided to part company.

Of the original idea of naming the east-west streets after Union generals of the Civil War, only the name of the main business street, Sheridan Avenue, survived. The other major east-west streets were named after the directors of the company at the time of the founding—Beck, Alger, and Cody south of Sheridan, Rumsey, Bleistein, and Salsbury on the north side. Two parks, named Irma and Arta after Cody's daughters, were set on the west end of the business district. Although the plat was for the town of "Shoshone," the centrality of the Cody family argues that it was not undertaken in any fit of pique against Buffalo Bill. And the Colonel had not had his last word on the name of the town.[15]

The effect of planting a new town two miles downriver was to cut Hymer completely out of the town business. It appears that this was just what Buffalo Bill, as well as Beck and others, had in mind. In fact, as Beck's account indicates, Cody set about making sure that the new town carried the right name. It was not a simple matter. When they set up the new town, Mrs. Minnie Williams, wife of a Marquette-area rancher, applied to become postmistress. Beck wrote to Congressman Frank Mondell to ask his assistance in getting the post office at "Shoshone" instead of Cody City. Mondell replied quickly that he had been just in time to prevent the appointment of the storekeeper at Cody City as postmaster, but he had been assured that Mrs. Williams and "Shoshone" would go through. When the Post Office later rejected that application, they asked for a new name, and Mrs. Williams sent in "Richland." In August the directors learned that "Richland" had been accepted. They were not pleased with Mrs. Williams's choice. Nate Salsbury was in Cody at the time. He, Beck, Hayden, and some others determined to press for the name "Cody," as Cody City had not yet secured a post office.[16]

Bill Cody remained interested from afar in the fate of the new town. At the beginning of August he wrote from Muskegon, Michigan, to ask: "what is that town to be named? As I paid for surveying Cody City, and no one has a title to the land why can't that name be annulled or discontinued. Do so if you can attend to it George. I don't want anything to do with that town—& Hymer."[17] Then, in September, when he heard what Minnie Williams had been doing, he exploded: "I see that women are nameing and running the town. If so I won't put up another dollar. I don't care a damn whether water ever gets there or not, and how quick all work stops. My interest in the damn town is ended."[18] It is doubtful that this letter stimulated the men in Cody to act. After all, they had come a long way to share in the reflected glory of the Cody name and it was not time to give that up now. Hayden is quite clear that they made their application for "Cody" in August, and from August 26, most correspondence went out with "Cody" as the return address.[19]

The post office business did not settle that easily, however. In October 1896, Beck had a conversation with Congressman Frank Mondell, who was running for reelection, and learned that the post office designation had been held up by a petition from Hymer "which has a great many signatures on it" protesting against the name Cody, on the grounds that Cody City was already incorporated 2½ miles away. In order to get around the petition, Mondell had suggested that they assign the name "Westfield" so they could at least have a post office in the new town. If Beck is right that Buffalo Bill sent his secretary to Washington to pull what strings he could, as fast as he could, it was probably upon hearing this piece of news. It is barely possible to imagine the history of that piece of ground if Mondell's choice of name had stuck. In the event, it was not until December that the final approval for the post office at Cody arrived in Wyoming; to no one's surprise, E. A. Goodman, Buffalo Bill's nephew, was named postmaster.[20]

The Shoshone Irrigation Company did not incorporate the town of Cody. They did not even form a real town-site company as they laid out the town and began to sell lots, for the company was barred by law from going into the townsite business. It was easy enough to conceive of a way around that law, of course. Elwood Mead himself suggested a plan late in 1895, which Cody and Salsbury implemented in January 1897. The two of them, plus Beck and Rumsey, had each filed entries on a quarter of Section 32-53-101 in July 1896. Now they agreed to dispose of the land in the interest of the company. Beck took the south half of the north half-section and Bronson Rumsey took the north half of the south half, giving Beck his power of attorney. The northernmost and southernmost quarters were taken by Salsbury and Cody, respectively, but were not platted or sold for some years to come. Then, in February 1897, the directors resolved to form the Cody Townsite company, with Alger as treasurer and Rumsey to act as trustee of the lands held by all four directors. During the course of that summer they hired a man to irrigate one-eighth of section 32, which met the requirement for cultivation under the Carey Act.[21]

Every little town, in addition to a saloon and a boarding house, needs a newspaper. Buffalo Bill founded, in 1899, the newspaper that survived the twentieth century in Cody, and therefore is regarded as the man who brought journalism to the north end of the Basin. It appears on closer examination that more of the credit, such as it was, should probably go to George Beck; Bill Cody was involved, of course, as in everything else. In his report to the company directors at the end of 1896, Beck expressed concern that the town of Cody might almost be abandoned over the winter for lack of employment, and this could have adverse consequences for the future of their enterprise. He thought something should be done to keep Cody alive in the public eye. "The most feasible thing . . . is the continuation of the Newspaper which has been started and if necessary I believe that some financial aid should be given to it during the first year."[22]

He referred to a sheet called the *Shoshone Valley News*, the first issue of which had appeared November 26, 1896. Beck had identified the need for a newspaper as part of the campaign to make Cody the county seat, and had sent teams to Lander to pick up the presses and a man who had agreed to come run the newspaper early in October. The board of directors agreed at their February 1897 meeting to subsidize the paper $50 a month for six months. But it soon became clear that Mr. Rathbone, the man hired to run the paper, was no newspaperman. Beck concluded in April that Rathbone was just living in Cody to collect his salary. The paper was not at all satisfactory, but the contract—signed by Buffalo Bill himself as company president—gave no grounds for firing him as long as the paper came out on time. The contract was not renewed, and the first experiment in newspapering along the Shoshone came to a merciful end.[23]

The company chose to start its new town just as a new county, Big Horn County, was being carved out of three others to make a single jurisdiction in the Basin. To George Beck and Bill Cody, this was an opportunity not to be missed. If they could land the county seat for Cody it would guarantee the success of their town and the colony. The idea appears to have originated with Beck, but Cody took to it like a natural campaigner. Early in August, before the name of the town was even settled, Beck took a trip through the Basin to look into the matter. Cody wanted to know what the prospects looked like. Recognizing that no one would vote for a county seat without water, the Colonel used that vision to whip Beck on with the ditch work.[24]

Buffalo Bill's imagination, of course, ran far beyond the ditch. The county seat idea fit in with his strategy of bringing Cody to the attention of the world. To that end, they would have to overcome its isolation. Bridging the river was one of his first concerns, and then laying out a road to Red Lodge so they could establish a mail service. "If a bridge can be built across river for a $1,000 I will agree to build it—And wait for my money if I can ever get it *back*." He urged Beck to write other directors to "get them enthused," and then he made the same appeal to Beck: "Now George I wish you would pump in with all the energy and enthusiasm you can muster—And lift things now is the dark time to show your strength." Cody's idea was to set some stakes and put a grader to work on a Red Lodge road. In other words, "Make a bluff—let it be known over south [southern end of the county] that a shorter road is to be built through our Town to the R.R." For his own part, he promised to push hard in Washington to get the post office business settled. He also wanted an estimate of the cost to bridge the river. He closed urgently: "Now or never George—Don't weaken—but get an excitement started. . . . George—you and I started that enterprize. Lets carry it through."[25]

Beck and Cody agreed that this was not the right time to fold tents; rather, they should push ahead with construction on the ditch and, in addition, start building a bridge across the Shoshone to open the road from Red Lodge to the Basin, start a newspaper, and start building a road to Yellowstone Park. All of these things would make Cody a logical county seat. But Buffalo Bill vaccilated. Within a single week in September, he seemed to accept the inevitability of a shutdown, then swung back into the fight with as much energy as ever. The catalyst may well have been a bold move by George Beck, who traveled to meet with the new county commissioners early that month and made them a grand offer. The Cody Townsite Company would give them a city block and a city park adjoining, and invest $5,000 in a courthouse if they would settle county government there. This was in the nature of an investment that Beck expected to recoup through lot sales, the price of which would jump dramatically if they won. When he learned of this, Buffalo Bill came fully alive again. It looked to him like a chance to get the reluctant board members back into line, "and in Nov. we will be hammering away at the bluff with all kinds of powder, and a strong force."[26] He wanted Beck to spare no tricks in the county seat fight; he especially approved of the court house offer.

The Colonel even offered to take on and operate the company hotel in Cody, as long as the company understood that he was doing it for the good of them all and not just to make a profit for himself. He thought it was an important part of the push for the county seat. In place of criticism and abuse, he heaped praise and encouragement on Beck. He wished he could be there campaigning with him: "I am as much interested in that election as I am in the Presidential election." If Beck could hire a good man or two to work on the campaign, Cody would see they got paid. "Keep this thing red hot and win if possible."[27] Beck was ready to play the game. When the Burlington and Missouri River Railroad sent one of their construction engineers out to run a survey up the North Fork toward Yellowstone, Beck made sure everyone in the Basin knew of it. When he told Buffalo Bill of this, the Colonel raised the ante yet again. He was trying to get state engineer Mead to work up an estimate for the North Side proposition; if Mead came to Cody, Beck was to get him all the help he needed and make sure people heard of it. "We want to make all the bluff we can this month, everything goes in a county seat fight. So don't be afraid to exaggerate—even to lieing [sic]. Tell them Mead is coming."[28] A new road to Red Lodge, a rail connection to Yellowstone through Cody, and a dramatically expanded irrigation scheme, with Elwood Mead personifying the unity of interest between the State and the Shoshone Irrigation Company: how could the people of the county not see this as the way to go? How could his fellow directors hold back when the prize was so close? This was the imagination of the celebrity developer at work.

Once again Nate Salsbury stands as a foil to Buffalo Bill. Beck made another attempt to convince him to help them with the county seat fight in October. He suggested to Salsbury that they put the bond issue up as collateral for a loan to finance the county seat fight. Nate thought it a decent idea, but stood utterly certain that no one would loan them anything on the bonds until they could honestly say they were earning enough on the ditch to pay the interest. From there he moved to a more general observation: "As you say, 'The Company has ventured so far &c, &c.' That has been the trouble from the start. It has been nothing but venture all the time." There had been no assurances that the company could meet the obligations all these ventures entailed, or provide for future liabilities. "It has been a kind of trust to luck game from the first."[29] He offered his support as a director to Beck's plan to bond the company to build a courthouse, but would go no further.

As it happened, the election did not go Cody's way; the equally new town of Basin City, on the banks of the Big Horn River, won out. Beck rode up and down and across the Basin pushing Cody, but he labored alone. At one time he thought they had 500 votes, but in the end only 243 citizens bought the vision of Cody wrapped up in that glittering package, and most of those surely worked for the Company or lived under the ditch. That total was less than a quarter of the votes cast, but considerably greater than the actual population of the town. It is hard to see how anyone could have thought that a little town a few months old with half a dozen buildings, no real post office, and no working water supply had a chance, or that the kind of bluff Buffalo Bill was trying to run could succeed outside the show business world. Still, it is impossible not to admire the willingness to take on the fight, to run the risk, that infused Bill Cody's attitude—and George Beck's as well—not just toward the county seat but toward his entire enterprise in the Big Horn Basin.[30]

Water was, of course, an issue from the beginning, in the town as well as on the farms. Beck talked optimistically in the summer of 1896 about getting water to the town, but was unable to accomplish it. In September, Buffalo Bill gave thought to the plight of his settlers in the coming winter. What would people at Irma do for water when the ditch did not run? Should they not have a cistern, and should it not be built now to be ready? "I know that's their looks out, but they should be told and warned, and persuaded to build them. Same for the Town. Let me know if you are providing for these things."[31] Beck was pleased to reply that he had been urging people for two months to build cisterns. He nevertheless thought the company would have to build a public cistern at Irma and another one at Cody. He promised to get everyone who expected to draw from it to join together in the building of it. He fully appreciated the seriousness of the winter water question.[32]

It was not only a question of winter water in that arid environment. While the men were working on the townsite in 1897, before the irrigation lateral reached the town, they needed water for domestic purposes in the few buildings they had managed to construct. The river ran by Cody through a canyon fifty feet below the townsite and a quarter-mile from where they were working. Beck had a well dug beside the river, where they struck good water only six feet down: water taken directly from the river frequently carried too much silt to be potable. They lined the well with stone from the quarry and began hauling drinking, washing, and cooking water up the hill. Individuals set up water hauling businesses, and water barrels became the indispensable adjunct to every building in the new town until a water system was finally installed in 1905.[33]

On April 30, 1897, the water first ran in the ditches of the new town of Cody. Because it was a year later than everyone had hoped, Beck restrained his excitement when he reported this momentous event, but it is clear that he was proud of the achievement. He took pictures of the laterals bringing water to town gardens for the first time. The following day, which was coincidentally Arbor Day, Beck sent a crew to the river to dig up some five- and six-year-old trees for transplanting to Irma and Arta parks, grace notes in the town plan on the west end. The mighty cottonwoods that shade those parks today could have been among the wagon loads brought up May 1, 1897. Beck irrigated the parks, the eight acres of farmland plowed on the townsite, and an eighty-acre farm adjacent to the town taken by a Mrs. Polhamus, a stenographer with the Wild West, which he openly referred to as Col. Cody's land.[34] Beck made no attempt to disguise his satisfaction as he told his fellow directors of each increment of growth on the new townsite.

The townsite was useful to the Irrigation Company even before they started to sell it. When Beck resumed operations in the spring of 1897, he had Buffalo Bill's ranch manager, Charley Trego, plowing land in the townsite—particularly Cody's quarter-section—in which he planned to plant a great variety of seeds in one-acre sections to see what did well there, and to grow seed to furnish to settlers when they came. He hired one Albert Blummel to live in town and supervise the planting and irrigation; Beck called him their "farmer," and the land on the town-site he worked was the "experimental farm." They spent the spring leveling land, burning sagebrush, and plowing the townsite, including the parks named after Buffalo Bill's two daughters. In that spring they also began to build in the town, and Beck hired one of the last of the Nagel Germans, a man named Ammon who turned out to have skills as a mason, to operate a stone quarry and lime kiln near town. Early buildings were as likely to be stone as wood, since lumber was scarce. Once water was available, Beck tried to plant as much land as possible, both to provide object lessons to settlers and to keep the prices of grain and vegetables within reason in the area. He planted both the townsite and Bill Cody's holdings under the canal.[35]

The company built a hotel to accommodate workers and visitors. George Canfield came over from the Sheridan Inn, probably to help them set it up. The hotel doubled as a church when a minister happened to be in town on Sunday. Toward the end of April a schoolteacher arrived, whom Beck regarded as a very important addition, and they began planning to build a school. Late in May, after several trips to investigate, the Yegen Company of Billings sent a man to open a general store in Cody. Whether that venture succeeded or not is hard to say, but in August, H. P. Arnold, one of the founders of the original Cody City, told Beck he was going to move his store to Cody. Company workers found time to fence all the crops in and around the town that same month using fence posts they had cut and stacked at Irma. They also fenced the new parks to protect the newly planted trees. The company had extensive gardens of cabbage and tomatoes, and Beck tried to seed wild rice and watercress along the banks of the reservoir above town.[36]

Late in June the new town experienced its first blast of foul weather when a hailstorm a mile and a half wide roared through and in about fifteen minutes nearly ruined the season's work on the town garden. Beck thought the field crops, though hurt, would survive the storm better than the vegetables. The hail also nearly ruined the roof of the hotel and commissary and broke out several windows. A week or so later the garden looked good again, after considerable replanting by Mr. Blummel. As it turned out, only the tomatoes did not produce a decent crop. When the company work force was completely laid off in August, the remaining staff and the work force employed by Colonel Cody on his lands combined in a single mess and the garden supplied them all. It was a tiny town, but they hired a teacher and got their school running in November. There were only twelve students and they met in the unused premises that had once housed the *Shoshone Valley News*, but it was a start.[37]

One of the things they needed to supply their settlers was fuel for the winter. Wood was not a practical source for any number of people, so coal became essential. Cody and Beck located good coal deposits near to town in the first year, and Buffalo Bill incorporated a company to mine and market it. He had men working the mine, on Sage Creek, through the winter, and those who used it found it a good grade of coal. The mine, with attached house and stable, was still running the second winter. Beck determined to employ his irrigator, Blummel, as a coal miner during the winter season. There was also a small vein of coal right on the edge of the townsite, at the western end of Salsbury's claim, that produced good fuel.[38]

Others who were crucial to the success of the colony, particularly the Burlington Railroad people, were interested in coal. The Burlington could not sustain its plan to build across the Continental Divide without good coal supplies along the route. In the summer of 1897 no less a person than Frank Mondell came through Cody to look the country over, especially to look for coal. Mondell, who was first elected to Congress in 1894 and went on later to represent Wyoming for twelve more terms, had been washed out of office in the Populist tide of 1896, so he was in the Basin as a working citizen. He had worked for and with the Burlington for years, especially in the development of his hometown, Newcastle. He was also interested in the Shoshone valley, having only recently given up a state water right lower down the river that was large enough to supply a major development. Bill Cody and Nate Salsbury had taken it up as soon as Mondell let it go. On this trip, Mondell and a companion were going on up the South Fork, following the Burlington survey, prospecting for coal and looking for any other resources the country might offer.[39]

Another significant arrival late in the fall was Buffalo Bill himself. It was always a big event when Cody came to Cody, but in the early years it must have been particularly important. Not only was he the president of the company, but he was far and away the biggest landowner in the area and he also owned the blacksmith shop, the livery barn, and other businesses in town. Probably half the population of the area worked for Bill Cody, in addition to those who worked for the company. A man named Frank Houx, later to become a mayor of the town and secretary of state for Wyoming, had started a stone house on the main street but moved away, leaving it unfinished. Beck got a man to finish it off and plaster the inside so it would be ready for Buffalo Bill's party to use. Beck was told to expect him November 4, with "quite a party including several of our stockholders." Colonel Cody also "requested" that there be water running through town when he arrived, so Beck had to put some men to work repairing the flume, even though irrigating season was behind them. Freezing weather and Buffalo Bill arrived November 5; ice caused some breaks in the canal, so water was turned off as soon as the president had seen it. When the great man arrived he was accompanied by only five guests, one of whom was Henry Gerrans of Buffalo, a friend of the Buffalo directors, soon to become a major investor and one day join the board himself. Gerrans contracted for 160 acres before he left.[40]

It had already become a settled practice for Buffalo Bill to go immediately to the high country to hunt when he arrived in the fall. He took his party up the North Fork of the Shoshone this year, leaving on the 7th and returning on the 11th. The day after they got back the Colonel hosted the entire town at a party in honor of his guests, an event that showed "a decided gain in the number and character of the population of Cody." Buffalo Bill and Henry Gerrans also decided to invite the gentlemen of the company to go in on the building of a general store and a flour mill. Beck expected those improvements to centralize the trade of the entire county at Cody. Clearly, when Bill Cody was in town the energy level shot up, and the prospects of the town started to look better.[41]

As if to solidify that sense, Colonel Cody and a local rancher, A. C. Newton, made large donations to start a public subscription for a bridge over the Shoshone at Cody. The bridge, much discussed a year earlier, would be a large, tangible step toward connecting the new settlement with the outer world, via the railroad at Red Lodge, fifty miles away. Buffalo Bill personally contracted with two local builders to do all the construction for $350, and Newton donated the logs. Beck had the approaches graded and he and Okie Snyder, one of the Colonel's men who had taken 160 acres near Irma, donated 500 feet of 1½-inch wire cable. It was a community effort, led by the little town's principal citizen.[42]

The bridge soon revealed a divide within the company's board of directors. When they met the following March, an "informal" gathering at Nate Salsbury's house attended by only four directors, they took the position that the company should own the bridge. A few weeks later Cody and Salsbury told Beck they thought it should be turned over to the county. Obviously, there were cross-currents within the company board of directors. Cody and Salsbury were the most reliable sources of cash for operations, and expected their opinions to carry a little more weight. They had both been present at the March meeting but must have had second thoughts as they considered the impact of the bridge on the town and collective energy and money already devoted to it. George Beck, on the spot as always, had to navigate the swirling waters of the board as best he could. He finessed the issue by reminding the directors that keeping the bridge as company property would make it a taxable asset, while a county bridge would be maintained by the public.[43]

After his stay in the tiny outpost along the Shoshone, Buffalo Bill returned to North Platte for Christmas 1897, then went down to Cheyenne to do a little business with Elwood Mead. In fact, he appears to have failed to meet Mead. As he explained later, "I went to Cheyenne to see you and the Govenor, but went with too gay a party, but the great mistake was I went to the Fort first." This seems to indicate a rip-roaring drunk with the army there. He continued in the same vein: "I did meet the Govenor in Denver but I was still trotting quite a pace and I did not get to say to him what I wished to," and closed, "Well I am down to business and have joined up with the water wagon train for annother year."[44] Cody asked Mead to please write him in Buffalo, and told him about the beginnings of settlement success at Cody, including the plans for a general store and flour mill. It seems clear that he had been so incapacitated by drink that he was unable to conduct business for days. Successful capitalist entrepeneurs, even in the 1890s, generally held themselves to a higher standard than that.

At the end of January 1898, Buffalo Bill was back in Cody. He continued to pour out to Mead his satisfaction with their progress. He was letting a contract for a store building, thirty feet by eighty feet, which was to be built in forty days, and which would become a warehouse for a new store to be built in the summer. He was also contracting for a foundation for the flour mill.[45] In fact, most of this was taking place in Buffalo Bill's imagination, not on the ground. No doubt the store building was real enough, but it would be years before a new one was built or a foundation laid for a flour mill. Although the directors had talked about a mill, there had been no final determination to build one, for all of Cody's wishful thinking. One wonders how well Mead recognized the confusion between dreams and reality that plagued Bill Cody's business ventures. However that played out, it is clear that keeping Mead thinking positively about the Cody Canal was important to Buffalo Bill.

The flour mill question absorbed a lot of directorial time and attention during the spring of 1898. Beck backed the idea enthusiastically, arguing that it would draw the trade of the entire county to Cody if they got a mill going. The flour mill, which was apparently the subject of considerable discussion at a board meeting in March, was not to be strictly a company project. Some directors wanted to invest in it, but it would be independent of the irrigation work and open to other investors. The new store building was nearing completion at the beginning of April, giving Beck more ammunition for his campaign to build a flour mill. Bleistein met Buffalo Bill in Detroit to talk about the mill, and Gerrans peppered Beck with questions about the amount of wheat grown around Cody, the length of a proposed milling season, and the like. Still, by the end of May, Buffalo Bill saw clearly that the growth of the town was going to depend upon him and Salsbury; the others would spend no more money.[46]

Cody, typically, swelled with energy and enthusiasm when the picture of the flour mill arose in his mind. "I am just as anxious as you are for the mill," he wrote Beck in the summer, in the same spirit he had approached the county seat earlier. Beck was to talk to everyone in town about purchasing stock; Cody himself would put up $2,000. "Now George jump to it. And lets get the work started. Wire me soon as possible what can be done. P.S. I believe Newton will take $500 or a $1000 worth of stock. If work is commenced. *Rush it.*"[47] Then, only ten days later, the Colonel acknowledged that the mill would have to wait another year; the Buffalo men simply would not put up any more money, and he refused to go it alone. He did allow as how the timber might be sawed, for lumber would keep and they would have it ready when they had the money to build.[48]

The town of Cody in 1899. Note the irrigation lateral running in the lower left corner.
Courtesy of Park County Archives, Cody, Wyo.

Of course, there were other pressing needs in the struggling town.
By March of 1898, they had run their school for four months, but they
had only enough money to pay the teacher for two, and more students
were coming in to the district. Local subscription pledges got up only
around $30 a month for the teacher, so they owed her another $20 for
each month. Beck urged his fellow directors to make up the difference,
which they did. The Buffalo men who were taking on the store independently of the company sent out a man to set it up and run it, but he
was dissatisfied with the structure they had built and soon left. The
Shoshone River bridge construction proceeded on schedule, and the
first teams crossed the river there on April 19. However, that bridge did
not survive the challenge of the first year's high water: it washed out in
June 1898, and they had to rebuild. When the second bridge was completed the following spring, Salsbury could not restrain his mordant
humor: "I am glad to hear that the bridge is done, and hope that it will
stay there at least a year, so that we can get the reputation of knowing
how to build a bridge, to offset the last disaster."[49] Buffalo Bill tried to
find someone other than George Beck to blame for the bridge collapse;

perhaps he had begun to see how much good work Beck was doing for them. For instance, when he could not find anyone to lease the farm-land at the western edge of town, Beck took the lease himself rather than let the land lie idle. Although there would be more troubled times in their relationship, Cody seemed to respect the work Beck did in building the town.[50]

The Shoshone Irrigation Company found it difficult to get their town of Cody up and running. A panoramic photograph of the town in 1899 shows so little development that a claimed population of over five hun-dred in 1900 seems impossible.[51] Annual resolutions to see that a flour mill was built were set aside each year as debt and general uncertainty made such an investment perilous; not until 1905 was it constructed. Water supply problems that plagued the entire project did not spare the town. They managed—barely—to get a school set up for the children. Well-supplied with saloons but rather short of churches, the town used one of the former to fund the construction of one of the latter. As George Beck told it, he and Colonel Cody were playing poker with Tom Pursell and a couple of ranchers one night in Pursell's saloon. They opened a jackpot and everyone stayed in until the pot reached $500. Before the last hand was dealt, they agreed that the winner would have to donate the money toward the building of a church. Beck won the hand, so the first church in Cody, built some time around 1900, was an Episcopal Church, with a building fund of $550. By such shifts was the town patched together until it could get a good hold on the ground.[52] That required the arrival of a railroad.

CHAPTER FOUR

Settling the Land

Building even a medium-sized irrigation system is a difficult and complicated enterprise. Certainly the Shoshone Irrigation Company encountered problems for which it was not prepared in constructing the ditch, but the directors' lives were additionally complicated by the fact that their task was more than a matter of digging a ditch. While the construction went on, there were matters of settlement to manage. They needed to find colonists to take up land under that canal and they wanted to attract citizens to live in the new town they were founding in the middle of the project. The complications attendant upon these human affairs often made the construction work look like child's play. George Beck's urging of his fellow directors to take hold of the settlement problem at the end of 1896 was propelled by the problems they encountered in their first year of operation.[1]

Wyoming statute governed the administration of the Carey Act. The Shoshone Land and Irrigation Company had signed a contract with the State stipulating the cost of settlement. The land was virtually free: colonists were required to pay only fifty cents per acre filing fee to the State to cover the costs of administering the act. The company was allowed to charge settlers ten dollars per acre for the water rights. Legal settlement of the land was to follow the terms of the Homestead Act of 1862 (for which see below.) Settlers typically entered claims on 40- and 80-acre lots, although some claimed 160, the maximum allowed under the Homestead

Act. A settler who wanted 80 acres would owe the Company $800; he could pay it at once or spread it over five years at 6 percent interest. After having paid off their obligations to the company and fulfilled their obligations under the Homestead Act, the settlers would own their land and the irrigation system that watered it; each 40-acre lot entitled the holder to one share of ownership in the new canal company. If everything worked as it was drawn up, this settlement program had great potential for getting farmers on public land in the West. Certainly the State and the Shoshone Irrigation Company regarded it as a great opportunity. Unfortunately, a great gulf lay hidden between their vision and the reality of frontier colonization at the end of the nineteenth century.

As noted earlier, Buffalo Bill was negotiating with prospective settlers before construction even started on the canal. From the beginning, he took a more active interest in the colonization aspect of the enterprise than any of the other partners. He was attuned from his show business experience to the public relations aspect of colonization, and he was eager to use the publicity arm of the Wild West to encourage Americans to seek their fortunes in the Big Horn Basin. From the fall of 1895, Cody pestered Beck for information from Wyoming. He wanted pictures to show people, examples of minerals, anything to get people into conversation. "Send me some more of that building rock, gypsom, sulphur, asphalt and anything I can show or talk on. Send it quick and please write me whats being done."[2] He was avid for the game. Only after several years of hard experience did he ever learn just how difficult the business of development could be.

The "German Colony" (as he called it), first got Buffalo Bill excited about settlement prospects. It was a shadowy bunch, apparently composed of immigrants, whose agent was a man named S. V. Nagle, an associate of the firm of F. A. Nagle, Commission Merchants, of Chicago. Cody frequently talked to newspapers of his dreams for the Big Horn Basin, and Nagle sniffed out an opportunity. He first contacted Cody in September 1895, long before formal advertising had begun. He convinced Cody that he had a big group of German families, people with some money, who were looking for a new home. The two stayed in touch over the winter. In the spring of 1896, Nagle traveled out to the Basin to look over the canal and the country. After he returned to Chicago, he arranged a meeting of the potential colony (and their parish priest) with Buffalo

Bill. Cody was supremely confident; he told Elwood Mead they would have a thousand people at Cody by the first of June! Once again his imagination was running ahead of his accomplishment.[3]

Nagle had driven a hard bargain as settlement agent for the company. He wanted $300 per month for office and expenses in Chicago in addition to his commission. Apparently, he was to receive his entire commission from the first payment on the lands, although he agreed to leave the first $10,000 with the company as a guarantee of good faith. He also persuaded them to allow the settlers to pay only 10 percent cash as their first annual payment. Cody insisted that subsequent colonists would have to pay 20 percent annually from the beginning, as the standard contract read, but he obviously had lost that argument with Nagle for this first group. Eagerness to have a group commit to their new colony would explain this financial arrangement. Cody was nevertheless proud of the deal he had worked out with Nagle.[4]

Again, Buffalo Bill was completely unrealistic about the complexity of combining construction and settlement. He was, of course, paying out more money than anyone else for the construction, and consequently more worried than the other directors about acquiring a steady income to help support the cost of construction. But it was plain folly to bring settlers to the land before there was water available for them to work the ground. Beck knew this better than anyone, but his attempts to inject some reality into Cody's view of their problem met with incredulity and bluster. "Cunningham [one of the original partners] writes me he has a good colony ready to go—and men with money. And I don't see why they are bared [sic] George."[5] Flurries of action were Cody's metier; he had neither time nor taste for careful, considered planning.

Nagle led the company a long and difficult way to an empty and frustrating end. Early in April 1896, Bill Cody was in Chicago with Nagle, supposedly getting the colony ready to depart for the Basin. After leaving Chicago, he rushed to Buffalo to arrange for some money.[6] Nagle chose that moment to wire Beck a bombshell: "Unless you meet me at Omaha prepared to conclude mercantile arrangements colony will not start Have based all preparations on your proposition answer quick."[7] Apparently, Bronson Rumsey, who had been in Wyoming when Nagle was there, had offered Nagle the prospect of operating a general store in the new settlement. Beck clearly knew of it and had probably gone along with it. Buffalo Bill had conferred with Nagle in Chicago in March and in April, but they apparently did not talk about the mercantile enterprise. That was a significant omission, for Nagle expected the company to place some funds at his disposal in a special account for what he called "the Western Mercantile Company." He needed other things from Beck: examples of cereals grown in the Basin, building stone, etc., none of which Beck was able to provide. Nagle was clearly annoyed with Beck on a number of counts, but the real sticking point was the mercantile company. Beck obviously knew the mercantile offer had not come from the full company, and he found himself surprised and embarrassed when Nagle pushed it so hard. Nagle had made arrangements with wholesalers for purchasing the needs of his colony on credit, but needed the final authority from the company to establish his accounts. Beck was unable to provide that.[8]

Beck did travel to Omaha to meet Nagle. Cody, who was in Philadelphia, wired Beck in Omaha, inquiring what was going on and urging him to contact potential investors while he was in town. He also wanted Beck to get his business done and get back to work on the canal.[9] Both Nagle and Beck sent Buffalo Bill messages from Omaha, which he claimed he could not understand. "Nagle had no agreement with me about starting store & yesterday wired would load today. Fearful blunder some place[.] We cannot buy wagons for Colony[.] Wish you would please write."[10] The reference to the wagons suggests that Nagle also expected the company to buy the equipment necessary to get the colony there. Cody understood the Germans to have enough money, perhaps $400 per family, to support the expense of moving, and suggested that Nagle give up his first commission payment to cover the cost of wagons and collect it from the settlers later. Beck moved on to Chicago, where Cody ordered him to find an interpreter and interview each family to find out what Nagle had promised them, particularly about farming implements. Beck was also to try to find out who the middleman for the settlers was, and why Nagle dealt with Rumsey instead of Cody himself.[11]

The next day he wired Beck to come to Philadelphia at once, and also reminded him that the colony was very important to their success, so he should give every concession possible.[12]

We can only imagine the fireworks when Beck, Cody, and the other investors met in Philadelphia. Buffalo Bill seems somehow to have emerged from this crisis with his confidence in Nagle intact. He was, as we have seen, already upset with Beck, and this debacle can only have made that worse. But Cody's own vacillation in dealing with Nagle put the company in a difficult spot. The directors swallowed hard and authorized an expense of $4,200 to move the colony to the Basin, but insisted that all purchases be handled by the company store of the Shoshone Land and Irrigation Company; Nagle clearly lost out on his "mercantile proposition." Thinking he had solved the problems with Nagle, the Colonel then ordered Beck to tell Dennis Cunningham in Omaha to get his settlers ready, although Beck had already said he did not think they were ready for them. For his part, Nagle made a show of following through; he told Beck the families would leave for Billings at the end of April, where he expected to find wagons with groceries and implements for them.[13] A week or so later they completed their journey, a grand total of seven families, without resources and at the mercy of this fledgling water company and the wild Wyoming summer. It was not an auspicious beginning.[14]

When June arrived, all the directors were in Chicago trying to sort out the ditch business, and Buffalo Bill was talking with representatives of another big colony interested (so they said) in the Big Horn Basin. Nagle's contract earned him a 10 percent commission for each settler he secured. Buffalo Bill hoped, by dealing directly with potential colonists, to avoid paying commissions and thereby secure the entire income to the company. He tried to get other directors, particularly Beck, to help him, to avoid having to turn the prospects over to Nagle or some other commission agent.[15] But he got no help, and they continued to rely on agents. Cody's energy was prodigious, but even he could not simultaneously run the Wild West and manage the recruitment of colonists for the Big Horn Basin.

Cody enlisted Elwood Mead in the colonization work, implicitly relying upon Mead's own determination to make a success of the Carey Act in Wyoming in order to get from him work that fell quite outside the ordinary definition of engineering. Even before President Cleveland had signed the papers authorizing the project, Buffalo Bill had Mead writing copy for an advertising folder. Mead sent maps to an office in Chicago that the company had set up to handle colonization, and worked with the Burlington and Missouri River Railroad to establish freight rates to the colony. He confessed he "found it rather a difficult matter to handle."[16] He joined Cody in urging Beck to keep at the ditch work so there would be water for settlers in the spring.[17] What Beck needed was someone to rein in Buffalo Bill, but what he got was another rider on his own back.

Although a few colonists did arrive in the summer of 1896, the only people to make formal application for entry under the canal that year were directors (Cody, Salsbury, Beck, and Rumsey) of the company and employees of the Wild West. There were eight of these entries, seven for quarter-sections, in July of 1896.[18] These entries were more in the nature of investments than genuine colonization. They were also involved in unknowable ways with the business of the Wild West and the unceasing patronage Buffalo Bill extended to members of his own family. He sent Alger money to pay the first water right payment and state fees for two of his men, William Sweeney and George Berch. He sent another check for three others to pay their state fees and asked that the water right charges for their parcels be charged to him personally "and I will take chances on collecting it." To complicate matters further, Cody wanted his nephew, Ed Goodman, to act as agent for these new colonists. Goodman would get a 10 percent commission, but only half of it out of their first payments; Cody himself would pay him that 5 percent. He wanted Beck to sort this out and answer fully, "*at once.*"[19] The Colonel would work himself around the clock to avoid paying a commission to legitimate land agents, but here he went out of his way, at his own expense, to steer that 10 percent to his sister's son.

The company laid out a small village on the upper reach of the canal and named it "Irma," after Cody's young daughter. It built several structures there for the colonists, one of which was a house for an irrigation specialist who would help the colonists learn this method of farming. The families who arrived took up some land on the upper end of the project, in the area that came to be known as Irma Flat. The company sold the priests who were leaders of Nagle's group a block in the new town it was laying out. The colony intended to farm on the European pattern: they would live in the village and go out to their farms to work. Even though the settlers had made only small down payments, they still needed help. Colonel Cody worried about them from afar: "George, I understand some of those Germans Nagle brought are broke already," he wrote in July. "I wish you would have a talk with them and find out just how they are situated and if Nagle is treating them squarely. You might say its none of our business but I say it is."[20] The directors of the company helped them with farm implements, some stock and horses; they even furnished seed for planting. But the colonists were few and poor and they did not stick. Beck recalled later that when it came time for them to put up the second payment they appeared in a body, all in their shabbiest clothes, and protested they could not pay. Eventually, all left except for one family.[21]

In addition to the considerable hardships involved in immigrating to this lonely frontier outpost, the Germans faced a typical western problem of getting along with their new neighbors. The cattle and sheep ranchers who had had the Shoshone valley to themselves were not happy to see the land plowed and planted. The settlers had neither time nor money to fence their farms, and had to adopt a night watching system to keep the ranchers from running their stock on the new crops. The ranchers regarded the whole country as open range, and would not accept any limitation on where they might graze their stock. Some apparently herded their cattle down to the Irma settlement and personally headed their stock toward the open farm fields. Somehow bloodshed was avoided, but there were uneasy relations between canal settlers—and consequently the canal company—and ranchers for many years. Here, in a classic face-off between Old West and New West, we find Buffalo Bill entirely on the side of the sodbusters.[22]

It also appears that Nagle may have acted in bad faith toward the Shoshone Irrigation Company. He could, of course, have had his own doubts about the capability of the company to deliver water reliably, and in that case "bad faith" would be somewhat mitigated by the company's own dismal performance. In August, Beck suspected Nagle was diverting colonists to "the Sweetwater country"; he may have been referring to another Carey Act project underway in the southwestern part of the state. But Cody continued to have faith in Nagle. Nagle communicated directly with Frank Grouard at Cody's ranch, putting him on notice that he would need two hundred teams in the late summer. As late as mid-August, Cody still believed that Nagle would "land nearly one hundred men there in Sep." He urged Beck to allow these men to work on the canal, and to pay half in cash and half in credit on their water right payments. Salsbury and Bleistein, he noted, had no objections. He reminded Beck that the company had a duty to be as accommodating as possible to their new colonists while they were getting settled: "It will go a long ways toward making them feel at home and that we are glad to have them, etc. Will you instruct all our employees to be pleasant to them people[?]"[23]

By the end of August 1896, the bright prospects Cody had allowed to grow in his mind came crashing down. Beck wrote him that no one in Wyoming had any faith in Nagle, least of all those early colonists he had brought out there. At the same time, Cody learned that the new group Nagle had talked about had fallen through. It seems that Nagle wanted a guarantee of $15,000 worth of work on the canal for them, and the company could not give it. Cody himself told Nagle that his colonists would need to have $1,000 apiece if they expected to make it through the winter. It is hard to imagine that Beck was very disappointed. He found the Germans a difficult group to work with, always grasping for advantage and presuming upon those who tried to help them. He told Cody in August that it looked like those who had worked the summer at Irma might get a fair crop, but he wanted no more to do with Nagle. He had heard that Nagle was using Buffalo Bill's picture and the Shoshone Irrigation Company sign on his Chicago office to enlist settlers for the Sweetwater project, and he thought they should shut Nagle down and take their sign and picture away. Beck would not long lament the departure of Mr. Nagle.[24]

Although Nagle seems to have absorbed most of the time and energy of the company that season, there were other ideas afield. In April 1896, Nate Salsbury urged Beck to use his Omaha connections to get some of them to go out and see the Cody country: "[If] we have *really* got a farming country out there, they will influence a lot of Nebraska people to pull up stakes and come to us." Salsbury also was working on the *Philadelphia Daily Press* "to take up the matter on the same lines that Horace Greely did in Colorado." He thought they might make that work if they could make it valuable to the paper; he was considering proposing to newspapers in all the large eastern cities "to start colonies in the same fashion, for it will give us the benefit of their columns."[25] Obviously, nothing came of this, but the air was pregnant with possibility in those early days.

At the end of 1896, in spite of all the big talk and high hopes, there were still only eight certificates of entry issued under the Cody Canal. Although some of Nagle's Germans were apparently working on land on Irma Flat, none of them had actually signed contracts with the company to begin the legal process for locating land under the Carey Act. The company seems to have allowed them to rent water, not an uncommon tactic where people were without the resources to enter into a purchase contract. Nor did they produce much in the way of a crop. A building put up at Irma for Nagle had been taken over by the Irrigation Company, which also claimed virtually all the produce of the Flat for the year.

Under these conditions Beck urged his fellow directors to reconsider their approach to finding colonists. He urged that an agent be employed to work in Colorado and Utah, where there were already people familiar with irrigation farming. He thought the long-term chances of success would be better with some experienced irrigation farmers on the land. He also thought they should do everything they could to promote the town of Cody, such as building a telegraph line to Red Lodge and starting a newspaper that could advertise Cody to the rest of the world.[26]

Buffalo Bill was, of course, very much in favor of an aggressive advertising campaign for Cody and the new land. He had already placed a great deal of newspaper advertising in major dailies across the land. Truth was the first casualty in these ads, which sometimes took the form of interviews with the Colonel himself, a favorite fictional tactic of Major John Burke and the publicity operation of the Wild West. The one that appeared in the *Omaha World-Herald* on July 15, 1896, may unfortunately be typical. Envisioning a future when the Big Horn Basin was filled with productive farms "conceived and built by 'Buffalo Bill' to perpetuate his memory," the paper went on to speak of three thousand eighty-acre farms and a canal one hundred miles long and projected a population for the town of Cody of five thousand within a year. Both Cody and Beck received letters throughout that fall and winter from people who had read advertisements in papers like the *Portland Oregonian* and the *Los Angeles Times*. It is not clear that they ever produced much in the way of colonization; Beck himself, admittedly a jaundiced observer, thought that with all their Wild West ads they ultimately had attracted only one family to the Basin.[27]

In 1897 the company took steps to improve its recruitment of settlers. Members prevailed upon Mead to compose a formal letter promoting the project that they could show to investors and colonists, an idea that Nate Salsbury had first put forward in 1895. "I regard the Cody Canal as one of the most important and valuable projects ever inaugurated in this state, and believe it is destined to exercise great influence on our growth in wealth and population," he began, and he went on to praise the climate, the abundant water supply, and the plan to transfer ultimate ownership of the land to actual settlers.[28] The letter was then incorporated into a lavish twenty-six-page illustrated brochure promoting both the town and the irrigated farming possibilities of the colony. This was apparently put together by the company's newly hired colonization agent, D. H. Elliott, and it was printed in Buffalo. It marks a dramatic escalation of effort over the modest six-page pamphlet put out by the original company in 1895.[29]

The new brochure, titled "Homes in the Big Horn Basin," featured a plat of the town of Cody, hinting at a solidity of settlement that no photograph of the town would have sustained. It also included, in addition to Mead's letter, one from Governor W. A. Richards, disquisitions on the geology of the Big Horn Basin, the history and prospects of irrigation farming, photographs of ranches and farm fields near town, copies of the Carey Act and of Wyoming's statute accepting the Carey Act, even the full text of the contract a settler would sign with the Shoshone Irrigation Company and the prices that would be charged for the land. All this more or less official material provided a nest for a promotional text that made the Big Horn Basin, and particularly Cody, sound better than the fabled valley of the Nile. Not only would superb and varied agricultural products spring from the ground at the touch of water, but crops would never fail: "Under ordinary conditions, no legitimate business is so precarious as farming. In the Big Horn Basin it will have the certainty of a mathematical demonstration." As for the climate, "it is hardly possible to describe the charms and health-giving qualities of this region without indulging in what would seem to be extravagance." Statistics were cited that appeared to show that people lived longer in Wyoming than in the East. As most readers know, land promotions stand near the top of the list in any history of American fraud, and "Homes in the Big Horn Basin" was a fine example of the kind of advertisement that sustained such promotions. For all that, this brochure by itself could never have saved the Cody Canal.[30]

The new brochure made strikingly different use of the fame of Buffalo Bill than the first one had done. The 1895 brochure was titled "Ideal Western Lands selected by the famous 'Buffalo Bill'" and featured prominently on the cover a portrait bust of Cody from Wild West publications. The text began with reference to Buffalo Bill and essentially based its appeal on the fact that Bill Cody had chosen to live in this land and therefore others should. On the cover of the new publication, a man who might be Cody is shown standing in a field, but no identification of the figure is made, and although W. F. Cody is clearly listed as president of the company, only one reference is made to him in connection with the irrigation project. When Buffalo Bill appears in this new brochure it is in connection with a game preserve he intended to establish upriver from Cody; symbolically, he is the hunter, not the farmer, and the experience he is invoking in these photos hearkens to a time and place ruled by guns rather than plows.[31] This is an early intimation of an important shift in the way Bill Cody approached his venture on the upper Shoshone.

Buffalo Bill loved the upper Shoshone River country principally because it was some of the best country left in America for big game hunting. The high mountain parks above both the South Fork and the North Fork of the Shoshone were filled with game—elk, big horn sheep, bear, deer—in majestic isolation from the money-making world to the east. Hunting was what Bill Cody did when he was most himself, and hunting, he believed, would set his irrigation project apart from the run-of-the-mill farming operations elsewhere in the West. Each year when the Wild West closed down, Cody would bring a group of wealthy and influential men out to his new home and take them up in the mountains to hunt. He invited Wyoming governors and other political and governmental leaders to join him and his eastern friends, showing each party how much he meant to the other. These hunting parties were in a sense the first instances of the bridging of local and metropolitan cultures that became a hallmark of Cody's life and legacy. They were also instrumental in establishing and expanding his own celebrity, which was such an important element in his strategy as a developer.[32]

Buffalo Bill's close personal interest and supervision of the colonization in and around Cody in the early years was manifested in many ways. In November 1896, the first winter of the new town of Cody, Buffalo Bill brought a hunting party to town for two weeks of hunting, partying, and taking the waters of the springs. The company included Wyoming governor William A. Richards, who was familiar with the Big Horn Basin and the plans of the Cody Canal. Another of the hunters was D. H. Elliott, whose experience included service as land promoter for the Kansas Pacific Railway. After looking over Cody in the company of Buffalo Bill, Elliott accepted Buffalo Bill's offer of a position as land commissioner for the company. When Elliott set to work on a new advertising brochure, Buffalo Bill himself devised a relief map of the West that showed the Big Horn Basin on larger scale and indicated the several routes of access by railroad; he had apparently been using it in

Wild West advertising that year. Programs from 1897 to 1903 displayed prominent advertisements for the Cody Colony.[33]

When Elwood Mead traveled into the Big Horn Basin in the spring of 1897, he took the opportunity to offer some more help in the way of advertising the Cody Canal. It has already been seen how Mead used the office of state engineer to support the project, and how Buffalo Bill patronized him to encourage further help. In fact, Cody had even asked Mead to examine the potential for a colony moving from Crawfordsville, Indiana, his hometown, when Mead visited there the previous winter. He took photographs in the Basin while he was traveling the country with George Beck. Beck then developed the pictures for him, and also gave Mead a file of the best ones he had taken himself, because Mead had said he intended to use a great many pictures of the Basin in his next Biennial Report. The company left no stone unturned in its effort to attract settlers.[34]

The Wild West often built its season around a long run in New York. The show had always provided Buffalo Bill with opportunities to talk about colonization in the Big Horn Basin and plenty of access to news-papermen eager to attract readers through the use of his name. The *New York Journal* of May 23, 1897, carried what Beck termed "a nice article" about the Shoshone Irrigation Company, and this produced several letters to the land commissioner in Cody inquiring about settle-ment. Elliott also had letters from people in Iowa and Illinois, one inquiring about possible excursion rates to Red Lodge. But Beck was not happy with the decision to employ a land agent. Answering the occasional letter did not look much like work to Beck. Acutely conscious of the need to conserve funds, he requested of the other directors that they let him terminate Elliott and stop the drain of expenses for an office that appeared to him to do nothing. The other directors seem to have thought he wanted to shut down the land office itself, and put him off. Beck protested that he wanted only to get rid of this agent, who had spent as much as they had spent on construction and after six months could show no results whatever.[35]

One of the land commissioner's jobs was to classify the land they had for sale. From his first examination of the land, Elliott offered his opinion that no more than 15,000 acres could be sold and cultivated. Beck took issue with this estimate, since all but 1,400 acres had been selected by

Elwood Mead himself. His own conclusion was that possibly 5,000 acres might be hard to sell because they were "more or less rolling or rough." Elliott completed his survey at the end of May, at which time there had been 1,231 acres sold or disposed of. He concluded that of the remaining land under the canal, 6,005 acres were good land, 8,962 acres were "of doubtful utility," 6,400 acres were useless, and 3,840 acres could only be sold when the canal had been extended to Sage Creek. This information (which events showed to be quite accurate) could not have been welcome to men who had invested on the expectation of selling water rights to 26,000 acres! Beck rejected this classification and set Charles Hayden to classifying land under the canal in the summer as if Elliott had never done it.[36]

Cody exchanged letters with Elliott weekly through the summer of 1897, even when on the road with his show. (Elliott's half of this correspondence survives, but none of Cody's letters do.) They wrote in considerable detail about the many and varied means they could imagine to promote the town and the project. In May, Elliott received a letter from the manager of the Afro-American Land and Colonization Company inquiring about possibilities in the Basin. Elliott did not respond favorably; he told Cody that his experience in Kansas with a colony from the South did not fill him with confidence in the ability of poor blacks to thrive in new surroundings. Elliott considered trying to get the Salvation Army, which was planning to move some poor people out of urban areas, interested in the Cody Canal.[37]

One of the more interesting roads not taken in the colonization of the Cody Canal involved Eugene V. Debs, whose Social Democracy movement was contemplating creating a Socialist colony somewhere in the West. Elliott received communications from both Bill Cody and Nate Salsbury at the end of June, directing him to find Debs and to talk to him about setting up a colony at Cody. When Elliott met Debs he judged him to be favorably impressed with the potential at Cody, but Debs could make no commitment, as they were in the early stages of setting up their colonization scheme. Elliott encouraged them to consider taking up the land and leasing the water rights. While claiming complete political neutrality, Elliott was quite enthusiastic about this group. He, Beck, and Cody exchanged several letters in the summer of 1897 concerning the possibility of a Socialist migration to Cody. George

Beck had also exchanged letters with Debs, perhaps even before Elliott got involved.

It is impossible not to wonder how Bill Cody understood Social Democracy, in particular the goals of the colonization movement, which included establishing a political base for Socialist power in a sparsely populated western state. When Elliott wrote to Cody he kept these details out of the letter, preferring to dwell upon his own communication of the virtues of the Big Horn Basin and the possible melioration of the human condition that would follow from such a plan. He even went so far as to say his conversation with Debs had nothing to do with politics. An earlier letter to Salsbury, however, contains a perfectly frank description of the Socialist plan to find a thinly settled state where a concentration of Socialist voters could exercise real influence on electoral politics. Salsbury, a self-described "Black Republican," apparently made no objection. Politics could not stand in the way of success in this suddenly parlous venture. A Socialist plantation would have been a wonderfully colorful addition to Wyoming and the Big Horn Basin, but unfortunately the colonization scheme fell casualty to tensions within the Socialist Party before it could get off the ground.[38]

Elliott and his agents put a great deal of money and time into enticing colonists to the Basin in the summer of 1897. The company formalized with the State a plan by which they could lease water to new people who did not have enough money to begin purchasing a permanent water right. Elliott worked with men in several towns across Illinois, Indiana, Iowa, and Nebraska; at least one of these was suggested by the ever-helpful Elwood Mead. In the spring, these men seemed to have groups interested in moving, but complicated matters, such as working out railroad fares, coordinating people from different places, and caring for crops already in the field (they were recruiting, of course, all farmers) defeated them; in the end none of the excursions planned ever went to the Basin. Buffalo Bill ordered his men in Wyoming to be ready to transport prospective settlers from the railroad at Red Lodge to Cody for a nominal rate, but they were not called upon. All the grand ideas and network of agents had produced virtually nothing by the end of the summer of 1897.[39]

The lack of success in getting colonists led to distress among the company directors. Buffalo Bill and Beck were always the most heavily engaged in the work. Cody relayed some of Elliott's weekly reports to Beck, and seems to have begun to lose faith in Elliott by the end of July. Beck, of course, had run out of patience with Elliott before June. He referred to Elliott as "unemployed" and complained that he spent his time in Cody rather than out on the road. On May 22, he warned Elliott that there would be changes in the land department soon, since it was running high expenses and showing no results. After weeks of complaining about Elliott, Beck received a telegram from Cody and Salsbury in June ordering him to send the land commissioner on the road to stimulate migration. Elliott had actually departed for Omaha before the telegram arrived, but Beck still thought he should be fired. When no immigrants arrived by September, Elliott was paid off and those who had been working with him were instructed to deal only with Beck at Cody.[40]

Some part of the problem with the land commissioner may have been that he considered himself working for Buffalo Bill rather than for the company. This would be the down side of Colonel Cody's strong personal engagement in the settlement operation. There was a similar problem with the employment of Al Goodman as company bookkeeper. George Beck felt that, as manager of the company's business on site, he needed to know what all the employees were doing. After Elliott left Cody, Beck was in the dark as to his activities virtually the entire summer. He learned from Buffalo Bill only in late July that Elliott intended to have an excursion ready to visit Cody on July 27. He complained to the directors that he needed some warning to be ready for such an event (which never, of course, materialized). Cody was a frontier outpost, with few buildings and limited supplies, and it would take significant advance planning to be ready for any kind of invasion of potential settlers. Neither the organization nor the personalities of the Shoshone Irrigation Company conduced to that kind of orderly procedure.[41]

Elliott seems to have been a man of wide interests. He understood Eugene Debs's efforts on behalf of working people to have considerable support among good people, and saw it as an attempt on the part of "the better class of people" to organize charity. The government was becoming, as he said, a "vast trust," and it was in the interest of the monied people who ran the government to make some provision for jobs for the poor. The Cody colonization scheme could fit into that. If they could not find people to come farm under the Cody Canal, perhaps the company could organize a syndicate and cultivate the lands on its own account, to provide employment for the poor. Elliott appealed directly to Buffalo Bill in a letter early in August, in which he began by flattering him, referring to his "mind fruitful in resources for great enterprises." He urged Cody to turn that mind to "evolving some practical scheme" to better develop the natural resources of the country and improve the condition of the people. Cody's varied experience, in Elliott's view, uniquely qualified him to "present a practical plan for solving the problem of civilization, good government, charity and prosperity, the want of which seems to worry the public at present."[42]

This letter might reveal why it was that Cody was impressed with Elliott in the first place. The Colonel enjoyed talking over big issues and was not above being flattered. However, what it shows most clearly is how each of them misjudged the other. Elliott must have known that Buffalo Bill was a McKinley Republican; he seems to have thought that he could influence Cody, a determined capitalist, by appeals to loftier social interests. It is no wonder that Elliott failed as land commissioner, but Cody has to share the blame for putting him in that job in the first place.

Throughout the summer of 1897, Cody's faith in Beck, never really strong, began to fray seriously. He had repeatedly begged Beck for reports on crops, construction, settlement, and expenses. He worried about money and kept a close eye on the work of land agents. In August, he complained bitterly to Beck, "I understand that a daily mail route is going to be put through the Basin, and its not going to strike Cody. This is discouraging news to me, and it looks like lack of energy of Cody." He was sure he could have got it through Cody if he had been informed in time. He closed bitterly, "I will not tire you with any suggestions or consult on any business matters, as I never know whether you receive them, as I never get an answer from you on anything what ever."[43] Stung by this communication, Beck immediately wrote to the postmaster general to get the situation remedied, using his own connections rather than working through Buffalo Bill. He soon had it straightened out; in October he reported that daily mail service would be in effect from July 1, 1898. And some of the land agents, particularly one C. B. Jones of Galesburg, Illinois, began to produce some potential settlers.[44]

Beck reached an agreement in August with Jones, one of whose businesses was titled "The Wyoming Colonization Co.", to pay him expenses up to $75 a month. He knew as he did it that the expense of traveling to find settlers would be greater than the treasury would support, and that Jones's money would have to be paid out of the land sales for which he was responsible. Beck expected to superintend the immigration effort himself, and told the other directors again that it would be better to be scouting in Colorado or Utah, where people knew something about irrigation farming. The crops the company had been growing at Irma and on the townsite would be harvested soon, and he felt he could spare some time for the work. Then, when he was back in Chicago in September on legal business, he met Jones, who had two men with him on the way to the Basin. Later one of these men took out a contract for water rights under the canal.[45]

Beck also thought that some work on the mineral front would help improve settlement prospects. In early September 1897, he had the gravel beds at the mouth of Alkali Creek surveyed and located placer claims there in the names of the company directors. He left it to them whether they would put up the money to develop their claims, but on his own account he set some men to work washing gravel. He was afraid the country would seem too quiet with all work on the ditch shut down; there obviously needed to be a way for people to make money or there would be no town. He named the place "Shoshondyke" and kept eight men working there into October. Several of the other directors were interested in this activity, and Beck traveled to Basin to register the locations with the county in December.[46]

In early October, Beck received a bill from a publishing company in New York for setting up illustrations for a new advertising folder and a proposition for publishing it. This was a project Elliott had begun. Beck knew they were running low on the old material and they needed to be able to advertise, but the money would have to be raised, $190 to $425 for ten thousand folders, depending upon variety of colors and covers to be used. There were to be some improvements on the brochure designed by Elliott in the spring, particularly changing some of the pictures and fitting in the text of the *New York Journal* article from May. Beck encouraged the directors to support this initiative, which he thought he could bring in for $280. He also urged them to come up with some money to pay for colonization efforts, which had run around $150 per month under Elliott. Alger had reported that the treasury was completely empty. Beck reminded everyone that there were also salaries to be met and running expenses that could not be avoided; they needed to face these facts and respond appropriately.[47]

Late in October, Jones arrived in Cody with two men from Kewanee, Illinois, and both talked as if they were going to buy. Jones claimed also to have sold Nagle's old place at Irma and expected a man to arrive soon who would purchase 640 acres. Beck refused to get too excited, saying they had heard enough of hopeful talk and "not one of our land salesmen has as yet made a single sale."[48] Within a week, however, Beck signed the first contract with a settler, John Hoff. Hoff had no money, so Beck kept the papers while Hoff went to work to get the money to make the first payment. A week later Jones brought in three more men who took up 320 acres on the upper stretch of the canal. All of these men wanted to defer their first payment until the new year, to which Beck agreed happily. These prospects offered the first solid grounds for hope that anyone had seen in some time.[49]

C. B. Jones succeeded in bringing seven or eight families from Illinois to settle around Irma during the late fall and winter of 1897–98. After the company directors appointed him land commissioner in March 1898, Cody sent him a long letter of appreciation and encouragement, intended to be shared with the colonists. The letter reached back through American history to the Pilgrims for comparisons to what the Cody settlers were aspiring to do. Florid and overblown as it might have been, the very fact that he chose to send the letter at all shows Buffalo Bill's idea of his role as grand patron of the settlement. After comparing the Big Horn Basin favorably to Utah and expressing his conviction that a season's work would show results as great in Wyoming as already shown around Salt Lake, he assured Jones he would help make the Basin all that it could be. He thanked the people for their patience and promised to see them when his Wild West season was over.[50] This was a genuine letter. Buffalo Bill wanted people to feel good about what they were doing, and he offered his vision of the West and of the future as an aid to that goal.

Years at the pinnacle of American show business, thinking of himself as an educator as well as an entertainer, had apparently given Buffalo Bill a sense of personal responsibility for the morale of the American people in troubled times. He massaged popular feelings through the Wild West show and he expected to do the same along the Cody Canal. Whether he fully understood their motivations or not, he knew very well that people enjoyed being around him. It was not, therefore, an empty promise, but an offer of genuine reward when he told Jones he would see the settlers at Cody after he had done his own work. People might well have felt that they participated in some way in the mighty civilizational work represented in the Wild West show itself by laboring on Cody's project in Wyoming and associating with him when he returned there. Cody certainly encouraged that kind of association.[51]

Before the Colonel left the Basin in the spring of 1898, he gave Beck a set of quite particular instructions, which Beck in turn communicated to the rest of the board, as much for self-protection as for information. Cody's orders were:

1. Keep Jones's promises to settlers; show them all possible attention; keep them pleased if possible.
2. Give the settlers a house for a school.
3. Class all the lands so the Company knows how many acres can be irrigated.
4. Provide a statement for Company farming in 1897.
5. Make recommendations for Company farms in 1898.
6. Estimate the cost for the flume for the lower canal from Sulphur Creek.
7. "What about school here in Cody?"
8. Plant trees all around the park.

These orders reflect the comprehensive but disorganized cast of Buffalo Bill's mind when it came to colonizing: no matter was too large or too small to merit his concern, but nothing commanded his continuing attention.[52]

Beck's letter reporting these commands to the other directors revealed his impatience with the Colonel. He claimed not to know what Jones had promised the settlers, and could not therefore pledge anything in that regard. He would do his best to see them satisfied in their settlement at Irma. The matter of donating the schoolhouse he referred to the decision of the board, although he clearly favored it. Land classification was still a sore point with him. As far as he was concerned, land classification had been completed, and there were 20,000 acres of good land under their canal. He offered a summary report on the Company farms, where the hailstorm had held yields well below expectations, and advised that for 1898 they should lease their acreage to another farmer. Their goal of getting twenty acres of each quarter-section in the townsite under cultivation had been met, and he did not want to be in the farming business. He thought he could get $1.00 per acre per year on a three-year contract. As for school in Cody and planting of trees, these were matters he had well in hand.[53]

Colonel Cody's fretful and inconsistent interventions in the settlement business continued even after the Nagle and Elliott disasters, and there is no evidence he ever learned very much about the business, or about the effect of his own activities on the working of the company. In the summer of 1899, George Beck received, out of the blue, a letter from one John Gilman, a lumberman and land agent with interests from Boston to Idaho. Cody had appointed him agent "to co-operate with you in selling the Big Horn Valley lands." He asked Beck to send him maps and circulars with information as soon as possible, and hoped to be able to stop in to see Cody on his way to Idaho in a few weeks. As with so many of Buffalo Bill's plans or visions, nothing ever came from the Gilman appointment but resentment. We cannot know what Beck did or said when this letter arrived, but he was growing increasingly unhappy with his position in the Shoshone Irrigation Company. A free-lancing company president who showed open disrespect for his work was making his life hard to bear.[54]

This little matter has no consequence but to show how the company worked against itself, or rather how the president carried on without regard to the rest of the company. Things had reached such a pass along the Shoshone, in fact, that the directors of the Shoshone Irrigation Company resolved in 1898 to sell the whole project to anyone who would put up $150,000. Buyers did not step forward, but the directors continued to pursue ways of getting out from under the mountain of obligations the colony had piled upon them. Nevertheless, Buffalo Bill wrote to his friend Mike Russell after Christmas 1899 that "everything is booming at Cody. The Mormon Church want to buy us out—the ranch and all our land—everything but the townsite of Cody—that we wish to keep."[55] Of course, if everything had in fact been booming they would not have been thinking of selling out. The plain facts of the land settlement situation under the Cody Canal were extremely depressing.

By the end of 1899, only twelve people had filed for patents on land segregated to the company, and all twelve of them were connected either to the Wild West or to the company itself. A number of others had contracted with the company for water rights and had not yet filed, but overall it looked very little like a boom.[56]

Settlers on public land in the West took up their acres under one or another of the laws passed during the nineteenth century to provide for orderly passage of government land into private hands. Under the Homestead Act of 1862, the most famous but not the most important of these laws, this involved filing a claim at the nearest U.S. Land Office for a 160-acre parcel one had located according to the government survey, that is, a particular quarter of a particular section of a particular township under one of several major surveys of the West. Once legally described and filed, the homesteader moved to "prove up" on the land, either by payment of $1.25 per acre (after six months had expired), or by continuous occupation and improvement of the land for a period of five years. Proving up gave the settler a patent to the land, a certification from the Land Office that he owned the land outright. Although there is evidence that homesteaders in earlier times had been able to use claims as collateral for loans, by the end of the nineteenth century no bank would loan money on any security less than a patent. Consequently, on projects like the Cody Canal, those who took up a contract with the Shoshone Irrigation Company were eager to get their patents, and the Company was eager to help them.[57]

On a Carey Act project, there were some special case considerations, although the basic process was quite similar to simple homesteading. The land was withdrawn from public entry and segregated to the State by the General Land Office once a project was approved. The State then monitored the process of securing title. A settler, first of all, had to sign a contract for a right to water a set amount of land; under the Cody Canal the contracts were for units or shares of forty acres. Proof of settlement and improvement required the irrigation of at least one-eighth of the land claimed and residence for three years. The settler submitted this proof to the State Land Board, which applied then for patent from the federal government and passed it on to the settler for a $2 fee. After two years of experience, this cumbersome process was streamlined somewhat to allow the State to acquire patent on all the land under a canal once the canal was completed, thus removing the settler's period of waiting after making proof to the State Land Board.[58]

There were further particular complications on the Cody Canal, stemming perhaps from the fact that it was the first Carey Act project in the state to be carried to final proof. From late 1897, George Beck was in communication with the state engineer and the U.S. General Land Office, seeking information and government forms for applying for patents. Buffalo Bill pushed Elwood Mead, to move the process ahead. They learned in October 1898 that the State had initiated the process of acquiring patent to the land under the Cody Canal. This required Mead to certify that the canal was complete. He submitted the certification to the governor for transmission to the Department of Interior on October 18, without having visited the work in more than a year, relying only on the word of George Beck that the canal was performing as it should. The application covered 11,131 acres. They had not sold nearly that much land, but the 1896 amendment to the Carey Act allowed the state to receive patent for all the land that the canal could water at the time of application.[59]

The application was sent to the U.S. Land Office in Lander early in December. A clerk apparently noted it as received, but the agents in the office, who were nearing the end of their term of service, not only took no action but failed to inform their successors that the papers were ready for action. These were the same people who had routinely rejected applications for segregation submitted by the state in 1895; this was apparently the last, petty act of men who disliked the Carey Act from the beginning. After waiting a decent interval, the company began to inquire after the success of the application, and when the GLO in Washington could find no record of it, they descended upon the Lander office, where the entire package was discovered gathering dust. Everyone on the Wyoming end was furious, of course. Governor Richards promised to do what he could to push it through.[60] But the Land Office mill ground excruciatingly slow and exceedingly fine, and there were one or two more kernels to crack before this grinding was done.

The process of patenting public land always required a period of public notice to enable anyone who desired to contest the patent to present reasons why it should not go through. Ordinarily, this amounted to little more than a formality, but in Cody the formality presented itself as an opportunity to a man who had already developed a grudge against the Shoshone Irrigation Company, Hudson W. Darrah. Darrah was a sawyer and a teamster who operated his own sawmill and had worked under contract for the company since 1896. He felt he had been denied income and opportunity by the company. He had failed in an earlier legal contest with them, but was ready to try again. The list of lands to be patented was advertised from May 6 to June 10, 1899, as required by law. The Lander office then inexplicably held the papers until November 1899, and when the agents there sent them to Washington they transmitted also a protest from Darrah against patenting 6,200 of the 11,131 acres under the canal, including the Cody townsite itself, which he had not filed until October! Darrah was a man of some substance for a place like Cody; his protest was treated with a great deal of respect by the Lander office, and was subsequently allowed by the GLO to proceed to a hearing. It seems likely that this was a matter of political hangover from the Robert Foote protest of 1895. Federal land managers did not want to open themselves to charges of collusion with well-financed companies against the interests of the people. The company responded by sending Beck and Alger to Washington to examine the papers in the General Land Office. There, they called on everyone, including the congressional delegation, and were cordially received, but they left town having failed in their mission to expedite the hearing.[61]

Darrah's protest against patenting such a large section of the project was based upon his assertion that "said lands have not been irrigated and reclaimed by said State of Wyoming or by any corporation, person, or persons nor has there been supplied the necessary canals for the irrigation of said lands and the reclamation thereof," and that some of it was too hilly and rocky to grow crops, good only for grazing.[62] A considerable portion of the 6,200 acres was actually unfit for cultivation, as Darrah alleged, but just as much was manifestly good land, including the townsite of Cody. The assertion that that land had not been reclaimed amounted to a charge that the irrigation system itself was insufficient or did not work. Later history of the canal would suggest there was merit in that allegation as well, but Darrah himself was unable to carry his point. In fact, when the U.S. Commissioner went to hear the case in Cody in July 1900, Darrah refused to comply with the judge's order for more particulars on the allegations in his affidavit, and he was unable to produce any confirming witnesses. The commissioner concluded the complaint had been "made for delay" and dismissed it on July 31.[63]

The Land Office had carried through the granting of patent to 4,495 acres under the canal that were unaffected by the Darrah protest. Virtually all of these were along the upper reaches of the canal around Irma flat. Patent to the state for these lands was issued on June 9, 1900. Patents on the protested lands were subject to further delay, as another Cody citizen, Frank O. Thompson, submitted a second protest after the Land Office had announced the rejection of Darrah's. It was virtually copied from Darrah's but included some land already patented. From the response to this protest, we learn that both Thompson and Darrah thought that the law required more of the company than the construction of the main ditch and laterals. In fact, the contract between the State and the Company considered it sufficient for the company to bring water within three miles of a tract to be irrigated, and subsequent Land Office regulations had adopted a similar standard. As this never appeared in individual contracts, people might easily conclude that the digging of main ditches did not constitute reclamation of land miles away from the ditch. However, the commissioner refused to accept Thompson's protest since Elwood Mead's affidavits showed clearly that the main work had been completed. At long last, in January 1901, the remainder of the land on the original list for patent was cleared to the State.

As noted in the case of Elwood Mead, such pliable conduct on the part of state officials enabled Buffalo Bill to believe, and to ask others to believe, that his own fortunes and the interest of the State of Wyoming ran hand-in-hand. Governors, state officers, and everyone involved with Carey Act development at the top seemed to see things his way. Investors, of course, wanted secure investments; delays and difficulties in getting title to the land would surely constrict investment, and without investment Wyoming would wither and die. But, as seen earlier in the case of Robert Foote, not everyone accepted that the interests of the state and the corporations formed under the Carey Act were identical.[64] To Foote, and probably to Darrah, what was good for Bill Cody and other agents of incorporation was likely to be inimical to the interests of the ordinary individuals who hoped to make their fortunes on their own terms. Both corporate developers and individual citizens saw life in Wyoming through the lens of opportunity, but the full exercise of opportunity by either side shut out the other. Looking back, it is clear that the days of small-holding irrigators were past and that only large-scale investment and development could make use of Wyoming's agricultural resources. But that was not yet clear to ordinary settlers seeking their place on the land at the turn of the 20th century. Darrah's failed protest might be seen as the death rattle of the small-holder's vision of opportunity in Wyoming.[65]

CHAPTER FIVE

"I wish to God I had never seen the Basin!"

The first construction seasons on the Cody Canal and the earliest years of the town of Cody brought out clearly the size and type of the problems faced by the Shoshone Irrigation Company and its redoubtable president. The logistics of both projects were formidable, due to the character of the Wyoming mountain environment and the distance from the nearest point of settlement. Stresses and strains among the company's directors caused by cost overruns and perceptions of mismanagement by both George Beck and William Cody nearly sank the entire enterprise. However, these two men refused to let it sink. Beck learned that he needed to keep his colleagues informed as to what was happening in Wyoming, to provide some shield against sniping from Colonel Cody. Buffalo Bill did not learn his lessons as well; indeed, he could not, as his style of management was one with his helter-skelter style of living. He continued to send money, however, which (with a big boost from Beck) kept some hope alive during dark times.

The Shoshone Irrigation Company $50,000 bond issue remained unsold at the close of 1896. The directors knew that they could not proceed with construction without raising more money. Buffalo Bill had talked the previous summer about selling the bonds himself in the winter, but he did not follow through. George Beck decided to use some of his father's connections, and traveled east in February 1897 to Washington, D.C., and to New York to see what good he might be able to do. In Washington, he went to see Phoebe Hearst, the widow of an old family friend, Senator George Hearst of California. Mrs. Hearst said that she would take $30,000 of the bonds. "Go back to my New York office," she told Beck, "and tell my manager there to give you the money immediately. If he refuses, have him call me by long distance." The manager was furious with her. He stormed at Beck, "You can't raise money on Government bonds, much less cash on a ditch in Wyoming!" Mrs. Hearst stuck to her promise, however, and Beck got his money, although the manager did force him to accept a 10 percent discount up front.[1]

With $27,000 cash in his pocket, Beck went back to the Hoffman House to pack for his return to Wyoming. In the hotel, he ran into Buffalo Bill and Nate Salsbury, who were getting ready for another Wild West season. He bragged to them of his success, and they in turn begged him for $5,000 that they needed to raise in order to be able to open on schedule. Beck gave them the money and they promised to repay it within sixty days. "Times being what they were, it was nine months before I got it back."[2] This was perhaps the only time that cash flowed from the Shoshone Irrigation Company to the Wild West; it generally drained in the opposite direction. The company's directors were happy with Beck's work, of course, and cancelled the remaining $20,000 of the bond issue. A year later, no doubt after a good talk with her financial manager, Mrs. Hearst sent Beck a quiet note asking how they proposed to repay the bonds, and assuring him that "at any time you wish to retire these bonds it will be entirely agreeable."[3]

The 1897 construction season began the first week in April, with money in the bank from the bond sale and a reduced force on the ditch in order to spend as little as possible of it. Buffalo Bill and George Beck had gone to Red Lodge and paid off a note at the bank there; the company paid half and Cody himself covered the other half. No more than seventeen men were on the work crew in the spring, and they used Bill Cody's mule teams, plows, scrapers, and other equipment from his ranch; Cody got credit on the books, of course, but that was far better for the Company than paying someone else real money. The teams were not in good shape and had to be fed well and worked carefully to build up strength, which was not easy when feed was in short supply, as it was at that time of year. George Beck thought the ditch was in generally good shape. One big flume had been blown away by winter wind, and there were places where rock slides required to be cleared away before water could be let in, but these were not serious issues in his mind. They cleared the canal and let water in on April 19. Then they began to fill the Sulphur Creek dam and construct the laterals into the town of Cody. Things were going well enough that Charles Hayden, the company engineer, took off for Buffalo Bill's ranch on Carter Mountain to survey a 5,000-acre tract the Colonel was going to lease from the State, and most of the men were set to work grading and plowing on the townsite.[4]

As they were getting underway, Beck took a shot across his bow from Buffalo. The *Shoshone Valley News* had run an article on the resumption of work and talked grandly of building the ditch on beyond Cody. George Bleistein squealed, "Upon what authority and what conditions is this done?"[5] Even with the money from the bonds, Bleistein said, the company had only $8,000 with which to work. He insisted that Beck go ahead only after consultation with Elwood Mead. At virtually the same time, Nate Salsbury wrote Beck to find out why work had not started sooner and proceeded faster. It seems that the Colonel was upset that his teams had been taken in but no work was being done with them; this way of working seemed hard on him. It is entirely possible that neither Salsbury nor Cody knew the teams were in such poor shape that they could not work. The Wild West could always buy feed for its horses, but up on the Shoshone, men and animals often had to wait for grass to grow. Beck tried to calm both sides, assuring them all that he was working as well as he could, waiting for Mr. Mead to come up from Cheyenne and approve the next stage, and defending the ways he had cut costs. He sat in a familiar, uncomfortable seat, pushed from behind by the Wild West directors and held back by the Buffalo men.[6]

The most effective thing Beck could do was to send out reports each week to all the directors so they would not feel anxious for lack of information. He had begun this practice in the summer of 1896, but no copies of such reports before 1897 have survived. From 1897 there are copious reports, and it is clear how helpful they would have been to the other investors. Beck, however, seems to have regarded preparation of the reports as a substitute for personal communication when time got tight, and Buffalo Bill continued to complain that Beck never sent him enough information.

Colonel Cody apparently also complained about the quality of the bookkeeping on the project, part of his general dissatisfaction with Beck's work. A good part of Beck's first weekly report was devoted to describing just how much work had to be done to get the books in order. In a private letter to Salsbury, he laid a large part of the blame on Buffalo Bill's nephew, Ed Goodman. The Colonel had not been satisfied with the bookkeeping the year before, so Beck gave the job to Goodman. Goodman did not satisfy Beck, leaving the books unbalanced, "saying that he would give one [a balance] to the Colonel." Beck felt strongly that he could not run the work without having charge of the employees, and "for reports to be made from outside sources or from employees to other members of the company without the same having at least been presented to me is wrong & can result in nothing but confusion."[7] Apparently, a partnership with Buffalo Bill brought with it a family full of other partners and a set of working relationships that were not always smooth. But Beck clearly did not feel he could challenge the Colonel openly on such matters.

On April 30, irrigation water came down to the bench where the town was located. The teams began constructing dams for a storage reservoir on the bench above the town. But about that time, they began to experience troubles with the canal around the Red Bluffs, both above and below the long flume. At considerable expense, and under Elwood Mead's direction, they had dug the section of the canal leading to the flume through what looked like solid rock, expecting to avoid the difficulties they had encountered with soil banks slipping away on sandy side hills. The sandstone through which the canal ran there, however, turned out to contain veins of gypsum, which swelled and cracked when wet, causing the canal to leak prodigiously. Turning off the water, they patched the leaking stretch of canal, but this was just another sign that keeping the canal full would require a constant duel with the environment through which they had dug it. Patching with earth sometimes held for a while, but for some stretches they had to build more flume to run the water above the gypsum rock. Whatever they tried, they found more trouble in response. They did, however, manage to keep enough water coming into town to start irrigating crops there.[8]

Elwood Mead arrived in Cody on May 12, and immediately went to Buffalo Bill's ranch with Charles Hayden to complete the survey of the land there. When finished with that work, he moved across the Shoshone River from Cody with a group of surveyors and began to prepare the maps and other engineering work for what they called the North Side project, which was now a development plan to be run by

Buffalo Bill and Nate Salsbury in a completely separate company. Mead did not get around to consulting with Beck until more than a week had gone by. When he did go over the ditch, he pronounced everything done as he would have liked, and apparently discussed the design of laterals that would go beyond the town to irrigate land toward Sage Creek. His principal work on this trip was to run surveys for Cody and Salsbury, rather than supervise the Shoshone Irrigation Company. Beck was disappointed to get so little of Mead's time, and complained specifically that he did not examine the work more carefully. Mead made a point of requesting his quarterly retainer of $250.[9]

While Mead was at Cody, Charles Hayden undertook to survey some new canal lines. He calculated that a second, smaller dam, lower down on Sulphur Creek, would enable them to run a lateral to the town bench more effectively than their present arrangement, which involved a drop into town from the upper bench. This would mean the irrigation water for the town would be freed from dependence on the big flume around Red Bluffs. It would also be clear and sediment-free, coming from a settlement area rather than from the main ditch. The new town lateral would be almost a mile long, but it would have no drops on it, as opposed to three drops on the first plan. It would therefore be easier and less expensive to build. However, late in June, Beck heard from Cody and Salsbury that Company funds would not support further work after the 26th. His response was to push work on the new lateral as hard as he could until he had to lay off the men, aiming to get it to a point where it could be easily completed when money became available. He eventually worked the crews two more days than had been authorized. On June 29 the entire work force, save three men, was discharged.[10]

The 1897 construction season was reasonably good while it lasted. The town lateral was running and crops planted in town and east of town were being watered for the first time. The reservoir on the bench above and south of town was partially filled, although work on the dam had not been completed when the men had to stop. They had begun work to extend the canal beyond Cody toward Sage Creek, in addition to the construction of the new town lateral from Sulphur Creek. Beck's work crews had had to fight constant battles with collapsing banks on the main canal above Sulphur Creek, but they maintained the upper hand until the workmen had to leave. The upper canal, around Irma, provided excellent water supply to farms, mostly operated by Bill Cody and by the Shoshone Irrigation Company. Although clearly frustrated at having to stop, Beck felt good about the work that they had done.[11]

The work never stopped entirely, of course. The few men Beck had kept on waged continual struggles with the ditches and the dams. Their ditches were continually developing sinkholes, which would have to be filled when they were discovered. The sides of the canal would collapse in places when run full for any time at all. Gypsum in the soil continued to give them problems. The flume around the Red Bluffs tended to wash out at both ends, and the foundations under the supports also gave way with distressing frequency. When the water had to be shut off to make repairs, the flumes—made, as they were, of wood planking—dried out and shrank, and thus leaked prodigiously when water was started up again. There was no water on the townsite for quite a few days in July and August when things were particularly bad. Beck remained optimistic that the problems could be solved, although they would probably have to build a permanent flume around the Red Bluffs. But other problems cropped up. They found that the canal was also leaking water into geyser cones in the Sulphur Creek area, at one time losing the entire flow of the canal into a hole in the ground! Temporary fixes allowed them to keep water flowing intermittently, but an impartial eye would have seen this canal as a fundamentally shaky proposition.[12]

Beck took the opportunity of the lull in construction to contract with two men who had a sawmill to produce lumber from trees logged during the past winter. He hoped to have lumber available for settlers to build with "if we are to get any settlers at all." A settlement operation in what was more or less a wilderness required that the company be prepared to provide everything people would need. They could charge for it, of course; Beck figured they could get $10 per thousand board feet for the finished lumber, and they were going to pay the sawyers only $5 per thousand. Of course, the company would have to invest some money in order to make this paper profit. Beck signed a contract with Sonners and Johnson, who owned the mill, but he had no idea where the money would come from when it came time to pay.[13]

The directors of the Shoshone Irrigation Company were all more or less interested in the possibilities of precious metal mining in the area. Horace Alger arrived July 11 with a Mr. Darlington, a mining consultant whom they brought in to help assess potential developments. Beck and Alger took him up the South Fork to look at possible claims they had found. After five days there, they rested a day and took off for Sunlight Basin, an area along the upper Clark's Fork River that was drawing a great deal of attention from gold and copper miners. Altogether, they were gone nearly two weeks, and when those trips were finished, Darlington went over to the head of the Greybull River to look into mining work near Kirwin. Darlington thought highly of the Kirwin camp, and found the Sunlight much better country than upper South Fork for mineral prospects. Beck thought that mining in either of those places would help the little town of Cody quite a bit, as they would be the natural suppliers of food, grain, and other supplies to the miners. Beck remained optimistic about the South Fork mines, from which Darlington took samples to assay. They also went down the Shoshone to Alkali Creek, where panning produced small quantities of gold distributed widely enough to keep their attention.[14]

At the end of 1897, Beck was desperately concerned to hold down the payroll and expenses. All ditch work except emergency repairs had been shut down in August, and Charles Hayden, the engineer, had been notified he would be paid by days actually worked instead of annual salary. Beck inquired of the directors what he should do if Elwood Mead applied for another installment of his $1,000 annual retainer. Mead had already been paid $500 that year, and Beck thought it unnecessary to keep him on, "especially as I do not know how I should meet it, should he draw on me for another quarter."[15] As noted above, however, things began to look up late in 1897, with parcels of land actually selling and people chipping in to build a bridge over the river. Perhaps 1898 would be the year the project got over the hump.

It was the ditch construction that mattered most to Beck. He was prepared with the estimates for flumes from lower Sulphur Creek to the town because he had had Hayden at work surveying alternative sites and plans for the work. He envisioned that the lower Sulphur Creek dam would not only supply the best water for the city but it would also provide a head of water that would enable them to run the flour mill, "if such were to be determined upon." He thought it could be done for $2,000. Spring was the time the company had to decide what would be done on the ditch in the coming year. Beck was particularly eager to get going in 1898 because most of the land around Irma had been sold and they had begun to sell parcels east of Cody. People were arriving and the company would have to be prepared to deliver water. Beck was anxious that things be decided properly, and urged the directors to schedule a meeting in Cody where they could see the Company's position clearly.[16]

The board gathered, however, for their March meeting at Nate Salsbury's New Jersey home. There were only four men present: Gerrans and Bleistein from Buffalo, Salsbury and Cody. They elected C. B. Jones, from Illinois, who had been largely responsible for the small surge in settlement, to serve as land commissioner. They decided to open a general store as a company business and to build a flour mill in the summer. Regarding the ditch, they determined to proceed with the dam on lower Sulphur Creek to bring water into Cody, and dedicated $2,000 to its construction. They agreed to donate a building and grant some money to start a school in Cody. These are the actions of men who were committed to the future; at least some of the reluctance of a year earlier seemed to have evaporated, owing perhaps to a little success in the land department. Bleistein and Bronson Rumsey had been generally tight with their money. Buffalo Bill was frustrated when they refused to take chances, and he talked frequently, even in the first year of the new company, of buying them out. In 1898, however, even they seemed eager to get started.[17]

As the managing partner, Beck had to plan the work and then beg for the money to do it. He was relieved to learn of the decision to build the Sulphur Creek dam, but he told his colleagues in April that he needed at least $3,000 to get both upper and lower ditches working. He had to keep track of the debts and obligations of the company on the ground; he could not make do with airy promises. In March, for instance, Buffalo Bill had told Beck that Jones would have $1,000 for him when he arrived from Illinois. The actual amount turned out to be $160, and this immediately had to be turned over to their lumber hauler, who had not been paid for months. Beck was quite unhappy to learn of the appointment of another land commissioner, which would mean paying a full salary that he did not think they could afford. Jones had done good work as a land salesman, but Beck saw no reason to put him on salary. A further complication was that Jones had been offered a job with Cody, "and if he accepts this and remains land commissioner, his value to us will be again curtailed—it will leave us with practically no one representing us in the land business."[18]

Beck requested opinions from the other directors on this matter. Cody, hearing of Beck's concern, let him know that no salary had been set for Jones; he appears to have expected Jones to work on commission for his land sales. Forgetting entirely the work done the year before by Elliott, Buffalo Bill stated that they needed the land graded and classed, and if Jones did that they would have to pay him something. Turning to more pressing matters, he urged Beck to get busy on the dam: "If no one else will pay for it I will but I want to know if you will do it or contract it done at once. There is no time to lose."[19] This is, once again, management by flurry of energy and promises, doomed from the outset.

It was one thing for the board to make decisions, and quite another for them to come up with the money to make them happen. As Horace Alger, the company treasurer, put it, "There seems to be a misunderstanding between Col. Cody and our Buffalo friends."[20] Buffalo Bill would tell Alger that Bleistein had money for him, but when Alger wired for it Bleistein would claim he had never promised Cody any money. "It is a shame and a big one the way the financial part of our company is arranged for. We are told to do work & then no provision is made for payment & those who get & give us credit are not justly dealt with."[21] Buffalo Bill's habit of broadcasting his hopes as if they were accomplished facts when talking with the press or the state engineer was perhaps harmless, but carrying on the financial affairs of the company in that fashion, as these letters reveal, made life for his colleagues difficult.

After the resolutions at the March meeting, Cody and Salsbury directed Alger to assess each stockholder proportionately to raise the money for work in 1898. They hoped to be able to spread the burden of expenses more widely. All three Buffalo men refused to contribute any more to construction. Bleistein had subscribed $1,000 a short while before, and the other two had all the ditch stock they wanted. Cody and Salsbury had to find the money to get work started in 1898, to pay off some of the debts held over from the previous year, and to make the first interest payment on the bonds sold to Mrs. Hearst. They subscribed $2,000 ($1,500 from Buffalo Bill himself) to clear obligations but there remained the matter of $2,100 to pay Mrs. Hearst her interest before any money was available for construction. These were large sums of money for two men to keep raising. Alger and Beck, who were not supposed to carry any of the financial load, did their part by scrambling in Wyoming to keep the company solvent and working.[22]

The subscriptions from Cody and Salsbury, in fact, allowed Beck to begin tentatively on construction in May. He had only about $500,

enough for a week or ten days, and then he would have to stop again
unless someone sent some more money. The directors seemed to be
interested in everything but the ditch. Rumsey wrote repeatedly about
the prospects of finding working mines on some of the placer claims he
and Beck had located at various points along the South Fork and downstream at Alkali Creek. Bleistein and Gerrans apparently saw the flour
mill and the general store as investment opportunities. Bleistein was an
active hunter and supporter of Buffalo Bill's hunting preserve idea. They
all had purchased land around Cody and up the river. Obviously, as they
continued to be interested in the Shoshone country, Cody and Salsbury
could continue to work on them to keep up subscriptions to the company. Early in June, Beck concluded that he had no choice but to stop
work, and he went so far as to pay off the men. On June 6th he drew up
the books and told the directors how much the company owed.[23]

Company affairs, and particularly George Beck's job, were complicated
that spring by more impatience and free-lancing from the president. In
April, Cody was already complaining about not hearing enough from
Wyoming. He particularly wanted to know if the new settlers had got
discouraged during the cold snap. In May, exasperated that he and
Salsbury were left to carry the financial load, he took some of his frustration out on Beck for changing his weekly reports into monthlies. He
returned to what he saw as Beck's habit of procrastination: "Mr. Salsbury
is very much put out that you gave him no answer about the mill. Business men like Mr. Salsbury cant see why business cant be done promptly.
I tell him he hasent lived in the Basin."[24] In fact, Beck had already sent a
detailed reply to Salsbury discussing the matter of building a flour mill in
Cody. With only Buffalo Bill's letters to go by, we might think Beck an
incompetent fool, but his judgment and patience were critical to the
success of that enterprise, perhaps as important ultimately as the energy
and money of the Old Scout himself. Certainly in the critical year of 1898,
when Buffalo Bill was distracted by the notion that his own participation
was needed in the invasion of Cuba, Beck's no-nonsense approach to the
work of the Company shines by comparison.[25]

Working arrangements within the company remained chaotic. The
Wild West show was having a difficult spring season, with constant rain
and intermittent illness, and these only increased Cody's anxiety about
work in Wyoming. Anyone there with any kind of complaint, particularly
unpaid bills or wages, wrote directly to the Wild West, and then Cody

railed at Beck. The Colonel also independently remained in contact with C. B. Jones, the land commissioner. A few days after Beck had paid off the work force, Cody wrote to him, from Lyme, Massachusetts, that he had wired the contractor to stop work on the dam at Sulphur Creek. It is not hard to imagine how Beck felt as manager, dealing with the occasional interventions of the company president from his outpost on the Atlantic Ocean. In this case no particular harm ensued, but this meddling was symptomatic of bigger problems. In that same letter, Cody told Beck that the Buffalo men were finally going to put up some more money for the ditch, but that Beck needed to get all the bills paid and stop the heavy expenses. After another plea to hear more frequently from Beck, Cody closed with an almost audible groan, "I wish to God I had never seen the Basin!"[26]

It was becoming clear to the directors that their project was in danger if they did not get their business in order. Cody called an emergency meeting of the board for June 27, in Buffalo. Beck was to bring the company books and pick up Alger along the way. The meeting appears actually to have taken place on July 1. Although the president called the meeting, he was not present. Beck, Alger, Bleistein, and Salsbury were the directors present; Gerrans was there as a major stockholder, not yet a member of the board. They looked over all the accounts and pronounced themselves satisfied with the treasurer's report, which showed that at the end of June 1898 they had put $128,007 into their project and had taken in less than $4,000 on water contracts. For the future, they resolved that no official of the company should make any contract in its name without prior approval of the board. Further, they resolved that the manager should present estimates of the cost of future work at each biennial meeting, and that none of it was to be done until the treasurer notified him that there was money to cover it.[27] The first resolution was probably aimed at curbing some of the free-lancing of Buffalo Bill, although perhaps Beck could be considered guilty as well. The second was clearly aimed at controlling the way Beck did his job.

While the meeting was going on, E. H. Clark, Mrs. Hearst's financial manager, wired Beck on July 1 that he had presented his coupons to the bank that day and payment had been refused; he required an immediate explanation. The Wild West was in Pennsylvania that week, and Beck took it upon himself to go there to convince Buffalo Bill that they were ruined if they could not cover these coupons. By July 15,

Cody had found the $2,100 to do it. Trying to decide how to move ahead, while wiping clear a trail of debt from where they had been—such uncertainty kept the affairs of the company in a constant state of crisis.[28] Bill Cody's response to the bond crisis was typical: he dipped into one of his many pockets and produced the money the company needed to stay alive. Whatever else he may have said or done, this one thing was constant in his conduct. Not only did he rescue the company in emergencies, but he also used ready cash to jump-start essential projects like the Shoshone River bridge at Cody. He was a maddening colleague, no doubt, but he was determined to succeed and to take a lead where circumstances required it.

Living in the Wyoming high country (the elevation at Cody is 5,000 feet) exposes people to the elemental fury of mountain weather. In 1897, it was a hailstorm that destroyed gardens and fields. High water in June 1898 had washed out the new bridge over the river. On July 12, 1898, a storm poured torrents of rain down the mountainsides, washing out sections of the canal and utterly destroying the large dam on Sulphur Creek that had regulated the supply ditch to the bench above Cody. Although he must have been staggered by the events, Beck moved quickly. He communicated the news to his fellow directors, including a plan that he had drawn up to re-route the ditch so that they would not need to rebuild the dam. He told the directors that he probably could do it in two weeks' time if they could find $800 to pay for it, and urged them to act at once. He was afraid that the company would be liable for failing to deliver water to the settlers' crops if they could not get the ditch repaired immediately, and he was prepared to meet the challenge.[29]

Bill Cody responded immediately to the news of the washout with humor and determination. "As Gen. Manager you should bar cloud-bursts," he told Beck. "Well it cant be helped. And you done perfectly right in repairing the damage and getting water to the farms and Cody as soon as possible."[30] So Beck got the money and proceeded with his repairs. The work required a new 12-foot dam in Sulphur Creek 2,200 feet upstream of the original one, then 2,200 feet of new ditch leading to a new flume across Sulphur Creek gulch at the site of the old dam; this flume would be set 27 feet above the creek and run 240 feet across to the canal leading to the big flume around Red Bluff. They also had to clean out that ditch leading to the flume, as the washout had completely filled it with silt. Beck managed to finish the job by August 7.

That was a prodigious feat of construction to accomplish in such a short time, and—perhaps predictably—it was not very good work. The first day water was turned in to the new ditch there was a rainstorm upstream, which led the farmers there to turn back their water into the main canal. The full head of water flowing into the new ditch caused it to break just below the dam, and they lost their lake. Beck had the canal repaired a second time by the 17th, and could only hope that it would hold.[31]

In his August report to the directors, Beck also gave a detailed account of his trip to the county seat to see about county road matters, which had resulted in his appointment as road supervisor for the Cody District. There was a Democratic Party caucus in Basin when he was there, and he was nominated to be a delegate to the state convention at Casper, which he had to forgo "on account of the condition of our work." He had hoped to work for Horace Alger's nomination for governor, which Alger had won without any assistance from Beck. The manager included a detailed report of his activities in Basin because he had learned that Okie Snyder had told Cody that he had left work to go help Alger, "and Col. Cody had written to me saying he would report me if such were the case."[32] Beck went on to assert that his Saturday in Basin City was the first day he had been away from the work since returning from the East. It seems clear, however, that Buffalo Bill had set Snyder to watch Beck, an indication of serious deterioration in relations within the board.

Although the company had found the money to keep the water running to town, they faced other serious problems. The lumber men had completed their contract sawing, and now the company had 350,000 board feet of sawed lumber stacked and ready to use, if they could find the money to pay the contract. "This, of course, I cannot do without money," Beck wrote, "and I wish the Directors would let me know, as soon as possible, what they propose to do about settling this contract; something must be done and done quickly."[33]

Bill Cody, probably well supplied with comment from his dependents in Cody, took Beck to task when he learned of the washout of the new ditch and the debt come due for the lumber. As to the ditch, he was "surprised that more judgement was not used. It was neglect and carelessness that the water should be allowed to wash out the new canal. I don't know as I could express my mind any more clearly on the subject." And on the lumber matter, he foresaw that the bill would fall to him for payment. "But I don't propose to do it. From this [time] on the stock holders are to do their share. They ordered the lumber sawed."[34] It is easy to be wise after the fact and from a distance, and the Colonel was obviously not in a mood to go easy on his manager in Wyoming. But repeatedly, as already seen, he urged the work on, apparently ignorant or careless of the consequences of hurried construction. The Cody Canal ran through some of the most difficult terrain imaginable for an irrigation canal. Beck knew of the dangers of washing out and also of the needs of people for water. Trying to balance these ends and dodge the bullets that arrived in the mail must have more than once made him rue the day that he, too, first saw the Basin.

The harder nut to crack proved to be the cost of the lumber. A month passed without any solution to that problem. Late in September, again after no one else stepped forward to share the burden, Bill Cody bought the lumber himself, "rather than have the Co. suffer the disgrace of not being able to pay for it, and the mill men take it for the sawing of it, and still leave us in debt to Darrah [the hauler]."[35] He was angry at Beck as he did it, saying—against all evidence—that if only Beck had told the company how much it would cost and what the stakes were they would have come through. In fact, Beck had given them all the information they needed to figure out what the bill would be—$1,750—and had warned them several times that it would come due at the end of the summer. Cody's attack on Beck was unfair and unwarranted, and it did not stop there. He went on to more general accusations of malfeasance: "I cannot help but believe that many things have been neglected that could have been done, and should have been done." After his familiar complaint of not having been informed, he assailed Beck again: "If not yours, whose duty is it to keep the Directors posted. . . . All I know is what I accidentally hear."[36] The surviving records of Beck's reports to the directors are sufficient to absolve him of the worst of Cody's charges. We cannot know whether Cody received every letter Beck sent, but there is little reason to doubt it. It is clear that this relationship was in danger of breaking apart, and Buffalo Bill's anxiety was the biggest single reason.

Recollecting himself in a less harried time, the Colonel came to his senses soon after that last letter. In October, he wrote Beck from Indiana, to express his hope that they might meet as friends when he got to Cody. He knew Beck had had a hard time managing with no help from the company: "You and I have had to stand the brunt, and I expect we will have to do it." The Buffalo men were talking about getting out, and he would not mind seeing them go. He offered his favorite olive branch in closing: "I hope we can have a nice time this winter if we don't make a cent. We generally have a good time when we get together—let's go up South Fork to its head & have a hunt.[37] This was the man people loved to know and touch, not the irascible old man fulminating from afar.

As Cody intimated, the morale of the directors of the Shoshone Irrigation Company reached a new low in the fall of 1898. At their meeting, Bronson Rumsey offered a motion that Beck be authorized to sell all the company's property "to any would-be purchaser for $150,000." They tried to figure out ways to get their ditch finished by paying people with water contracts, "no money to be demanded on either side." However, they also decided to draw up papers to make a townsite company; low as morale obviously was, they were not totally discouraged. Salsbury and Rumsey were still quite interested in the progress of the placer mining operations, and the Buffalo men had sent one of their protégés, young Jacob Schwoob, to Cody to run the mercantile operation.[38]

Nor would one have suspected from Beck's letter to Elwood Mead in October that things were not going well at Cody. The ditch was in good repair, he said, and the colonists at Irma had done very well. They had a full reservoir on the bench above the town, and the town lateral was constructed far enough to irrigate farms east of town. His claims on the size and strength of the canal were clearly overstated, but much of the correspondence between the Shoshone Irrigation Company and the State was conducted in that vein. Beck was pleased, at least, to learn from Mead that their settlers would soon be able to apply for final proof on their homesteads.[39] Of course, that was an illusion as well, as we have seen. Mead had been cooperative to a fault with their company. Time would tell how wise that had been.

CHAPTER SIX

Corporations along the Shoshone

Four years into their project, prospects did not look bright for the Shoshone Irrigation Company. It was mired in debt, the canal was in parlous condition, and external legal and social challenges exacerbated its continuing internal dysfunction. Its mission to establish corporate control of even the first stage of the empire envisioned by Elwood Mead in 1894 looked in danger of ignominious failure. The year 1899 would be the time for them to reverse their downward slide or to fold their tents and go home.

The president of the company, as was his habit, pressed on regardless of the troubles. It seems never to have occurred to him that they would not prevail somehow. We have seen how relations among the directors had been strained to breaking, and how close they had come to throwing over the entire enterprise the year before. In the midst of the organizational crisis, however, Buffalo Bill brought his family to the new town for the first time, and began building his home ranch. Both George Beck and Bronson Rumsey appeared to be throwing their youth and their family fortunes in with Cody and the Big Horn Basin. Although Rumsey did not move out west, Beck had a home and a family in Cody. As others faded, it was these three who carried the load, although they did not share it equally, nor did they always pull in the same direction.

The company's year did not begin well. The second bridge it built over the Shoshone stayed up, but other things seemed to fall apart. In February, Hud Darrah filed a lawsuit against the company for failing to

pay him for hauling lumber as contracted; he also sought an injunction
to prevent the sale of the lumber. While the company won that suit, it
lost a countersuit for malicious trespass against Darrah. Darrah had built
a road to the sawmill at his own expense, and then plowed it up, rendering it unusable, when he was not paid. Beck thought there was some
prejudice against the company in the jury; the directors were learning
that things did not always fall out as the incorporators would have them.
Winning the first suit at least allowed the company to sell the lumber
to the Cody Trading Company, the mercantile operation owned by the
Buffalo men.[1]

But the problems with the ditch that had shown up late in 1898 had
not gone away. The directors agreed in the spring to appropriate $1,000
to rebuild the canal, to avoid entirely any dam in Sulphur Creek. This
would require more new ditch upstream of the Sulphur Creek flume,
and, as usual, no one but the Colonel would put up any money. Moreover, Cody seemed to be unable to send money without also sending
along a familiar dose of heavy criticism. After telling Beck that Salsbury
would put up no more money because it had been so badly handled, he
returned to his familiar litany of complaint about Beck's mismanagement of the men. If Beck would promise to stay close to the work and
see it done right, and if he would write Salsbury promising to do so,
Cody guaranteed that the $1,000 would be placed to his credit imme-
diately.[2] In effect, he was making further payment depend upon Beck's
acceptance of Cody's view of the situation.

Buffalo Bill was in New York early that year, but his thoughts apparently remained in the Basin. He wrote Beck every few days throughout
March, reiterating his promises and complaints. Tradesmen knew that
the Colonel was the man who paid bills, and the larger of them even
sent their bills to him in New York, which he had to relay to Wyoming
to see if they should be paid. The Yegen Company in Billings was still
trying to collect money owed since 1896. Cody urged Beck to collect
money due them in Wyoming to cover those debts, but it is not clear
that whatever was owed them would have covered the bills. At the end
of the month, Cody appeared to consider his demands about supervision of the ditch work satisfied, and he, with Salsbury, promised to get
the money together. The Colonel ordered his own man in the Basin,
Okie Snyder, to tell Beck to go ahead with the ditch work, but still he
held back the money.[3]

The Wild West opened in New York in April to overflow crowds, taking in nearly $40,000 the first week. Although the Colonel had already ordered work to start on the ditch, he continued trying to get Beck to commit to do it *his* way Finally, in the middle of the month, Cody sent the money, saying as he did, "I hope you will make a success of work and get water to town without fail. But I find a man cant make a success of anything if he don't look after it himself." Buoyed by what he called "the greatest show success of my life," he also paid off the creditors.[4] A week later he picked his manager up with another injection of energy. "I told you I would send the 1000—did I ever fail yet?" He predicted colleagues would be more willing to put up their shares "when we get a rail road . . . and our town numbers thousands and land worth $100 an acre."[5] But April passed and there was still no water in Cody.

Having to wait for cash created difficult conditions for George Beck. He complained that he had been unable to start work when the directors wanted him to, due to the failure of the directors to provide any money until Cody first put up his $1,000. He had gathered mules and equipment, but finding men to work was proving difficult, even when he offered $1.25 a day plus board. No doubt the experience of previous summers made many potential employees wary of tying their fortunes to the Shoshone Irrigation Company, but even a good employer like the Burlington and Missouri River Railroad had difficulty hiring for the 1899 season as the railroad considered starting its line into Cody. Beck searched as far afield as Red Lodge to put together the small force that he managed to assemble.[6]

Other investors, less mercurial in temperament than the Colonel, were also less sanguine. H. M. Gerrans had begun to sour on his investment in the general store, and said he would sell his interest in it for 75 cents on the dollar. He also refused to contribute any more money to the ditch; he had put in what he could, "and rather than put any more in will lose my stock."[7] Nate Salsbury, who must have been sharing Buffalo Bill's good fortune, nevertheless remained unhappy with the way the company handled its business. He wanted Cody to call a meeting to plan work on the ditch; he had always disliked the "piecemeal way" the company proceeded. And he thought Cody was unrealistic about the cost: "I believe it will cost nearer six thousand dollars to put the ditch right than it will one thousand. Query? Where is them thair six thousand comin' from?"[8]

Salsbury was much closer to the mark than his partner was. Bill Cody was sure the job could be done for $1,000 if Beck personally took it in hand, even though he obviously had no clear idea what needed to be done. He projected these bold visions and then expected George Beck to bring them to reality or he would know the reason why![9] Even Salsbury was losing patience with Beck. The directors had stipulated at the Buffalo meeting that there should be a full statement of the financial condition of the company prepared every six months, "and from that day to this I have never had such a report, or one regarding money collected or money spent for the interest of the company." He urged Beck to start producing these reports, if only to protect his own interests.[10]

In June, the annual interest obligation on the Hearst bonds came due, and once again the company found itself scrambling. At first the Colonel seemed resigned to picking up the tab again, but by the end of the month he was furious with his partners, who voted in meetings to spend money and then refused to carry their share. "I have wired them I would pay my share and no more. They shant make me stand for everything. Let Clark [Hearst's manager] step in and foreclose, then I will have to pay the $30,000 with interest. Then we will see who owns the layout. Am I not right?"[11] Of course, this was bluff, and the Buffalo group knew their man. They all kept their hands in their pockets, and Buffalo Bill, "rather than give Mrs. Hearst a moment's concern" paid the $2,100, as he had each year since she purchased the bonds.[12]

The summer of 1899 was a relatively rainy one in the Basin, which was a stroke of luck for the Shoshone Irrigation Company; Mother Nature provided what the company could not. Ditch and flume repairs, only just begun at the end of April, were overwhelmed by collapses in the canal, and at the end of June there was still no water in the ditches at Cody. Lack of news about the water was creating serious anxiety in Buffalo Bill's excitable breast. As the Wyoming spring snowmelt was due to begin, he wrote, "Every day now every mail every telegram boy I see I say [is there] water running in the streets of Cody."[13] A month later he confessed "my heart will be broke if you don't have water running in the streets of Cody" when Mrs. Cody and friends arrived there in two weeks.[14] Eventually, with little money and few hands, Beck managed to complete sufficient repairs to the ditch to get water flowing by early July, but as always, both in construction and finance, the Shoshone Irrigation

Company was just patching leaks. In fact, in August Buffalo Bill still claimed not to know if water had reached Cody and farms beyond.[15]

Although the year had begun inauspiciously, the summer of 1899 brought major events to the town of Cody. Buffalo Bill's wife and family had never accompanied him to Wyoming, but he was eager for them to see the Big Horn Basin and the new town. He and Beck arranged the visit for August. Besides wife, Louisa, and daughters, Arta and Irma, the visiting party included Mr. and Mrs. Frederic Remington. Although he had ridden a decade earlier in the Pryor Gap country just north of the Basin, this was the painter's first visit to Wyoming. He and Buffalo Bill had known each other for years, and formed a kind of mutual admiration society. When the Colonel told Beck of the visit he referred to him as "Fred Remington," and a couple of weeks later he reminded Beck that "Remington has a mouth and likes his toddy—so stay with him. Gerrans says that whiskey is the best."[16] Beck was very much on his mettle to make this visit a pleasure trip. His own good friend, W. Hinkle Smith of Philadelphia, who would one day invest money in Cody, also came to town in August, and Bronson Rumsey brought his new wife to see the Basin as well. Considering that Beck's young wife, Daisy, had just given birth to their first daughter, it was a time of youth and high spirits all around.[17]

One plan for the Cody family party was to go up the North Fork of the Shoshone, along the route that would one day carry the highway to the East Gate of Yellowstone Park. Buffalo Bill began urging Beck to fix up the road to Ned Frost's ranch on the North Fork early in June. He first thought of asking Okie Snyder to take the family on their mountain tour, but he feared Snyder would get drunk and not carry through, so Beck agreed to take charge, and added his wife and daughter to the entourage. In addition to this trip, Beck arranged for an excursion to the Carter Mountain ranch that Cody had started in 1895. The centerpiece of that trip was a party at Irma Lake, where Cody had built a small cabin. Everyone in the county was invited, a pavilion was constructed for dancing, and all manner of food laid on. Rain, as it so often does on summer afternoons in the Wyoming mountains, drove the dancers into the cabin (which was not built for crowds) but did not dampen their spirits. Remington produced two sketches that afternoon, each featuring Buffalo Bill's daughter Irma. He also did some other incidental pieces, but put off serious painting until he could return to Cody in 1908.[18]

"Irma Going to Irma," a pen and ink drawing by Frederic Remington of Buffalo Bill's daughter, Irma, riding to the party at Irma Lake on Cody's Carter Mountain ranch in the summer of 1899. Courtesy of Buffalo Bill Historical Center, Cody, Wyo.; 77.69.

Everyone enjoyed this trip very much. Later, Louisa and Arta wrote glowing reports to the Colonel about their time in Cody and up the river, paying especial compliments to Beck and his wife. Cody obviously appreciated what Beck did for his family, but the affairs of the company were so strained in the summer of 1899 that he could not stop with simple thanks: "Am ever so much obliged for all your kindness to my family & friends. How I wish you would take the same interest in business affairs. Your friend, Cody"[19]

In the course of arranging for his family visit, Cody dropped another nugget on the town: "George, I am going to start a newspaper there, and see if I can't hoop up things a little. My man will be there with press and everything complete to be brought out with the teams that takes Mrs. Cody & party back to rail road. I hope the bridges don't go out."[20] J. H. Peake, who had been serving as editor of the paper Colonel

Cody had bought for his sister, Helen Cody Wetmore, in Duluth, was the man, and the press was coming with him from Minnesota. Peake was an old friend from North Platte, where he had run the local paper. Buffalo Bill had long wanted a newspaper in his town. As seen earlier, the first venture had failed, but this one was better founded and better timed. They named it the *Enterprise*, after the North Platte paper that Peake had run twenty years earlier, and under that name it has published continuously in Cody since August 31, 1899.[21]

With a newspaper on the way, the bridge holding, and water in the town ditches, there remained one more dish to be delivered to Cody's little summer picnic. The Shoshone Irrigation Company had been betting on the Burlington and Missouri River Railroad from the beginning, none more vociferously than the company president. In 1899, the Burlington took the first steps to bring this dream to life. Edward Gillette, the regional superintendent, led a team of surveyors into the Big Horn Basin, establishing the line for what was to become the Cody-Toluca branch of the B&M. Those surveyors were nearing Cody in July. Not only did they promise real progress, the surveyors offered other potential to the Colonel's fertile imagination. He had heard that two sons of Burlington directors were with the surveying party. He urged Beck to invite them to join his family excursion, to see if they might be interested in investing. And he directed Beck to take photographs of them if they surveyed through Cody, so he could use the photo in a magazine article or a new folder about the colony.[22] The promoter engine in Buffalo Bill never rested.

Toluca was a junction point on the Crow Reservation in Montana, 101 miles north and east of Cody. The Burlington people were interested in opening up the Big Horn Basin and had explored the possibility of constructing a transcontinental line that would run through Cody. Gillette had run preliminary surveys for that line in 1891, before George Beck ever entered the Basin.[23] As the surveyors moved toward Cody, Beck reminded Buffalo Bill of the coal seams the two of them had located. These were turning out to be right along the line of the proposed rails. Cody's response was, "I think we had better do some stakeing and filing, don't you?"[24] The Colonel was prepared to do everything he could to scratch out some return from his enormous investment.

The company's legal problems with Hudson Darrah did not go away with their first success in court. Darrah sued again in July for damages, as he had been prevented from fulfilling his contract by the sale to the

Cody Trading Company. He secured attachments of property belonging both to the Trading Company and the Irrigation Company, and Beck's lawyer down at the county seat in Basin worked tenaciously to get them dissolved. By mid-August Darrah had been defeated on the Trading Company matter but continued to make trouble for the Irrigation Company on other fronts, and the legal fees were mounting. In the midst of all the other debts they lived with, the company now owed $260 to lawyers in Basin and Sheridan.[25] Horace Alger asked Cody to pay the lawyers, but Cody refused to do so until he could get a statement of credit out of Beck. By Cody's own account he had already provided the company $3,296 that summer.

By the end of August, the Colonel was again nearly out of patience with his company. No one would put up any money, and there was no certainty that money would bring good results on the canal. If he thought the work would be done well and he would get credit for it, he might put up some more himself, but he was in a terrible end-of-summer funk.[26] Then, as summer turned to fall, Cody's mood improved. He heard more frequently from Beck, and consequently seemed pleased with his manager and the work he was doing. He promised to find money to take care of all manner of things, even to the point of paying water right obligations for some of the settlers who had not been able to find the money. He expressed his unhappiness that their settlers could not prove up on their homesteads (see Chapter 3); he asked Beck to tell him where the problem was and he would try to take care of that, too.[27] Unhappy as he might have been with the Buffalo men, his energies still were fully committed to the Basin.

Some of the change might have been owing to the approaching end of the show season, which meant the beginning of hunting season, Cody's favorite time of the year. There was other big game on his mind as well. Early in October he wrote that General Nelson Miles would surely be coming out this year, with a party of nine around the 26th. Some of these men were wealthy enough that he did not want it generally known that they were coming; he expected that Miles and some of the other would want to invest. He wanted to take them up South Fork and he hoped Beck would have some elk located. He even thought Admiral Dewey might be with them: "We must treat this party out of sight if it busts me."[28] He signed the letter with the familiar, "Col," a sign that he was feeling good. When he was not, it was "W. F. Cody, Pres."

Having talked for so long about getting General Miles to come out with him, Bill Cody could hardly contain his excitement at the prospect. Over the next few days, he wrote more letters, setting out in detail how the affair was to be managed. Miles wanted to ride over to Cody, so Beck would have to arrange for saddle horses and saddles and supply wagons, but Cody would tell him how many and where they would change and so forth. Menu planning was not too small a detail for him: he asked for some game and some trout for the party when they reached Cody on the 27th. He left very little for Beck and Okey Snyder to handle. He seems to have thought Miles was a genuine potential investor, one who could bring others in and really give the Irrigation Company a boost. He even asked Beck to have the water running in the ditches if the weather was not too cold![29]

Of course, although they came and hunted (without Dewey), neither Miles nor any of the others joined the company, nor is there any reason to believe that such a prospect existed anywhere outside Bill Cody's fevered imagination. Instead, another prospect arose from an entirely different quarter. Charles Kingston, a land agent in Evanston, Wyoming, served as the Wyoming representative for the Church of Jesus Christ of the Latter-Day Saints in the Church's efforts to mount colonial expeditions into the state. A small group of Mormons were already established at Burlington on the Greybull River. Kingston wrote to George Beck in mid-October that he was coming to the Basin to visit the colony at Burlington, "and also to look over the Big Horn country with a view of its settlement by our people." He wanted to stop by Cody around November 1 to see the canal and the country, to get a general idea of the facilities the country offered to new settlers.[30] This opened a vision of their long-awaited settlement success in the minds of all the company directors. Mormons were a good deal more prosaic than the Commanding General of the Army and other, unidentified, wealthy easterners, but they seemed for a while to promise a more tangible result.

A general convergence of interest on the part of the Mormon Church, the State of Wyoming, Buffalo Bill Cody, and the Shoshone Irrigation Company enlivened the next few months. It is not known whether Buffalo Bill was in town when Kingston came to Cody, but what Beck heard from Kingston gave him the idea that a Mormon enterprise directed at the Basin might come to Cody and take up all their land. He communicated this prospect to the other directors. Some of them looked upon this as salvation for their investment; Cody wrote his friend, Mike Russell, that the Mormons wanted to buy them out.[31] By mid-January 1900, the company had learned from Kingston that some Mormons might choose individually to settle at Cody but that the Church party Kingston was organizing would go elsewhere. This did not completely end the matter. Beck was directed to try to negotiate a sale to the Church of the entire Cody Canal enterprise. Founded as they were on a dream, those negotiations soon fell apart, but even then the dream of salvation from Utah did not die.[32]

Nor did this rejection end Bill Cody's flirtation with Mormon colonists on his own account, independent of the Shoshone Irrigation Company Wyoming governor DeForrest Richards and his secretary of state, Fenimore Chatterton, traveled to Salt Lake in January 1900 to confer with the president of the Church, hoping to promote Mormon migration to Wyoming. There was a large Mormon colony in the Star Valley of southwestern Wyoming, but the State was specifically promoting the Big Horn Basin. An early Carey Act project along the lower Shoshone River, organized by some capitalists from Cincinnati, had fallen apart by 1898 without any work having been done on a canal. The State hoped to find someone else to pick up that project. Soon after the governor's visit, Elder Abraham O. Woodruff took out a water right for the area, known at the time as the Cincinnati Canal, and the Church made plans to send a group to the Basin to assess the feasibility of making a success of it. When that group of fourteen came into the Basin from the railhead at Red Lodge in February 1900, Bill Cody himself was waiting at the Eagle's Nest stage station, sixteen miles downriver from Cody, to welcome them.[33]

Buffalo Bill might have thought that there was still some possibility of working out a sale of the Cody assets to the Mormons. He would have learned on meeting them that the Church had other plans. But Cody was the president of two development companies with interests in the Shoshone valley, and if things would not work out for the Shoshone Irrigation Company, he might well find another way to benefit from the Mormon presence. The company he and Nate Salsbury had formed to build the Cody-Salsbury Canal had a water right for 169,000 acres, mostly on the north side of the river all the way from Cody to the place where the Cincinnati Canal would begin. Buffalo Bill looked very much like becoming the dominant landowner and town developer for the entire river valley. Looking around the Eagle's Nest station that night in February 1900, Cody surely thought of himself as greeting neighbors and potential customers for the little empire he had in hand in the Basin.[34]

The gathering at the stage station was certainly memorable to the Mormons who listened to Buffalo Bill spin tales far into the night. Cody also spoke of his respect for the Mormon pioneers in Utah, and especially for Brigham Young. If the Mormon account is to be believed, Cody announced that night that he would relinquish a part of his water right on the north side of the lower Shoshone so that the new colony could build their canal and villages there. Cody and Nate Salsbury did, in fact, relinquish their rights to the water needed to irrigate the old Cincinnati Canal property on March 9, 1900, only a month or so after the meeting at Eagle's Nest. As the story goes, Salsbury protested that they should have made the Mormons pay $20,000 for the rights. In reply, Buffalo Bill stated that the Mormons would help fulfill his dream of a great agricultural empire on the Shoshone. When Salsbury protested a second time, the Colonel said to him, "When you die it will be said of you, 'Here lies Nate Salsbury, who made a million dollars in the show business and kept it,' but when I die people will say, 'Here lies Bill Cody who made a million dollars in the show business and distributed it among his friends.'"[35]

This fine gesture of cooperation with the Mormon colonists could not have sat well with the other directors of the Shoshone Irrigation Company. Although they had been rebuffed in their attempts to attract the Mormons to the Cody Canal, they did not give up easily. Abandoning the early plan of working with Charles Kingston, three of the directors—Bronson Rumsey, Horace Alger, and Beck—decided to try a different strategy. In May 1900, Rumsey wrote to some Mormons settled at Burlington, long after the Cody-Salsbury relinquishment had gone into effect, and even after the colonization company had begun to move toward Wyoming. This was indeed a forlorn message, a measure of the continuing desperation some of the Company felt about its prospects. The directors offered to give the Mormon colony water rights to 30,000 acres under the Cody Canal east of town, if they would undertake to enlarge the canal and extend it instead of starting on the Cincinnati Canal project on the lower river. The land Rumsey described was over a low divide from the land segregated for the Cody Canal: it would have been a revival, on a small scale, of the South Side Plan first laid out by Elwood Mead in 1894. The company could have expected nothing in the way of income from the land, but it would have brought a large group of citizens into an area tributary to the new town of Cody. Income from land sales might have seemed a smaller matter than town development by the summer of 1900. But, of course, this proposal fell on deaf ears. Bill Cody had dealt his partners right out of the game, as he had so often threatened to do.[36]

Hud Darrah truly had made 1899 a year of pain and trouble for the Shoshone Irrigation Company. In apparent collusion with Land Office agents, he manipulated the public notice provisions of the Carey Act to prevent any of the land proceeding to patent. The proceedings in the General Land Office initiated by Darrah dragged on into the summer of 1900. And he found other ways to harass Cody and Beck. When Beck returned to Cody after his visit to Washington to try to clear up Darrah's protest there, he learned that Darrah was going to try to foil their plans to profit from selling coal to the railroad. Beck tried to defend their interests by transferring the coal lands to Louis Decker, Cody's brother-in-law, but Darrah filed a protest in the summer of 1901 on 160 acres containing the coal seams. If the land were adjudged to be valuable principally for coal, it would have to be removed from the Carey Act segregation and be opened to entry under the mining laws.[37]

Attorney General J. A. Van Orsdel took note of the special character of the land patent contest. Although the State did not customarily intervene in this kind of matter, Cody had convinced him that a success for Darrah "would be inimical to the interests of the Cody company and also to the early settlers under the Cody ditch."[38] It is not clear what interests the early settlers might have had in the affair, but Van Orsdel was certainly right in his observation about the company. This was a forthright example of the values and vision of a company setting out to establish corporate control of the resources—and thereby of the life—of the land where they chose to do business. Colonel Cody himself was hopping mad. He wrote to Curtis Hinkle, chief clerk of the State Land Board, urging him to make a good fight in the Darrah contest. "If he wins that suit no one will feel like putting in another dollar in ditches— it will put Wyo. back ten years, if he gains it."[39] One might reasonably suggest that Darrah would have had a better idea of the interests of ordinary settlers at Cody than Buffalo Bill himself did. At any rate, Hud Darrah certainly drew the lines in the dirt where issues of incorporation would be fought out.

In the summer of 1899, Elwood Mead moved on to a new position in the federal government. Casting about for a new agent in Cheyenne, Buffalo Bill's eye fell on Hinkle, and for the next few years he directed to him the same kind of pleas for help and promises of reward that he once showered upon Mead. Cody's position in the state was further strengthened when Van Orsdel, his Cheyenne attorney, was appointed attorney general. As noted above, Cody's direct connection to Van Orsdel put what might have been an ordinary land dispute in quite a different light. Cody kept up the pressure on Van Orsdel. When the case had not been settled by midsummer, the Colonel wrote him, "I hope you will put a stop to this disturber Darrah so that Wyo. can have a chance."[40]

The law works too slowly for men like Cody and Beck. Van Orsdel asked Beck to find someone who lived near Cody to represent the State at a hearing on the dispute, since it was too difficult and expensive for any-one to travel that far from Cheyenne. Complaining that the State was not showing proper interest in the case, Beck engaged a Sheridan attorney to represent the company and to cross-examine witnesses at the hearing before Judge Stillwell. After that initial hearing, the contest was set to be heard in Lander in late May. But that hearing was actually held in Cody as well, after which the matter was forwarded to Lander for decision. In the interim, Beck learned from the commissioner of the General Land Office, former Wyoming governor W. A. Richards, that the inspector had recommended against the company on the coal contest. Seeing that the chances of winning the suit did not look good, he took it upon himself to bargain with Darrah to split the interest in the coal land however the contest came out, and Darrah accepted the arrangement. When the decision came down, only forty acres were opened to coal entry. Darrah immediately filed on them and soon took patent to the land, the north-east quarter of the southwest quarter of section 23-53-101. In any case, the significance of the coal land had begun to decline in Beck's mind as he saw the B&M engineers working on a line for the new railroad that by-passed the seam they had first located.[41]

The coal contest was actually the lesser vexation visited upon the company by Hud Darrah. It has been pointed out how he pursued a protest against the issuing of patents on the land under the Cody Canal. As late as June 1900, George Beck was still trying to talk Darrah into dropping his protest. Even the agreement on the coal land did not imme-diately bring Darrah around on the larger point. The company and its agents were quite distressed about the continuance of the protest into the summer of 1900. C. W. Burdick, Van Orsdel's partner and now the company attorney, even asked Buffalo Bill if he knew of any way Darrah "could be reached by outside influence" and induced to withdraw.[42] Buffalo Bill's only response was impotent rage: "That cuss of a Darrah should be run out of the country," and "this damn Darrah out [*sic*] to be cut & driven out of the country. Don't leave a stone unturned to down him."[43]

Probably at Darrah's request, the hearing was postponed to the end of June, and then to the end of July. Important business of the Shoshone Irrigation Company with the new railroad had to be put on hold. Beck suspected that breaks in the canal over the summer, coinciding as they did with his own absence from town on this and other business, were not unrelated to the protest. Buffalo Bill continued to fulminate from the Wild West: "Let's down this man Darrah. If he wins in one court, appeal it. Law him to a stand still."[44] However, during the delay Beck managed to convince Frank Houx, who had originally joined with Darrah in protesting the patents, to withdraw, and when the hearing was finally held, on July 31, Darrah himself, being denied a motion for further continuance, refused to testify. Judge Stillwell declared the case closed at last, although (as we have seen) another protest followed immediately and the legal troubles were not entirely out of the way for another year.[45]

The spring of 1900 brought a strange and potentially catastrophic personnel crisis to the affairs of the Shoshone Irrigation Company. George Beck resigned. President Cody had ridden general manager Beck mercilessly, had listened to Beck complain to other directors, and yet through it all—sometimes in the midst of construction crisis and sometimes in the calmer times at the end of the summer—they had remained friends and partners. In March 1900, this kind of relationship seemed to be proceeding as usual. Cody wrote Beck a letter each week, urging him to do particular things (such as getting a mineral filing on their coal fields) but generally to communicate jolts of energy. "Please George wake up and help me look out for our interests. . . . Let me hear from you. Keep mum. Get up steam and lets make a fortune in the next two years. Cant do it without work & energy."[46] That was March 1st. A few days later, as he took off for Cheyenne to see that the Land Board did their business on the Darrah suit, he wrote, "I hope you will *push* at that end, dont let the bunch grass grow under your feet for the next two years, and you will feel better. And we will take our families to Europe."[47] The next week Cody warned him that the stockholders could forget to pay his salary if he did not push things. "This continual nagging from me is disagreeable I know, but if I shut up nothing is done, so I would rather keep some one mad than have nothing done."[48] He underlined the importance of getting the water down early that spring.

It was between the writing of these last two letters that Beck announced his resignation to the board. "Due to a difference with the President of our Company and to written criticism on my conduct of affairs by him, I feel that I no longer wish to retain the management of this company. . . ."[49] Since there was nothing new in the way of criticism, it is probable that the resignation was Beck's response to a rumor hatched somewhere in the East that his salary might be withheld as a way of stimulating him to work harder. Beck surely suspected that Cody was at the bottom of it, and the resignation was probably his way of calling Buffalo Bill's bluff. He asked to be relieved of his duties by April 1. Cody and the Buffalo men met near the end of March and concluded that Beck should prepare a complete audit of the company books, and they would pay him whatever was shown to be due him. However, they also seem to have concluded that they needed him. It is interesting that Buffalo Bill, recognizing that he was part of the problem, left it to other directors to communicate with Beck about the resignation. The only letter mentioning the matter that survives was written by Nate Salsbury early in April, smoothing the waters a bit; in fact, the resignation was never carried into effect and Beck appears to have been paid. It was not until June, however, that Beck and Cody effected any kind of reconciliation. The dispute was surely behind them in July, when Cody signed a letter to Beck about townsite business, "Your friend, W F Cody."[50]

Events were moving swiftly on several fronts in the early spring of 1900; Beck could not have chosen a better time to threaten to withdraw his services. Buffalo Bill learned early in March that the General Land Office had ordered an inspection of the Cody Canal before they would allow any of the land under the canal to be patented. His Cheyenne attorney advised him to make sure Beck took good care of the inspector when he got to Cody, which they had been told would be very soon. Cody immediately fired off a letter to Beck communicating that advice and guaranteeing, whatever the other directors might do, that Beck would have the money he needed to get water flowing to the town and farms beyond town by the time the inspector arrived. Beck got crews started on the canal March 20, and added more men within the week, in expectation of money from the directors, which this year actually did come. And when the inspector came to the Basin he found water in the ditches and filed a favorable report to his superiors in Washington. At long last, something had gone right on the Cody Canal.[51]

When the Darrah patent dispute seemed settled in their favor, Beck sent word to all the directors, and also sent a full account to Attorney General Van Orsdel, as it was the State's authority to receive patents that was contested. That was in August. Final disposition of the Darrah case seemed to have arrived in October, at the Land Office in Lander, with a confirmation of the victory of the State and the Shoshone Irrigation Company. Buffalo Bill thought it was done and wired everyone, including President Morrill of the Lincoln Land Company, the land development subsidiary of the Burlington Railroad, which was in the process of acquiring an interest in the Cody townsite.[52]

Still, the case would not go away. The General Land Office required some final assurances that the proper notices had been sent to Darrah before the several hearings. In early December, the Lincoln Land Company took the lead in dealing with the government. To be in the best position to profit from land sales, they needed to have clear title to land in the townsite before the railroad actually got there. The attention to detail and single-minded pursuit of objectives that the Land Company brought to these matters is striking, in contrast to the conduct of business by George Beck and Bill Cody. They immediately directed Beck to hand-carry the evidence of service and of Darrah's withdrawal of protest to the federal land office at Lander, a journey of more than 160 miles, and to stay there until all the papers had been corrected and forwarded to Washington. Bringing decades of business experience to the Wyoming frontier, as an agent of incorporation the Lincoln Land Company was more formidable in the course of ordinary business than the Shoshone Irrigation Company was even on its best days.[53]

Having consolidated his position within the Shoshone Irrigation Company (which he had surely never intended to give up), George Beck undertook to prepare the fledgling town for the future that the Burlington connection seemed to promise for it. The first order of business was to create a commercial club to boost the town. By late July of 1900, the Cody Club, with George Beck as president and J. H. Peake as treasurer, announced itself to the world. Buffalo Bill greeted it wryly: it "should be a success, properly officered."[54] A few months later, Nate Salsbury, apparently fortified for something more strenuous than letter-writing, devoted a page of rollicking prose to Beck and to his presidency, concluding, "Commend me to my friends indeed, and those who would like to be. Say that I am not impervious to the spoils of office, and that some day I will aspire to put you out of the business of being president, if you do not read this letter with due care for punctuation and the rights of authors."[55] Salsbury and Beck brought aid and comfort to each other as they pursued their life works in the company of Buffalo Bill. Nate had only about two years to live when he confessed to this modest ambition; it is unfortunate that he never had the chance.

In the fall of 1900, Buffalo Bill laid the last ghost of the Nagle experience from 1896. Several of the priests who traveled to Cody with the German immigrants had bought lots in the town. Beck must have borrowed some money from some of the priests against the security of their town lots. Three of the priests sold notes totalling $200 to Nagle and subsequently refused to pay any more on the notes, so Nagle tried for years to get Beck to pay off the notes. The persistence of these unpaid notes and the generally acrimonious character of the breakdown between Nagle and the Shoshone Irrigation Company led Nagle and the priests to make life difficult for the company in every possible way, poisoning the minds of anyone who might be considering a move to Cody. By October 1900, the Colonel had had enough of it. Pressed anew at the end of September, he told Beck, "Those priests have called me a swindler until I am tired of it. They have 16 lots that they claim cost them $1600. I have just wired you that I am buying them."[56] He wanted to know for certain from Beck that the lots would be worth $1,600. Among the many reasons Cody found to empty his pockets on behalf of the company, maintaining his and the company's credit was surely near the top.

Colonel Cody also continued to keep close watch on the mineral possibilities of his settlement. Traveling through the southern states late in October, he inquired closely after the situation with the coal mine they had located. He was concerned that the mineral filings be transferred to him immediately, and wanted to know whether the Shoshone Irrigation Company would get the present coal mine (over which they and Darrah had struggled earlier). He wanted to be sure he could work the mine that winter, and that he could get the land patented. Ultimately, his Wyoming Coal Company was organized and made some small money, but probably nothing like what he had hoped at one time.[57]

When the board of directors met a few days before Christmas in 1900, Horace Alger presented the balance sheet for the Shoshone Irrigation Company after five years of operation. They had spent $152,488 in that time. They had sold capital stock in the amount of $92,425 and raised $27,000 on their bonds from Mrs. Hearst. They had, however, sold only $11,375 worth of water contracts, far less than the $18,485 borrowed from individual directors, in addition to their stock subscriptions. Bill Cody, of course, had lent close to half of that sum, $6,300 of which had gone to pay interest on the Hearst bonds. This is not the picture of a company in thriving condition, but the prospect of better days with the arrival of the railroad line kept them all in an upbeat frame of mind.

Throughout the fall and winter of that year, the volume of mail inquiring about land under the Cody Canal increased dramatically, due no doubt to the advertising of the Burlington. Many individuals wrote to Beck in Cody, seeking a new location for themselves. In the midst of these communications came one from a Gustav Wallenberg of Chicago, who claimed to be interested in locating a colony in the Big Horn Basin. Wallenberg had been in touch with the Wyoming state engineer and knew something of Buffalo Bill's business there. There would come a time when Beck would rue the day he ever answered Wallenberg's letter, but in early 1901 it must have looked like more of the good news for which they had waited so long.[58]

Nor was the arrival of the railroad an unmixed blessing. The enterprise of the Shoshone Irrigation Company was, among other things, an attempt at incorporation of that out-of-the-way corner of the nation. Land and water were to be managed by the company, for the company's interest. There were opportunities for individuals in Cody, but where freedom of opportunity for a Hud Darrah conflicted with the freedom of opportunity for Bill Cody, Darrah was to be forced into line. As a force for incorporation, however, Cody's company was not especially efficient. Events took them by surprise, and their own mistakes made them needlessly vulnerable to those who resisted falling into line. Cody certainly thought of himself as a benefactor, and consequently anyone who opposed him had to be simply wrong-headed. The Burlington Railroad and the Lincoln Land Company entered the valley of the

Shoshone as experienced and successful corporations. They knew how to do their business and did not need, as Bill Cody did, to be loved by those with whom they did it. The incorporation of the Big Horn Basin was about to change character in a big way.

CHAPTER SEVEN

The Burlington Comes to Cody

As railroads moved west, they moved carefully, with every eye trained on long-term advantage. The Chicago, Burlington, and Quincy Railroad was the last to enter into the cross-country sweepstakes. Although only a decade later they were to change course and cast their lot with the Great Northern and Northern Pacific lines, in 1890 the CB&Q was still actively planning to construct its own transcontinental system. From 1890, one of its most attractive prospective routes across the Continental Divide ran up the south fork of the Shoshone (then the Stinking Water), across Two Ocean Pass, and then through Jackson Hole and down the Teton River to the Snake. Edward Gillette, the first CB&Q surveyor to explore the Big Horn Basin, entered the Basin from the north in 1893 to stake out this route. The Burlington had decided in January of that year to build on from Sheridan, Wyoming, to Billings, Montana; Gillette was sent out to keep the company ready for the next step beyond Billings. No doubt George Beck knew Gillette in Sheridan, where the Burlington rails had reached by the end of 1892, and would have talked to him of his trip; it is hard to imagine that Beck decided casually to interest himself in irrigation on the Stinking Water. Bill Cody, who had put a company together to manage the Sheridan Inn for the Burlington, knew all the railroad people. It is impossible to believe that Cody offered to join Beck's group on a mere whim. From the beginning, the success of their plan depended on the railroad building to their land. Cody and Beck had every reason to believe they would not be going into the Basin alone.[1]

In later years, Buffalo Bill frequently took credit for bringing the railroad to Wyoming. He mentioned it when he communicated with officers of state government, hoping to build or to extend his reputation as one upon whom they could depend to bring large affairs to successful conclusions. He spoke of it to journalists all over Wyoming. A rambling conversation in January 1910 with the former editor of the *Big Horn County Rustler* may be considered typical. It was all about his determination to see a road built into the Basin. As Cody told the story, after he had described the wonders of the Basin to President Perkins of the CB&Q, "he told me if I would come in and help in its settlement he would build the road at the earliest opportunity." Later, just before he was to retire, Perkins recalled, "I promised Col. Cody to build that line, and I am going to do it before I quit." Cody ended the interview with his famous brag, "If it had not been for me you would not have had your railroad."[2]

There can be no doubt that Cody and Perkins were friends. The Wild West was surely a good customer for the CB&Q, and Perkins, in common with many wealthy businessmen, enjoyed the reflected celebrity of a relationship with Buffalo Bill. The Burlington's historian notes that Cody was a "favorite and frequent" guest on Perkins's private car.[3] But anyone who knew Buffalo Bill Cody knew that he was not shy about taking credit for things. As this chapter will show, it is rather more likely that the Burlington brought Cody to Wyoming than the other way around.

The earliest surveys of the Basin by Gillette and others make it clear that the Burlington was interested in this territory for its agricultural possibilities and its mineral potential. Agriculturally, it was clearly the best and largest area remaining undeveloped in the state of Wyoming. Gillette wrote of the coal fields already discovered and the prospects for significant finds of gold, silver, and copper. Mining was already underway in the Sunlight Basin, high up in the Absaroka Mountains, tributary to the Clark's Fork of the Yellowstone but as easily reached from the Cody area as anywhere. There were also working mines near Cooke City, at the northeast corner of Yellowstone Park. He was also aware of the potential of an entrance into Yellowstone up the north fork of the Shoshone River. Even leaving aside considerations of a transcontinental route (which by 1894 seemed more likely through central Wyoming than the north), all of this territory could be captured by the Burlington if its line were extended south from Montana. Gillette's recommendation was to build from a junction point at Toluca, on the Crow Reservation.

It would be an easy road to build, and it might make possible the removal of the Crows from Pryor Creek to more eastern parts of the reservation, which would allow the opening of the western section of the reservation to white settlement. This report seems in retrospect as much an advertisement as an analysis; Gillette may have known what his supervisor wanted to hear.[4]

George Holdrege, general manager of Burlington lines west of the Mississippi, kept a very close eye on economic development along all possible Burlington routes. He backed a line from Toluca to Cody as early as 1896. He had an agent in the Kirwin gold fields up the Wood River from Meeteetse who kept him posted on developments there, and he kept an ear to the ground where the Northern Pacific tracks ran as well. Clearly, he thought the Big Horn Basin was going to be a prosperous area. He had sent T. E. Calvert, his general superintendent, into the Basin in the summer of 1896 to recheck Gillette's 1893 survey and to work up another assessment of the situation there. Calvert thought Cody held the best position to command the trade of the Basin, since most of the people already in the Basin took their trade to Billings. He observed that the "Cody Company" could not get much further on their present scheme without good transportation facilities. That, in turn, appeared to him to depend upon finding "mineral in paying quantities." He traveled to Yellowstone Park with George Beck, along a route Beck had marked out earlier, and urged the Shoshone Irrigation Company to convince the government to open a road out to the Timber Reserve on the eastern border of the park, so that wagon travel to Yellowstone could go through Cody. If those two things came through, Calvert expected a road from Toluca to Cody to do well.[5]

Mining and tourism were not the primary reasons why Cody and Beck had embarked upon this colonization scheme, but others who were being asked to bet on its success saw those as the best reasons. In the fall of 1899, C. H. Morrill, president of the railroad's land development arm, the Lincoln Land Company, visited the Basin to provide more up-to-date information for President Perkins. He was not encouraged by what he saw. There were fewer than a dozen houses in Cody, and only a single store. There was no water in town; the ditch scheme was a failure up to that time. There were only about ten settlers along the upper canal, and probably no more than 600 acres being farmed. More had been there earlier, but many had become disgusted and left.[6]

Morrill was struck by the difficulties of making the Cody irrigation project a success, with the long flume that was always in derelict condition, and too small even if it was kept in repair. He estimated that the company would have to spend $250,000 to make their ditch big enough and good enough to water the land they had segregated. Further, he specifically discouraged speculation on the prospects of mineral deposits. There was no coal of engine quality in the Basin, only lignite. The gold and copper mines of the Sunlight country had rich ore, but in very small quantities. He referred Perkins to Holdrege's man for an estimate of Kirwin possibilities. But he was enthusiastic about the future of agriculture in the Basin, where he thought a million acres could be irrigated some day. In conclusion, he offered his opinion that it was too early to build into the Basin, though acknowledging that a railroad would stimulate the development of industries there.[7]

Morrill sent Perkins another report a week later, one prepared by the Burlington attorney in Wyoming. "I thought perhaps you might like to know the facts in the [Cody irrigation] case," he said, "as Cody has stated he could put three or four hundred thousand dollars in it almost any time if railroad was to be built. I think most of the money he has put in their [sic] has been invested in wines, and probably will be in the future."[8] The attorney was not especially well informed on the details of the Shoshone Irrigation Company's financial situation, but at least he saw clearly that their condition was precarious. "Am not advised as to what has been done on the ground, but understand that but little of value exists, the large amount paid in having been swallowed up by extravagance and incompetent management."[9] Morrill also learned in Cheyenne that the Carey Act projects in the Big Horn Basin were not doing well. He thought there were only about twenty settlers at Burlington and no more than ten at Cody. He reported that the state land commissioner thought that the Cody scheme was not likely to succeed unless someone else took it over.[10] These reports would seem calculated to instill caution in anyone considering building into the Basin, but they arrived too late to deflect the plans that Holdrege had set in motion.

Expansion into the Big Horn Basin and a new connection to Denver from Guernsey, Wyoming, were the main construction items on the CB&Q table in the summer of 1899. Holdrege wanted to go full ahead on both, but Perkins insisted that the Denver matter be settled before they took any proposal to the board regarding the Toluca extension. He asked Holdrege to prepare a detailed map for the board, with construction estimates, traffic projections, and a statement of the best arguments for building it. When Holdrege replied, he emphasized the glowing future of the Basin and the opportunity they had—but could not count on having for long—to build there now while the Northern Pacific was busy elsewhere. He urgently recommended starting the line: it would pay from the start, he said, and they could hold the territory against the Northern Pacific with a relatively small expenditure. Grading and bridging the road to Cody would cost in the neighborhood of $615,000, but $200,000 spent over the coming winter would settle the question of occupancy of the territory. Holdrege reemphasized his belief that the mountains surrounding the Big Horn Basin would contain important mineral deposits. He even went so far as to use the freight figures from Deadwood as a yardstick for what they might expect from this new line.[11]

Although the prospect of mining riches seemed nearly certain to Holdrege and some other officers of the CB&Q, one of whom observed that a hundred miles could not be built in the mountains without finding some valuable mines, others thought a "purely mining road" was not a good bet. Although Holdrege certainly had his eyes on mining prospects, it was never a "purely mining" proposition to him. When he learned from a correspondent that the Northern Pacific was building new track in Montana as well as Idaho, he again urged Perkins to take the opportunity to secure the Big Horn Basin. With word that the Mormons were going to send five hundred families into the Basin early in 1900, it became more imperative to keep the NP out; he wanted to begin grading and bridging work in the spring of 1900 and to plan on laying track in 1901.[12]

Traveling as many miles as he did by rail each year, and enjoying as he did the company of men of wealth and fame, Buffalo Bill naturally made friends with the men who ran the railroads. In a conversation with Holdrege in the fall of 1899, Cody learned of his hope to start crews to work in 1900 on the line from Toluca to Cody. In the spring of 1900, Cody was in Chicago talking with Charles Manderson, the Burlington's general counsel, who told him that $2,500,000 had been set aside to build their road. Reporting this conversation to Beck, Cody suggested that they "put him into something good" to reward him for his work on their behalf. "How would it do to give him some stock in our mining co.?," he asked. "Suggest it to the boys. Allso Holdrege & Perkins, it will help us."[13] But was there anything "good" they could offer to men like this in a project that was staggering from one year to the next? Only the kind of bullheaded optimism that Bill Cody could not keep under wraps could make anyone think so.

Buffalo Bill would have learned in his conversation with Manderson that the final decision to start work was still hanging fire. From his North Platte ranch, he wrote a long letter extolling the virtues of his new Wyoming home; the letter was directed to Manderson, but it seems likely that it was written for Perkins, to whom Manderson immediately forwarded it. Even for one as given to hyperbole as Bill Cody, this was a remarkable letter. He began by noting that General Nelson Miles had been there the previous winter. He and his friends had bought ranches and intended to settle. What better recommendation could there be for a place? And then there were the Mormons. The ones who already were there were the most prosperous Mormon colony in the West, and thousands more could be expected if a railroad was built. There were mines of all kinds, and "every kind of building stone from the finest marble down." Timber and water, enough to irrigate 400,000 acres, made it "the richest portion of America." In conclusion, he asked, "What are the stockholders of the Burlington thinking of?[14]

From this fustian blend of overstatement and outright fabrication, one might conclude that Buffalo Bill himself bore as much responsibility as Major John Burke for the hyperventilated prose of the Wild West publicity. Miles did come hunting with Cody, but there is no evidence he or his friends ever bought any land. The elevated claims that fill the rest of the letter contrast dramatically with the sober evaluation produced a few months earlier by Charles Morrill. Manderson seemed somewhat embarrassed by the letter he probably had stimulated: "Of course Buffalo Bill's interests in that locality compel enthusiasm" was his partial disclaimer to Perkins. Nevertheless, he sent it, and concluded his cover letter: "I thought it well to send this letter to you as it is an encouragement to proceed with what is underway."[15] It may have been this letter that led Buffalo Bill to think, many years later, that he had convinced the railroad to come to Wyoming.

That letter to Manderson could be considered a general advertisement for Cody's Wyoming project. A month later, back in New York and about to begin another Wild West season, he sent off a more particular letter directly to Perkins. The railroad had apparently asked Horace Alger if the Shoshone Irrigation Company would grant right-of-way across their segregation and enough land to build a depot on the town site. "We will do so with pleasure," Cody told Perkins, and further assured him that they could have right-of-way across the Cody-Salsbury segregation along the north side of the Shoshone. "You may be sure of the hearty cooperation of all concerned to further the interests of the Burlington in the Big Horn Basin." He then inquired of Perkins if he could assure potential investors in the Cody-Salsbury project that the Burlington would extend its line to Cody in the near future. Cody talked of these shadowy "potential investors" frequently, and they may or may not have been the real consideration on his mind as he wrote. He may have wanted nothing more than reassurance that the CB&Q was ready to start building. Perkins replied in a few days that they were "considering . . . the expediency of beginning construction this summer," and further observed that "the value of that region, as a contributor to a railroad, must depend largely on what is developed in the way of mines of one kind or another." Rich mining developments would stimulate everything, including the railroad construction.[16]

The same day Perkins wrote to Buffalo Bill, he sent a note to Holdrege, with a copy of Cody's letter. When Holdrege knew what he needed at Cody, or elsewhere, Perkins wrote, he could just ask the company to give the railroad the necessary deeds. Moreover, "now that Col. Cody has promised co-operation, and said we can have everything he can give us, no doubt the officers of the Company will execute the necessary papers, when the time comes."[17] An air of self-satisfaction permeates this short letter, as if he felt they had bested Buffalo Bill in industrial combat. And they had. They knew that Cody needed them more than they needed him, and that they could drive a hard bargain if they needed to.

Of course, the Burlington needed to complete its survey before building the railroad. At the north end, near Toluca, it was ready for work, but at the Cody end, the survey was still unfinished when Buffalo Bill wrote his letters. What the railroad was trying to decide was how to enter Cody and where to cross the Shoshone River. Edward Gillette's original survey crossed the river several miles east of town, at the mouth of Sage Creek, and ran tracks right through the section set aside for the townsite. On that plan, they would locate a depot on the west side of the new town. The crew of surveyors and engineers sent out in 1900 were considering keeping the track north of the river until they got to the hot springs two miles west of town, and bridging it there. Either of these plans would work with the original Burlington plan to carry the line up the South Fork and on west. Beck thought that they would cost roughly the same, but the Burlington engineers thought they would save some money with the north side line. It was not a trivial matter for the Shoshone Irrigation Company. One line would bring the depot into town, the other would locate it possibly two miles from town on the other side of a canyon. Beck, as was his wont, put it down to personal rivalries between the leaders of the two engineering parties, and proposed that the directors weigh in where they could in favor of the old line: "If there is any understanding between our people and the Burlington people, or if any influence can be brought to bear, the south side proposition should be insisted on."[18]

Using influence was what Buffalo Bill did best, and he swung immediately into action. He wrote to Perkins from New York at the end of April. People in Cody were alarmed to see a line being surveyed on the north side of the river. "Can I assure residents of Cody that when you *do* build into that country that you will build to Cody? You know I have spent six years of time and lots of money to open up that unknown country."[19] There is no evidence that personal rivalry between surveyors had anything to do with the siting of the railroad line. Cost and corporate advantage were almost certainly the only things considered in the decision. However, corporate advantage may have looked different to different people. T. E. Calvert, B&M superintendent, recommended to his boss, George Holdrege, in May 1900 that of the several lines run to and through Cody the one that stayed north of the river would be best. They would have difficult communication with the town on the south bank of the river, but they would be in a better position to build on west toward Yellowstone and would save nearly $100,000 in construction costs. Holdrege, however, passed up to his superiors a recommendation that they cross the river and build to a terminus adjacent to the town of Cody. He also forwarded Calvert's detailed letter with its different recommendation, but the separation between these two on the issue was perhaps significant.[20]

Engineering issues aside, the siting of the line was apparently not a simple decision for the CB&Q leadership. President Perkins was still thinking about it in early 1901. He thought it was probably best to stay on the north side of the river because of the complications with land titles at the townsite, but he was sensitive to the situation of the "old proprietors of the town of Cody." They needed to be satisfied, he thought, "because we told them definitely that we were going to build to Cody, and they may have invested money, or gone to expense, which would give them a claim upon us."[21] This was, of course, the argument that Bill Cody had made to him. Holdrege was caught between a president who was perhaps too close to Buffalo Bill and a staff whose views were not tainted by personal acquaintance with Cody.

While Holdrege was trying to sort out his position, Calvert weighed in again with information from the Basin. When the Burlington started thinking about the Basin, he noted, the Cody Canal looked like a good proposition, and Cody looked like "the proper place to land from both the commercial and strategical considerations." He still thought Cody was the best point strategically, but the work accomplished by the Mormons below Corbett "has changed the situation somewhat commercially."[22] A large and rigorous community of Mormons on the lower Shoshone compared favorably with the struggling little town of Cody in terms of potential value to the railroad. He recommended building to the Cody vicinity, but thought it a bad idea to spend much money getting into the town. They could locate on the north side. They would need to locate their own water supply, but that was not a great drawback: "I have little faith that Cody will now succeed in making permanent arrangements for getting and keeping water on his Cody town site; it will require more money and care than his organization will probably put into it."[23] These arguments echo strongly those of Charles Morrill from late 1899. They indicate that the Burlington staff who went over the ground in Wyoming saw the situation without any of Buffalo Bill's smoke getting in their eyes.

Holdrege, although he had originally supported building into Cody, was apparently convinced by Calvert's arguments. He told Perkins that he now thought it best to remain on the north side. Perhaps, he suggested, Morrill could convince Colonel Cody and the others to move their town interests across the river, and that would be a way of satisfying them. As it happened, Buffalo Bill himself came to Omaha in February to meet with Holdrege. Morrill, Calvert, and Holdrege had already concluded that there was not sufficient room north of the river to locate a full-fledged town-site, but they were pretty well decided they did not want to build across the river. They would save nearly $300,000 on a road to Yellowstone by staying on the north side, and crossing the river would not bring them any significant business they did not already expect. Cody talked hard to get them to build to the town, but ultimately had to agree that the

Shoshone Irrigation Company could live with a railroad terminus on the opposite side of the river. The distance would be only half a mile, and a good wagon bridge would make the town accessible. Perkins immediately concurred in the arrangement with Cody, and the board followed suit in April, after construction had already reached Corbett. The board determined not only to stay on the north side, but approved the location of a line on beyond Cody, through the canyon west of town and up the north fork of the Shoshone to Yellowstone Park. However, the railroad built only the seven miles from Corbett to Cody as the first stage, and that is where the line remains to this day.[24]

Buffalo Bill's first venture into town-building had taken place when he was quite a young man. In 1867, twenty-one years old but married and a father, he went into partnership with a contractor he met at Fort Hays, Kansas. They knew the Kansas Pacific was building westward, and Cody was looking for a way to get out of scouting for the army and to settle down. He and the contractor, William Rose, laid out a town where the railroad was scheduled to cross Big Creek, and started a saloon and a general store. They gave away lots and the town had, according to Cody, two hundred houses, several other stores and saloons, and a hotel within a month. Then a railroad agent stopped to see them and proposed that he be admitted to partnership in the hustling new town, called Rome. Confident in the superiority of their location, Cody and Rose refused. The railroad went down the track a mile, announced they were going to set up a town to be known as Hays City and make it an important railroad town, and almost immediately the population of Rome packed up and moved to Hays City, leaving Cody and his partner high and dry.[25] From this experience, Buffalo Bill drew life lessons that came very much into play as the Burlington approached Cody in 1900.

Although they had laid claim under the terms of the Carey Act to section 32, where the company planned to locate the town of Cody, and Beck had even sold some lots in the new town, the directors had never taken any further steps to organize a townsite company. The approach of the Burlington Railroad caused at least one director to urge that they proceed immediately to get that done. By the early part of the summer, the railroad itself, through the Lincoln Land Company, had let the directors know that it intended to take a leading role in developing the new town. Charles Morrill journeyed with Superintendent Calvert to Cody in May and put a proposition before Beck, Alger, and Rumsey. The Land Company would take half of the town, paying the Shoshone Irrigation Company $10 per acre, if they concluded to make Cody a railroad town. They further offered that if they chose to start another town, they would sell the Shoshone Irrigation Company half-interest in that town. With their north-side survey in hand, the threat to start another town was clearly not an idle one, and the directors who met Morrill and Calvert in Cody accepted on the spot. Buffalo Bill had already given them the benefit of his early Kansas experience to teach the folly of taking the railroad for granted.[26]

Townsite matters suddenly moved to the top of the Shoshone Irrigation Company's business list. Beck traveled to Lincoln, Nebraska, early in June to try to get things started properly. They faced immediately the problem that the claims of Beck, Cody, Rumsey, and Salsbury, a quarter-section each, had to be patented; without that they had nothing to offer the Lincoln people. The Hudson Darrah protest against patenting land around Cody consequently assumed an importance out of proportion to its simple troublesome nature. Buffalo Bill could see that, and it added to his distress with Darrah. He wrote repeatedly to Attorney General Van Orsdel, sending copies to Beck, urging him on against Darrah. Beck did what he could on his trip to Lincoln in June, and railroad officers journeyed out to Cody. It was determined that the claims and water contracts of the four directors would be relinquished to the Lincoln Land Company, which business Beck took in hand. For their part, the Land Company bought one claim and took an option on another in or near the townsite, and Beck started building houses for them. The Shoshone Irrigation Company was doing everything it could to create a good working relationship with the Lincoln Land Company.[27]

The first plat of the town of Cody covered about 230 acres of the designated section. Of the 925 lots platted, only 183 had been sold by the summer of 1900, many of those to the founders. The directors of the Shoshone Irrigation Company agreed to sell half-interest in each of the 742 unsold lots, and half-interest in the unplatted remainder of the section for $10 per acre. There things stood for the first year, but by the summer of 1901, the Lincoln people were talking again about moving the town. The people of Cody opposed it, of course, and the result was a compromise that resulted in a re-survey, a new plat, and a vacation of the original plat. The major change was to reshape the part of town west of Third Street The original plat had a pair of parks interrupting

Sheridan Avenue, the main east-west business street, with offset streets named after Civil War generals, one of Buffalo Bill's cherished ideas from the beginning. It was a graceful civic plan, but perhaps it looked inefficient as a business proposition to the hard-headed men from Lincoln. Whatever the reason, the new plat ran all the east-west streets (except for Sheridan, these were named after directors of the Shoshone Irrigation Company) through to the western limit of the town and left the question of parks to be settled at a later date. The Lincoln Land Company submitted this amended plat on July 9, 1901. That done, the two companies agreed formally that they would participate equally in the growth of the town site. Bronson Rumsey was appointed trustee for the partners in the Shoshone Irrigation Company. The Lincoln Land Company was established as legal owner of the townsite, and they issued confirming deeds to those who had bought lots from the Irrigation Company before the new arrangement had been formalized.[28]

There were still significant matters to be sorted out between the new townsite owners and the town's founders. In particular, Colonel Cody himself needed to get his holdings in good order as he set about building his great Irma Hotel in 1901. The contract between the two companies had stipulated that lot exchanges from the old to the new plat would be allowed. Cody owned a considerable chunk of the town from the beginning. He asked in late 1901 to have all of block 7 of the old town and to be allowed to select eighteen residential lots in the new town, in accordance with the agreement. The next year he proposed to Morrill a slightly different arrangement. Instead of taking the residential lots, he asked for the lots on the block where his hotel would be located. If he owned the entire block, he could select purchasers who would erect good buildings and keep away undesirable neighbors from his hotel. George Beck and Rumsey supported Buffalo Bill's request, and Morrill agreed to it. The papers were signed at the end of 1902 in Lincoln.[29]

The arrival of the railroad stimulated sales of water-right contracts for irrigated land under the Cody Canal. The volume of inquiries expanded dramatically, starting in 1902. Only 24 people had purchased water contracts by the end of 1901. More than 120 filed claims in the first six years the project was served by the Burlington; these covered 11,960 acres and represented potential sales of $125,483. Nearly one-third of that land remained unpatented when the Irrigation Company handed the Canal over to the settlers in 1907, so probably something less than

$90,000 was ever paid in on those land accounts. Still, compared with their record of sales before the railroad arrived, that was a significant amount of money. On balance, a reasonable estimate of land sales and town real-estate business would amount to something less than $100,000 by 1907. Beck estimated near the end of his life that their venture had cost the company nearly $22 per acre and they had sold most of the water rights for $10 to $15 per acre. It is impossible to know how he calculated those costs, and one cannot compare his estimate to the documented company expenses that survive with any precision at all. However, the December 1905 statement shows that the company had incurred expenses and interest charges of more than $240,000. All of the directors had loaned money to the company, in addition to their capital investments of $92,425. It may have cost Beck only $22 per acre, but Cody and Salsbury had loaned over $36,000 to Beck's $439; it surely worked out worse for them. However one counts, it is quite clear that the Shoshone Irrigation Company was a losing proposition for its investors. Only the late surge of business that came in with the Burlington enabled the Cody Canal investors to come away with anything like half their investment intact.[30]

George Beck did a little better than the others out of the townsite. They all kept an equal share when the land was transferred to the Lincoln Land Company, but Beck did not rely only on that. As managing partner of the Shoshone Irrigation Company, he managed most of the transition to Lincoln Land Company ownership of the town. It was natural, therefore, that the Land Company employed him as their agent in the sale of lots in Cody, for which he received a commission. As he was also mayor and president of the school board, he was essential to the growth of the town in the early years of the twentieth century. He negotiated the trade of lots that freed up a block on which to build a school building in 1903. Beck did not make a great deal of money out of this arrangement, but he concentrated a great deal of power in his hands and quietly built a foundation that may well entitle him to a higher claim as Cody's *pater civitas* than the man for whom the town was named.[31]

Beyond question, the Burlington kept Bill Cody and his partners from total financial collapse, and it may have saved the entire project. The Shoshone Irrigation Company had taken in only $1,535 on lot sales by the end of December 1900. The Lincoln Land Company not only paid the Irrigation Company $3,200 for half the townsite, it set about selling lots faster than the original owners had ever been able to do. However, when a series of judgments went against the company in 1907 and 1908, its income flow came to a halt. No record of the transaction survives, but the Land Company, now full partners in the fate of the town and the project, must have come up with the money necessary to balance the Irrigation Company's books prior to handing the water system over to the settlers, accepting the Irrigation Company's share of town lot sales as a means of repayment. At any rate, annual accounts of Cody lot sales from that time refer to Bronson Rumsey, trustee, as debtor to the Lincoln Land Company.[32]

Money from lot sales was paid into Rumsey's account with the Land Company for debt service until 1928. In some of the early years it was as little as $600, but in 1926 it was over $4,500. In that year Rumsey expressed his hope to George Beck that they would soon be evened up with the Lincoln Land Company, and two years later they achieved that. In 1928, the Land Company made $8,000 available for distribution among the members of the Shoshone Irrigation Company. When Rumsey sent a check for his share to Beck he sardonically remarked that Beck could "buy some golf balls with the enclosed." Although they had made a very small amount of money in the early years from lot sales, it was more than twenty years before any of the original investors saw another nickel from the townsite investment. Even in 1928, however, Buffalo Bill (or his heirs) had made no profit from the town. He apparently had incurred a debt to the Lincoln Land Company outside of the debt owed by the Shoshone Irrigation Company, and his share of the distribution remained with the company to be applied to that debt.[33]

The railroad not only saved the men who built Cody, it helped to establish the future of the town. Cody immediately became the "end of the line," the meeting point between wilderness and civilization. The Burlington took on the job of mediating that encounter through its promotion of the Cody country. They advertised irrigable land as long as that made sense, but they soon saw that the growth industry in that part of the world was going to be tourism. They had already recognized in their planning that Yellowstone Park would make Cody a significant point on the map of the West, and that a Park entrance on the east would give them equal standing with the Northern Pacific and Union Pacific lines when it came to building a tourist industry there. Although there is no evidence that Cody struggled against its destiny as a tourist town, it is worth noting in passing that in this, as in everything else, the Burlington called the shots and led the way. As with the advent of federal reclamation in this corner of Wyoming, it was the Burlington Railroad that brought in modern industrial tourism.[34]

The first Burlington brochure advertising the Big Horn Basin appeared in 1902. To a remarkable degree, the railroad incorporated text and pictures from the 1898 Shoshone Irrigation Company brochure. Only their maps and the Burlington insignia on the cover were a significant departure from the earlier publication; it was the Burlington badge, signifying the integration of this outpost in Wyoming into a known national network, that surely carried the most weight with the public. Interestingly, the Burlington brochure also carried a letter to prospective settlers from "Buffalo Bill, Great Showman and Scout." Alongside the boiler plate about the limitless potential of irrigation agriculture in the Basin, Cody found space to tout the government road to Yellowstone, then under construction, and to rhapsodize over the hunting between Cody and the Park. He straddled, rhetorically as well as actually, the agrarian and the "white Indian" traditions in American culture, and positioned his town along the same divide.[35] No one then could have had an inkling that such macrodevelopments as federal reclamation and modern industrial tourism, each mediated by the Burlington Railroad, would pave the way for the incorporation of this last corner of the West, for good and for ill.

CHAPTER EIGHT

The Demise of the Shoshone Irrigation Company

The business of building and colonizing Cody and the Cody Canal proceeded on their own courses in 1901, independent of the activities of the Burlington Railroad and the Lincoln Land Company. George Beck had much to do managing for the new owners of the townsite, but at the same time, he set up a contract with Gustav Wallenberg of Chicago to take on the ill-fated position of supervising the settlement of farmers on the land. Buffalo Bill started promoting the Cody Club as a hunting club to people he met on the road with the Wild West, and this in turn led to more work for Beck (whose name Buffalo Bill passed around as manager of up-scale hunting trips).[1] Nevertheless, the Colonel was consumed with worry about work on the ditch even while traveling with his show. His crew was starting work on the Irma Hotel, and needed water to help produce mortar for the stones. At the end of April, micro-managing as always, he demanded to know from Beck if the new ditch and flume were perfectly secure, their support beams placed on large rocks in trenches. "Please give this your personal attention, and keep a *good* ditch rider continually on the ditch."[2]

Back in Cody, George Beck was dealing with business as usual on the canal. Buffalo Bill filled out his letters about the Military College with worries about the canal, asking Beck to be especially careful about maintaining it. "Just think what a black eye it would give us if anything should happen to the ditch now. I beg of you to guard against it."[3] The summer of 1901, however, brought Beck another master to mind. The

Lincoln Land Company pushed him weekly until he produced titles for the quarter-sections they had purchased for the townsite. They also, with specific encouragement from Bill Cody, began to pressure Beck to get water into the canal and to keep it running. "Is the water running yet through the new ditch? If not, what seems to be the matter? Don't let up on the water business until you have it running in all the ditches."[4]

As summer approached, the Shoshone Irrigation Company faced more than the usual annual worry about paying interest on the Hearst bond; the bonds were due to be repaid in full on July 1. Beck thought the Lincoln Land Company would put up the money, on what authority one can only guess. Buffalo Bill wired Horace Alger, company treasurer, to assess each director prorata by the number of their shares, which he did. Henry Gerrans and Bronson Rumsey refused to pay their assessments, as they had for years, and this time Cody and Salsbury could not simply take the burden upon themselves. Once again Beck applied to Mrs. Hearst, this time for an extension, and she granted it. Cody and Beck had to give a $50,000 bond to secure the extension, which would require the company to pay interest in 1902 and 1903 and then interest plus principal in 1904. It was serious business, but it saved the company for a few years at least.[5]

The closing months of 1901 brought yet another crisis to the Cody Canal. Judging from the comments Charles Morrill had picked up in Cheyenne a couple of years earlier, the State of Wyoming was losing patience with the Shoshone Irrigation Company. At the end of October, the state board of Land Commissioners, which administered the Carey Act, resolved to send the state engineer into the Big Horn Basin to look into Carey Act projects there, and especially to inquire into the construction of the Cody Canal. In November, Fred Bond, Elwood Mead's successor as state engineer, visited Cody and conducted a thorough personal investigation of the canal. He did not like what he found. The time allowed under the Carey Act for completion of canal work had expired and the company was requesting an extension. Bond concluded that the work had not been prosecuted or, where undertaken at all, completed in accordance with the requirements of the permit. "For nearly half its proposed length there has been no construction whatever and a considerable proportion of that upon which work has been done is totally inadequate to carry the water required and is neither substantial nor durable in character." Bond pointed out that 1,800 acres of land patented to the state and 15,000 acres of land within the Carey Act segregation were wholly without water. Other colonists were moving into the Shoshone valley, able and anxious to use the water. He could not grant the requested extension "unless it be preceded by a thorough demonstration by the Shoshone Land and Irrigation Company not only of their intention but also of their ability to begin and complete this work without further delays."[6]

After the degree of cooperation the company had received from Elwood Mead, amounting almost to a state partnership, this must have come as a shock. Mead, after all, had certified the canal as completed in order to facilitate the patenting of the Carey Act segregation to the State. But Bond understood that in attracting settlers the reputation and credibility of the state was as important as its resource development, that indeed the latter depended upon the former. The state government, however, did not want to have the whole project fall back into its lap; this was a very forceful reminder to Beck and the others of their contractual obligations, but it left them a way to work themselves clear. Bond required the company to let contracts for the work, to get crews into the field early, and to work until the job was finished. If he had evidence by July 1 that the work would be completed without delay, they would get their extension, "otherwise such action will be taken as may be deemed proper in the premises."[7]

Coming as it did, just when the arrival of the railroad seemed to open a possibility of salvaging a bad investment, Bond's letter got immediate attention from the company directors. In fact, they must have anticipated the results of Bond's investigation before the formal notification arrived. At a directors meeting early in December, they voted to complete the canal, enlarging and extending it as originally planned. Moreover, before Bond's letter was written, George Bleistein, the strongest of the Buffalo directors, had already opened communication with a civil engineer in Salt Lake City, the man who was employed by Buffalo Bill to design his new Cody-Salsbury project downstream from Cody. He asked him to step in and provide corrected surveys and work estimates for finishing the canal as planned and bringing their present canal up to the state's standards. This is an important measure of how seriously the company viewed the situation: it was the first time in six years that anyone but George Beck or Bill Cody had taken any initiative on the ditch. The engineer, Frank Kelsey, wrote back within a week to tell Bleistein what fee he would charge to get the plans ready, and agreeing to contract to do the work once he had completed his estimates. Throughout the winter, which Buffalo Bill spent at his TE ranch on the South Fork, company members corresponded with Bond and Kelsey and each other, obviously serious about making the needed improvements.[8]

The other major private irrigation project in the Big Horn Basin at this time was that of Solon L. Wiley, an Omaha businessman, who was building a canal from the Greybull River known as the Bench Canal. Wiley had bigger ideas than that, however, involving tapping the Shoshone above Cody and bringing water to thousands of acres south and east of the town. This would eventually become known as the Oregon Basin proposition. Wiley's plans overlapped with some of Elwood Mead's original vision for the Cody Canal. It is unlikely that there would ever have been enough water to support both the Cody Canal and Wiley's project, and it occurred to him in early 1902 that it might be simpler if he controlled all the irrigation on the south side of the Shoshone. Consequently, just as the directors of the Shoshone Irrigation Company were resolving to spend the money they would need to bring their work up to the standard set by the state engineer, Wiley approached them with an offer to buy them out. Sensing the deliverance that had eluded them earlier, Cody brought Wiley to Buffalo to meet with the directors in early March, and at the end of that month the board voted to accept a proposition from Wiley to take over the canal and all their obligations to the state and the settlers. Wiley, however, had the same financing problems that everyone else in the irrigation business had, and the deal fell through within two months. Bill Cody was more than a little angry at Wiley. He suspected Wiley of attempting to steal his water rights, and resented the fact that the Shoshone Irrigation Company had wasted two months when they could have been working on the canal, dickering with a man who could not deliver. It is, however, revealing of their desperate condition that they ever entertained the offer in the first place.[9]

Slowed and diverted by the Wiley negotiations, the company tested the patience and resolve of the state engineer in the spring and summer of 1902. The directors decided not to hire Frank Kelsey to undertake full repairs, probably because they could not come up with the money. Buffalo Bill stated quite frankly to Beck, "You know every member of our Co look to you to keep water coming through old ditches this summer."[10] Beck undertook to keep Fred Bond happy, telling him they were working on the canal. Bond continued to press for a plan, particularly a plan to finance the construction. Apparently, Bond knew better than to deal with Beck alone, for he made sure that both Cody and Bleistein were kept in the conversation. Cody's approach was to delegate the hard numbers to others and try to manage Bond as he had managed Mead. He reminded Bond that they had worked to build up northern Wyoming, and took credit for the railroad presence there. He and his fellow directors were not speculators, but were determined to make Wyoming their home. And he had the nerve to ask for some consideration from the State, as they were "the pioneers doing the work under the Carey Act and had many obstacles to overcome that those following us did not have."[11]

Bond appeared less susceptible to Buffalo Bill's charms, or at least more determined to manage his office for the public good, than Mead had been. At the end of June, the company resolved to raise the money to complete the work, and it was Bleistein who took the lead in that decision. He insisted that the work be done by an independent engineer and contractor. Buffalo Bill suggested that Fred Bond might be the one to do the job, but Bond refused. Bond recommended another man, and the company contracted with him. Bleistein, at least, had obviously lost faith in Beck as a construction manager. Negotiations with the new engineer stretched out over the rest of the summer, complicated somewhat by the fact that George Beck got himself nominated to run for governor on the Democratic ticket.[12]

As the political campaign began in the fall, Buffalo Bill thought he could use it to stimulate Beck to get busy, his preoccupation for so many years. He was finishing work on the Irma Hotel that same summer, and all these projects melded together in his active imagination. He urged Beck to help him get the hotel finished; it would help with the election. Beck was also to get the ditch work completed. If it was not done, his opponents would use that against him; conversely, "the more Cody town booms now the more it will help your Governorship." Get the work going, send the news out across the state: "Politics is something like show business—keep your name in the paper to beat the band if you expect business."[13]

A month later the issue seemed more urgent. Bleistein and Salsbury were complaining to Buffalo Bill about Beck's failure to keep them informed, to collect money due from settlers, or to get moving on the contracts with the engineer. Cody in turn reminded Beck that everyone in Cheyenne knew that the finishing of the Cody Canal had been left to him, "and if its not *done* soon they will make political capital out of it, and it will be hot stuff. . . . the truth will come fast and hard and it will hurt you and our company."[14]

Beck lost the election, but Wyoming's persistent Republican majority probably had more to do with that than any problems on the Cody Canal. Both Salsbury and Cody seem to have genuinely supported Beck's candidacy, in spite of their Republican politics. There was obviously nothing of ideological importance at play, and it would have been very good for business if Beck had won. And, although the election did not go his way, Beck did get the ditch work started that fall. Buffalo Bill was touring the West Coast, but not too busy to keep up a constant rain of letters on Beck telling him what to do and criticizing him for not doing it sooner. The work was finally completed in the spring of 1903, at a final cost of just under $43,000.[15]

Completion of that job, however, did not bring peace to the affairs of the Shoshone Irrigation Company. In his correspondence with the state engineer that summer, Beck reported that they had had a good season "with the exception of some breaks" and had supplied water to all who were ready to use it. However, a group of settlers calling themselves the Ranchers Mutual Protection Association wrote to the state engineer, alleging that water was not evenly distributed or always available when needed. Clarence Johnston, who had succeeded Fred Bond as state engineer, discussed the situation with the State Land Board in the fall of 1903 and then traveled to Cody in October to examine things for himself. He found that the canal was still not adequate to irrigate the land segregated, and estimated that some 9,000 acres of the segregation never could be watered from it. Although he did not specifically mention Elwood Mead, he did point out that the original survey "could easily have been complete enough to have designated such lands." He ended his report by listing four more significant repairs that would need to be accomplished before the State could finally accept the canal. When he returned to Cheyenne, Johnston recorded a conditional notice of completion of the canal, extending the time for repairs to July 1, 1904.[16]

The directors of the Shoshone Irrigation Company met in Cody at the end of January 1904. They examined their corporate accounts and decided how much they wanted to spend on their placer-gold claims up the South Fork. On January 31, they had a conference with a committee of the settlers. "Had long talk came to nothing" was Beck's diary reference, followed by a note that they "were notified that settlers considered that they had no agreement with us."[17] Such a conclusion to a board meeting should by rights have caused more consternation than apparently it did.

Johnston's report to the State Land Board on the management situation he found at Cody may afford some explanation. He found that "all difficulties brought to my attention can directly or indirectly be attributed to the management." While George Beck had few enemies, "an unusual condition," everyone agreed that directly or indirectly he was to blame for the failures along the canal. The state engineer's conclusion was that Beck "has not been as active as he might have been in affording relief during the time when no water supply meant no crop. It is indifference rather than incompetency."[18] Time and again over the years, Buffalo Bill had said more or less the same thing to Beck. He knew Beck could do the work, but was vexed beyond bearing at times that he would not do it. Beck's unhurried approach to life and work contrasted, sometimes violently, with the mercurial energy that Bill Cody brought to everything he did. But Cody never would have stayed to do the work, and in the end that was Beck's contribution to the canal, indifferent as it seems to have been.

The state engineer revisited the Cody Canal in August 1904 and pronounced himself satisfied that the canal was in decent working order. It was apparently carrying a sufficient amount of water to irrigate all the land being farmed under the canal that summer, and he thought it could carry more without difficulty.[19] However, he returned in 1905 in the course of a survey of water rights and resources in the Big Horn Basin, and produced a much more critical examination of the canal. He was very unhappy with the Shoshone Irrigation Company. It had made no effort to reconcile its land and water permits to reflect the large amount of land that could not be irrigated. Furthermore, the company had failed to collect money from water users for maintenance of the canal, as stipulated in the water contracts, because it would make no public accounting for the expenditure of the money. "Practically no attention has been given the canal by the local representatives of the company and the recommendations for improvement made by me two years ago have been carried out only in a half-hearted way." He now saw how poorly designed the canal was: ditches on hillsides regularly gave way, flumes washed out at both ends, the canal silted up, alkali was carried out to farmers' fields. "Unless a radical change is made during the next year or so, much of the valuable lands lying south and west of Cody must be injured."[20]

As an engineer, Johnston made some specific suggestions for improvements, including a pipeline almost three-fourth of a mile long through the worst part of the terrain; altogether his suggestions would have cost about $20,000 in addition to the $43,000 they had recently spent. And he went beyond technical recommendations. He suggested that the State provide someone to manage the canal for the next two years. He thought people would welcome the change, and a new man would be able to collect and manage maintenance fees so it would not be a financial drain. The Cody Canal was at a critical point, and the irrigators needed some protection by the State. Taking control away from the company "would be an object lesson for all other similar enterprises."[21] This would have amounted to a state receivership. It would surely have stood as a warning for other developers, but no one on the Land Board wanted to take such a drastic step. There was no precedent for this kind of administrative takeover of a private company, and the Republicans in control in Cheyenne were less likely than most to initiate one, particularly as it would have run directly athwart the interests of Buffalo Bill Cody.

Despite these and other problems, the Shoshone Irrigation Company by 1905 had sold a significant amount of land and had taken in enough money to pay off most of their current debts and complete most of the repairs ordered by the state engineer. At the end of 1905, they had sold approximately 125 farms totaling over 14,000 acres. The company's accounts at the end of that year show that it had taken in nearly $82,000 in payment for water rights, and expected close to $45,000 more, as time payments came due. Expenses and debts totaled nearly $262,000 on December 1, 1905. The company had repaid the Hearst bonds, but had had to take out a bank loan in Buffalo to cover them. It had had only $27,000 from those bonds to start with, and had paid $16,800 interest over the time it held the bonds; Beck's coup in selling those bonds was not, in retrospect, a great financial play. Even if it had been able to collect the greater part of what was owed for water rights, the company would have lost over $100,000 on the entire canal proposition.

Flood damage to one of the wooden flumes on the Cody Canal on the side of a hill above
Sulphur Creek. It is easy to see how a flume became a weak spot in a long canal. Courtesy
of George T. Beck Papers, American Heritage Center, University of Wyoming.

The 1905 books showed that Bill Cody was carried for loans totaling
$15,724 and the Nate Salsbury estate for $20,386; interestingly enough,
these amounts were counted as income, not as debts payable. Nor was
that the extent of Buffalo Bill's financial support for the canal: at the
end of 1905 Cody personally picked up the tab for four of his extended
family who had taken land under the canal—Frank Powell, Helen Cody
Wetmore, Bess Isbell, and John Martin—at a cost of $3,381. Overall, it
was a dismal picture for the Shoshone Irrigation Company, and it was
about to get worse.[22]

In the absence of action from the State to bring some relief to people
who had settled under the Cody Canal, a number of the water users took
legal counsel and initiated lawsuits against the Shoshone Irrigation Company. The first of these, and the one that set the pattern for all subsequent suits, was filed September 15, 1906, by one Orin McGhan. He had
purchased a water-right contract in March 1905 for eighty acres, and

had expended $3,000 erecting buildings, improving his land, digging his laterals, etc. He planted a variety of crops in 1906 and used properly what water was furnished, but claimed that the company failed to deliver a reliable supply of water—indeed, any supply at all for long periods—and consequently he lost his crops. As the case dragged on into 1907, McGhan amended his complaint to add that the company had not completed the canals and laterals to irrigate thoroughly all the lands entitled to water, substantially the charge Clarence Johnston had made in 1905. He complained that he had paid his maintenance assessment, but that the company had done no maintenance. He and some others had had to spend their own money and time working on the canals to get any water supply at all in 1907. He further stated that the officers of the Irrigation Company had told him they were insolvent and he could expect nothing from them if he won a judgment against them. Finally, after the company initiated foreclosure proceedings against him in May 1908, McGhan added to his case an appeal for an injunction against foreclosure.[23]

These cases amount to a staggering indictment of the Shoshone Irrigation Company. The complaint of Fred Houston includes details of the activities of farmers on the project in the face of continued refusal of the company to meet its obligations. Fearing they would lose everything they had invested, Houston, McGhan, and the others in effect took over the canal, and in the spring of 1907 put up $20,000 worth of labor and cash, and the following year another $10,000. They provided more water to their farms in 1907 and 1908 than the company had ever furnished, and testified that it would take $50,000 more to repair everything left undone by the company. Another suit filed in 1909 against both the Shoshone Irrigation Company and its successor, the Cody Canal Association, alleged that virtually everyone on the project lost all or a large portion of their crops in 1906. In that year, 115,000 cubic yards of silt were washed down the poorly constructed canal, choking canal and laterals, and spreading across fields.[24]

The company's defense was simply pathetic, a tissue of legal dodges and wordplay to cover its incompetence. The only matter of substance they chose to include was a contention that difficulties on the canal had been caused by "unforseen and unavoidable accidents," against which the terms of their contract specifically protected them. The accidents were, in fact, rainstorms. The judge in the McGhan case instructed the jury that "unforseen and unavoidable accidents" were not to be taken to mean "a mere surprise," or anything that might be a result of the company's mistakes, carelessness, or lack of competency. If the storms referred to were of the character usually expected in that country, they did not fall within the protected category: "It would be the duty of the defendant to so construct this ditch or canal as to guard the same against the usual rainfall or storms in that section of the country."[25]

Judgment was for the plaintiffs in every case. They were awarded damages due to nonperformance of the terms of their water contracts, and quieted in the titles to their farms. Their monetary awards were in most cases more than the amount of money they owed in total for their water contracts, so most of them at least had to pay no more for their land; it is unlikely that the company paid them the difference they would have had coming, nearly $3,000 in total. The company apparently tried to dodge paying any settlements at all by a legal device of assigning water contracts to a trusted third party after the McGhan judgment, thereby protecting company funds from a real and present danger. At the end, the important decisions appear to have been made by Harry Weston, Cody banker and assistant treasurer of the company, and George Bleistein. Buffalo Bill and George Beck were not involved; Bill was so far out of the loop that he had to write Beck from Michigan to ask if the company had done anything about water rights or Wallenberg. The loss on unpaid water contracts was close to $22,000. Years later, when George Bleistein performed his last act as trustee for the Shoshone Irrigation Company, he distributed $5757.60 among all the directors, except William Cody (who had received his share in water rights), and that was an end to it.[26]

While the lawsuits were proceeding, the Shoshone Irrigation Company initiated the process of turning over the canal to the settlers, who formed the Cody Canal Association to accept it. Clarence Johnston had reluctantly agreed to accept the irrigation system in 1906; he still did not think it a good job, but so much money and time had gone into it he thought approval was the best course overall. In April 1907, the parties agreed to the terms of the transfer. The transfer was not supposed to take place until 90 percent of the land had been sold, but the parties simply agreed to say that condition had been met when it had not; of 19,000 acres patented to the state, 6,000 remained unsold. The Cody Canal Association agreed to enforce debts owed to the Shoshone

Irrigation Company, but it is doubtful that they did. The State was not satisfied with the April agreement and insisted that a new contract protecting its interests be worked out. In October, the State cancelled its contract with the Shoshone Irrigation Company and signed a new one with the Cody Canal Association. But turning over the canal did not cause the cloud of litigation to lift.[27]

None of the suits against the Shoshone Irrigation Company were finished before the new Cody Canal Association took over, but the Association was clear of those. Many of the farmers, however, undertook a lawsuit against both the old Company and the new Association, asking the judge to compel a condition of receivership that could do what Johnston had recommended in 1905. It was a very complex suit, with water users divided against themselves, as both plaintiffs and defendants, and it was ultimately dismissed.[28] Hard feelings and recriminations must have remained in the air for years. On the ground, however, the uncertain legacy of the Shoshone Irrigation Company is beyond dispute, as it took years of work and expense to bring the water system into the kind of working order that had been promised from the beginning.

In the summer of 1912, the Cody Canal Association voted to sell $95,000 worth of bonds to rebuild the system they had acquired with such difficulty.[29] One allegation that surfaced time and again in the lawsuits was that the company was attempting to hold onto money for itself by deferring maintenance on the canal, and there can be little doubt that was true. For all the posturing of George Beck and Buffalo Bill Cody, the first Carey Act enterprise in the state of Wyoming was a dodgy affair from start to finish. Nate Salsbury had seen this clearly enough back in 1902. "We seem to be up against a stump in irrigation affairs," he told Beck. "I am waiting events, with a pretty sure guess that I will lose every dollar I have invested out there, and also what I have loaned to help along the enterprise. It is a pretty hard knock, but it has taught me something."[30] No doubt it was also a learning experience for all the families who came to Cody to farm under the canal.

These lawsuits were not the only legal problem that dogged the last years of the Shoshone Irrigation Company. Over the winter of 1901–1902, Bill Cody had met a man in Chicago named Gustav Wallenberg, a Swedish immigrant who worked as a land agent. As land sales were still slow at Cody, it seemed a good idea to hire an agent who would work entirely on commission, in spite of the dismal experience the company had had with land agents. Accordingly, Cody and Beck signed a contract with Wallenberg in January 1902, by which he would sell all the water rights under the Cody Canal, allowing the company $10.00 per acre and taking his income from whatever he could charge over that amount, up to $15 per acre. The contract specifically excepted, in a handwritten note, "parties now negotiating for rights," which Wallenberg tried (without success) to have limited to specific individuals. He was afraid that was a wide gate through which would march many buyers who brought him no profit. When Wallenberg started reading the *Cody Enterprise* he grew more agitated because the Irrigation Company advertisement there still talked of land for sale at $10 per acre, as it always had. In other words, there was mistrust between the parties virtually as soon as the arrangement was made.[31]

Wallenberg soon discovered that there were other uncertainties in the Cody land business. The State actually allowed the company to charge more than $10 per acre after the canal had been constructed (not an easy point to determine where this canal was concerned, as noted above). In fact, the directors of the company had decided at their November 1901 meeting to raise the price they were asking for water rights. The least expensive rights were to go for $12 per acre, and the most expensive, those near the town, for $16. It is astonishing that Cody and Beck made the contract they did in light of this decision. Wallenberg protested to Beck that Colonel Cody had only spoken to him of $10 per acre. Cody himself held the terms of the Wallenberg contract very lightly. Although they had agreed that Wallenberg would be the exclusive agent of the Company, Cody continued to sell pieces to cronies and friends, and to ask Beck to hold out a few 160-acre tracts to sell.[32]

Wallenberg worked in good faith, arranging an excursion train from Chicago in the spring of 1902 and getting out a new brochure. He asked Beck not to show the old one around, and to please have the laterals in good shape when his colonists arrived. As it turned out, the company did not complete their canal work and Wallenberg found himself dealing with some angry migrant farmers. At the same time, Buffalo Bill (whose name was displayed prominently on Wallenberg's stationery, of course) began to make life difficult for Wallenberg on the other side. "I have written Wallenberg that was an unlucky and foolish contract we made with him, and its been a lesson to me," he wrote Beck. "So nurse Wallenberg. Dont let him go into court."[33] Cody had something to worry about, as Wallenberg made clear in a formal letter specifying breaches of contract that summer. He was selling water rights on the company's promise that the canal would be extended to irrigate tracts where he had located settlers, and the company was not holding up its end of the bargain. Over the course of 1902, he sold water rights to 3,053 acres to thirty-three migrants, mostly from Illinois, Iowa, and Nebraska, and followed that with 809 acres the following spring. But inquiries continued to come directly to Beck in Cody based on earlier advertisements, and the company was loath to let Wallenberg have any income from them, no matter what his contract said.[34]

In the autumn of 1904, Beck recommended to the board of the Shoshone Irrigation Company that they could get along without a land agent. At its December meeting, the board agreed with the recommendation, and charged the manager with selling their land, at $10 to $30 per acre (the State had allowed another increase in the prices of land on Carey Act projects). This action apparently took place without consultation with Wallenberg. After some deliberation, Wallenberg set an attorney on the company in September of 1905, to remind it that he had a contract that made him sole agent to sell water rights under the Cody Canal. The company was very worried about the suit; the directors even considered initiating lawsuits of their own against the company to protect their status as creditors. Gerrans, in particular, believed that Wallenberg had a very good case against them. For his part, Wallenberg tried to work with the company; tired of being put off by Beck, he took to writing directly to Cody, hoping to get some cooperation.

When Wallenberg did eventually initiate a lawsuit, in the fall of 1907 in Cook County District Court, Illinois, the company chose as a defense the assertion that the contract had been an unauthorized action by its president that had never been ratified by the board. They contended that all parties to the contract had had a spoken understanding at the time of signing that such ratification would be necessary to bring it into effect. This is the kind of convenient after-the-fact interpretation that Buffalo Bill had attempted to maintain against the federal government on a far bigger land deal playing out at the same time. It did not work with the government, but it appears to have carried some weight in the Wallenberg suit. Of more weight, perhaps, was the fact that the company did pay Wallenberg $3.00 per acre for the land that he sold for it. The judge found for the defendants, giving them their only good courtroom news of the closing-out years. The entire Wallenberg affair, however, starkly underlined the feckless managerial practices of Bill Cody and George Beck.[35]

The short history of the Shoshone Irrigation Company was not a happy one, nor was the ending of it. Begun with the highest of hopes and dreams in 1895, there were only ashes and dust in the legacy of the company in 1907. It had undertaken a major irrigation project in country where water would not easily run, without either the professional guidance or the financial backing necessary to make irrigation work in that environment. The management, especially Cody and Beck, was simultaneously hyperactive and shortsighted, distracted and desperate to stop the dollar drain. Nate Salsbury, who had seen it all coming, died before the final curtain fell; his estate simply absorbed his large share of the losses. The canal was totally inadequate to the demands on it, and it required enormous additional expenditure to make it adequate; it was never more than that, and never watered more than 16,000 acres. Elwood Mead had thought to make of the Cody Canal a model for Carey Act development. It probably eventually served more as a warning to others, not at all what Mead had in mind.

Bill Cody, who set out to make a name for himself as a corporate mogul through this development, ended by revealing himself to be the same kind of impostor in the corporate world as he had been on the frontier. As Louis Warren has shown, Cody's life and fame had been based on dubious claims to performance in the Pony Express and elsewhere. William Cody's approach to the colonization of the Shoshone valley grew from similar claims to competence and consequence in the corporate world. This latter imposture, it should go without saying, had nothing of the success and staying power that the first one had. But although his Cody Canal was a technical and financial failure, there were other enterprises in and around Cody town where Buffalo Bill and his friends left their marks.

CHAPTER NINE

Having It All

"While you were about it why didn't you make application to control all the air in the Basin? You seem to have pinched everything else in sight."

Nate Salsbury to William Cody, February 1896

The difficulties along the canal did not deter any of the Shoshone Irrigation Company directors from pursuing other avenues of enrichment. Mining, ranching, and other investments attracted all of them to one degree or another. As Salsbury's words above suggest, William Cody found more outlets for his energy and capital than any of the others did, but everyone was in on the ground floor; they were the big fish in that small pond. As already seen, they had in mind enterprises in trade, in mining, and in milling. These were straightforward matters of investment and management, the kind of ordinary capitalist activity that builds towns and fortunes. Bill Cody took part in some of that, of course, but his real heart and energy seemed more engaged in grandiose schemes that would make him a name as well as a fortune.

The first of these projects he took in hand in 1901. He conceived the idea of founding a military college near his new town. His idea probably grew out of the experience of the Spanish-American War, for the company he incorporated to set up and run the school was titled

Cody Military College
International Academy of Rough Riders.

He envisioned a school that would teach young men all branches of military science. In April 1901, he planned to establish a military camp in tents near Cody by the beginning of the summer, and commence construction of a permanent set of barracks. The school would be commanded by General E. V. Sumner. Cody claimed the school was first intended to go to Colorado, but at his personal intervention it had been shifted to Wyoming.[1]

The short-lived excitement over the Cody Military College affords an opportunity to study the mind of the celebrity developer at work. Although there surely were earlier conversations, the idea first surfaced in a letter to Curtis L. Hinkle, clerk of the State Land Board in Cheyenne, and Cody's man in state government. Cody had business with Hinkle regarding his lease of a section of school land near his Wyoming ranch. Although the Land Board had nothing to do with water permits, Cody asked Hinkle to look into a filing he had made several years earlier, jointly with Charles DeMaris, for use of the mineral waters of the hot springs along the Shoshone west of the town of Cody. By way of incentive to get Hinkle to help him with the water permit, the Colonel let him know that he was "doing something that will be of great interest to the state," namely, his Military College. In this way, he reminded the men in Cheyenne that he was no ordinary seeker after water permits, effectively implying that they would best serve the state by serving Buffalo Bill. It was a trick that had worked frequently with Elwood Mead, and he clearly expected that it would work again with Hinkle. Cody even gave Hinkle permission to use the letter as a press release if he chose, and enclosed some advertising material.[2]

At about the same time, Buffalo Bill sent George Beck a packet of information on the new college. Cody reported that his new company had held their first meeting in New Jersey on April 19. He was certain it was going to be a great success, and a great help to the town. "Why no military Government Fort near a town will be a starter to it." He claimed that in only four days he had raised enough money to start it.[3] General Sumner was going to set up camp at Fort Custer, Montana, where he would receive recruits and buy horses from the Crow reservation before coming on to Cody. Buffalo Bill could not keep his excitement under control: "When a hundred recruits are equipped and mounted, they will march through Pryor Pass to their new home near Cody."[4] Judging strictly from his record, we are entitled to doubt that any significant money had in fact already been raised, but that did not cool the Colonel's ardor a bit. Buffalo Bill could talk himself—and sometimes others—into a positive frame of mind just by the force of his imagination. He could already see the college nestled in the foothills of the Absaroka Mountains, bringing glory to his town and his name. And he wanted to make sure that those people partnered with him in the new venture got all the flattering attention he could manage for them.

Hinkle apparently reminded him that his earlier application for a permit on the springs had not been granted, but failed to point out that it was because Charles DeMaris already had a valid permit there.[5] Buffalo Bill wrote him immediately, asking him to follow the matter, reminding him (as if he needed reminding) that he was bringing the Military College to the state. "And as I was the first man to make application to the state for those mineral waters I should be considered. . . . Please find out what I can do to get use of those springs." Then, to cement the deal, he added a P.S.: "Hinkle fix this business up for me and I will make it all right with you. I want to get control of those springs."[6] The springs were part of his plan for the Military College, but Buffalo Bill had always wanted to find a way to build Cody around the springs. The first town he laid out on the Shoshone centered on the springs. Now that the new Cody was growing two miles downstream, he wanted to pipe mineral water from the springs so people could "take the waters" at his new hotel in town. The mineral hot springs would help make Cody into a popular western destination. Cody, Buffalo Bill, and Wyoming would all profit from the development. The Colonel attempted to use his celebrity status both to influence the working details (that is, the matter of the water permit) and to ensure the ultimate achievement.

DeMaris heard of the Colonel's intention to monopolize the springs and hastened to reassert his right to appropriate water there. When Cody learned of this from Hinkle, he protested that he had no intention of harming DeMaris. He made a separate application for 130,000 gallons of the spring water per day "for the use of the Military College and for my hotel and for bathing and shipping purposes. I think that the water should be shipped all over the country as soon as the railroad gets there—it will advertise the state." He asked Hinkle to fix this up for him, reminding him what a benefit it was going to be for the state.[7] A couple of weeks later he wrote Hinkle again, somewhat more forcefully. He set forth the claim that he wanted to develop the springs "for the benefit of humanity," and it was going to cost a lot of money. He had surveyors at work near Cody on his new irrigation project, and he could have plans made for state officials "that cannot fail to convince them that it is for the benefit of the whole public that these springs be given over to capital that will improve them and bring within reach of the public their health giving qualities."[8]

This appeal was based on the good that Buffalo Bill, a big entrepeneur with money to devote to development, could do, compared to the paltry enterprise that DeMaris operated on the site. As in the matter between the Shoshone Irrigation Company and Hud Darrah, the opportunity of DeMaris, a little man seeking to make a living by his work and wits, clashed with the opportunity of organized capital to shape this new frontier environment to its own benefit. Much as he labored at it, Cody's *pro bono publico* argument would not hold water. DeMaris was confirmed in his rights, and Cody dropped his mineral springs plans; the next season DeMaris announced plans to build a hotel and bathhouse at the springs.[9] Celebrity was not enough, nor was the kind of bribery Cody intimated; the water laws of the State of Wyoming were designed to foster development, whether by little men or big corporations, and neither Buffalo Bill nor his favorite land clerk could find a way around them. To this day the springs carry DeMaris's name, and within a few years Buffalo Bill himself was a regular wintertime visitor at the cheap little bathhouse DeMaris built there.

The Military College idea collapsed of its own weight and disappeared from view during the course of 1901. It is impossible to imagine a company run by William F. Cody building and operating that kind of complex institution, and only the colossal egocentrism of the great showman could have thought for a day that the nation would locate this college at Cody. Nate Salsbury told Cody as much late in that year.[10] As it faded away, however, the idea shifted shape into another, equally unrealistic proposition. At the end of May 1901, Buffalo Bill, still promising that the Military College was going to be built, told Governor DeForrest Richards that he was out to bring to Cody the national home of the Benevolent and Protective Order of Elks. He himself was a member of the Omaha Lodge, and knew that the order was considering establishing a home for aged and infirm members. He offered to his brother Elks as many acres of free land as might be required to build the home there. In the promotional letter, which he apparently prevailed upon a senior member of the order to mail out to every lodge in America,

Presentation portrait of William F. Cody, looking every inch the capitalist. This copy was given to Curtis Hinkle, chief clerk of the State Land Board, in 1904. Courtesy of Wyoming State Archives, Cheyenne, Wyo.

on Cody Military College and International Academy of Rough Riders stationery, it appears that the College has already been located at Cody. The letter speaks of the mineral springs, the salubrious climate (including the "health giving ozone which soon makes new beings of all who locate there") and the wealth of building materials available close at hand. After touting those benefits, Cody asked that the members consider his offer at their coming Grand Lodge session.[11]

Free land was not going to be enough to swing the Elks to Cody. Buffalo Bill knew that Colorado Springs was working for the home, offering free land and a subvention of $20,000. He asked Beck what the Shoshone Irrigation Company might do to help, rather a desperate play when most of them would not pay assessments for the canal. He also wrote to the Burlington Railroad and Lincoln Land Company, hoping to interest them in the proposition. Nothing came of it, despite Cody's advocacy. The Elks did apparently decide that summer to proceed with a plan to establish a national home for "indigent Elks." The order purchased the Hotel Bedford, in Bedford, Virginia, at a bankruptcy sale in 1902, and put it into service the following year. Obviously, the great weight of membership of the order, especially aged membership, was in the East, and a cheap hotel in an established area must have met their needs better than a bare patch of ground on the Wyoming frontier.[12] Nevertheless, Buffalo Bill got a lot of mileage out of this clinker. As late as May 1902, long after the idea of the Military College had been dropped, Cody was still stringing state officials along on the prospect that the Elks would locate in the Basin. By that time, his main focus was on his very large Carey Act development downriver from Cody, and he needed as much cooperation from the state as he could get. Once again, he was playing his national celebrity for all it was worth in Wyoming, while no doubt making clear to those he dealt with elsewhere (for instance his brother Elks) what a power he was in the state. Fame and influence are the currency of the celebrity developer, but they are a poor substitute for real money and a good record.[13]

The other directors, unburdened by the demands of fame, proceeded to try to get wealthy in more traditional ways. They had all been interested in mining possibilities from the very beginning. In December 1896, they drafted articles of incorporation for the Shoshone Mining Company, with Cody, Beck, and Cody's nephew, E. A. Goodman, as directors. That company was not legally incorporated until March 1900; Cody was president, Beck vice-president and general manager, and Jake Schwoob was secretary-treasurer. In addition to these three, the directors were Bronson Rumsey, surely the most avid of the Irrigation Company directors when it came to precious metals, John "Reckless" Davis, one of

Buffalo Bill's retinue who lived up on the South Fork and more or less actively kept at the mining business for the owners, and a couple of other Cody men. They also incorporated a more mundane operation in 1896, the Shoshone Coal Company, created by Beck, Cody, and a third man in December of that year.[14]

Rumsey, Bleistein, and Beck seem to have been more actively interested in finding gold on the Shoshone than any of the others. Bill Cody was involved in a couple of mining companies in southern Wyoming, near Encampment, one of which was incorporated by his close friend, Frank Powell, and he would later lose a fortune in mines in Arizona. He seemed generally to have many other things on his mind when thinking about his new town and irrigation project. Cody and Salsbury were not entirely immune to the attractions of a little gold, but they seem to have regarded it as an instrument to interest others, either capitalists or settlers, thereby making the success of the colony a better bet. Buffalo Bill did take some samples out to have them assayed, which kept Rumsey quite agitated, wondering what they would show. Beck actually hired prospectors for Rumsey, and kept them busy checking out mountains in the neighborhood while waiting for Rumsey to arrive in Cody. Rumsey, in turn, solicited capital in Buffalo to help develop their placer claims while he utterly refused to raise any more money for the irrigation project.[15]

There was already some gold, silver, and copper mining in progress in the mountains around Cody. To the south, up in the Greybull Mountains, a mining camp named Kirwin was provoking enough interest that George Holdrege, CB&Q general manager, kept in close contact with developments there. It has been pointed out how concerned all the Burlington advance men were to assess the mineral potential along their new line. When he heard of Beck's prospecting along Alkali Creek, fifteen miles east of Cody, Holdrege asked one of his men to get a large sample of the gravel; he wanted to be able to produce a favorable showing for the Cody country. North and west of Cody, on the headwaters of the Clark's Fork of the Yellowstone, an old prospector named John Painter had been trying to drum up interest in gold and copper claims for years. For the most part, directors of the Shoshone Irrigation Company concentrated their mineral exploration efforts along the Shoshone River, west of Cody on the South Fork or east at Alkali Creek. In the summer of 1997 they brought in a mining engineer named Frank Darlington to explore all possibilities within fifty miles of Cody. He traveled up the South Fork with Beck, Alger, and Cody's man, Okie Snyder, and when they returned, Frank Mondell joined them for a trip up into Sunlight Basin to look at Painter's claims. They found that at least one of Painter's mines was shipping high-grade ore, but it was a long and difficult route to haul ore. The mine was actually located near the head of the North Fork of the Shoshone, which Darlington thought much more promising country than the South Fork. Beck also took Darlington down to Alkali Creek, where they panned gravel and Darlington was surprised to find it as good as it was. It would, of course, take a great deal of work to determine if it was capable of producing in paying quantities. Beck put a force of men to work at the mouth of Alkali Creek in September, after staking placer claims in the names of each of the directors, to prospect the gravel banks for gold.[16]

They were rather a comical lot in their vast but vain hopes for instant riches. Once again, the steady business experience of the Lincoln Land Company shone a light on the methods of the Shoshone Irrigation Company. In the summer of 1901, Beck received a letter from the president of the Lincoln Land Company. John "Reckless" Davis had brought Morrill some samples of ore and asked to have them assayed. They were so badly mixed up that he could do nothing with them. He asked Beck to have Davis send him other samples, properly labeled to indicate where they were from and the thickness of the vein there. He did not want to go to the expense of analysis unless he knew there was a reasonable amount of ore to be mined.[17] Rumsey had complained in much the same way about Buffalo Bill's placer assays: one bag assayed at $.12 per ton and another at $24.00 per ton, but no one could say how much of the high-grade sand there was. Davis (or "Davies," as he signed himself) made a good thing for himself, working claims for Rumsey and Gerrans up the South Fork.[18] Their heads turned by dreams of wealth, the directors of the Shoshone Irrigation Company were bumbling amateurs alongside men like Morrill and Holdrege. It is not surprising that they never turned up "mineral" in paying quantities.

In 1901, they turned their attention to oil. George Beck entered into correspondence with Professor Wilbur Knight of the University of Wyoming to come look over oil possibilities at Cody. A group of Cody men, among them Bill Cody and George Beck, formed an association in September 1902 to coordinate the exploration of what they called the "Bonanza Oil District." C. H. Morrill, president of the Lincoln Land

Company, induced several of his Nebraska friends to join with him in some oil claims on the Cody field. Oil was pursued in those days under the same placer laws as gold or silver, meaning that a claim stayed in force as long as those who had filed the claim could provide evidence of continuing work (defined as $100 worth per year on each 160-acre claim) toward development of the property. This was what the organization was formed to do. A large group of Cody and eastern men, including Congressman Frank Mondell and all of the Irrigation Company directors except Bill Cody, filed oil placer claims east and south of the town. In October, Beck and two of his Cody friends announced the formation of the Cody Oil Company, to exploit an oil spring discovered a couple of miles from Cody a few weeks earlier. They bought drilling machinery and set to work, financed in large part by Irrigation Company directors George Bleistein and Bronson Rumsey. By August 1903, they were down 500 feet, and by October they were sufficiently encouraged to start a second well. However, they encountered insurmountable problems with water, and this first burst of oil energy produced indifferent results.[19]

A second wave of oil activity began around 1909. In April, Beck and C. E. Hayden staked and filed 115 oil placer claims about ten miles south of Cody, on behalf of Bill Cody, Bronson Rumsey, Bleistein, Gerrans, and others, again including Congressman Mondell. It is not possible to tell what kind of payday came out of that work, but it is worth noting that they were in the area of the Oregon Basin field, which became one of the most productive in Wyoming.[20] Back in New York that spring, Buffalo Bill was carrying pocket flasks of oil to show his friends in the East and attempting to interest eastern investors in his oil field; some of them called him (with what degree of seriousness we cannot know) "Bill, the Oil King." That fall, while planning a hunt near Pahaska with Beck, Cody offered his services to bring men with money to look into their oil fields around Cody. In April of 1910, the *Enterprise* reported significant strikes in the oil field east of the railroad depot and north of town. All of this activity clearly had some effect, as the newspaper noted in late November 1910 that an agent of J. P. Morgan was spending a week in town to look at oil and gas prospects in the area.[21]

The Shoshone Oil Company had been incorporated that year, and although none of the town founders were involved in the formation of the company, Buffalo Bill owned 2,500 shares (worth a dollar per share), and George Beck was in for 46,666 shares! They and other Shoshone

"Bill, the Oil King," at his new well near Cody, 1902. Courtesy of Buffalo Bill Historical Center, Cody, Wyo.; P.6.172.

Irrigation Company directors were interested in leasing undeveloped areas of the Cody townsite for oil and gas development. They tried to convince the Lincoln Land Company to go along with the plan, but Morrill did not like the lease they proposed; once again, the business standards of the Cody men fell short of those of the Lincoln men. The Buffalo directors were apparently willing to finance the drilling of at least one well.[22]

Once again there is no evidence that this activity produced anything of significance. In 1915, Colonel Cody announced his intention to organize the Buffalo Bill Oil and Gas Company and to invite people to buy shares. When he told his friend Arbuckle about the company and the 1400-acre oil field he owned and leased, he closed by asking, "Don't you and some of your Friends want to come in on the ground floor—and make a real clean up?"[23] Perhaps his old friends had had enough ground-floor offers, for the company seems never to have been formed. In that same year, he wrote to his cousin, Frank Cody, that there was big oil excitement in Cody, claiming to have struck oil in one well on his property and expecting three more rigs to be set up on his land. He wrote of a meeting to be held in Cody at the end of the month to consider leasing part of the townsite to an oil company.[24]

If such a meeting was ever held, it did not make the newspapers. However, the *Enterprise* did note significant new oil drilling activity east of town on both sides of the Shoshone River in the winter of 1915–16. It is not clear what this would have meant to Bill Cody. He might have picked up some money in the form of oil leases, but whatever plans he might have talked about, the development was in the hands of other men.[25] Moreover, oil development near Cody was soon completely over-shadowed by discoveries of four much larger and more productive fields within a fifty-mile radius of the town. Oil field service and refining were to become important parts of the Cody economy, and many men in Cody—including George Beck, who built his own refinery—were to profit mightily from the oil business, but that was long after the days of Buffalo Bill. The relationship between Bill Cody and oil was, for the most part, the same old story of heavy promotion and little performance.

Bill Cody's principal preoccupation in 1902 was the construction of the Irma Hotel, soon to become famous as "Buffalo Bill's Hotel in the Rockies." For years, he had advertised Cody as the home of fine building materials, and the Irma, built from locally quarried stone, was, in part, a demonstration of this quality. He started crews quarrying stone and building the foundation in the summer of 1901. The foundation was in place by March of 1902, and over the summer they worked at putting up the building and finishing the rooms. He convinced his recently widowed sister, Julia Goodman, to come to Cody to oversee the purchasing and the kitchen for him (he described her position as "the Mother of the house, not to work yourself but to see that the help does"). He did not want to let anyone else run it, "for I am going to furnish it to [sic] fine & costly to rent it to anyone. I am going to have the finest of furniture, am going to run it on the European plan—right up to date. . . . The prices will be so high that the tough & bums can't hang around."[26] In addition to the fine furnishings, he hung paintings everywhere, including his favorite, Charles Schreyvogel's rendering of the Battle of Summit Springs; he expected to have some by Frederic Remington, but that plan fell through. He also planned to bring out a chef from the Hoffman House in New York and to install two pianos: "I tell you I am going to have this hotel out of sight—I will make it the talk of the West."[27]

The grand opening of the Irma, which took place on November 18, 1902, also served as the engagement party for his daughter, Irma. Buffalo Bill sent out one thousand invitations, when the population of Cody was less than five hundred. The practice of building destination hotels as centerpieces for development was only beginning to take hold in the West. Cody's Irma pioneered in this regard. People came from all around the nation for the gala, including Charles Wayland Towne of the *Boston Herald*, there at the suggestion of the press agent of the Wild West. Dignitaries from the Burlington Railroad and the Lincoln Land Company, as well as friends from Cheyenne and most of the Colonel's living relatives, plus many of his old cronies, made up a large crowd. The Colonel was apparently unhappy with Towne's account in the *Herald*, as it emphasized the presence of cowboys in chaps and spurs instead of the civilized dress suits that many, including Cody himself, had worn. The party went on through the night, and the next day Buffalo Bill took a dozen or so men— including Towne—up the South Fork on a hunting trip.[28]

The Irma was an expensive undertaking. Estimates of the cost of construction range from $60,000 to $100,000; common consent seems to have settled on $80,000. Don Russell believes the hotel lost $500 a month on its operations. But true to the character he showed on the canal work, Cody no sooner had the hotel up and running than he began to plan for an addition. Julia Goodman tried to temper his enthusiasm. Buffalo Bill had left for London with a new Wild West production in the spring of 1903. He attempted to micromanage the Irma from England, as he had tried to micromanage the canal from Massachusetts, and perhaps with equal success. He patted Julia on the head when she urged caution on him, claiming she did not have the kind of faith in the town's future that he did. In a rare (and fleeting) moment of self-awareness, he said to her, "I like you to warn me for I am liable to get speedy . . . But you know I am a broad gazer. And I am willing to back my judgement. I expect to let the contracts for the addition this week."[29] Of course, he never built the addition. In fact, by the summer of 1903, he had changed his tune quite dramatically. "Darn the old hotel," he told Julia, "we can close it up if it is going to be such a worry to us all."[30] He never seriously considered closing it, but as his financial affairs deteriorated over the following years, he mortgaged it twice.[31] Running a hostelry was not a bed of roses, and, as with the irrigation scheme, provided no guarantees in the way of income.

Whatever worries it caused the Cody family, the Irma was also a problem for the town of Cody. The sewer permit for the hotel required laying a pipe 1,700 feet to dump waste out of town near the river. Cody, of course, had neither a municipal water nor a sewer system in 1902. When every other building in town had its own outdoor privy, the problem of the concentrated sewage of forty hotel rooms must have been considerable. The Town Council established a sewerage committee that spent a lot of time dealing with the Irma over the first decade of its existence. Sanitation remained a problem, even after the town decided to install a sewer system in 1912, because it was two more years before it got a functioning water system. In fact, the town did not get around to sewage treatment for decades.[32]

The Colonel maintained a private suite of rooms in the hotel to serve as his town headquarters for the rest of his life, and he received notables from all over America and Europe there.[33] Clearly, the Irma was more hotel than the town of Cody needed, but it was intended as Buffalo Bill's pledge to link the wilds of Wyoming with the metropolitan East, and in that it succeeded dramatically. The Irma was continuous with the Wild West in Bill Cody's life-long project of educating easterners about the West, or, rather, presenting a particular and self-serving version of the West for public consumption. The presence of this relatively grand hotel effectively domesticated the West, smoothed off the rough edges and made the experience of Wyoming palatable, just as the show domesticated the history of the conquest of western lands and peoples. Both the show and the hotel provided a nice soft sheen on the experience of the West, anodynes for a population drawn more to entertainment than to knowledge.

Russell's estimate of the Irma Hotel's losses must have been based on the early years. By 1915, when there is some solid evidence on the point, the hotel made a steady profit, averaging around $500.00 a month. Expenses at other Cody properties, his two ranches (TE and Sweeney) and Pahaska Tepee, were paid by the overage at the Irma. The balance sheet, however, for the Colonel's "Interests at Cody, Wyoming" was not pretty overall. He was carrying roughly $20,000 in notes payable and from $7000 to $10,000 in current liabilities, and not bringing in enough to reduce either of those figures significantly. The correspondence between Buffalo Bill and W. L. Walls, his attorney in Cody, reveals that the Colonel had lost none of his determination to try to manage affairs in detail from a distance. Walls tried to get him to see that things were not as bad as he thought they were, but Cody was ready to fire his son-in-law, Fred Garlow, who was managing the hotel, and he repeatedly urged Walls to set someone to watch the bartenders at the hotel, to see if they were putting everything into the till.[34] Those were hard times for the Old Scout.

Buffalo Bill had a number of other enterprises in and around Cody. He founded the town newspaper, the *Cody Enterprise*, in 1899, and owned it five or six years. The paper was edited most of that time by J. H. Peake, an old friend from North Platte days. The Colonel's sister, Helen Cody Wetmore, who had been in the publishing business in Duluth, was active on the *Enterprise* during that period; it was part of the full employment program for members of the Cody family that Buffalo Bill supported in his new town. Eventually, Cody and Peake had a falling out. Bill must have known of Peake's politics when he took him into partnership, but by 1903 he was complaining about them. That summer Cody told Wyoming's Republican acting governor, Fenimore Chatterton, that he hoped soon to be resident in Cody full-time, where he would work "to keep that part of our beloved state in line for our Party." He told Chatterton that he was going to get rid of Peake if he had to sell the paper to do it, and then buy it back later. "If I dont buy the Enterprise I will start another paper and wont have a *Democrat* to edit it."[35] It

Bill Cody, George Beck, and some others in the bar of Cody's Irma Hotel, 1906. Courtesy of George T. Beck Papers, American Heritage Center, University of Wyoming.

Bill Cody with his sister May and her husband, Louie Decker, in the Colonel's apartment at the Irma Hotel. I am indebted to Paul Fees for pointing out the portrait of P. T. Barnum on the wall behind Cody. Courtesy Buffalo Bill Historical Center, Cody, WY; P.6.335.

is not clear exactly when Buffalo Bill sold out his interest in the newspaper, but it is clear that he did not get back into it. Peake died in 1905, and his widow ran the paper for a while, the first in a series of short-term publishers. Cody's letter to Chatterton was perhaps only part of his public relations campaign with the state as he prepared for another big development venture.

Buffalo Bill had high hopes for Cody's Wyoming Coal Company. As noted earlier, he fought Hud Darrah over a coal lease on their Carey Act land, and was anxious for George Beck to keep a strong legal hold on their coal claims. In pursuit of this goal, Cody worked through a bewildering variety of proxies and agents as he tried to fight his way through the federal land laws. Prior to the formation of the coal company, one of his local agents, John Martin, had entered a piece of land along the Burlington Railroad right-of-way east of Cody. Martin held the land under the mining law as "Coal claim no. 10." Cody paid Martin $2,000 for the claim in the fall of 1903. To that 160-acre parcel he added an adjoining eighty acres, claimed by several of his men serially under both the Homestead Act and the mining law, in a process so confusing that the General Land Office could not keep it straight. In a classic case of possession being nine-tenths of the law, Cody sold this parcel to his coal company for $5,000 in February 1904, although he did not own it. It was, in fact, not clear until some time in 1907 who held the land and under what law, but Cody's Wyoming Coal Company built their buildings and dug their shafts and took coal from it the whole time. Cody also tried throughout those years to expand his coal holdings.[36]

Buffalo Bill obviously enjoyed being president of companies. The prospectus for Cody's Wyoming Coal Company made the usual claims for the quantity and quality of the product, the ease of its extraction (the mine was located in the Burlington Railroad cut), and the strong market for coal all along the Burlington line. It went on to point out that "not the least important ingredient, guaranteeing the success of this enterprise, is the forceful personality of Col. Cody." As a "true pioneer," possessed of "varied experience, rugged honesty and indomitable energy," he had the "resources to surmount whatever difficulties he may encounter."[37] Despite all these advantages, there was not a great deal of profit for Cody in the coal business. The coal sold in Cody, a captive market, but was not good enough to sell elsewhere. It is interesting, however, that the company attempted to attract investment by reference to the imagined qualities of its president. Once again, the celebrity was at work, this time as a promoter rather than a developer. Cody's persona, created on the stage, was expected somehow to bring people and money running to his side in real life. A well-advertised claim that the coal was first-class could not make it burn hot, but this was the way Buffalo Bill knew to do business.

He did do some ordinary business; it was not all big ads and posturing. Probably the business Cody knew best was the livery stable. When he first went into business in Wyoming, it was with a livery barn and wagon company in Sheridan. He opened a livery barn in Cody the first year of the town's existence, and maintained it steadily. This operation was not glamorous, but was essential to any town's life, and as it catered to visitors, it was particularly appropriate for Buffalo Bill, the man who brought so many outsiders in. The Irma was located just around the corner from the Buffalo Bill Barn, and the two made business for each other. This business merged seamlessly, in Buffalo Bill's mind, with a larger and more glamorous transportation company that would operate wagons and then automobiles over the new road to the eastern entrance into Yellowstone National Park. But again, his way of going about this extension of the livery business shows a rather different idea of the working of the marketplace than that of his competitors.

Celebrity being his second nature, Cody wrote directly to W. A. Richards, former governor of Wyoming and South Fork hunting partner, now commissioner of the General Land Office in Washington. He asked Richards to help him get a concession to operate an automobile and horse line from Cody to Yellowstone. If Richards would help him achieve this, he promised a liberal compensation. He also reminded Richards that President Roosevelt was a good friend and might be able to help.[38] The road went through the Yellowstone Timber Reserve, so perhaps the idea of a federal concession was not in itself out of the question; transportation within the Park was managed in that way. Nor was the offer of reward for the commissioner's assistance unusual in a time when government officials often lined their pockets by doing special favors. However, he was clearly trading upon his reputation even to try to use Richards as his agent, and his reference to President Roosevelt needs no elaboration.

Although he had his own way of going about it, Cody showed in this application an eye for business that kept up with the leading edge of technology. The year 1903 heralded the first transcontinental automobile trip, a race among three cars that attracted great national attention. The possibilities of automobile travel were just becoming apparent when Cody communicated his idea to Richards. (He probably did not ride in an automobile himself until two years later.) Not until 1909 was it demonstrated, by Cody auto enthusiast Jake Schwoob, the manager of the Cody Trading Company, that automobile travel between Cody and Yellowstone Park was genuinely possible. Bill said of himself more than once that he was a "far-gazer," and in this instance he saw truly, if beyond his own immediate grasp.[39]

He continued to believe in the automobile as a vehicle to move Americans around and to fill his own pocket. In 1915, nearing seventy years of age, he "got into a new layout," as he told his cousin Frank. He was going to invest in a Salt Lake City company that was set up to use automobiles as public transportation, running on streets parallel to the trolley. "This looks like about the best thing I have got into."[40] It quickly proved another dead end, and we have no way of knowing whether he earned or lost any money on this one, but nothing shows his indomitable spirit, as well as his clouded eye for the main chance, better than this last project.

Of all the enterprises beckoning an immigrant to the Big Horn Basin, land was probably the one that Buffalo Bill knew best. He had owned a fine ranch in North Platte, Nebraska, for many years, and the life of the rancher appealed more to him than any other. It is no surprise, then, to find him actively engaged in buying, selling, leasing, and otherwise acquiring land throughout the upper Shoshone country from the first year he arrived there. His first adventure was to file a Desert Land claim and a Homestead entry on the north slope of Carter Mountain, where he expected to build his first ranch. This property lay along the upper reaches of Marquette Creek and included five small lakes, which he named after female members of his family. He built a cabin there, but a couple of years later he found land farther up the South Fork that he liked better. In 1898, he decided to relinquish the first claims and file a new Desert Land Entry for 320 acres of river valley about ten miles farther west. This became the TE, but not without a struggle.[41]

Cody surely knew that he could not file more than once under each of these public land acts. He submitted a sworn statement that he had "lost" his first filings a few months before making the new Desert Land Entry, in which he was required to swear that he had not made any other DLE. It apparently did not trouble him to so testify. He then took out water rights to irrigate pastures on the new ranch and proceeded to erect buildings and fences. In due time, in February of 1905, he applied for title to the land. Title was held up in Washington, however, because Cody neglected to transmit an official copy of his water permit from the State of Wyoming. At roughly the same time, Cody, or his attorney, determined to change the legal description of the land he was claiming. The land he had filed upon, known locally as the BN ranch, originally located by a Captain Belknap, had not been well surveyed when he claimed it. The government survey had been completed only in 1904, and Cody wanted the proper legal description for his land, so he amended his original filing in January 1907. The General Land Office insisted that Cody readvertise his claim in the terms of the new survey. In all this time, it appears he neglected to provide the GLO with the water permit it had requested, so the case dragged on into 1908. Given all that time, a clerk must finally have realized that this William F. Cody

Buffalo Bill on horseback in the yard of his beautiful South Fork ranch, the TE. Courtesy of Buffalo Bill Historical Center, Cody, Wyo.; P.6.641.

was the same one who had filed DLE 140 ten years earlier. It is impossible to know if anyone in Cody dropped any hints that might have led a clerk to inquire.

In April 1908, William Cody was charged to show cause why his Desert Land Entry for the TE ranch should not be cancelled for illegal misrepresentations. Cody, of course, immediately applied for more time in which to present evidence, which was granted. When his reply was filed it was another tour de force of misrepresentation. He swore that he had relinquished his earlier Desert Land Entry believing that the lands were improperly described, due to the confusion of the survey. It was his intent to reenter the same land under a correct description, which he thought he had done. He had no recollection of any homestead entry; if he had made and relinquished one, it would have been for the same reasons. This was bald-faced lying. There had been no improvement in the survey in the late 1890s, as the Land Office must surely have known. Moreover, the errors of the survey had been serious but not so totally disconnected with reality as to move a piece of ground ten miles. It was probably true that he did not profit from his relinquishments, but there can be no question that he was playing fast and loose with the regulations and the Land Office people. But his tactic worked. Perhaps helped along by a favorable recommendation from the Shoshone Forest supervisor, and probably some others as well, it was apparently decided to let this case slide. It surely was not the only land title case in Washington to be concluded with a convenient untruth.[42]

Having relinquished his public land claims on Carter Mountain, Cody nevertheless maintained an interest in ranching on the lower South Fork. He bought a small place (160 acres) near the junction of the forks of the Shoshone that he called Buffalo Meadows. In November of 1900, he bought 640 acres on Carter Creek at the foot of Carter Mountain, for $3,000. This land was about five miles closer to town and a thousand feet lower than his Irma Lake claims. He did not abandon the Irma Lake country entirely. He bought a quarter-section next to his original claim from his brother-in-law for $1 in 1906, reasonable evidence that it had been his in all but name.[43] These two pieces of land bracketed the extensive tract of land he had leased from the State of Wyoming through the good offices of his friend, Elwood Mead. (He had leased over 6,000 acres on Carter Mountain before he decided to let his desert land and homestead claims there go.) In all, he had accumulated 8,400 acres of state land tributary to his Carter Creek ranch by the time he sold it in 1911. He paid the State only $.05 per acre per year and accepted the obligation to fence his leased land. It was a very good deal for the Colonel.

Land leases in Wyoming were managed by the State Land Commission, for which the state engineer was the principal staff officer. Public land was donated by the federal government to the newly formed western states to provide endowments for agricultural colleges and other public institutions. The State had a strong interest in getting the land leased to generate income, and large leases were not unusual. For instance, Otto Franc, a pioneer rancher on the Greybull River, was awarded a lease for 11,162 acres in 1896. Big operators were probably better bets to make their lease payments than small ones just starting out. However, when Buffalo Bill, as agent for his syndicate of New York hunters, requested in 1897 a 50,000-acre lease for his game preserve project, the Land decided it was time to consider some principles to govern the leases.

They concluded, after careful consideration, "that the smaller selections requested by the farmers and ranchmen residents of the state should have primary consideration."[44]

When he learned that his game preserve lease would not go through, Cody quickly telegraphed a request to Mead for 5,000 acres to use as pasture. This stimulated further discussion, in which the Commission determined that requests for leases of less than 1,000 acres would be considered first, and the larger ones would get secondary consideration. When all was done, however, more than a few men got large leases. Former U.S. senator and future governor Joseph Carey got one for 13,400 acres, and future governor DeForest Richards got 2,000 acres. In Big Horn County, Bill Cody received a lease for 5,720 acres, and his friend A. A. Anderson, a wealthy New York artist who owned the Palette Ranch on the upper Greybull, picked up 5,040. Both of these men were particular clients of Elwood Mead.[45] These were no doubt good business judgments for the State, but in the context of the 1890s, they were also politically charged decisions, given the populist cast of the Commission's original intent.

Mead worked with Buffalo Bill to help him acquire more state leases. Cody had already taken a school section (640 acres) adjacent to the land that became his 5,700-acre lease. Mead had been given authority by the Commission to select up to 10,000 more acres in Big Horn County, and he funneled 1,080 of those acres into Cody's hands. Some of this was done by more or less open collusion to avoid the land laws. Since Cody already had a school section under lease, he could lease no more school land, but the fence he built around his big pasture included two half-sections of school land. Mead's advice to him was not to take down the fence and run it only around his own lease, but to find someone else to lease the land for him. The same applied to two other quarter-sections, not yet fenced. In the face of this kind of official manipulation of regulations, the Land Commission's populist posturing for the cause of smaller ranchers lost all meaning. Mead and Cody, both Republicans, with interests that far transcended the mundane world of struggling little men, worked to put in place an early version of the corporate farm, what we might call the corporate ranch for corporate cowboys, on the western slopes of the Big Horn Basin. Mead was quite aware of the protests against the decisions of the Land Commission, but was confident of his ability to manage them. Speaking particularly of the Shoshone valley, he bragged to one of his assistants, "Shaped up the selections along the Stinking Water in such a way as to make converts all along the line. All are pleased."[46]

Cody bought and sold a great variety of parcels of land in the Shoshone valley. He employed a wide array of resources to stay active in the land market. Consequently, it is not remotely possible to trace and catalog all his land deals. He bought land in the names of other people—or paid for their public land claims—who later conveyed it to him for little or nothing, or for a decent sum that might have been offered in lieu of wages. He financed a Desert Land Entry for his sister, May Cody Bradford, in order to increase the size of the TE. Similarly he used a homestead claim by his brother-in-law, Louis Decker, to keep some land up near Irma Lake, and another one by his mistress, Bess Isbell, to hold a ranch upstream of his Carter Creek ranch. Between 1900 and 1910, when he was well supplied with money, he bought and sold six or seven parcels of land between Cody and the TE. After the hard years, when he had had to sell just about anything that he could move, he was reduced to his home ranch, the TE, and a small place on the edge of Cody known as the Sweeney ranch. The county tax roll in 1911 assessed him on 118 cattle and 70 horses at TE; it was a good ranch, worth $10,021, but not the biggest in that end of the valley. He also paid taxes on land worth $6,920 at the Sweeney ranch, and $4,050 worth of town lots. By 1913, he had deeded over both the TE and the Irma Hotel to his wife, Louisa, to keep them safe from creditors. He was well set for land and property but crucially short of money to get out of debt. The colossal ambition he had brought into the Shoshone River valley left mostly an empty echo from the surrounding mountains.[47]

It might be instructive to look into the affairs of George Beck by way of comparison with Bill Cody's way of doing business. Beck's curious lack of energy in Irrigation Company matters did not carry over into those places where only his own profit was concerned. Perhaps his awareness of other opportunities distracted him from Company business, but it is also true that the financial failure of the Irrigation Company hurt him less than it did the other directors; he had far less money invested in the canal company than any of the others. As a result, he had resources to take advantage of other opportunities. Hydroelectric power is a case in point. Power generation had been on the minds of the Shoshone Irrigation Company from the beginning. The contracts that settlers signed when they bought into the canal included a provision that the company had conveyed to "the Shoshone Power Company" the rights to power generation along the canal, and as soon as the SPC began to employ water in the canal to produce electric power, the company would pay 3 percent of the annual maintenance of the canal. The provision never came into effect, because the canal was barely adequate for its main purpose and could not have generated electricity in addition.

The need for electricity in Cody was real nonetheless. As the Shoshone Irrigation Company was averse to putting any more money into Cody, and as Buffalo Bill himself began, after 1902, to allow other interests to occupy his mind and empty his pocketbook, George Beck determined to go into the power business on his own. In the spring of 1904, Beck applied for a permit for 500 cubic feet per second of Shoshone River water to operate a power plant along the river just upstream of the bridge to the Burlington depot. He raised the money on his own, and in 1905 he completed installation of his machinery and began to supply the town with electricity. After all the work and worry on irrigation matters, this power plant provided Beck with a steady flow of income—several thousand dollars per year—for the following three decades. Of course, he hired a man to run the plant for him.[48]

For most of the Shoshone Irrigation Company directors, minerals meant gold or oil. Beck expanded his interest in minerals to include such a proletarian element as sulphur. He started work on a pair of sulphur placer claims in 1901 west of Cody (near Sulphur Creek, in fact). In 1904 he leased these claims to a man from Denver for $10,000. Sulphur mines near Cody were a paying proposition for more than twenty years, and Beck more than recovered his financial losses on the canal with his sulphur claims.[49] He was also a partner in the flour milling plant in Cody, and he invested in one of the banks. He did not lose interest in richer minerals, of course. As late as 1911, he, along with Cody, Bleistein, and Henry Gerrans were considering patenting some placer gold claims high up the South Fork, and, as already noted, he became active in the oil business in the early years.[50] The point here is that George Beck, who actually performed as a capitalist, took a very functional approach to identifying and taking advantage of opportunities. Beck invested where he thought he saw a potential for profit, without much consideration of how the world would regard him. As a result, ten years after the demise of the Shoshone Irrigation Company he was the wealthiest man in Cody, in a far better position than his famous friend.

In summary, William Cody, addicted to the spotlight, seemed to choose undertakings with at least one eye on reputation. He also attempted to use the weight of the reputation he had earned in the Wild West arena to swing money and authority his way in economic transactions in Wyoming. He had convinced himself of the truth of his "frontier imposture" and built fame and fortune on it. He then convinced himself that he was a man of affairs, the equal of great capitalists and political leaders across the nation. This, a kind of "capitalist imposture," proved a tremendous handicap for him to carry in the world of exchange, away from the show arena. For one thing, it depended to an extent on people who had given him the full credit of his frontier imposture now being willing to put their money on the line with him because of his supposed role in "the winning of the West." For another, people are generally more careful in assessing performance where their own money is concerned, and Buffalo Bill, the great performer, did not perform well in this arena. One wonders what George Beck expected in 1893, when he and Bill Cody met. Did he ever think that in twenty years he would be looking downhill at "the best advertised man in America?" Probably not; surely, Cody never saw it coming.

CHAPTER TEN

The Cody-Salsbury Proposition

A traveler going west up the Shoshone valley in, say, 1950 would probably have been most impressed by the wide, green expanse of cropland in the central valley, centered upon the prosperous town of Powell, and the great network of canals that feed it. Continuing upstream beyond Cody, through the Shoshone canyon, our traveler would have found and admired the life source for that vast garden twenty-five miles to the east, a reservoir containing 465,000 acre-feet of water held back by a great concrete arch dam, both named after Buffalo Bill. That reservoir provides plentiful water to irrigate 93,000 acres around Powell, on what is today known as the Shoshone Project of the U.S. Bureau of Reclamation. Although he built none of it, Buffalo Bill envisioned something like this verdant valley from his earliest days in Wyoming. It requires no stretch of historical imagination to connect his memory to these monuments of the early days of federal reclamation, although, as we shall see, there is a certain irony in this.[1]

Bill Cody frequently referred to himself as a "far gazer," by which he meant one who dreamed big dreams. The Cody Canal was never the whole of the picture he carried in his mind of what he could do in the Shoshone River valley. It is likely that he knew, when he decided to join George Beck and Horace Alger in the scheme that became the Cody Canal, that Frank Mondell of Newcastle had already applied for a water right to develop 155,000 acres of land along the north side of the river. Mondell had been elected to Congress in 1894, and he was well

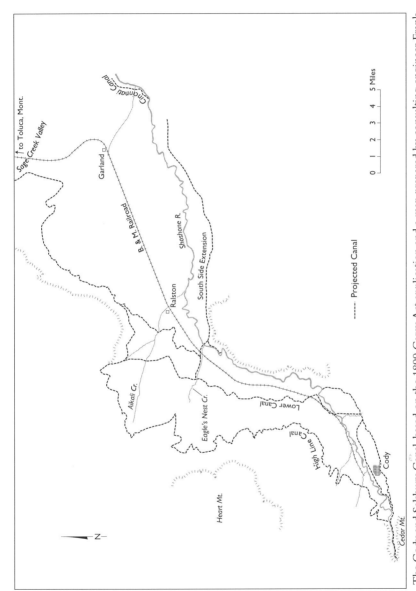

The Cody and Salsbury Canal, based on the 1899 Carey Act application and a map prepared by consulting engineer Frank Kelsey in 1901.

known as an energetic man who worked closely with the Burlington Railroad, as Buffalo Bill did. Once Cody began work with the Shoshone Land and Irrigation Company, which brought him into close contact with Elwood Mead, Wyoming state engineer, he kept an eye out for other possibilities downriver. When Mondell's congressional career superseded his development plans, Cody was ready. In spite of the considerable difficulties they were already encountering with the Cody Canal, he and Nate Salsbury took up Mondell's water right as soon as they could. They were careful to maintain a distinction between this new project and the one they continued to pursue with the Shoshone Irrigation Company. It was probably inevitable, however, that confusion between the two would arise.

The first of these confusions involved Elwood Mead himself. Mead had surveyed the Cody Canal project in 1894, as part of a larger enterprise that he grandly called the South Side Canal. In that report, he casually mentioned irrigation prospects north of the river, which obviously caught Cody's attention. Mead continued under retainer with the Shoshone Irrigation Company at the rate of $1,000 per annum through the summer of 1897, but from the fall of 1895 he was actively in correspondence with Buffalo Bill about what they called the North Side project. His *Irrigation Age* article of February 1896 described a project that covered both sides of the river, and he began the survey for it that year. When he visited the town of Cody in the summer of 1897, he spent almost no time working on the Cody Canal, where George Beck could have used his help. In addition to laying out a large lease of land for Buffalo Bill, he spent a great deal of time running the survey lines north of the Shoshone River, taking steps toward giving some reality to Cody's second irrigation project. Mondell's permit had not expired, but it was clear that he was doing no work on it, and Mead's determination to see Wyoming developed would not allow him to hang back on a legal technicality. But until Cody and Salsbury took out their own water right, it was not clear what the relationship between the Cody Canal and this new enterprise would be. Given all this, it is no wonder that contemporaries, as well as historians, have suffered confusion when looking at Cody's irrigation projects.[2]

At first, Colonel Cody himself was not too sure just who would be with him. Irrigating land on the north side of the Shoshone had been part of company discussions even before the Shoshone Irrigation Company was formally organized. While waiting for the secretary of the Interior to sign the papers for the Cody Canal, Buffalo Bill was urging his new Buffalo friends to get money together to push the ditch down the north side. In September 1896, although he recognized that money was tight in the East and that his Wild West income would have to carry the Cody Canal, he apparently had not ruled out participation by his other partners in the big north-side venture. If they did not join him, "then I will go to Europe & organize a company that can build anything."³ A month later he told Mead he was out to raise a million dollars for the new project. His plan was to take water out of the river in the canyon west of Cody to water the tableland around Cody, plus a 90,000-acre tract below Eagle's Nest stage station, about fifteen miles downriver from Cody. He wanted Mead to survey it and estimate the cost of the project; it was this that would occupy Mead the following summer when Beck wanted him to help on the Cody Canal.⁴

But before Mead could travel to the Basin, he received an application for a competing irrigation proposal for the north side, near Cody, from W. E. Hymer, a director of the defunct Shoshone Land and Irrigation Company. Mead was puzzled, it seems, and told Cody he thought he probably would have to approve the application "unless your company files objections thereto." But, having no water right or interest of record north of the river, the Shoshone Irrigation Company had no grounds for complaint; Cody's conversations with Mead were the only things that held that land. These were a far cry from contracts and permits, but Mead knew that cooperation with moneyed men like Buffalo Bill was the only road to water development in Wyoming. So he put Hymer off with an objection to his dam design, perhaps knowing that Hymer would go away if pressed. He surely knew that Cody and Hymer were on the outs, and might have expected Buffalo Bill to take care of Hymer on his own.⁵

Apparently on behalf of the Shoshone Irrigation Company, Horace Alger had told Mead that he was making arrangements for Mead's survey of the north side of the river, but Mead (who was aware that he was in legal no-man's-land) needed clearer direction. At that point, in the early spring of 1897, Buffalo Bill was brought to see the need for definite legal action. He and Salsbury, he told Mead, would undertake this development in their own names, and arrange for a big company to handle it. They would need first right to dam the river and take enough water for 150,000 acres. "Its easier to float a big enterprize than a little one, but we must have the first water right and plenty of it."⁶

Salsbury had some questions about the advisability of this new investment. Specifically, he wanted to know from Mead if there was any prospect of getting more time than the ten years allowed by the Carey Act to complete the reclamation. Whatever answer he got must have satisfied him, because in October 1897 he put his name on the line with Buffalo Bill to take out a water right permit from the Shoshone River and inaugurate officially the Cody-Salsbury project. Mead and three assistants had performed the survey work and had drawn up the maps necessary to make application for segregation of the land under the Carey Act. Proud of his work with Buffalo Bill, Mead sent a special copy of the map prepared for the Cody-Salsbury segregation to his patron, Senator Francis E. Warren, to hang as a wall decoration in his office. At the same time, he was worried about the size of the enterprise. There was an abundance of water and, in his opinion, no better land anywhere for the purposes of irrigation. He thought the canal line was entirely feasible. "If built and the land occupied it would sustain more people than the state contains today. I don't believe private enterprise can afford to build it. Can we not enlist government aid on this matter?"[7] Warren agreed that it was a "big enterprise," but confessed that he knew of no way to enlist the government in aid of it.[8]

Mead and his office worked all through the summer of 1897, preparing the paperwork connected with the application to the General Land Office to segregate the land that Cody and Salsbury wanted under the Carey Act. One of his assistants forwarded to Cody, in Lafayette, Indiana, slips of paper indicating the tracts to be irrigated, asking him to check them as to correctness. Asking Bill Cody to do this kind of detail work would have been unrealistic under the best of circumstances; when he was traveling with his Wild West show it was nothing short of ridiculous. One historian of Cody's water rights has concluded that this ill-advised procedure explains why significant tracts of land were left out of the Carey Act application.[9] In September, Cody told Mead he was ready to put his company together to finance the big development. Permit no. 1586 was issued to Bill Cody and Nate Salsbury on October 8, 1897, allowing them sufficient water to irrigate 120,000 acres. In December, Cody intended to visit Mead in Cheyenne, but that was the trip where he got drunk and stayed that way for days, unable to do any business. Afterward, he told Mead that he planned to meet with John McKay and some other wealthy men in New York.[10]

Apparently, Mead was not dismayed by this kind of performance; drunk or sober, Cody was still the biggest thing on the Wyoming horizon. When Buffalo Bill told Mead that McKay wanted to send an expert out to Wyoming to look at the irrigation proposition, Mead immediately volunteered to shepherd the visitor around the Big Horn Basin. Cody evidently neglected to tell Mead that he was trying to interest McKay in investing in gold mines as well as irrigation canals. They arranged the visit for early March of 1898. It was subsequently postponed a couple of times, but by the middle of May, the men (McKay sent more than one) were back in New York. McKay's men recommended favorably on the agricultural proposition but were against the placer mining, and that seems to have put an end to his interest in Wyoming. Cody chose, as he usually did, to blame something other than the quality of his own plans. This time it was the war fever over Cuba. "Its simply impossible to get capital to invest until they see the war clouds pass over. Had it not been for the war work would now be going on and the North Side canal an assured success."[11] He then requested, in light of the difficulties entailed by the war, that Mead get a year's extension for him on the North Side work. It is wholly characteristic of Buffalo Bill Cody that he was actively planning this huge new venture at the same time he confessed to George Beck his regret that he had ever seen the Big Horn Basin!

Mead arranged the extra time that Cody needed to begin construction on the Cody-Salsbury Canal, and Cody continued to report meetings with wealthy eastern investors. During the course of 1899, they carried on their discussions about the design of the project and possible starting dates. Mead prevailed upon Cody to submit a revised application when it became clear that Cody was considering changing the point of diversion for the Cody-Salsbury Canal. On May 22, 1899, permit no. 2111 was issued as an amendment to no. 1586, containing new deadlines for beginning and completing construction, but in size and intent identical to the earlier one. Actual construction under this permit began in May 1900. Ever the optimist, and needing to keep Mead thinking he could deliver, Cody tried to picture the Burlington Railroad survey as his salvation; if they would start that railroad, he said, "I could raise a million in no time and put ditch through quick." However, that proved to be another blast of hot air. As it happened, no financing was ever secured beyond what Bill Cody and Nate Salsbury could supply from the Wild West. The Cody-Salsbury Canal consequently lived a short and parlous life.[12]

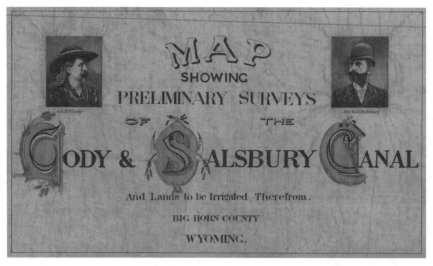

Cover page of the application to segregate land under the Carey Act for the Cody and Salsbury Canal, 1899. Courtesy of Wyoming State Engineer, Cheyenne, Wyo.

None of the action and revision concerning water rights moved the Carey Act process along, except for the fact that without the water right permit from the State, the General Land Office would not entertain an application. Mead worked on both state and federal goals at the same time. In the summer of 1898, Cody prepared the bond required by the State for a Carey Act project, and Mead gave him detailed instructions to accomplish the filing. When the water right was renewed the following spring, Cody had to file another set of papers. Only in the spring of 1900 was a proposal submitted to and accepted by the Arid Lands Board for the segregation of 79,000 acres of public land under the Carey Act for the Cody-Salsbury enterprise. The tract stretched along the north side of the Shoshone from the mouth of the canyon almost thirty miles downriver, and included as well a sliver of land south of the river on the lower end. After they paid $990 in fees and the president and secretary of Interior had signed off on it, Bill Cody and Nate Salsbury had their second irrigation project in the Big Horn Basin.[13]

Another Carey Act project received State approval in May 1900. As noted earlier, when a company of Mormons traveled through the Shoshone River valley in the winter of 1900, Buffalo Bill met and entertained them. The governor of Wyoming had been to Salt Lake City to encourage Mormon colonies to move to Wyoming and take up irrigation farming. The group that Cody met in February 1900 returned to Utah and constituted themselves the Big Horn Basin Colonization Company. An apostle of the Church, Abraham O. Woodruff (who was only in his twenties and was the son of Wilford Woodruff, past president of the Church of Latter-Day Saints), led a group of more than four hundred families. They came together in April and moved their households from settled Utah towns to the unsettled frontier along the Shoshone River in northern Wyoming. They took over a failed Carey Act project known as the Cincinnati Canal. The land under that unbuilt canal was available (that is, not part of the Cody-Salsbury segregation), but Cody and Salsbury's water right was so large that the state required a relinquishment to guarantee a sufficient water supply for the Mormon colony. Cody and Salsbury relinquished water to irrigate 21,000 acres in March of 1900.[14]

When Charles Kingston, agent for the Big Horn Basin Colonization Company, had first gone over the land in the Basin, he took note of the tract that was part of the Cody-Salsbury project south of the river. He asked state engineer Fred Bond at the very beginning of his Wyoming negotiations if there was any way of getting that land for his colonists. Since it was under Cody's water right filing, and particularly since the Wyoming state engineer had worked hand-in-glove with Cody, he was told that it was tied up until December 1902. He and Woodruff protested directly to Governor Richards that the law required work to be done in order to keep a water right current, and no work was being done there, but they were told that work done anywhere on a project holds all the land segregated and there was no legal way to take that land from Cody. However, the Mormons remained interested in that land (which they came to call Willwood, in honor of Apostle Woodruff's father), and did not allow the issue to go away. They argued that Cody planned to irrigate only 8,000 acres or so south of the Shoshone, and their own surveys indicated they could manage more than twice that. After contemplating the energy with which the Mormons went about their business, while nothing ever happened on the Cody-Salsbury tract, Governor Richards made up his mind to try to separate the Willwood piece from Cody's larger project.[15]

At the end of the summer of 1900, Richards composed a careful letter to Buffalo Bill, explaining that the Mormon colonists had nearly completed their first canal and would like very much to take up the south-side land that was part of the Cody-Salsbury segregation. He was anxious, he said, to see the Big Horn Basin settled. Cody's north-side project impressed him as "large and difficult." He had spoken with engineers who regarded Cody's plan to water the Willwood sliver by means of a long flume as "a difficult and expensive engineering problem." It seemed to him that "the chances for the reclaiming of this section of the country within a reasonably short time are not good," and, knowing that Cody desired to see that portion of the country settled by good people, he asked the Colonel to consider relinquishing that bit of his segregation to the state.[16] In response to the governor, Cody said that they would consider it, but they must have some compensation if they gave it up, for the outlay they had already made. "I did not know that they had spent a dollar" was Richards's observation on that request.[17]

The Mormons tenaciously pursued the Willwood land. Governor Richards repeatedly told them it was beyond his power to get it for them, that their only hope was to appeal directly to Buffalo Bill. In the summer of 1902, driven by the persistence of Woodruff and others now settled in Wyoming, Richards again addressed a long letter to Cody. Apparently, the Mormons, who had balked a year earlier when Cody mentioned $19,000 as compensation for giving up the land, were willing to consider paying "a reasonable consideration" by this time, so the governor was attempting to serve as a broker. He reminded Cody that he would still have quite a large tract to develop, which if he succeeded in reclaiming, "would be an accomplishment sufficient to immortalize anyone's name in the State for time immemorial." He repeated his earlier arguments, adding that surrendering Willwood might actually be a benefit rather than an injury to his enterprise. He protested than he had no interest in the matter beyond that of seeing the arid parts of the state settled, and closed with a forceful request to "please let me know what substantial progress you are making toward the earnest beginning of the work of reclaiming the large tract segregated for you."[18]

Although the governor's position was both logical and reasonable, Buffalo Bill was not persuaded. Cody obviously felt the governor leaning on him, as he wrote Richards twice in the next two weeks and caused the governor to protest mightily that he had never intended to pressure him to do anything, and that he deeply appreciated everything Buffalo Bill had done for Wyoming. (These particular letters have not survived, but references to them and others like them are abundant in the papers of state officials of that period.) No one was ever allowed to forget or over-look the work Bill Cody had done for his new home state. Moreover, whatever Governor Richards might think of his long flume across the Shoshone, Cody had just paid Frank Kelsey for a brand-new survey of his entire enterprise, and had no reason to doubt the competence of his own engineer. Finally, it made no economic sense to him to sell off the Willwood. It was good land and easy to irrigate, and the prospect of having this land to sell made the larger development more likely. As he told George Holdrege, "The Mormons want only the cheap end . . . and if they get that the upper end will never be irrigated."[19]

It is impossible to know how much time or energy Buffalo Bill put into the financing of the Cody-Salsbury Canal in the years 1899–1902. What is not in doubt is his determination to make important people believe he was working on it. A letter written from Chicago to Curtis Hinkle, clerk of the State Land Board, is quite typical. "I am here seeing some gentlemen who are talking of building the Cody & Salsbury canal," he wrote. "In a few days they may send their attorney to consult the Board and Engineer. I am using my best energy to get that canal built." Returning to the earlier issue with the governor, he said "it was lucky that the Mormons did not get any more leased off the lower end or this great expansion & canal would never have been built." It would, of course, be expensive, and the State would have to allow him to charge accord-ingly for the water rights. Then the classic upbeat conclusion: "I expect to get five thousand [colonists] men women & children into the Basin inside of two years. . . . Rest assured I am not idle and am doing my best to build up Northern Wyo."[20]

This time he apparently did get someone to go out to look over the land, but nothing came of it. By the end of the summer, he told Hinkle to expect a visit from M. P. Pels, president of the Great Maxwell Grant in southern Colorado and New Mexico. Pels, Cody said, was interested in the Cody-Salsbury Canal. In his mind the project was now swollen to 120,000 acres on both sides of the river. "I know this is asking much of you and giving you extra work," he said to Hinkle, "*but* you wait till I land this enterprise." He went on to say he had the money in sight in England, but if he could get it sooner here he would take it. "So try and land Mr. Pell. Introduce him to the Governor and Board—and Mr. Bond."[21] Then, ten days later, Cody wrote Governor Richards that the Pels deal had fallen through. He still had his English friends, of course, "and I expect to bring them and the money with me when I come back from England in February."[22] At approximately the same time, Cody told George Holdrege of the Burlington that he was negotiating with the Spreckles Beet Sugar people.[23] Who can say whether Pels or the Spreckles people were ever seriously interested, or just who the phantom English friends (who stayed conveniently to hand throughout the following year) might have been? We have seen too often the gap between Bill Cody's words and his actions to give easy credence to any of this.

The fact that Cody was once again thinking of his project as a north- and south-side canal may be confusing, but nevertheless it was the way his thoughts were tending. In the summer of 1901 he and Salsbury hired Frank Kelsey, a prominent civil engineer from Salt Lake City, to go over the entire ground of their project and to make a series of construction recommendations. Kelsey made use of the survey Elwood Mead had run for the 1897 permit, which had been incorporated in the 1899 water right and formed the basis of the Carey Act segregation, but he also ran his own survey lines and set out to answer a number of questions that had not been raised in of any of the earlier planning. The printed docu- ment he handed to his employers in September contemplated not only the irrigation of the Cody-Salsbury Carey Act land, but also a gravity water supply system for the town of Cody and a canal that operated a hydroelectric power generating system for Cody. Although the water right on file with the State indicated that water for the big irrigation project would be diverted from the Shoshone about four miles below Cody, Buffalo Bill directed Kelsey to base his plans on a diversion dam to be built in the canyon six miles upstream of the town. This allowed sufficient drop for the water and power canals, and it also took water out at a high enough elevation so that they could—by means of another of those high flumes—irrigate land close to Cody on the north side of the river. The line of the canal that would do that was part of Mead's first survey, denominated in decades of newspapers and correspondence as "the High Line."[24]

There would have been a considerable benefit to Buffalo Bill's new hometown had Kelsey's plans been put into shape on the ground, and a considerable profit would have run into the pockets of both Wild West partners, to the exclusion of the other directors of the Shoshone Irriga- tion Company. Kelsey's survey represented, then, a big step toward what Cody had often threatened to do (get rid of partners who would not put up when the going got tough) while it also expanded the horizon of his irrigation planning. The other directors, of course, had actively been looking for a way out for years; there is no evidence that they resented what Cody and Salsbury were doing. And when these plans fell through in their turn, George Beck, with help from other eastern friends, built the modest hydroelectric plant that powered Cody for decades. It would have required another amendment to the Cody-Salsbury water right to move the point of diversion as Kelsey's survey did. The record of their dealings with the state engineer leads one to expect they would have had no trouble getting it, but events caught them out before it came to that.

In June of 1902, President Theodore Roosevelt signed into law the Newlands Reclamation Act, so named for the senator from Nevada who was its principal sponsor. There had been considerable agitation for a national irrigation law since it became clear that the Carey Act was not going to be the tool to bring about the full development of western water resources that western politicians and capitalists wanted. Among those working hardest for federal support for western water development were the western railroads. Federal dams, irrigation systems, and settlements promised to bring money, people, and business into all corners of the West. The United States Geological Survey, under the direction of John Wesley Powell, had been at work for more than a decade mapping the West to determine the best ways to develop water resources. Powell had retired by June 1902, but men who had trained under him—Clarence Walcott, Frederick Haynes Newell, and Powell's nephew, Arthur Powell Davis—led the new Reclamation Service as it set about its business. Within two months of the passage of the Newlands Act, these three traveled to Cody "as guests of the Burlington." Buffalo Bill was in Oregon, but his Wyoming agent, John Martin, gave them a blueprint of Kelsey's survey and showed them all around. Martin wrote Cody that they were greatly impressed with the Cody-Salsbury scheme. He believed that if Buffalo Bill did not do it, the government would be sure to take it on.[25]

When the federal government came into the Shoshone valley, brought in on the newly laid tracks of the Burlington Railroad, development prospects for the Big Horn Basin changed entirely. As soon as he received this letter from Martin, Cody wrote Governor Richards. He still had his English friends, but would not stand in the government's way if it wanted to take up the Cody-Salsbury project. "I am as anxious to see that land under cultivation as any man in Wyoming and am doing my level best to bring it about. . . . I am putting $80,000 in my new hotel in Cody and I want to get people to support it. No one is more interested in the prosperity of the country than I."[26] The Burlington Railroad began to try to move Cody aside as soon as the Reclamation Service men left for Washington. Cody played a little harder to get with them, holding out the possibility of another financing scheme, but George Holdrege and his associates pursued the goal of a government development single-mindedly from the time the Newlands Act passed. As soon as he had heard from Buffalo Bill that he was still negotiating for financing, Holdrege sent a copy of the letter to Charles Walcott at the USGS, saying, "I hardly think it probable that he will succeed this time in arranging with Mr. Spreckles to undertake the enterprise," and concluding, "If you can see your way clear to arrange for the construction of the proposed irrigation works, I have no doubt it will be entirely satisfactory for the State of Wyoming to cede back the necessary lands to the United States Government." He felt certain that Colonel Cody would relinquish his claim upon the water permit.[27]

Walcott was actually less aggressive in pursuit of the federal project than Holdrege. He rejected the proposal that they go to the State with their plans. He did not want to interfere with private development or with State prerogatives. The Reclamation Service thought the Cody-Salsbury project was a good candidate for federal reclamation, but they preferred to wait until the State came to them. That was not good enough for Holdrege. After the show season was over, he arranged for Buffalo Bill to sign a conditional relinquishment of his water right for the Cody-Salsbury project. The indenture may well have been drawn up by Burlington lawyers, and it was witnessed by Charles Morrill of the Lincoln Land Company. In it, Cody and Salsbury abandoned to the State of Wyoming the 1899 water right granted them by Elwood Mead, the relinquishment to come into effect "in the event that the Government of the United States shall have commenced the construction of a canal over said lands, or any part thereof, . . . before the end of the year A. D. 1903."[28]

This document is remarkable in any number of ways, and extraordinarily revealing of the power relationships that grew up around development issues on the Wyoming frontier. In the first place, although the relinquishment is from Cody and Salsbury to the State of Wyoming, there was no one from the State present at the signing, nor was the paper subsequently transmitted to any state official. Instead, it remained in the hands of George Holdrege, "in escrow" as they said. Secondly, Nate Salsbury's name was obviously signed by Bill Cody himself. Salsbury was, in fact, on his deathbed in New York as the deal was being struck, and may never have known the first thing about it. Third, the indenture was shot through with errors, starting with the number of the permit being relinquished; 2111 at the state engineer's office, it was referred to here as 22111. It is unlikely that it would have been defensible at law should any party have cared to renege upon it. However, it seemed to satisfy Holdrege. He must have recognized that Buffalo Bill was a difficult character with whom to do business, and he hoped that a document like this would help keep Cody marching to the Burlington tune. As for Cody, he probably believed that the conditions he wrote into it left him some degree of control, even as he turned the project over to the United States government.

Governor Richards confessed a month or so later that he had been "casually informed" of the relinquishment, but had had no official notification of it. Word of it had the effect that Holdrege obviously intended, however, for in the course of January 1903, Richards conferred with the State Board of Land Commissioners, and they agreed to turn back the Carey Act segregation on the north side of the Shoshone to the federal government for development under the new Reclamation Act. In the letter communicating this resolution to Walcott, Richards closed by mentioning that he had been assured "that the Burlington Railroad will enter into an agreement, also, to bring abundant settlers upon these lands so soon as they are ready for settlement."[29] They were doing much more than making promises. Holdrege was in direct communication with Senator Francis E. Warren in Washington, who set to lobbying Walcott and Newell, the head of the new Reclamation Service, to get going on it. "I have explained to the officers of the survey," Warren told the CB&Q attorney in Cheyenne, "the interest of Mr. Holdrege in the matter, and his desire to see the project utilized and the lands under it reclaimed by the Government."[30] Obviously, in Warren's mind, if the Burlington wanted it they should have it. The railroad was now running the game for all it was worth.

The State of Wyoming under the guidance of DeForest Richards seemed less impressed with Buffalo Bill Cody than earlier administrations had been. As already seen, the State was holding the Shoshone Irrigation Company to strict performance of its contract on the Cody Canal. Now it moved quickly to return the Cody-Salsbury Carey Act segregation to the federal government, apparently without even seeing the relinquishment Cody had signed. The prospect of federal money for development was a powerful magnet, of course, and much more certain than Cody's talk of "English friends." However, Richards was surely being honest when he told Abraham Woodruff that he was as proud of bringing that colony of Mormons to the Shoshone River as anything he had done. Good agricultural development required dedicated, hard-working people. The Mormons were all of that and experienced in irrigation farming as well. Balked by Cody in his first attempts to get more Shoshone land for the Mormons, Richards found a second opportunity in the breaking of the Cody-Salsbury segregation. That is why he proposed to return to the United States only that part of the segregation north of the river. When questioned about this by Walcott, he stated his determination to dispose of the land south of the river "in another way," by which he meant his Mormon clients. For those representing the State, this was good policy: they attracted more of a very good class of agricultural settler (most of whom supported Governor Richards politically, by the way) and they got the big federal investment they needed.[31]

While the State was charging ahead, Buffalo Bill was off in London with the Wild West. His heart was still in Wyoming, however. He wrote Governor Richards and others in Cheyenne frequently, inquiring about the status of his leased State lands and checking up on the progress of the government in the Cody-Salsbury business. Richards wrote him late in February that the government was definitely going ahead with the project. To this, Cody replied that he hoped they would start their canal above Cody, so as to irrigate the land opposite the town and develop water power near the hot springs. He claimed to have spent $15,000 on the project and to have a syndicate ready to go, but he would step aside in the interest of getting the job done quickly. To support his arguments for using Mead's "High Line," he forwarded a copy of Kelsey's survey which incorporated that line. Cody hoped the government might pay him something for the Kelsey survey, but he would not protest if they did not. "Anything to benefit our State, and especially during your administration."[32]

The U.S. Reclamation Service, while remaining respectful of the laws and rights of the State of Wyoming, nevertheless kept Governor Richards

at arm's length where the Willwood land for the Mormons was concerned. They intended to base the design of this project on their own
surveys and their own ideas of what was best, and were not completely
happy to have only a part of the Cody-Salsbury land segregation turned
back to them. USGS director Walcott told the governor that their early
examinations indicated that including Willwood might be feasible, and
asked him to leave matters open so the government would not be limited
in any way in its design of the project. Richards, however, had leaked word
to his Mormon clients about the change in Cody's plans, and Mormons
were in the field surveying a canal line while all these letters were traveling
back and forth between London, Cheyenne, and Washington. Then, early
in May, ill health caught up with Governor Richards and he died, leaving
his secretary of state, Fenimore Chatterton, to serve as acting governor.
With this single stroke, the entire political environment of the Cody-
Salsbury proposition changed.[33]

Chatterton was young and, as it turned out, reckless. He liked to think
of himself as an enemy of the Republican machine by which Senator
Francis E. Warren dominated Wyoming politics. It was clear that Warren
and Congressman Mondell championed the government takeover of Bill
Cody's development scheme. Whether their support shifted Chatterton to
opposition or whether he was genuinely convinced that private developers could do better than the government is not entirely clear, but from
the outset he approached the question of developing the Shoshone far
differently than Governor Richards had. His first letter to Buffalo Bill
emphasized that his relinquishment had not been filed and that the project
remained in the hands of the State until the federal government agreed to
"take up the proposition and bring it to a successful conclusion."[34]

As the Reclamation Service had already given enthusiastic testimony
to their desire to take up the project, Acting Governor Chatterton was
showing, at the very least, an excess of caution. Jeremiah Ahern, the government's project engineer, was already in the field, beginning the careful
survey of the entire valley that would enable the most effective distribution of the water. Chatterton actually traveled to Cody at the end of
May to see what the engineers were doing. He concluded that they
would not be able to tell him until September what they were going to
do. Although he seemed to believe that the Reclamation Service would
take on the work, he asked Cody to stand ready to pick up the project if
they did not. At the same time, Chatterton pursued Governor Richards's

policy with respect to the Mormons and the Willwood land south of the river, which Cody had himself opposed.[35]

Chatterton unfurled his colors at a state Industrial Convention in Sheridan in October, decorating his opening address with a highly prejudiced and wildly inaccurate attack on the Reclamation Service. Hearing of this performance, USGS director Walcott wrote to answer him point by point and stated forcefully the need for cooperation between state and federal authorities in the work of reclamation, but Chatterton, without getting down to particular cases, put him off.[36] Things got worse around Christmas, when Chatterton actually saw the Cody-Salsbury relinquishment for the first time. He clearly hoped to use his acting governorship to move up to the top, and he needed some help to throw into the balance against the expected opposition of Senator Warren. He thought he might find that help from the Colonel's friends in the Big Horn Basin. However, when he put the word out that the government's right to develop the project would be forfeited January 1 because it had not begun work on any canals, he got a great shock. Public opinion in Cody, Buffalo Bill's hometown, did not want to hear that the big development was going back into his hands. Townspeople had endured years of incompetence and malfeasance at the hands of the Shoshone Irrigation Company, and had no reason to expect that another Cody development would bring any better results. One citizen wired Walcott at USGS to say that "nine-tenths of the people are opposed to it."[37]

The acting governor thus found himself in the open and exposed to fire from all sides. He spent the entire month of January 1904 trying to find cover and preserve some of his fast deteriorating political hopes. In letters to the USGS and to Wyoming's congressional delegation, as well as in leaked releases to selected papers, he tried to present himself as the champion of western men and western methods against the devious and untrustworthy representatives of the federal government. They had wasted an entire summer, he said, on topographical surveys "of a country upon which a practical western irrigation engineer could run a ditch line and make accurate estimates of the cost of construction within sixty days." They were planning a dam at the head of the canyon that would flood some of the oldest and finest ranches in that corner of the state. They had not met the time limit stipulated in Cody's relinquishment. Colonel Cody had organized a big company with prominent and influential eastern men at its head, and would move quickly to effect the reclamation of this large tract of land. "It has been our experience that Wyomingites through practical business methods rapidly push things to completion, and it is the intention of the land board to stand by Col. Cody, one of our citizens who has demonstrated his ability to do things."[38]

A knowledgable reader of this letter, someone like Frank Mondell or Francis Warren, would have seen through it instantly. People had had experience with sight-and-scrape western irrigation developments, and confidently expected better from more careful, better-funded, government work. They surely knew also that the Reclamation Service had never known of the January 1 deadline, since the State had only just learned of it. And they probably saw Buffalo Bill with clearer eyes than did Fenimore Chatterton. As much as they would have kept it quiet on the hustings, Mondell and Warren would have recognized Chatterton's peroration about practical Wyomingites and Cody's demonstrated ability to get things done for the hogwash that it was. They wasted no time in letting Chatterton know what a stupid game he was playing. The Reclamation Service, in the person of F. H. Newell, questioned directly many of the key assertions in Chatterton's letter, effectively refusing to accept that Chatterton had the power to alter so fundamentally the plans that had been in operation for more than a year.[39]

More to the point, perhaps, George Holdrege and the Burlington people would not let the project be derailed by a reckless engineer. Holdrege simply refused to believe that anything other than a federal solution was possible. He kept in close contact with the Reclamation Service and with Buffalo Bill. He learned that Cody's plans were "entirely indefinite," and that, although he seemed to think he could raise the money, he did not want to stand in the way of the government. Holdrege encouraged Newell to persevere in his course of developing plans from the Ahern survey. The Buffalo Bill to whom Holdrege was talking was quite a different man from the one Chatterton spoke of. The governor tried to make it sound as if this whole upset had come about because Cody appeared in Cheyenne with his relinquishment and demanded his rights. No one else who dealt with him in these months represented him in that way. Mondell in particular was convinced that there was nothing at all to the story that Cody had the money in hand and was ready to go.[40]

Chatterton grasped at one last straw when he saw things running against him. The Reclamation Service had inquired at the General Land Office whether Solon Wiley's large Carey Act segregation south of the

Shoshone, known as the Oregon Basin project, would conflict with the water right for the Cody-Salsbury development. This was a perfectly ordinary thing to do in the land office business, but Chatterton chose to see it as a plot by the Reclamation Service to monopolize all the water in the Basin and cheat Wyoming out of a large private development. Mondell, who had actually worked for two years in the General Land Office, tried to set him straight, but no amount of information could budge him from this conviction. Taking this line enabled Chatterton to pose as the defender of Wyoming's right to maximum development, while he searched feverishly for a way to climb down from the tree he had got himself stuck in. He worked his way around to the position that the State would allow the Reclamation Service to proceed with the Cody-Salsbury work only if the government would agree to segregate the Oregon Basin land. Since the Land Office had already decided to do just that, he was on safe ground. He chose to announce this shift in policy in a letter to George Holdrege, a week after the *Laramie Republican* editorially undermined his antigovernment positions.[41]

What Bill Cody himself was thinking while all this was going on is not clear. Leaving his Wild West show in England, he was spending the winter in America initiating his divorce suit.[42] He spent the last two weeks of November in Cody, at his ranch and probably hunting. When he left he was still talking of spending up to a million dollars on the North Side development; he was on his way east to put together a syndicate of American and English capital to finance the job. He then went to Cheyenne, while his press agents publicized a "gigantic" coal discovery near Cody and his plans to form a syndicate of wealthy Englishmen to finance a transportation company from Cody to Yellowstone Park. After conferring with Chatterton about his relinquishment, he moved on to Washington, where he dined on successive nights with Senator Warren and General Nelson Miles. Warren would certainly have tried to keep him thinking of federal reclamation of the Cody-Salsbury tract, but Miles was frequently mentioned as a major investor with Cody in one or another of his schemes. Cody was reported to have told the *Washington Post* that he was going ahead with his big development. In fact, the *Cheyenne Leader* reported a couple of weeks later that Miles would be president of a new $3,500,000 syndicate Cody had formed to develop his land; the paper specifically denied that Cody intended to relinquish his rights to the government. Like so many of Cody's press releases, this one was mostly fabrication, designed to keep the public convinced that he was the kind of man who got things done. However, General Miles did travel to Cody at the end of January, and Buffalo Bill's own newspaper, the *Enterprise*, talked in positive terms of the Colonel's rights to develop the land. A week later, it reported positively about federal development! No one seems to have known his mind very well.[43]

A shadowy group of investors, usually English, move through the history of these events and negotiations. In Cody and in Cheyenne at the end of 1903, Buffalo Bill spoke of them in the future tense; he was on his way east to get them engaged in his projects. In later years, when he was developing his own self-serving history of this period, he spoke definitely of them in the past tense: they had been with him and were fully ready to take on the project. These gentlemen never appeared in the present. No independent evidence shows that they had any existence outside the Colonel's imagination. He invoked them, with his flummery about multi-million dollar enterprises, to nurse the notion in the public mind that he was a capitalist of international consequence. It was never easy to penetrate the fog of unreality that Buffalo Bill could throw up around him, and those who, like Fenimore Chatterton, needed to believe found reasons to do that. A century later it is possible to see the "English investors" for what they were, props in a play the old showman was writing, one that never made it to a real stage.[44]

As the death of Governor Richards had shifted the political environment of this great irrigation enterprise, so another death altered the personal circumstances, and may have helped bring a year's uncertainty to an end. On January 30, 1904, Cody's daughter Arta died in Spokane. Facing the crisis of his marriage as he already was, this blow must have sapped vital energy from the old campaigner. Chatterton tried to encourage him to stay close to his London friends and be ready to take up the project, but he had no heart for it. Mondell and Warren, meanwhile, leaked word to the Wyoming press that the government was ready to devote $2,250,000 to begin construction of the great project, and as much more later. Chatterton attempted to enlist George Holdrege and the Burlington on his side, with his spurious arguments about Oregon Basin, but Holdrege took the opportunity to teach the acting governor a lesson in what was best for Wyoming. "Under the circumstances," he wrote, "it is of great importance for all interests that details should be arranged between the United States Government and the State . . . at as early a date as practicable."[45] He had also kept in close contact with Cody, and informed Chatterton that the Colonel was prepared to sign yet another relinquishment. A few days later, Cody told Chatterton directly that he was going to step aside, adding quixotically that he was going to Washington to see what he could do to get the Oregon Basin project through. He added, with apparent sincerity, "I cant see why the Government should try to hold that up."[46]

In order to make sure the matter was settled to his satisfaction, Holdrege sent his corporate attorney, Charles Manderson, to supervise the negotiations. This might explain why Cody's first 1904 relinquishment followed more or less the same form as the 1902 one, in that it returned his water right to the State. When they all gathered at Washington, Walcott and Newell suggested rather that Cody transfer his water right to the United States, thereby preserving the priority of May 1899, and giving the Reclamation Service senior rights to all other irrigation projects downstream of the Cody Canal. Wyoming water law, which the Reclamation Act pledged to obey, was based on prior appropriation. With the explosion of irrigation development along the Shoshone, priority of the water right was a consideration of great importance. From New York, Cody had mailed his relinquishment in the first form to the governor, and when he arrived in Washington the next day he learned what the government really wanted. He immediately sent a telegram to Cheyenne recalling and annulling his first relinquishment. Chatterton, predictably, balked at the request, and attempted once again to set up a bargaining situation over the Oregon Basin project. He also decided he needed to have his own representative at the closing of the deal, so he made plans to send the other member of the State Land Board, Thomas T. Tynan, the state superintendent of public instruction.[47]

In the end game that played out between February 15 and 24, there were players with markedly different motives, but the outcome seemed foreordained. Buffalo Bill surely knew in his heart that he could not handle this project himself, and government action gave him a way out with a good conscience. It surely was clear to him as well that in stepping aside he would be acting in accord with the wishes of the citizens of Big Horn County. At the same time, he took Chatterton's concern about Oregon Basin seriously enough to attempt to assure him there would be no problem there. Chatterton and Tynan were desperately trying to hold to a political course that was proving less and less tenable. Frank

Mondell and Francis Warren were attempting to insure that Wyoming got its fair share of the twenty million dollars Congress made available to initiate the reclamation program, and Warren was determined to squash the upstart Chatterton in the process. The Reclamation Service was trying to maximize their chances of success by getting the Cody-Salsbury project as far as possible on their own terms. In that, they were aided materially by the work of the Burlington Railroad people. Manderson was especially forceful in taking the lead and dragging the governor along: "If you insist on relinquishment to State you prevent action by Interior Dept. and work irreparable injury to Wyoming. Cody's telegram to you recalled and annulled relinquishment. You should return same to him without filing."[48]

Chatterton finally gave in, sending the relinquishment to Washington in the care of Senator Clarence Clark, another of Warren's rivals. Then he dispatched Tynan to Washington. First to last, Tynan was nothing but a fifth wheel, providing a cover for the acting governor's nakedness in the negotiation; his only function in Washington was to delay the conclusion everyone else had been working for. Finally, on February 24, 1904, the papers were signed, Buffalo Bill was off the hook, and Fenimore Chatterton was on his way out the door.[49] The big players—the railroad and the federal government—got the result they wanted. In the last analysis, it seems likely that Cody wanted this result as well. He almost certainly had lost his stomach for big irrigation developments, and he knew that local people wanted him to step aside. He may even have seen, as seems clear now, that his giving up of his rights made it much more likely that all those acres would one day be green and prosperous. Whatever his final motivation, it is from this angle of vision that a tinge of irony attaches to Buffalo Bill's name on the water system. Although it took a couple of generations, the federal reclamation people attached his name to a dam and a lake they had prevented him from building. Renaming the dam and the lake did, however, honor what they saw as his early dream for the valley.

It took a while for the last piece of the Cody-Salsbury puzzle to fall into place. When it looked as if he would have the Willwood land at his disposal, the acting governor started the Mormon colony on the Shoshone on a roller coaster ride. Before he had even communicated to the Wyoming delegation in Washington his intentions to cancel Cody's relinquishment, Chatterton wrote to Charles Welch, a leader of the Mormons in Cowley,

Shoshone Dam and Reservoir, west of Cody. Built by the United States Reclamation Service, 1904–1910, and named after Buffalo Bill in 1946, the centennial of his birth. Courtesy of American Heritage Center, University of Wyoming.

that he had prevailed upon Colonel Cody to relinquish his rights to the Willwood tract. This happened at the same time as Cody learned that the State of Wyoming expected him to take up once again the labor he thought he had handed off to the federal government. In light of Cody's repeated refusals to consider giving up that land, this strange piece of news could only mean he was truly exhausted with the big development scheme. Chatterton urged Welch to get busy and prepare a Carey Act filing for the tract in question. The Mormons were understandably elated.[50]

Although the land and water the Mormons wanted turned out to be legally and practically confused with land and water incorporated in the vast Oregon Basin segregation on the south side of the river, they persevered with their plans, as Chatterton urged. They applied for Carey Act segregation of 46,000 acres in all and set about designing their irrigation system. Over the course of 1904 and early 1905, after incurring expenses of approximately $1,500, and facing the possibility of legal confrontation with the Oregon Basin group, the Mormons were forced to conclude that it would not be as easy to incorporate that land into their colony as they had always assumed. In April 1905, they finally decided to abandon it and relinquish those Carey Act lands to the Reclamation Service. A small offshoot of the large Mormon colony had constructed a ditch and begun to cultivate about 3,000 acres on the far eastern end of the Cody-Salsbury land, and the negotiators of the settlement in 1905 asked only that these settlers (who had gone ahead without completing the permit process) be allowed to remain. Happy to have the larger prize, the government readily agreed to leave these people, on what was called the Elk Ditch, untroubled. By July 1905, the transfer of all but that tiny bit of the Cody-Salsbury segregation to the federal government was complete.[51]

CHAPTER ELEVEN

"I know thee not, old man"

Although he may have given up his big development dream with a feeling of relief, or even taken some pride in putting the good of the public before his own profit, Buffalo Bill did not simply put development and profit out of his mind and ride off into the sunset in 1904. The great, difficult, expensive work of damming and diverting the Shoshone River to irrigate the central valley he may happily have left to the federal engineers in the new Reclamation Service, but he still kept an eye out for opportunities that the federal enterprise might leave to an alert entrepeneur. In the pursuit of those opportunities, he relied, to his ultimate disappointment, on his friendship with men of power in Washington, in particular President Theodore Roosevelt.

It may seem obvious today that relinquishing his project to the Reclamation Service meant that Bill Cody would lose control of the design of it, but a century ago it was not obvious to him. We already have seen how he tried to use his influence with Acting Governor Chatterton in 1903 to convince the government engineers to follow his plan to take water out of the river high enough up in the Shoshone canyon so they could irrigate the land on the north side of the river opposite his little town. When he gave the Reclamation Service a copy of the Kelsey survey he wrote on its map, "Flume river at mouth of canyon and take the Mead survey," and further on, "This is the line."[1] He continued to push the High Line for years after he handed off to the government. At a dinner in Cody in December 1905 at the Irma Hotel, he told the assembled crowd that he had an understanding with the supervising engineer of the federal project, now named the Shoshone Project, that the High Line canal would be built by the end of the decade. The government had decided to start with a diversion dam and canal six miles below Cody, to open up the largest and easiest part of the project first, but the High Line plan would be built when that was done. Reclamation engineers present at the dinner agreed that such was their plan, saying only that they needed to have the income from the easier part before they could undertake the more difficult and expensive work on the High Line. In 1905 most parties seemed confident this scheme would work out.[2]

Of course, it did not work out. Construction and repayment problems bedeviled the Shoshone Project as they did all federal reclamation projects, and the High Line suffered a series of postponements. Bill Cody was increasingly upset as he saw his dream slipping away, as were others in town. In the fall of 1906, the Cody Club, a forerunner of the town's Chamber of Commerce, held a mass meeting to protest against the delay of the High Line canal. A letter from Buffalo Bill was read at the meeting, charging once again that the Reclamation Service had promised to build the High Line without delay and now they were reneging on that promise. Unable to get the answers he wanted from project engineers, Cody went straight to the top—to his friend, Theodore Roosevelt. Early in 1908, he spoke with the president personally, and then wrote to him, in hopes of getting help. The government was building a high dam in the canyon to store water for all the land they intended to irrigate, and Cody could see that the dam would make impossible the diversion canal he had envisioned for the land around Cody. He had been told of the Reclamation Service's plan to bore a tunnel through the canyon wall and take water out that way, but it apparently made no impression on him. He believed he had had an understanding with the government to build this canal when he gave up his rights. He even claimed that he only gave them up because the government could build a higher line, and therefore irrigate more land near Cody, than he could. He felt he had been tricked, and that the government was failing to carry out "that which was all but a written agreement."[3]

Cody dismissed the work on the lower section of the project, completed late in 1907, as "of no particular value in carrying out my plan and understanding," notwithstanding that those lands composed the major portion of his own Cody-Salsbury Carey Act plans. Cody's memory was a convenient tool, malleable to the needs of the moment. It is not entirely out of the question, however, that he really did expect the Reclamation Service to proceed first with the High Line. It may be recalled that the Cody Canal was initially envisioned as a grand, 200,000-acre south-side project, of which they only built the first stage, so it seems possible that he could have thought the same way about the north side. Whatever his ideas might have been, he did not like the way the Reclamation Service was proceeding now that they had control, and he sought to play on his friendship with Roosevelt to get his way. Presenting himself as one whose life had always had the single object of building up the West, he concluded, "I address this letter to you, Mr. President, in order that I may get justice.[4]

President Roosevelt sent Cody's letter on to the Reclamation Service before he replied. They reiterated the reasoning behind postponing the High Line canal, and emphatically denied that any understanding had ever existed with the Colonel. Their records indicated that their negotiations had primarily been with the State of Wyoming. Director Newell responded with bureaucratic finality. "We have a high regard for Colonel Cody as an entertaining companion and should be glad to do everything we can for him personally," he wrote. "He has, however, an apparently erroneous idea that something was promised him, or that there existed some understanding which has not been carried out. . . . Our people are very certain that no promises were made to Colonel Cody."[5] Over time and with some bitterness, the people of Cody came to understand that Buffalo Bill could not deliver the High Line and all its benefits. For several years, they wrote letters and held meetings. They regularly petitioned new secretaries of the Interior, but to no avail. It was not, in fact, until 1942 that the High Line—now known as the Heart Mountain Canal—was ready to deliver water (and then, ironically, only to the Japanese American Relocation Center at Heart Mountain, ten miles east of Cody). The land that Bill Cody had set his heart on was not opened to settlement until 1946.[6]

That letter about the High Line was by no means Cody's first attempt to bring his friendship with President Roosevelt into play to get his way with the Reclamation Service. Only a year after he relinquished his rights, he complained to the president that the Reclamation Service was developing plans that would deny him an opportunity to profit from a townsite he was planning on the edge of the first tract to be opened to settlement on the Shoshone Project. He had heard rumors that the government was going to build a town in the center of that tract, to which he took strong exception. He reminded Roosevelt that he was a pioneer, "and no one knows better than yourself what the pioneer has to contend with. I have spent nearly all that I possessed in opening up that country, making it possible for white men to live there."[7] When he gave up his Carey Act project, it was agreed that he could purchase some land along the railroad, at a point he called Ralston, about eighteen miles east of Cody, where he expected to build a town. Now he was aggrieved, and appealed directly to the president to "kindly see Mr. Newell and ascertain if he cannot lay out his Government town in some other place so that it may not interfere with the interests that I have there?"[8] Roosevelt replied immediately, saying he would refer Cody's letter to the Reclamation Service, and hoping it could be arranged to Cody's satisfaction. Newell responded a week later: he acknowledged Cody's townsite at Ralston and claimed innocence of any intent on the part of the government to build a town near to it.[9]

The right to purchase land under the proposed government canal and along the railroad line was the only concrete thing Bill Cody got in return for his relinquishment in 1904. In partnership with the Lincoln Land Company, he acquired 640 acres there, using land scrip purchased from a land company in Washington, D.C. that specialized in what are known as "lieu lands." Since 1891 the federal government had been setting aside forested land in the West as timber reserves, the nucleus of the national forest system. When it wanted to include a privately owned parcel of land in a reserve, it offered the owner the right to a similar-size parcel of public land elsewhere in *lieu* of the foregone land. The Aztec Land and Cattle Company had acquired rights in this way and sold them at a discount to the Collins Land Company, which in turn sold them to Cody and his partners. The land at Ralston was selected in the name of the Aztec Land and Cattle Company in November of 1904, and promptly conveyed to the Lincoln Land Company. Shortly after that, the Colonel must have heard the rumors circulating in Cody about plans for towns on the Shoshone Project.[10]

Buffalo Bill's Aztec Land and Cattle Company acreage adjoined an area of 220 acres taken up earlier by the Lincoln Land Company; when he entered into his long contest with the Reclamation Service over

Ralston, the partners controlled 960 acres in all. It seems likely that the Burlington people helped to persuade Cody to give up his big project by offering him half-interest in their townsites at Ralston and Corbett (halfway between Ralston and Cody, never developed). The size of the site may be taken as a measure of their hopes for Ralston; the Cody townsite, after all, was only 640 acres, and only half of that had been platted ten years after the founding. The Lincoln Land Company had also started a town called Garland, on the far eastern edge of the new Shoshone Project, eleven miles east of Ralston. It surely seemed reasonable to Cody that these towns would meet the needs of the project for trading centers, and the Lincoln Land Company, with a monopoly of townsites along their Big Horn Basin line, emphatically agreed. Cody thought he had set up at last a scheme that would actually make him some money in the colonization business.[11]

C. H. Morrill, president of the Lincoln Land Company, was an aggressive businessman. In the fall of 1905, he took advantage of a visit to Cody by H. N. Savage, the USRS supervising engineer for the Northern District, to press his case for exclusive townsite rights on the Shoshone Project. Morrill believed that it was right and proper for private interests to monopolize opportunities created by government initiatives like the Shoshone Project. Savage set him back by advancing a counter argument: there was a public good to be served, and the Reclamation Service was self-consciously dedicated to it. Where towns on the Shoshone Project were concerned, that would mean they would make no decisions until they had settlers in place, whose good would be their first consideration. Savage also made Morrill see that the Reclamation Service might well conclude that towns only five miles apart would better serve their settlers. They had already withdrawn land from homestead settlement at a point halfway between Garland and Ralston. At the conclusion of this meeting, Morrill had determined that it would be best for his company to sell off some of its land at Ralston. The railroad officials had done their best to bring the government into the Basin, apparently expecting to have their own way. They were learning that, as the government was paying the piper, they would want to call the tune.[12]

Not being blessed with the resources of the Lincoln Land Company, Bill Cody could not trim his sails to the new wind as quickly as they did. That winter he caught Savage in Cody and began to press his case for exclusive rights at Ralston. He told Savage that income from the sale of town lots at Ralston would be all he would ever get from the government for all his service, from the Civil War through Indian wars. Cody was en route to Washington to see his friend, President Roosevelt, in hopes of getting his way. Savage wrote Newell in Washington to inform him of his conversations, and to let him know that the people planning the Project had considered that a post office and other facilities accessible by railroad should probably be provided at five-mile intervals. Nor did they think it a good idea to turn over the site withdrawn in the center of the Project to the Lincoln Land Company, "notwithstanding a specific request has been received from them to do so." They were, however, planning a small reservoir along the main canal just above Ralston, which could provide water for Cody's town and the railroad there.[13]

President Roosevelt's daughter, Alice, famously married Congressman Nicholas Longworth on February 17, 1906. Preparations for another European summer tour with the Wild West kept Buffalo Bill from attending, but he made a dramatic impact by sending her as a wedding gift a silver inlaid saddle said to be worth $2,000. The president was so taken with it that he actually wrote Cody to thank him the day before the wedding: "I appreciate it, I think, as much as she does, for I was particularly glad to have her wedding day remembered by you."[14] There is no reason to doubt that the two men were good friends, but it seems obvious that such a gift, at a time when Cody was pressing hard for economic concessions in Wyoming, might carry other connotations. Buffalo Bill certainly thought it was important to his own future that President Roosevelt think fondly of him.

Cody had other friends in Washington. He and Congressman Frank Mondell shared an outlook on development in Wyoming, in addition to a large stable of mutual friends. Mondell had been present at the final negotiation leading to the relinquishment of Cody's rights to the Reclamation Service, and he stayed interested in the Shoshone Project. When the rumors of a government town on the project reached him in the summer of 1906, he wrote directly to Newell to ask if they were true. As Newell did not reply immediately, Mondell wrote again, inquiring more specifically: "I wish to express the hope that no townsite will be established within the reasonable sphere of the trade and influence of towns already established on the Shoshone Project."[15]

Newell's reply when it came was somewhat evasive. A temporary camp had been set up midway between Ralston and Garland; no decision had been reached about a town there, but it would be a good place. The decision would be made, of course, in the best interests of the project and its irrigators. Mondell's views as a congressman never strayed very far from those of the Burlington Railroad leadership, but in this case he was serving as well the interest of his friend, William F. Cody. He was also establishing in this correspondence the familiar triangular relationship by which powerful constituents used legislators to control executive branch bureaucrats who showed signs of independence.[16] Still, the Reclamation Service continued on its own course.

Cody had other issues to pursue with Newell and his men. Thinking about his townsite while touring Europe in 1906, he realized he had no water right certificate. Claiming to believe that the government would not allow him to take up land without also giving him water (although no land law ever in force would support that position), he asked Newell if he could expect to get a certificate: "You will readily see that the land would not be of any benefit to me whatever without water."[17] Newell initiated a conference of his engineers to attempt to discover if Cody had been promised water for his land at Ralston, and, of course, there was no record of any such promise. When Newell got around to replying to Cody, it was to tell him that his only recourse was to take water under the terms of the Reclamation Act. That would mean he would have to pay the same construction charges as any other settler, and could purchase a water right for no more than 160 acres, as that was the limit imposed by the Act.[18]

Newell's letter caught up with Cody in Germany, and prompted a three-page recitation of grievances once again directed to President Roosevelt. Cody forsook the "simple pioneer" line of earlier letters, and appeared here as the man who brought civilization to Wyoming and wanted nothing more than simple justice in return. He claimed to have laid out $25,000 on the Cody-Salsbury project (his first letter had mentioned $10,000, and a subsequent one $18,000) and to have been fully ready to develop the project when the government intervened. Although he did not claim a promise had been made regarding the water, he asserted again his understanding that he should have it, as the land was worthless without it. "It seems to me it would be bad faith on the part of the Government to refuse to let me have water after I turned my rights over to them without money and without price."[19] For twenty years he had poured every cent he could make into that country and had never got anything out of it. It did not seem a square deal to him that his land should be made worthless in this way. "What do you say?"[20]

Roosevelt responded immediately and personally to the letter. He gave Cody no reason to hope that he would be able to get water for more than 160 acres from a government ditch, but concluded, "If there is anything that can properly be done for you, I need hardly say that I shall be only too anxious to do it."[21] He then once again asked the Reclamation Service to send a report on the subject of this most recent complaint. There ensued another review of the relevant correspondence and another conference of the engineers, who at that point in the summer were spread all across the country. After more than a month of this, Charles Walcott submitted his report to the president. It was a familiar summation, and it did not offer any comfort to Buffalo Bill. Congress had passed an act in the spring of 1906 regulating the conditions under which townsites on Reclamation projects would be developed, and Ralston would have to meet those standards. In particular, this meant that no water would be provided at terms more favorable than those offered to agricultural settlers on the project. It would be no problem to supply Ralston with water, but it would have to be done according to law. Cody himself could have water for only 160 acres outside the townsite, on the same terms as any other settler.[22]

Even then, Cody could not let the matter rest. He kept after supervising engineer Savage throughout the following winter, when he was home from Europe. His partners, the Lincoln Land Company, also continued to push for water for the entire 960-acre tract they had at Ralston. The Reclamation Service continued to reject their demands, although they did respond favorably to a suggestion that Ralston be incorporated and make application for municipal water, but it does not appear that either Cody or the Lincoln Land Company followed up on that. Soon the matter of water at Ralston faded into insignificance.[23]

As they worked on the construction of the large central tract of land on the Shoshone Project, the Reclamation Service asked the Burlington to put in a siding halfway between Garland and Ralston for their construction camp, which they called Camp Colter. In the summer of 1907, as settlers began to take up land in that area, some enterprising merchants requested permission to set up shops at Camp Colter. Observing these developments, Bill Cody once again went right to the top, apparently set in his belief that for him the president could and would interfere with the orderly development of the project by the Reclamation Service. This time Roosevelt asked the secretary of the Interior, James Garfield, for a report on the situation. Garfield, of course, had to ask Walcott, so the effective reply was still that of the Reclamation engineers. Savage's planning from two years earlier had now attained a kind of inevitability. Camp Colter was more accessible for most of the settlers than either Garland or Ralston. "Apparently there must ultimately be a townsite" there, although no formal recommendation to that end had yet been made.[24] Interior did promise that Cody would be given an opportunity to present a protest if settlers did petition for a town there.[25]

The situation did not look good for Buffalo Bill, and it deteriorated further in October, when one of the merchants requested a post office at Colter and Secretary Garfield concurred. Mondell, still a soldier in the Cody-Burlington army, asked the secretary in December to take no action on mercantile leases at Colter until he could talk with him, to which Garfield replied that leases were already issued; he also reminded the congressman that his authority to do that was beyond dispute. Also in the fall of 1907, the Reclamation Service undertook to name the camp and siding, having learned that "Colter" was already in use elsewhere in the state. They actually submitted two names to railroad officials, asking them to choose between Powell and Newlands. The Burlington chose the former, associating thereby the future government-sponsored town with the patron saint of western irrigation. Major John Wesley Powell, former director of the United States Geological Survey, had trained all the leading figures of the new Reclamation Service, and they were no doubt pleased with the railroad's choice.[26]

Buffalo Bill held tight to his Ralston dream even as the ground began to shift beneath him. He wrote to President Morrill in Lincoln in January 1908 that he had spent a day there "and I am more impressed with the future of that town than I have ever been." He urged that the Land Company use its influence with the railroad to have a siding constructed and sleeping accommodations built. He also offered his observation that the people who were there were determined to stick. A few months later, however, a report by an agent of the Lincoln Land Company noted that the doctor and the largest merchant in Ralston were both leaving. The reporter offered his opinion that the government was discriminating against Ralston, and that the Reclamation Service was determined to have a town at Colter. He urged the company to do something to protect its investments at Ralston and Garland. Bill Cody's tack was to ignore the bad signs and try to keep the company engaged through force of his personality. In this situation, neither way offered much hope of success.[27]

Events had begun to cascade against Cody's hopes and dreams for Ralston. In February 1908, the project engineer at Powell requested authorization to prepare and file a plat of the town to enable the selling of lots. In May, he received the first petition from settlers and merchants that they be allowed to purchase lots in the new town. In June, H. N. Savage, responding to two petitions from entrymen on the project, requested from Washington the authority to subdivide a portion of the townsite and have lots appraised for sale. Cody and Mondell had made this otherwise routine matter so sensitive politically that Newell put the brakes on, telling Savage to hold off until Secretary Garfield could visit the site during a trip planned for August. Shortly after writing that letter, Newell received one from Senator Warren, attempting to bring to bear once again the influence of the Lincoln Land Company against the government town. Warren added a new wrinkle by requesting that the Reclamation Service headquarters be established at either Ralston or Garland. The letter from C. H. Morrill that he forwarded contained the most forthright statement of the Burlington's role in persuading Cody to give up his water right to the government, as well as the information that Cody was a partner in the development of Garland, in addition to Ralston. A great deal of power and influence converged on this small corner of Wyoming in the summer of 1908.[28]

Garfield made his trip to Wyoming late in July. He visited Cody and the Shoshone Dam under construction in the canyon, and then went up the new road to the east entrance to Yellowstone, staying at Buffalo Bill's new hotel at Pahaska, just outside the Park. He was accompanied by Congressman Mondell and several Reclamation people. Representatives of the Burlington interests took him on a tour of the townsites, although he did not stop at Powell. He endured more speeches on the matter of building the High Line canal at a dinner at the Irma Hotel. When he returned to Washington, he found another long letter from Bill Cody; he promised to give it careful attention, and then delayed his answer for five months.[29]

Cody's letter, dated July 27, was identified by the acting director of USGS as "the annual protest of W. F. Cody."[30] It contained the now familiar litany of complaint, listing all that he had done for Wyoming and all the money he had lost doing it. His hotels he ran at a loss; he had to sell Cody Canal shares at $10 per acre where private companies now got $30. He not only had had a company fully ready to go with the Cody-Salsbury scheme, he was to have received $75,000 in cash as the price of his concession to that company. This he selflessly gave up "to please the railroad officials and my neighbors." He hoped to get some of that back by developing Ralston; he had no idea "that the United States Government was ever going to dabble in town lots." He ended by asking Garfield's cooperation "in preventing a town at Powell, and making Ralston, the Headquarters of the Reclaimation [sic] Service, instead of Powell."[31]

As he postponed replying to Buffalo Bill, Secretary Garfield seemed to signal the Reclamation Service to proceed with their plans. Newell thought Garfield did not regard the matter of the Powell townsite as especially important. Newell took it upon himself to tell Senator Warren that Reclamation headquarters would remain at Powell, as that was the most efficient place from which to work. This action served as an administrative check to the senator, and the normal course of politics shook another pillar of Cody's support. Frank Mondell could count votes, and when he visited Powell with the secretary's party in July, he accepted a petition from a large group of entrymen on the project asking that the Powell townsite be opened. Probably seeing the future of the valley unfold before him, he told them he would be happy to use his influence with the secretary on their behalf. He had not yet abandoned Cody entirely, but he began to see that there was a double game to be played, and there was little Cody could offer against this pragmatic political calculation.[32]

In September, however, Garfield halted the process of opening up the new town. He was out of Washington most of that month, but made it clear to his acting secretary that he took a personal interest in the decision and had told Cody that he would investigate it personally when he returned in October. When he turned to the task he had a full file of letters and petitions, one from settlers around Powell asking for a town and one each from Garland and Ralston opposing it. Frank Mondell made one last attempt to swing the decision in Cody's favor, telling Garfield that "it is my knowledge and belief that Colonel Cody was given to understand when he turned over his Carey Act lands to the government that there would be no government townsite established in the vicinity of Ralston."[33] Senator Warren made another attempt, forwarding petitions from people opposed to Powell. Garfield's replies to these two gentlemen made it quite clear that he saw no reason to prohibit a townsite there if the settlers wanted one, and that he did not think this violated any understanding with Colonel Cody.[34] But still, he put off answering Cody's last letter.

Around Christmastime, Cody favored Garfield with a note, saying, "Please do not forget me regarding my townsite at Ralston." Excusing his tardiness by reference to the press of business, the secretary turned at last to the unpleasant but necessary task of telling Buffalo Bill some home truths. He rehearsed the history of the Cody-Salsbury project from the Washington point of view, emphasizing the uncertain progress of that work while Cody had it in hand and the desire of Wyoming officials to have it taken over by the federal government. "I cannot find that there ever existed any reason for assuming the slightest obligation, moral or legal, on the part of this Department to Cody and Salsbury for relinquishing any rights they may have had." With reference to Ralston, there was no record of any conversation about townsites at the time of relinquishment, and it seemed impossible that the engineers could have made any promises as they had at that time no authority to do anything in the way of townsites. It was entirely a matter for local settlers whether a town would be founded, as they would assume the burden of developing that country now. If they wanted a town midway between Garland and Ralston he could see no reason to object. He would not try to prevent a town from growing at Powell or try to force people to go to Ralston or Garland. "The profits to town owners should not weigh against the gain to the settlers."[35]

James R. Garfield, son of the assassinated president, was one of Theodore Roosevelt's new breed of elite public servants, a leader of the first generation of Progressive administrators in the federal government. He, with Gifford Pinchot and others, accepted and furthered the president's vision of a government actively identifying and pursuing the public good, a revolutionary concept in terms of the history of the federal government.[36] Bill Cody came of age in a different America, where the federal government took a narrow view of its responsibility to promote the general welfare, and all manner of men fattened off the government more or less as a matter of policy. He seemed unaware of the gulf growing between traditional and Progressive ideas of government as he kept after Roosevelt and Garfield to toss him his bone at Ralston. Garfield's January

1909 letter was direct and uncompromising, perhaps the most forthright communication of this new vision of government that Cody had ever seen. Cody's subsequent dealings with the Department of Interior reveal that he learned almost nothing from it.

Buffalo Bill's experience of the Old West injected another consideration into the debate over townsites on the Shoshone Project, one that not even Secretary Garfield ever brought up to him. Although he may have stopped drinking a few years earlier, Bill Cody still had a reputation as a bon vivant, and Cody was, by emerging middle-class standards, a wide-open town. The Irma Hotel was practically built around a magnificent cherry wood bar. There were more than a few saloons, where patrons could gamble as well as drink, and there was at least one thriving brothel. Both Ralston and Garland featured saloons, and settlers on the Project were said to reject farmsteads in the Garland neighborhood because they did not want their children to go to school near bawdy houses. The people who came to settle the Shoshone Project were in general a well-educated, upwardly mobile lot, determined to lead respectable, middle-class lives. These families wanted their own town so they could build schools instead of saloons.[37]

One of the new settlers wrote to Secretary Garfield that 90 percent of them would like to see a "covenant against intoxicating liquor" attached to their land.[38] The man who became the leading citizen of Powell in its early decades, S. A. Nelson, had come west from Iowa to live in Cody. He ran unsuccessfully for mayor of Cody in 1909 on a ticket favoring "law enforcement and such reasonable regulation of the saloon business as will give us the cleanest town possible."[39] After being painted with the Prohibitionist brush in the campaign, Nelson moved downriver and contributed his energy to building that kind of town from the ground up. He started a newspaper in Powell, having edited the *Enterprise* in Cody. His editorial in the second issue of the *Powell Tribune* argued forcefully that "the saloon must never enter Powell to blight its citizenship and work ruin to its varied and highly promising material interests."[40] The people of Powell were new citizens of a different West than Bill Cody had known; the distance from Powell to Garland or Ralston was not great, but the moral gap between them was large and significant. Cody was known to be pushing both Ralston and Garland; to people around Powell he was offering not just an outdated product but one that threatened their prospects for success in the New West. Nelson was sure that people moving into the Basin from the East would cast their lot with towns where families could live free of the taint of the saloon. In this they surely acted with the tacit approval of the educated professionals in the Reclamation Service.[41]

Within a few days of receiving Garfield's letter at Cody, the Colonel replied with yet another of his long, self-serving missives. First, he took all credit for introducing the Big Horn Basin to C. E. Perkins, president of the CB&Q. Then, he took credit in passing for getting Elwood Mead to survey the Basin and change the name of the river to Shoshone, and repeated his tale of having his project ready to go but graciously deferring to the wishes of the railroad and the people. He now included the charge that the Reclamation engineers were selling water rights only to land near Powell, in order to harm the outlying towns; H. N. Savage, by this account, had it in for Bill Cody personally. The malfeasance of Savage and his associates had resulted in land costs that were too high, and in exorbitant water charges for his town of Ralston. He ended by threatening an investigation to discover why water should cost double on the government project what it did under private enterprise.[42]

Several weeks later the Colonel must have reconsidered his earlier letter, for he sent the secretary another one of a far different tone. Perhaps he recognized that he had neglected to ask for anything in the first letter. Cody begged pardon for giving Garfield so much trouble. It was just that "being a pioneer of this country, having spent a fortune here in its development, besides being an old soldier of the Civil War and of the Indian campaigns, standing between civilization and savagery for many years on this frontier, I was in hopes of receiving a little benefit from the sale of town lots in Ralston, Wyo."[43] He was once again, as he had been with Theodore Roosevelt years earlier, the mendicant, the aging servant whose claim upon this one little thing would surely trouble no one. Garfield's last letter to Cody, just prior to leaving office along with Theodore Roosevelt, ignored the personal thrust of both of Cody's letters, taking care simply to note that the Reclamation Service was doing what it could to encourage settlement across the entire project, and had made particular provision for water at Ralston.[44]

Richard Ballinger succeeded Garfield as secretary of Interior in the Taft administration in March 1909. Buffalo Bill lost no time in attempting to take advantage of what he must have thought would be a change favorable to his interests. Early in April, he paid a call on Ballinger in his

Washington office to press his case for Ralston and against Powell. In February, Garfield had received a petition from virtually all the entry-men on the Shoshone Project asking that a town be established at the Powell site, and he approved the petition the same day it arrived. The Reclamation Service had proceeded with their plans. Although Ballinger was a conservative western businessman, one whom Cody must have expected to see things more his way, he did not hesitate to side with the Reclamation engineers. "Without very strong reasons being shown why the Government should not proceed with this townsite, I shall be disposed to confirm the action of my predecessor."[45]

As the great struggle between Ballinger and Gifford Pinchot later demonstrated, a change at the top could have a serious impact on the makeup and conduct of government bureaus, but that was an exceptional moment in the history of Progressive governance. In lesser affairs, partic-ularly where the issue was drawn between old style patronage politics and professional government in the public interest by civil servants, no new secretary would overturn the ongoing planning processes of those who worked for him. The behavior of the Reclamation Service and the secre-taries of the Interior in this matter afford classic instances of what we now see as the Progressive consensus that trained experts should have a central role in the making of government policy. Cody's behavior in 1909 in the matter of his hopes for Ralston marks him as a man of the old century, unable to see the times changing beneath his feet.

In the closing scenes of *Henry IV, Part II*, Shakespeare builds to the climax of his morality play involving Falstaff and Prince Hal. When word goes out that Henry IV has died and Hal has taken the throne as Henry V, Falstaff anticipates extravagantly that his friendship with the Prince will mean a great position at court and influence within the kingdom. Hal has given private signals throughout the play that he knows his new estate, when it comes, will mean cutting off the friends of his youthful dissipation. When first they meet and Falstaff lumbers toward the King expecting to be recognized as a friend and counselor, Henry stops him cold: "I know thee not, old man. Fall to thy prayers."

It may seem a long stretch from Henry V and Falstaff to Theodore Roosevelt and Buffalo Bill, but the pairings might help us understand the changes rung in this chapter. The fifteenth-century pair embodied a moral message about the responsibility of kings, drawn out in high drama because the fate of the monarchy depended upon everyone getting it right. No such fateful consequences hang upon the twentieth-century pair, but the lesson is quite similar. Roosevelt liked Cody and continued to like him, but he showed the mettle of one who understood the demands of modern government when he put Cody off, time after time, as the Colonel tried to play upon their friendship for his own ends. "I know thee not, old man" is perhaps too strong, but bouncing Cody time and again into the grinding bureaucratic processes of the Department of the Interior must ultimately have had the same effect as "Fall to thy prayers." The issue here was between government by cronies and the emergence of a professional administration in places like the Interior Department; Buffalo Bill, like Falstaff before him, stood on the wrong side of an important divide. And at the risk of overstating the parallel, the people of the Shoshone Valley who crushed Cody's townsite dreams in Ralston and Garland, were sending the same message. Here the divide was between an Old West they saw as undisciplined and their idea of a New West that could be made productive so long as rationality and self-control, primary middle-class virtues, held sway. Once again, Buffalo Bill was on the wrong side of the divide.

Cody's frustrated dream of developing a town on the Shoshone Project was not his only latter-day frustration with the Reclamation Service. As the Service expanded their planned dam and reservoir in the canyon above Cody, they set about purchasing the land that would be flooded. Neither of Cody's major ranches was threatened by the dam, but he owned two parcels totaling 240 acres that would be under the reservoir. The first sale went through without any difficulty, although it took the government close to two years to pay out. The second transaction did not go as smoothly. Although the land in question had never been part of the Cody Canal segregation, Interior Department attorneys developed a concern that its title might be clouded by a bond issued by the Cody Canal Association, and required the Reclamation Service to procure a release of the trust deed accompanying that bond issue. The amount of money was not especially large, and the time delay in this case only a year, but Cody's attorney took an egregiously outraged tone in his letter to the secretary of the Interior, exaggerating both the delay and the inconvenience to his client. Significantly, he wrote to Secretary Ballinger in the summer of 1910, after Cody's hopes at Ralston had been finally dashed. That perhaps explains the aggrieved tone of the letter. And it is not out of the question that $3,900, the amount of money at issue, could have seemed important to a man as strapped as Cody was in those years. Whatever the feelings involved, we cannot overlook the small irony that the bond issue that complicated this business for Cody was itself made necessary by the dismal condition of the canal that he and his partners handed over to the settlers in 1908.[46]

Buffalo Bill withdrew gradually after 1910 from significant engagement in governmental affairs. As a case in point, take the problem of Cody's municipal water supply. The Shoshone Dam was completed in January 1910 and began filling at once. The town of Cody depended upon the river for its water supply, with a system in which water was pumped from the river to a tank on a hill above town and thence distributed to houses and businesses. It had a state water right, and the Reclamation Service allowed sufficient water through the dam to meet that obligation, but it soon became apparent that quality of water, not quantity, was going to be an issue. In the first year there was a moderate amount of unhappiness as the detritus of abandoned farms and ranches under the reservoir showed up in the river and thence in the municipal water supply. That problem was superseded by a much more serious one in the following year, as the Reclamation Service allowed the dam to empty completely so they could work on some valves. The water that ran past Cody was muddy and filthy, unhealthy in the extreme. City government tried to get relief by haranguing the secretary of the Interior. William L. Simpson, town attorney and the progenitor of Wyoming's most famous political family of the later twentieth century, sent a nine-page letter to the secretary in August of 1911. Editorials and news articles in the Cody newspaper lamented the situation, casting blame on the perfidy of the Reclamation Service.[47]

The outcry from Cody got some attention in Washington, but not the result citizens wanted. A few years earlier, with help from Congressman Frank Mondell, the town had succeeded in having a sixteen-inch pipe inserted in the Shoshone Dam, from which they had hoped to draw a water supply. Town leaders had, however, been unwilling to bear the costs of constructing a main line eight miles down the river and then pay the government an annual charge for the water. They were already angry at the Reclamation Service for insisting on payment for the water, and the pollution of the river seemed too much. The townsmen seem to have hoped that the government would give in and let them have the water if they made enough noise. Nothing like that happened, of course, and as a result a second act played out in 1912. This time, it was begun with a long and barely coherent petition authored by Simpson, mailed off in April. More or less as a cover for the petition, Buffalo Bill wrote a paragraph "cheerfully" endorsing the petition and vouching for the accuracy of its descriptions, "as I have been here and investigated the situation." This effort produced a visit to Cody by a board of engineers who looked into the situation in June. They decided that the Reclamation Service could stop draining the reservoir at the end of the year, and that would take care of the problem. The solution was not completely satisfactory to the town, as it stopped far short of providing them with the supply from the dam for which they had been angling. Like most of Cody's previous letters to the Reclamation Service, this one seems to have had little or no effect.[48]

Nevertheless, Buffalo Bill remained the principal fount of information on Reclamation matters in Cody. While tempers were hot over the water supply issue, the town held its nearly annual dinner at the Irma in honor of their namesake. An address from the Colonel was always the centerpiece of these evenings. In the course of hammering the government for the ills his town was suffering from the big dam, he turned once again to the alleged betrayal that followed his relinquishment of the Cody-Salsbury project in 1904. Now he claimed that he and his shadowy group of English investors had spent nearly $100,000 on it before the government took it over. The government had made and broken many promises, including the one to irrigate the land around Cody first. Without the High Line ditch, the dam was useless—worse than useless when dust storms and polluted water were taken into account. This story became the orthodox account around Cody, reinforced by further comments from Buffalo Bill and repeated editorials. A few months later, in response to a question about the High Line canal, Cody said, "I feel toward the Reclamation Service as I always have. When a man gets into it he thinks he is running it all." When supervising engineer Savage left the Reclamation Service late in 1914, the *Enterprise* sent him on his way with a volley of recriminations, reciting in detail the list of his misjudgments and misdeeds that had brought misfortune to the town.[49]

In the last year of William Cody's life, the Wyoming Press Association convened in Cody. William L. Simpson was editing the *Enterprise* at the time, and he was a vocal and determined opponent of the Reclamation Service. He solicited a telegram to the Press Association from Buffalo Bill, who was on tour in Connecticut. No doubt following a suggestion

from Simpson, Cody charged the Association to use its influence to get
the water out of the dam (he called it a "monumental folly") and onto
fertile ground. Simpson clearly hoped that bringing in this big gun and
talking up the High Line canal with his colleagues from around the
state would jar loose the federal funds necessary to get that construction going. This was only sound and fury, signifying nothing, but it
shows the persistence of ideas of betrayal among the Cody elite. Finally,
it may not be too much to say that the continued poisonous relations
between this corner of Wyoming and the national government owe
something to Buffalo Bill's failure to deal intelligently with the federal
government, illustrated time and again in the self-serving stories he told
himself and his townsmen.

CHAPTER TWELVE

New Work for a New Century

Thoroughly established as a celebrity before he went into the development business, Buffalo Bill naturally used the one to further the other.
He brought Cody to the nation first through the ingenious device of
painting scenes of the upper Shoshone River country on the backdrops
of the Wild West show's stage sets. Advertising brochures for the Cody
Canal were available at every stop, and the Colonel took to speaking of his
love for the Big Horn Basin in newspaper interviews across the country.[1]
He was very free with newspapermen, and provided a dependable supply
of good copy for them. When he sat down to give an interview he told
great stories, of which he was the hero, and newspapers—building
upon decades of public acclaim for the Wild West—gave him a lot of
space. When he returned to America from Europe in 1903, he stopped
off in New York. A man from the *New York Tribune* met him in his hotel
and Cody gave him about six column-inches on his life in Wyoming.
The newspaper printed it under the heading, "Why Colonel Cody likes
Wyoming." The Big Horn Basin was, of course, a little corner of heaven,
made so by the vision and commitment of one William F. Cody. This
kind of journalism, along with broadcast media, helped to create a
relationship between the big city and the far corners of the country.
When he returned to New York with his show in 1907, after a four-
year absence, the final episode of the production was "a holiday at the
Colonel's ranch in Wyoming."[2] He never missed an opportunity to spread

word of Wyoming wherever he went, but the connection he seemed to work hardest to establish was that between Cody and New York City.

As he moved his off-stage life to Wyoming, Buffalo Bill returned to an identity he had more or less left behind when he permanently abandoned scouting for the army after 1876. During his scouting years he had developed the skills that would qualify him as a "white Indian," a figure famous in American lore and literature as one who bridged the "savage" and the "civilized" worlds. Possessed of the ability to track, hunt, and fight like an Indian, these figures devoted themselves to the service of white society. In some incarnations they were troubling figures, too close to primitivism to make white Americans comfortable. Even the archetype, Daniel Boone, may have crossed the comfort line. Davy Crockett did not, and he lived in legend after dying at the Alamo. Buffalo Bill Cody, with boosts from the dime novelist E. C. Z. Judson (Ned Buntline) and General Philip Sheridan, eventually won a place in the homes of Americans that none of his predecessors could have dreamed of. The effort of sustaining the Wild West show over decades, however, distanced him from the root experience of this particular class of men, hunting in the wilderness. In the Big Horn Basin, Cody found an arena where he could once again live wild (more or less). He also discovered, in America's Gilded Age, that a new way of living, with railroads running to every corner and excess wealth seeking new avenues of expression, presented opportunities for entrepeneurs with his package of skills.[3]

Cody started to explore these possibilities even before he entered upon his Big Horn Basin ventures. In 1892, John W. Young, a son of Brigham Young, enlisted his help in a scheme to create a great wilderness hunting preserve, featuring suitably high-toned accommodations for European aristocracy, on the Kaibab Plateau north of the Grand Canyon. In late November of that year, he led a party of English aristocrats and military men on a long and difficult ride from Flagstaff to Kanab, hunting along the way. Prentiss Ingraham, the playwright and hack novelist who had been associated with Cody since 1879, went along to keep New York readers informed of the company's activities, and Cody brought along a photographer from North Platte to take publicity views. As it turned out, the Englishmen in the group, who were going to bring visibility and probably some financing to the enterprise, concluded that the Kaibab was rather too remote to become the kind of destination hunting experience their countrymen would enjoy. Nothing came of this effort but a good hunt.[4]

Cody's personal connection to New York reached back before the days of the Wild West, and owed more to his reputation as a hunter than as a showman. By way of his famous "Ten Days on the Plains" hunt in 1871, and his 1872 hunt with Grand Duke Alexis of Russia, Cody established a high profile among the rich and famous of America and Europe who wanted to add North American big game to their trophy rooms.[5] In both of these cases, he benefited from the patronage of General Philip Sheridan, who made it part of his mission as commander of the army's Department of the Missouri to provide accommodations for wealthy eastern hunting parties. The 1871 hunt was described in detail by one of the participants, New Yorker Henry Eugene Davies, in a private publication intended only for those who had taken part in the expedition. Cody himself publicized the hunt to a much wider audience in his 1879 autobiography. Both accounts reveal how the young scout—he was only twenty-five at the time—worked to present himself as the beau ideal of the American hunter/guide. The hunt itself, as well as the subsequent advertisements and the fame that attached to his participation, especially in the 1872 hunt, helped to launch Buffalo Bill's career as a showman while establishing his public profile as a wilderness guide and hunter.[6]

By 1892, Bill Cody had devoted himself more or less exclusively to his show business for more than fifteen years, but early in the 1890s he began to recover those early frontier roles. When the Burlington Railroad arrived at Sheridan, Buffalo Bill was right behind them. In addition to operating the Sheridan Inn and a livery and transport business, he set up a business taking excursion parties of easterners into the Big Horn Mountains, his first venture into the tourist trade on his own.[7] Sensing the opportunity that Wyoming presented, he turned to self-promotion. In 1894 there appeared in *Cosmopolitan* an account titled "Famous Hunting Parties of the Plains," authored simply by "Buffalo Bill." It was a review of the supposed exploits of such famous hunters as Sir George Gore, Lord Adair (the Earl of Dunraven), Sir John Watts Garland, and the Russian Alexis. The historical parts of the piece, in which Cody was not himself present, are nothing more than recitations from other publications or rehashings of campfire legends. In parts in which he was present, the accounts are lively and interesting, especially when he turns to the hunt of the group he called "the New Yorkers," the hunt described in *Ten Days on the Plains*. Cody narrates an experience of humor, danger (the hunt took place where Indians were not reliably controlled on their reservations), violence and the excitement of the chase, all of which were counterpointed with highlights of luxury. He writes of waiters in evening dress and of French cooks, of floored and carpeted tents, and other marks of conspicuous consumption: "For years afterward travellers and settlers recognized the sites upon which these camps had been constructed by the quantities of empty bottles which remained behind to mark them." Cody concludes that, personally, he had never "enjoyed anything more than the New York party."[8] His new friends had invited him back to New York City, where he had never been before, and his relationship with the great city grew on that foundation. In fact, the article itself, which devotes twice as much space to this one trip as to any of the others, may best be understood as a kind of advertisement, an attempt to revive the memory of this particular kind of eastern venture into the West in the minds of latter-day New Yorkers. Here was a new kind of white Indian, one who could provide a packaged wilderness experience for eastern hunters, of whom there were a great many more than there had been twenty years earlier.[9]

The idea of a game preserve, where rich men from the East and Europe might come to shoot, stayed with Buffalo Bill after the Utah enterprise came to nothing. Such preserves had been a common element of the American hunting scene in the early nineteenth century, but by the 1890s they had for the most part been superceded by the rise of middle-class individualist sport hunting.[10] Undeterred by the anti-democratic character of hunting clubs, and drawn by the possibility of attracting men of wealth to his new Wyoming colony, Cody by the fall of 1896 was in conversation with Wyoming state engineer Elwood Mead about the possibility of setting up such a sporting operation along the upper Shoshone. The slaughter of big game in Wyoming, which in these very years was forcing the legislature to pass the state's first game laws, might be thought to give some color of conservation to Cody's plan, but the use of the term "Game Preserve" did not disguise from anyone that the game was to be preserved for the exclusive use of those who formed the club.[11]

Among Mead's responsibilities was chairing the State Land Commission, which managed the leasing of public land given to the state to provide endowment income for public schools, old soldiers' homes, and similar public institutions. In December of 1896, the Commission still had 125,000 acres unselected for lease and apparently eligible for this kind of use. In order to acquire a lease, Cody needed to show that he would improve the land—that is, fence it—and be willing to renew at the end of the first lease period. On such a showing, Mead promised to favor Cody's plan. He professed great interest in the plan, and thought the place Cody had chosen was not to be matched. He considered the plan to "have great interest and value both here and elsewhere."[12]

As with the business of the Shoshone Irrigation Company, Buffalo Bill depended upon the cooperation of state officials and attempted to impress them and employ them toward his own ends simultaneously. In January 1897, he confidently asserted to Mead that "the Game Preserve is a go." William Astor Chandler was to be president, and Clarence MacKay, son of John W. MacKay (the discoverer of the Comstock Lode in Nevada), vice-president. He promised a full list of members as soon as it could be printed, and he wired Governor DeForest Richards to get together with Cody's attorney in Cheyenne to prepare the form of the lease. He then asked Mead if he might be coming to New York soon, perhaps even the next week. Cody wanted to arrange a meeting with "the gentlemen of the Game Preserve" for him: "by your coming now I think it would clinch matters."[13] Here are contradictory sides of Buffalo Bill the entrepeneur. This business is "a go" but by the end of the letter, matters still need to be clinched, and he needs some help to get that done.

Bill Cody's enthusiasm led him to overstate his accomplishments and to outrun colleagues whose habits were to build on something more substantial than the promoter's vision. He was never the man to keep the details of his business in order, but he always seems to have thought that if he dropped enough important names (General Nelson Miles was a favorite) officials would fall in line. In a typical last-minute flurry, Cody wired Mead two days before the Land Commission was scheduled to meet to see what he had to do to get his application in. He had been fully informed by both Mead and Governor Richards that the State could consider his Game Preserve plan only if he would agree to pay the going rate for leasing of grazing land, five cents per acre, guaranteed for twenty years by the corporation formed to operate the Preserve, and to construct $50,000 worth of improvements. Cody had none of this in place when the board met in March 1897, and consequently missed out entirely on the land selection process. Mead held out as a kind of consolation the possibility that the state would get 300,000 more acres to lease. Cody seized upon it, and quickly began to imagine that they would be able to get a larger tract for the Game Preserve under the additional grant, but those hopes led to nothing.[14]

The idea, however, died hard in Bill Cody's conception of what he was doing in Wyoming. The Shoshone Irrigation Company brochure, rewritten in 1898 and continued in use for several years thereafter, included pictures of Cody out in the woods with his rifle and horses, one of them captioned "Selecting Site for Club House, Game Preserve." Whatever substance there might have been to the idea of the Preserve had disappeared in the spring of 1897, and the accompanying text speaks only about the facilities for hunting and packing that one could hire from W. F. Cody, and tours through the mountains and Yellowstone on his horses, mules, and wagons.[15] The brochure shows Cody's imagination balanced uneasily between the idea of a patrician elite club and the democratic reality of outfitting Everyman to be a hunter. Ultimately, Buffalo Bill could go either way, but circumstances soon showed him that only the democratic way was going to succeed.

Cody's *Cosmopolitan* essay of 1894 took an old-fashioned stance with regard to the slaughter of America's big game animals. Not only did Cody retail at face value the boasts of early hunters about the prodigious numbers of bison, elk, and deer they killed, but he stated simply and uncritically that the loss of these animals was an unavoidable consequence of the advance of American civilization. Within a few years, he began to shift his ground on the matter of preservation of game. As noted above, he first took up the idea of setting aside large areas of the mountains as hunting preserves for his wealthy and aristocratic clients. But local people objected ferociously to the very idea of game preserves, and looked askance at the creation of the Yellowstone Timber Reserves around the Park as possibly leading to the exclusion of local men from the forests.[16] Steering a course between local popularity and his own social and economic interest, Cody found himself moving inexorably to a more modern position on the matter of big game management.

His first public statement, in 1901, came, fittingly, in a New York newspaper. In January of that year the *New York Tribune* announced that Buffalo Bill had formed a hunting club headquartered at his ranch in Wyoming. "The first outing will be in the autumn of 1901, and among the guests will be Colonel Roosevelt, General Miles, and should he come to America to attend the yacht race, the Prince of Wales will be asked to participate."[17] That was standard press-agentry, reminding the readers how important a man the Colonel was at the time he was busy promoting his Cody Military College. The piece was probably written by Cody's publicists, since he is given sole credit for the founding of the club. In fact, it was a community effort, and was located in the town of Cody, not at Buffalo Bill's ranch. George Beck, whose name appeared in no New York press releases, was the president, and all of the Shoshone Irrigation Company directors were members.[18] Although Cody did his best to give the Club an aristocratic tone, it was nothing more than a gathering of individuals, mostly local, and involved no exclusive rights to land or game, as his first idea would have done.

Later that year, however, Cody turned to the theme of game protection in a more serious publication. He acknowledged that wild game had been devastated by unregulated hunting, but asserted that the passage of game laws in most western states would have the effect of saving populations of all except the bison. "Most of the Eastern men who go to Wyoming for the shooting are strongly in favor of the rigid enforcement of the law," he went on, and they were required to employ a local guide to make sure the game was not destroyed.[19] He also took the opportunity to promote the Big Horn Basin and his own shooting club. "This club contains many distinguished sportsmen. Vice-President Roosevelt is a member, and Colonel William Astor Chandler, and Clarence Mackay, and a number of foreign noblemen." The club's fall hunt would be organized competitively among teams of hunters, the object being not to bring in the most game but the best trophies. "That club, we expect, will be a missionary society, and will help to impress the idea that quantity of game is not the main point for the true sportsman to consider."[20] The governor of Wyoming, DeForest Richards, was also a member of the club. Although he did not expect to attend the hunt, he ordered his state game warden to have a strong force in the area, to be sure to collect state license fees.[21]

Most of the particulars about the club were made up out of whole cloth, but taken altogether, they make clear that Cody's ideas about hunting were undergoing a kind of transformation. The years bracketed by Cody's publications quoted here form the heart of the period identified by some scholars as the transformation of American attitudes toward big game hunting and game preservation. James Trefethen and John Rieger give most of the credit to the Boone and Crockett Club, founded in 1887 by Theodore Roosevelt and George Bird Grinnell, but Trefethen goes on to point out that, by 1915, it was just one of many such organizations. Trefethen mentions in particular the Camp Fire Club, which Cody joined in 1903, as one of the important organizations in bringing about this change of attitude. Game laws in the minds of these men served principally to combat poaching and market hunting, to preserve shooting for "sportsmen." The Boone and Crockett Club, according to Rieger, emphasized a code of sportsmanship enjoining a respect for wild game as an important part of American life.[22]

There is a comfortable illusion in this notion of sport hunting that has recently been exposed by a younger generation of scholars. Louis Warren, for instance, has argued that local elites in the West, immigrants to the hunting areas themselves, moved to make the land and its game "to a significant degree the property—or the privilege—of a national middle- and upper-class tourist public."[23] Buffalo Bill fits the model of the immigrant elite perfectly. Once he abandoned the idea of his shooting preserve, he could clearly see that there was an economic future for those who were in a position to mediate between the hunters and the game in a state-regulated environment. He and his partners in the founding of Cody began to lobby state government for strong game laws. Cody himself agreed to sign the bond for his man, John "Reckless" Davis, to become a state game warden on the South Fork.[24] Although opposed to poachers and "pot hunters," Buffalo Bill and his elite hunting friends were themselves participating in a commodification of Wyoming's big game on a more rarefied level. The hunting of game thus became a part of the general incorporation that the spread of wealth and power was forcing upon the far corners of the West. It does not materially detract from this point to note that market forces and popular habits emerging in the years after the First World War reasserted the right of ordinary people to join in the hunt, preventing the ultimate aristocratization of hunting in the West.[25]

The life I love. Camp head of
Shoshone River Wyo. Nov. 20ᵗʰ 1901.
W.F.Cody

A famous Buffalo Bill hunting party up the North Fork, near where he would build
Pahaska, in the fall of 1901. The inscription, "The Life I Love," is in Cody's own hand. The
Old Scout himself is seated with his back against a tree on the right side of the picture.
Courtesy of Buffalo Bill Historical Center, Cody, Wyo.; P.69.1061.

From the first year of the Cody Canal project, the Colonel initiated a
custom of inviting a few friends to accompany him to Wyoming at the
conclusion of the show season (usually in November) to spend a week
or two hunting, either up the North Fork or up the South Fork of the
Shoshone. An impressive roster of wealthy eastern businessmen, prominent military men (including Generals Nelson A. Miles and Leonard
Wood) and political figures traveled through Cody nearly every fall from
1895 to 1915. Cody apparently planned to take Theodore Roosevelt into
the backcountry in 1902, but the president had to cancel. Roosevelt's
nephew accompanied George Bleistein and his sons in 1903, but Cody
was in Europe and Bleistein went out with George Beck.[26] In fact, by
1903, men were traveling to Cody from Europe and New York and
Chicago to hunt without any expectation of going out with Buffalo Bill
himself. The Duke of Roxburgh hunted up the South Fork in October

of that year with two men who worked for Cody, and had a great time. "I know your townsman, Col. Cody, and think him a royal good fellow," he told the newspaper. "My people have a great regard for the Colonel and look upon him as a wonderful man. My experience has been so pleasant that I shall return in the future and have another hunt."[27]

The Colonel, of course, continued to hunt and to bring friends, although it is sometimes hard to know just which friends they were. In 1906, he returned unusually early to Wyoming. After the customary celebration of his return, he set off up the North Fork to Pahaska around October 15 with a large party. The local paper mentioned only the Oglala chief Iron Tail; Cody's old friend from Deadwood, Mike Russell; and a couple of men from Chicago and Omaha. George Beck, who has left an account of a trip (without the benefit of a clear date), says it was a big outfit, but named only the same men the newspaper did.

The party set off from Pahaska to cross the divide into the upper Yellowstone River country, known as the Thorofare. Caught by a great snowstorm, with as much as three feet of snow, they made camp with difficulty. As soon as the weather cleared, they persevered in their hunting, eventually making their way down to the Yellowstone. Beck recalled that, after four or five days on the river, Cody awoke to discover they were out of whiskey, so he and one of his men struck out for the TE (about two days away). Beck was left to bring in Iron Tail and the rest. When next Buffalo Bill was heard from he was in Cody, on November 1. "He has enjoyed his outing very much and is feeling well."[28]

Alongside the matter-of-fact local newspaper and the insider tales of George Beck, the notice of this trip that appeared in New York gives a flavor of the feeling for Bill Cody in the East. It was not front-page news, but on page eight of the *New York Tribune*, beneath a headline, "Fears for 'Buffalo Bill's' Party," there ran a thrilling current of alarm. The story was dated October 29, from Omaha, the last outpost of civilization on the way to Cody, and the party was now represented to consist of sixteen well-known European hunters and three Indian guides. They had sent word a few days into the trip that everything was fine, but had been out of communication since the great blizzard overtook them. "Unless they are heard from within a day or so a relief party will be organized."[29] We cannot know where so much misinformation originated, and it does not much matter. A newspaper story that combines aristocracy, celebrity, and danger in this way, connecting the present (in the East) with the past (in the West), gives us some idea of the power of the symbols with which Buffalo Bill was associated, and which he manipulated to his own benefit and that of his namesake town.

Important as he was, Bill Cody was by no means alone in working this change in the Big Horn Basin. Perhaps the most influential individual in bringing eastern aristocracy to this corner of Wyoming was Abraham Archibald Anderson, a Paris-trained New York painter. Possessed of considerable personal wealth, with a large Manhattan studio, he moved in the highest New York society. Anderson visited Wyoming to hunt in the late 1880s, and some time around 1890 acquired land and built the nucleus of his famous Palette Ranch on the upper Greybull River, one divide south of the Shoshone. He began the practice of inviting hunters and artists out to his ranch before Cody had imagined building a town in the wilderness. He personally brought emerging national standards of game preservation—and their particular commodification of big game— to northwestern Wyoming. One of the most famous of his visitors was Ernest Thompson Seton, who dedicated *The Biography of a Grizzly* (known informally as the "History of Wahb," the name he gave the bear) to the memory of days spent at the Palette. In 1915 Anderson brought the mayor of New York City to hunt bear with him. In 1897 he had joined with thirty-two other men to form the Camp Fire Club in New York; in addition to Seton, other particularly notable charter members were Dan Beard, cofounder of the Boy Scouts of America, William T. Hornaday of the New York Zoological Society (savior of the American bison, an ironic colleague for Buffalo Bill), and William E. Coffin. All of these men were outdoorsmen and hunters, and the Camp Fire Club quickly became one of the major organizations in the nation dedicated to game preservation.[30]

It is not clear just when Bill Cody and Anderson first met. Anderson included in his memoirs the full text of a 1903 letter to him from Cody, which is couched in fairly formal terms. They probably became friends and colleagues around that time. When Cody was admitted to nonresident membership in the Camp Fire Club in 1903, his address was listed "care of A. A. Anderson, Cody, Wyo." Since the Wild West was in residence in London at that time, Anderson probably took care of these details for Cody. Only males over twenty-one were eligible for membership, "and those only who have camped in the wilderness and are successful hunters, or painters, or sculptors of big game." Cody was quite well-qualified, of course. It is possible he was invited to give some frontier cachet to the meetings, although it is not clear how many of these he attended. At Hornaday's invitation, he appeared at a pioneer dinner given in New York in December 1909 by George Pratt of the Pratt Institute; the dinner was not a function of the club, but it was through Cody's club connection that Pratt (also a member) had him invited. He also attended a special meeting in January 1910, where game protection was the topic and Gifford Pinchot was honored for his service; of all that was said and done at the meeting, the *Times* chose to reprint one of Cody's Theodore Roosevelt stories the next morning.[31]

The Camp Fire Club produced at least one connection of great personal importance to Bill Cody and great general importance to the Cody country and the state of Wyoming. This was the acquaintance with William Robertson Coe, and it was also mediated by A. A. Anderson. Coe, a prominent man on Wall Street, who was married to a Standard Oil heiress, was far and away the wealthiest of Cody's New York connections. He joined the Club in 1908, the same year he took his first trip to the Big Horn Basin to hunt with Anderson. As recorded in the Club records, it was quite a successful hunt. His party killed four grizzlies and two elk, Coe taking one of each. Coe was impressed with the country and let Anderson know he would like to buy some land there. The next year Anderson told him that Cody was looking to sell some land. In the winter of 1909, he invited Coe to the annual dinner of the Camp Fire Club, seating him next to Cody at table. The next day they met to work out the sale of the Carter Ranch. Since Coe was not familiar with the area, he loaned Cody the amount of the purchase price and took an option for a year, waiting until he could go west to see what he was buying. He did know that Frederic Remington had stayed there and painted. In the fall of 1910, Cody arranged for John "Reckless" Davis to take Coe out on a hunt up the South Fork, and he first saw the Carter Ranch. He liked it, and paid Buffalo Bill a total of $33,000 for the ranch and the associated state grazing lease.[32]

The sale of the Carter Ranch, which Cody had told Coe was actually worth $100,000 (and for which Cody had paid only slightly more than $3,000 for the deeded portion), brought Buffalo Bill some desperately needed cash at a time when his mine in Arizona was beginning to bleed money. More importantly, it brought to Cody and to Wyoming one of the state's most important philanthropists of the twentieth century. Beginning with the gift of a $1,000 clock for the tower on the new Park County courthouse in 1911, and continuing through the funding of the Buffalo Bill Historical Center at his death, Coe gave generously to Buffalo Bill country for more than forty years. In addition to his munificence to Yale University, he also donated a new library and endowed the fledgling American Studies program at the University of Wyoming. The Coe family that remained in Wyoming is part of the heritage formed in the early days of the century by Buffalo Bill's metropolitan reach.[33]

Another A. A. Anderson connection resulted in what might well have been Cody's most famous Wyoming hunt. Anderson spent a great deal of time in Europe, where he became acquainted with Prince Albert of Monaco. The Prince was something of a sportsman, and the two of them arranged for Albert to visit the Palette Ranch to hunt for bear and elk in the fall of 1913. As fate would have it, Cody's Wild West show, which he was operating in partnership with Major Gordon ("Pawnee Bill") Lillie, crashed abruptly in July of that year, was foreclosed for a printer's debt and sold at auction.[34] Like it or not, the Colonel had some time on his hands.

Buffalo Bill at first saw an opportunity to return to Wyoming to see his ranch in the summer for the first time. Then, however, he got into conversation with some filmmakers about producing movies of the Wild West and historical accounts of great Indian battles. Cody's movie friends decided they would like to film a "real" Wild West celebration, and the Park County Fair seemed like a good opportunity. For a time it seemed that Cody would not be able to be present, but when dates were changed and filming arrangements were made, he returned to Cody in September. It is not clear when he learned that Prince Albert was coming out to see Anderson. He had one of his men negotiate with Crow chief Plenty Coups to bring a band of thirty warriors to the fair, but that appears to have been a part of his movie plans. Even a week before the Prince's arrival in Cody, there was no talk of him in town. When Buffalo Bill arrived on September 11, however, he knew of the Anderson hunting party, and he adroitly inserted himself into those plans. The town quickly drew up plans to have the Prince officially open the fair. Cody brought Plenty Coups and the Prince together to exchange gifts at the opening, which was thoroughly filmed and photographed. Albert had such a good time in Cody that he postponed his trip with Anderson for a couple of days. Then, after they had their hunt

Colonel William F. Cody introducing Crow chief Plenty Coups to Prince Albert of Monaco in Cody, September 1913. Courtesy of Buffalo Bill Historical Center, Cody, Wyo.; P.6.277.

on the Greybull, they returned to Cody and Buffalo Bill took them up above Pahaska, where a camp had been built especially for the Prince. There, they had a quite successful hunt, Albert killing a bull elk and a large black bear.[35]

Buffalo Bill always drew a press crowd, of course, and the visit of a reigning monarch, even of a tiny principality like Monaco, was big news in the West. The *Denver Post* covered the festivities and spread the word to the waiting world. Both for the town of Cody and Colonel Cody himself, it was a publicity windfall. The town newspaper celebrated the visit with a full-page headline: "ALBERT THE FIRST PRINCE OF MONACO! COL. W. F. CODY PRINCE OF GOOD FELLOWS!"[36] The Colonel played his two favorite roles, the mediator between East and West and bridge between the Old West (represented by Plenty Coups) and the New, under a national spotlight. This was not a bad way to turn the tide for one whose show business assets had been sold at sheriff's auction only two months earlier.

In addition to the opportunity to show off its county fair and cowboy celebration, the town now had its place as a primary jumping-off point for eastern and European hunters cemented in the public imagination. Associated for so long with the personal invitation and conduct of Buffalo Bill himself, that place was by 1913 no longer dependent upon the Old Scout. The Monaco expedition itself was put together by two

A. A. Anderson, Prince Albert of Monaco, and Buffalo Bill Cody around a campfire at "Camp Monaco," upriver from Pahaska on the North Fork of the Shoshone, 1913. Courtesy Buffalo Bill Historical Center, Cody, Wyo.; P. 69.1942.

local outfitters, Fred Richard and Ned Frost; Bill Cody was along more or less on the same terms as Anderson and Prince Albert. While they were hunting up on the North Fork of the Shoshone, another Richard and Frost outfit was afield with Charles Gates, son of the famous Texas oilman, John R. "Bet-a-Million" Gates, and Joe Jones had a group of New Yorkers up the South Fork. These men were so enthusiastic about their experience when they returned that they caused the editor of the *Enterprise* to gush that Jones and his men had "bound these Eastern hunters to Wyoming with links of steel."[37] Cody boosters were learning that their economic destiny depended upon the decisions of easterners to come west.

Within a few years, Cody area men, following in the footsteps of their founding father, could be found in attendance at Camp Fire Club meetings in New York. In fact, from 1909, Cody was listed on Camp Fire Club stationery as home to an allied club, along with Jamestown (New York), Detroit, and Los Angeles. A meeting held near the end of

June 1909 at the Irma Hotel (at the suggestion of none other than A. A. Anderson) determined that the club would be known as the Camp Fire Club of Wyoming. George Beck was elected president and William L. Simpson secretary. Colonel W. F. Cody was not present, but his spirit was, as Beck signed his name to the call for a permanent organization.[38] Not surprisingly, Joe Magill, partner with Joe Jones in the MaJo ranch on the upper South Fork, found the table decorations at a December dinner of the Camp Fire Club in the Gold Room of the Biltmore Hotel in New York constructed of sagebrush from Cody! Magill and Jones were in New York giving lectures, showing Wyoming pictures, and generally promoting the Big Horn Basin while lining up hunting parties for the 1915 season. Magill attended the December dinner and was invited back for another in January at Delmonico's, where the Camp Fire Club preferred to dine. On the way home, they stopped at Chicago, Sioux City, and Omaha, spending four months in assiduous promotion of their corner of Wyoming. There can be little doubt that Buffalo Bill opened some doors for them.[39]

Big game management, especially in northwest Wyoming, became a high priority for state government in these years. Wyoming pioneered the system of hunting licenses, including the premium charged to out-of-state hunters, and the state worked especially hard to sustain the population of big game that would keep it a favorite destination for hunters everywhere. George Beck, who was elected to the State Senate in 1912, had worked with Bill Cody to develop Cody's hunting economy. He was elected chair of the Game Committee of the Senate, where they were taking up the issue of expanding the state game preserves, places where animals would be left alone to breed to maintain the size of the herd. (The committee seemed primarily concerned with elk, the real Wyoming trophy animal.) Beck's wealthy friends and neighbors, A. A. Anderson and W. R. Coe, both lobbied him to have sections of the mountains near their ranches included in the game preserve system. Coe was, as always, quite frank in his appeal: "It is desired by Mr. Phelps, Mr. Anderson, and myself, as well as others, and I suppose we are the largest taxpayers on our side of the river."[40] Beck was able to add two areas desired by Anderson and Coe between 1913 and 1915. In this way, a nursery of game was designated near to the Cody hunting country.[41]

Accustomed as he was to the spotlight, the Colonel did not move off into the wings without some gestures at keeping his old role. In the summer of 1915, he announced that he had been talked into taking the largest hunting party ever assembled into the high Absarokas in the fall. There were to be about fifty hunters, and the expense of outfitting such a large group would surely run into thousands of dollars, "for it is to be the biggest hunt of all time." A week after announcing the hunt, he set the date for October 20 and the destination as the Thorofare country (south and east of Yellowstone Park, quite possibly the most remote bit of wilderness in the United States at the time, and one of Cody's favorite places to go). But, as with so many of his great ventures in the last decade of his life, this hunt dissolved before it began. Cody was on the road with the Sells-Floto Circus, and returned to Wyoming late in November that year. He may well have enjoyed a small hunting trip with friends, but nothing like what he had advertised in the summer. One cannot but wonder what moved him to set forth in such a public manner a project that obviously had no real planning or purpose behind it. At some point, it seems, we must conclude that the advertising of a thing was as real to him as the thing itself; if he could not actually conduct a hunt, he could at least talk about it, and thereby remind people that once upon a time he could do both. He may have been among the first Americans to recognize that having one's name in the news was good in itself, without regard to the truth of any claims attached to it.[42]

As noted above, the Camp Fire Club was part of the campaign that brought about modern ideas of game protection. The organization campaigned for protection of game in the national parks and against the commercial killing of seals. Dr. W. T. Hornaday, a charter member of the club, organized the American Bison Society and also raised the money to establish the National Bison Range in western Montana. However, when Bill Cody joined the club, presided over then by A. A. Anderson, it seemed to exist more to celebrate hunting than to engage in serious reform. Anderson served as the first supervisor of the Yellowstone Timber Reserve, and in that capacity had volunteered his district rangers as deputies to enforce Wyoming's nascent game laws. At the same time, he bred packs of dogs to enable the more efficient pursuit and extermination of mountain lions in the Wyoming forest. Like many of his peers, he seems to have regarded extermination of predators as a first principle of game management. Anderson served as president of the club for its first decade, but was removed because he did not lead strongly enough on matters of game preservation; he was replaced by Ernest Thompson

Seton in 1909. By that time, the club numbered editors of *Forest and Stream* and *Field and Stream* among its members, and was obviously more serious about game preservation. Cody was a member throughout these changes, and he probably learned a good deal about serious wildlife issues from them. By 1912 he was an outspoken advocate of new game laws that would reduce the harvest and sustain the population of elk and other big game. He directed those who would take the lead in shaping tourist hunting in the Big Horn Basin toward his Camp Fire Club connections. But when "Larry" Larom, co-owner of the Valley Ranch on the South Fork and pioneering dude rancher, headed east in December 1916, he carried letters of introduction from Buffalo Bill not only to the secretary of the Camp Fire Club but also to the Rocky Mountain Club of New York. This latter group had nothing to do with conservation or game laws. They were simply a collection of wealthy men with interests in the West, many of whom Cody knew. The most important connection Cody wanted to promote was that between eastern money and his new western home.[43]

Buffalo Bill's hunting parties were seldom simple affairs. They seemed designed to attract attention, both to the man and to his corner of the West. A considerable amount of press agentry, occasionally amounting to outright invention of facts, surrounded the workaday events of a trip to the mountains with an aura of high drama. As with his Cody Canal promotion, the Colonel worked to create a buzz about his hunting country, and with the same goal in mind. He frequently took painters along to memorialize hunts, and even referred to hunting camps up the South Fork as "picture camps."[44] Cody and those who followed in his path were making the hunting of big game into one of the core experiences of modern tourism. Commentators commonly speak of the "hunting industry" and its economic importance in Wyoming today. What makes it an industry is, in part, the fact that many men undertake the guiding and the outfitting that make the trips possible. Where once the celebrity, the "white Indian," initiated civilized hunters into the ways of the wild, now hundreds of ordinary men labor more or less interchangeably to keep up their part in the economy of the state. The industrial approach to the chase may be fathered upon Buffalo Bill Cody, not as a meat hunter for the railroad, but as the developer of a modern tourist hunting economy. And although Bill Cody himself had a particular

relationship with New York, his followers brought in hunters from wherever they would come, as long as they brought money.

Buffalo Bill also took the lead in establishing the general tourist trade
that has characterized the town of Cody in the years since his death. It
has been seen that, from the earliest days, the proximity of Cody to the
eastern border of Yellowstone National Park was on the minds of the
founders. Once again, however, Bill Cody assumed more credit than he
deserved. He liked to boast of how he had blazed the trail to Yellowstone,
and Theodore Roosevelt cited that as a reason for the federal government to build a road to the eastern entrance. In fact, it was George Beck
who marked out a route for a wagon road to the Park, just as it was Beck
who first took a Burlington Railroad agent up that road, in 1896.[45] Cody
made much of the road in his conversations with Burlington Railroad
officials before 1900, and, of course, it soon became identified with him
in the public imagination.

In 1901, he took a hunting party that included George Allen Beecher,
Bishop of Nebraska, up the trail to the edge of Yellowstone Park. One
evening Cody dramatically blazed a tree and proclaimed that he would
build an inn there and call it "Beecher Inn" in the clergyman's honor.
According to Beecher's account, Iron Tail, the Oglala chief who was
along on the hunt, suggested instead that the place be called Pahaska,
Cody's Lakota name, and such it became. Both Beck and Cody lobbied
hard with Wyoming's congressional delegation to provide federal funds for
the road in the Park and in the Forest Reserve. Beck asserted that it was
his influence with senators on the Appropiations Committee that got the
money for the road from the Park to the boundary of the Forest Reserve.
Congressman Mondell got money for the road included in the Sundry
Civil appropriation for 1902. Cody newspapers urged Big Horn County
commissioners to build a good road from Cody to the forest, and the U.S.
Reclamation Service helped a great deal by constructing the first section
through the Shoshone Canyon when they built the great Shoshone Dam.
Many people had a role in making sure a good road connected Cody
with Yellowstone.[46]

Buffalo Bill's dream of a transportation company went into abeyance
shortly after his 1903 correspondence with General Land Office commissioner Richards regarding a travel concession to the Park. Neither

his business nor his personal affairs went smoothly in those years. He spent most of the next four years with his show in Europe, and when he was in America, he was embroiled in his divorce trial.[47] When he returned from Europe on vacation in the winter of 1903–1904, he began making plans to build his Wyoming business around the Irma Hotel, by establishing two more tourist hotels along the road from Cody to Yellowstone. A new road was opened to travel in Yellowstone in 1903, running east from Yellowstone Lake over Sylvan Pass and then down to the eastern border of the Park. In the fall of 1903, Jake Schwoob traveled the wagon road from Cody to the Park and pronounced it "alright." In early 1904, Cody applied to the General Land Office for land and logs to construct "a hotel and road ranch" just outside Yellowstone on the Cody road, and another road ranch half-way between there and Cody. He acquired the use of 160 acres with the first one, and 20,000 board feet of logs for his hotel; this eventually became Pahaska Tepee. His second permit granted him half as much lumber to construct a small fourteen-room structure on five acres; this became Wapiti Inn.[48]

Leaving the field open for others to get established in the transportation of tourists to the Park, Cody set out to pick up some profit from catering to them along the way. He entered into an interesting correspondence with J. Barton Key, who was building a hotel at the St. Louis World's Fair, regarding the design and construction of a log hotel at Pahaska. His long-time friend, D. Franklin Powell ("White Beaver"), served as his agent in the construction first of Pahaska Tepee and then of Wapiti Inn. Powell applied in September 1904 on the Colonel's behalf, to the secretary of the Interior for a permit to build a station at Sylvan Lake in Yellowstone Park "for supplying food to tourists and feed for horses" on the road to Yellowstone Lake.[49] Cody seemed to be planning a monopoly of travel services between Cody and Yellowstone Lake. The park superintendent scotched that by rejecting his application, but Pahaska opened in 1904, and Wapiti the following year. Cody seemed in good position to control the tourist trade on that route. Although he had discussed with Key the possibility of a hotel at Pahaska that would house five hundred people, the capacity of the lodge and cabins was considerably smaller than one hundred in the first decade, and Wapiti, of course, was smaller than that. Key took no part in the design, which was accomplished by Cody's friend, A. A. Anderson. Before 1911, no

Buffalo Bill gazing off toward Yellowstone Park from the porch of his newly constructed Pahaska Lodge, 1904. Courtesy of Park County Archives, Cody, Wyo.

more than a thousand people entered Yellowstone by the east gate in any single year; Pahaska did not need more capacity than it had.[50]

Cody resurrected his plans for a transportation company in 1909. He planned to begin regularly scheduled service between Cody and Pahaska in a sixty-horsepower White Steamer. Delivery of the car was delayed until 1910, but in July of that year the car made its first run. It could leave Cody in the morning, stop for lunch at Wapiti, and arrive at Pahaska in late afternoon. Westbound trips left the Irma on Tuesday, Thursday, and Saturday, returning the next day, costing $5.00 for a round-trip ticket. The car trips were coordinated with the arrivals and departures of the Burlington trains, and, of course, Cody's were not the only cars on the road. In 1911, two more White Steamers were added to his fleet to accommodate the increasing crowds of tourists, and a fourth the following year. The Colonel employed a regular staff of drivers. They were not family, but many of the others in his hotel business were. His brother-in-law, Louis Decker, managed the Irma and both mountain inns until 1913, when his wife, Cody's sister May, took ill and they were forced to leave. Irma Cody herself and her husband, Fred Garlow, then took on those responsibilities. As the car travel increased, Buffalo Bill built a special log cabin headquarters for the Park County Automobile Association, which held annual meetings at Pahaska. By a judicious combination of proprietary and individual accommodations for all manner of travelers, Bill Cody set the stage for the dramatic growth of the tourist traffic through Wyoming's Absaroka Mountains and into Yellowstone National Park. Seeing this develop as it did, Burlington officials quietly abandoned early plans to build their rail line up to the boundary of the National Forest.[51]

All was not well beneath the surface, however. Burdened by debt and plagued by bad decisions, Buffalo Bill faced the possibility of the collapse of his carefully constructed tourist empire. He encumbered the Irma Hotel with a $20,000 mortgage to pay off his debt to Gordon Lillie in 1911. As his Arizona mine continued to require more than all the money he could make, he went looking for a buyer for his hotels around that same time. He wrote Augustus Busch, president of the Anheuser-Busch Brewing Company, offering them for sale, and then offered his friend Clarence Buell a 5 percent commission if he could close the deal with Busch for $150,000. "You know how the AnsHauser [*sic*] Busch people advertise that the sun never sits on their beer, etc. Well my hotels will give them a chance to advertise their beer in Yellowstone National Park."[52] Busch apparently could not be interested in this venture, but Cody did not give up. In 1915, he brought a California capitalist, P. J. Durbin, to Cody to look over his hotels, still hoping to sell out. This plan also fell through, and he was forced to look for other ways to raise money.[53]

Ever since automobile traffic had become common between Cody and Yellowstone, George Beck and other local leaders had lobbied constantly in Washington to allow cars in the Park itself. Finally, in the spring of 1915, Congressman Mondell sent word that automobile traffic would be allowed into the Park starting on August 1. The town immediately began to plan a celebration to coordinate with the opening, to be called Entrance Day. Within weeks Buffalo Bill shouldered his way into this spotlight with an announcement that he would ride in the first car into Yellowstone. "Think of Buffalo Bill," he wrote, "who used to guide the United States army in that wild country still advance scout for an army of a thousand automobiles into that weird land. I appreciate the honor and will ride at the head into wonderland."[54] In the event, he did no such thing. Jake Schwoob, proud owner of Wyoming license plate number 1, led a caravan of six cars bearing members of the House Appropriations Committee into Yellowstone on July 5. When general traffic opened in August, thirty-five cars went in on the first weekend, and Buffalo Bill was not in any of them. He obviously loved the idea of being there, but he was an employee of the Sells-Floto Circus that summer, and it would not be likely to release a primary attraction. Of course, he should have known that long before he promised to be in Yellowstone. The idea of bridging the Old and the New Wests, as well as sustaining with his celebrity the tourist empire he was building on the Shoshone River, overpowered anything as prosaic as good judgment.

Cody did undertake an advertising campaign for his "Hotels in the Rockies" when automobile traffic was opened in the Park. He produced a high-quality brochure titled "An Ideal Outing at Buffalo Bill's Hotels" in 1915, which touted the beauties of the eastern entrance to Yellowstone, the quality of his accomodations, and the excitement of traveling in his powerful "mountain climbing White Steamer autos." Ignoring the possibility of adverse publicity, he featured a picture in the brochure of himself sending off the Charley Gates party in one of his automobiles. With unconsious irony, the advertisement features the awe-inspiring federal dam in the Shoshone Canyon, then the highest concrete arch dam in the world, one that would never have been built if Buffalo Bill himself had remained in charge of that water. This little booklet stands at the beginning of tourist advertising in Wyoming, in which image is everything and inconvenient truth is masked or ignored.[55]

Thinking of other ways to turn a dollar off the land, Cody came up with two ideas, both of them retreads of earlier projects. The first one is rather shadowy, for it has left only a single track on the records, and probably never got beyond the initial stage of advertising. Although the "Cody Military College and International Academy of Rough Riders" vanished in a puff of prairie wind back in 1901, the idea was clearly close to Buffalo Bill's heart. While looking at the loss of his hotels and tourist business, he sent out a brochure advertising the Buffalo Bill Cavalry School. It was to be located at the TE ranch, offering five months of instruction "in the most thorough manner horsemanship, shooting, hunting, fishing, trailing, trapping, camping, camp cooking, packing, guiding and military tactics"

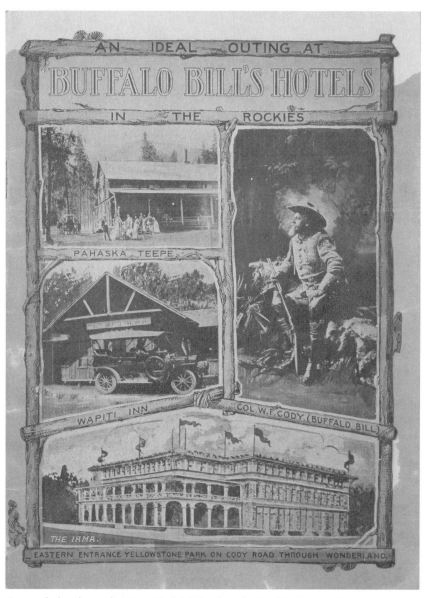

Cover of a brochure advertising Cody's "Hotels in the Rockies," emphasizing the connection with Yellowstone National Park. Courtesy of Buffalo Bill Historical Center, Cody, Wyo.; MS6.I.D.2/5.

Buffalo Bill sending the millionaire Charley Gates and his friends on a hunting party up the North Fork in one of his "mountain climbing" White Steamers. Courtesy of Buffalo Bill Historical Center, Cody, Wyo.; P.6.281.

for six hundred dollars. Students would wear uniforms, and would be forbidden to drink or gamble or misbehave in any way. Boys would have to be fourteen years of age to enroll.

The brochure based its appeal on an awkward combination of standard tourism ("unsurpassed natural beauty and scenic grandeur") and a vision of manly virtue like that represented by the contemporaneous Boy Scout movement. The instructors of Cody's school were to be "old timers," true western men: "the old hunter and trapper is a character worth coming hundreds of miles to meet."[56] This line of address echoes the likes of Frederic Remington and Theodore Roosevelt, famous for promoting the virtuous effect of association with western land and western men; Remington called them "men with the bark on." Buffalo Bill's Cavalry School may also be understood as part of the national conversation about bringing up boys so they did not lose the natural virtues of their forefathers amid the degrading environment of modern cities. The Boy Scouts and similar organizations for youth, as well as the rapid growth of summer camps in backwoods environments, testified to national anxiety on this point. Cody certainly talked over such matters with Dan Beard and Ernest Thompson Seton, cofounders of the Boy Scouts of America, at Camp Fire Club meetings.[57]

One could wish to have seen even one class matriculate at this extraordinary institution, but apparently Buffalo Bill shot too high for his public this time. Asking more of boys than the Boy Scouts did, but offering far less than a full military education, Cody's Cavalry School died aborning. And in contrast to his forward-looking vision of the automobile, the Cavalry School idea was frankly looking backward to the West as he first knew it. Evoking frontier excitement as a means of developing the virtues needed for modern civilization was a key to the success of the Boy Scout movement; Baden-Powell, Ernest Thompson Seton, and Dan Beard obviously had found the right balance. Buffalo Bill already had learned how to domesticate the Old West for popular consumption, but he did not immediately see that most Americans were not in the market for a more serious return to the middle of the previous century.[58]

Cody's other venture, again a reiteration of an old idea, was another attempt to capitalize on what he had built at his ranch on the South Fork. The big advertising brochure produced in 1898 for the Cody Canal included an invitation to interested parties to inquire at the TE ranch for guides and supplies for hunting parties in the Absaroka Mountains upriver. We have seen how the Colonel would casually refer potential clients to George Beck, confident that Beck would set up a good hunt for them. It is clear that from the very beginning Buffalo Bill had seen a potential to develop his own ranch into a paying proposition by farming people, rather than (or in addition to) hay and horses. By 1915, the Colonel seemed ready to jump feet-first into the dude ranching business. The *Enterprise* announced in its last issue of that year that Buffalo Bill was going to convert the TE into a resort, which would (of course) be "second to none in the West." Apparently on Cody's authority, the news-paper laid the credit for this decision to the persuasion of eastern friends, first among whom was the New York actor, William Faversham.[59]

The picture of the old showman yielding to the requests of his New York friends probably played well in the newspaper. Writing to his friend

E. E. Arbuckle, an automobile dealer in Greensburg, Indiana, he said it was a matter of family pressures and the familiar needs of the promoter. He wanted "Buck" to get some brochures as soon as Fred Garlow had them printed, and to promise to send some summer guests that way. "I'll sure show Greensburg with my show this summer. And I'll boom your game—you get busy and do as much for me."[60]

The advertising brochure for this new venture, identifying the summer of 1916 as the first season the ranch would be open to tourists, based the appeal of the experience on the fact that Buffalo Bill himself would be present, would be leading hunting parties, telling stories, overseeing the round-up. (As he was nearly seventy years old when the brochure went out, the unrealistic promises were perhaps a measure of the family's desperation.) Visitors to the ranch were warned not to expect resort accommodations; TE was a working ranch, and the work would go on. There were, however, croquet grounds and tennis courts, not usually to be found on Wyoming ranches, as well as barn dances and various rodeo sports. Cabins had been newly erected for tourists to use as bunkhouses; the Colonel's own ranch house dining room would serve them all their meals. Particular emphasis, as always with Cody publications, was placed on hunting, reviewing game laws and including specific encouragements to use the ranch as a base for hunting the high Absarokas. Fred and Irma Garlow were living at the TE and managing it, and it may have been—as the Colonel told Arbuckle—their idea to use the ranch this way.[61]

The decision to open up the TE to tourists led almost immediately to small explosions of publicity in eastern papers. The *Boston Evening Transcript* published a full page on life on the range and in the mountains around Cody written by Charles Wayland Towne. Towne had lived in Cody and worked for Buffalo Bill at the Irma and at the *Enterprise* for a while in 1902–1903, and he obviously recalled his Wyoming year with great fondness. He produced here a real puff piece for Cody and the TE. Without actually advertising any particular ranch (although the story was accompanied by a picture of the TE), Towne managed to make life on a dude ranch in Wyoming seem like a trip back to an ideal American democratic past. An article about life on the ranch and another about hunting were calculated to lead a reader to seek out reservations at the first opportunity. Buffalo Bill's life had always been for sale at Wild West productions. Now he was putting his personal life on the market. He could not seem to help himself: any notion of the private Bill Cody had vanished like a dream.[62]

Of course, he was not alone in this. Residents of Cody stumbled over each other in their haste to commodify the experience of visiting there. Other ranches along both forks of the Shoshone River between Cody and Yellowstone Park began to enter the dude business well before Cody took that step at TE. In the summer of 1917, the Burlington brought roughly a hundred tourists a day through Cody, although they did not spend enough time there to satisfy many of the town's leaders. Cody newspapers hosted the Big Horn Basin Press Club that same summer, showing off the string of dude ranches—and the exotic culture of the dudes and "dudines" who populated them—for more than twenty miles west of town. Tourism seemed like a great game, with Wild West entertainments and costume parties as well as fishing and riding. It was not possible to see, at that end of the century, just how thoroughly the tourist industry would change the land everyone purported to love so much. Only after midcentury, when everyone wanted to drive there in a car, so roads had to be built, and every wide spot in the road sprouted some kind of tourist accommodation, and every road became stacked with automobiles, exhaust, and dead animals—only then did the true price start to become apparent. When it was too late to do anything but pay the price, the devil's bargain, the inevitable destruction of what one loves through the act of loving it, began to be clear.[63]

When he first entered into the commerce of hunting in 1871, Cody took quite naturally to the role of the white Indian. There was no question of imposture here; as a hunter, he was the genuine article. As that role opened and expanded, first on stage and then most famously in the Wild West arena, he became, perhaps unconsciously, an artifice of his own creation. What the hunters from New York saw and admired on the Kansas plains became a show front. Shifting the base of his life to Wyoming gave him an opportunity to recover some of the authenticity lost in the show world, but he was too far gone in pursuit of money and fame to do more than gesture in that direction. By the end of his life, he had made his home, his family, his town, and his country into commodities and advertised them far and wide in the extravagant terms that had characterized the promotion of the Wild West. Visiting the Cody country was presented as the kind of peak experience that all modern advertising has striven to convince Americans is their birthright, available in exchange for cash. In this way Buffalo Bill led his town and his successors down the trail to the falsely glittering world of modern industrial tourism.

Conclusion

We have seen William F. Cody at close range in these pages. What this study has revealed is, not surprisingly, a complex and conflicted man, one who failed to realize his imperial ambitions in Wyoming but who nevertheless left an enduring mark on the country. His legacy is as complex as his personality. Louis Warren suggests that his real legacy is to be found in the Wild West show and the impressions generated over the decades of its performance. Does that mean that the real William Cody was the performer, Buffalo Bill? We have seen here that, in his Wyoming life, the performer, with all the habits that profession entailed, was not always separable from the real world actor. Cody also worked in the social and economic world, and there were consequences that attended his actions there. It has been important to try to sift through the claims made by William Cody, and by others on his behalf, to work toward a relatively solid grasp of just what he did and with what results. If, as Warren asserts, the real Buffalo Bill for most Americans is the Wild West performer, the real William Cody in Wyoming was something more—and less—than that. Off his horse and out of the arena, he was a "poor, bare, fork'd animal" like the rest of us, but one who seized a moment in the history of Wyoming's Big Horn Basin, and wrote his name across it.[1]

Everyone who knew Bill Cody remarked at one time or another on his physical strength and energy. His personal motor simply seemed to be set at a higher idle speed than most others. Few people today could even imagine, for instance, keeping up the voluminous correspondence

Buffalo Bill did, much of it apparently written on train journeys as the Wild West moved from one location to the next. He was known to boast he had never missed a performance in more than twenty years. When he focused that energy on the Cody Canal project, it threatened to overwhelm his colleagues, disrupting the company as a thunderstorm did their canal. He never stopped thinking of new things to do, never tired of telling others what they should be doing, and promoted his enterprises endlessly with whoever would listen. He saw great possibilities in every direction, and he had unquestioned faith in his personal ability to achieve whatever he set out to do. He was always willing to back up his words with his money.

At the same time, as the reverse of the same personal coin, he was frequently impatient with others who did not see and go as he did. He often could not keep to a single course, and he never developed a sure sense of how cooperative business enterprises needed to be organized and managed. He could not work well in yoke with others, and often was guilty of flagrantly self-serving behavior. Nate Salsbury, his partner in the Wild West show for nearly twenty years, offered as a title to his unpublished memoir (written probably three years before his death), "Sixteen Years in Hell with Buffalo Bill."[2] Salsbury was at that time engaged in a virulent scrap with Cody, which no doubt made it difficult for him to compose an even-handed treatment of their relationship. It is also worth noting that in the midst of this scrap, and in full knowledge of the man he was working with, Salsbury joined with Cody on the big new irrigation project downriver from the Cody Canal. Obviously, Salsbury was drawn to Buffalo Bill at the same time as he was repelled by many of the things Cody did. The same kind of relationship developed between Cody and George Beck; throughout Beck's autobiography, resentment of Buffalo Bill alternates with the pride Beck felt in associating with him.[3]

Cody, then, was not an easy or uncomplicated man. He functioned very well as the man out front, making perfect strangers feel close and comfortable with him, but he had problems with people in closer personal relations. Bishop George Allen Beecher told a remarkable story of traveling on the train to Cody with Buffalo Bill. Beecher watched people file through the train while the Colonel stood and greeted them, often by name, asking after their cattle, families, and so forth. Later Beecher mentioned this to Cody, praising his remarkable ability to recognize people and remember their names, and asked him how he did it. "The colonel looked to the right and left, and finding that we were seated by ourselves for the moment, said in a low voice, 'Mr. Beecher, I don't know a d—— one of them.'"[4] It was not that he did not have a gift for friendship, for he showed it frequently, and even Nate Salsbury seems to have been affected by it. Perhaps we could say that he intuitively understood the terms of relating to large crowds of strangers, and even trusted that they would forgive him as they walked away having been called by someone else's name. At close range, and particularly where business was the subject, it mattered much more how he conducted himself. It was not a matter of names then, but a matter of dollars, of honest estimates of tasks and accomplishment, less of playing the hero and more of acting the partner. Salsbury and most of his partners found him seriously wanting in this regard in the work in Wyoming.

Buffalo Bill came to Wyoming with extravagant, even imperial dreams of what he might accomplish in the Big Horn Basin. He died in January 1917, if not in poverty, yet with rather little to show for all the money he had made in his life. Even in the last summer of his life, exhausted and ill, he rode daily into arenas across America to introduce a shadow of his former Wild West because he needed the money to pay his debts. The centerpiece of his Big Horn Basin enterprise, the Cody Canal, where once he hoped to see thousands of farms on 300,000 acres of irrigated land, fed water to a couple hundred farms and watered no more than about 12,000 acres. His namesake town was doing well enough for a small town at the end of the line, but there was nothing imperial about it.[5] His home ranch was beautiful and productive, but he had had to deed it over to his wife to avoid creditors, and he had had to sell almost all his other land. His tourist hotels, particularly the Irma and Pahaska, had a reasonable future in front of them, but these things— more than enough to crown the life of an ordinary man—seem almost meager in contrast with the vision of what might have been, the vision that motivated Bill Cody when he came into the Basin. They were places where his children and grandchildren might hope to work for a living, but even then the death of his daughter Irma and of her husband, Fred Garlow, in the flu epidemic of 1918, cast a pall over the great man's inheritance.

It would be hard to imagine the history of Wyoming around the turn of the twentieth century without Buffalo Bill. He brought enormous, electric energy into the Big Horn Basin and to the state as a whole. He seems to have swept away state officials—most notably Elwood Mead and Fenimore Chatterton—with his cascades of plans and ideas for development. He brought hundreds of people, some of them famous, many not, into the Basin, and many of them stayed. His claims to having brought the Burlington Railroad into Wyoming probably did not hold water, but people used that road into Wyoming more times than we can know because Bill Cody's life and country were at the end of it. Joy Kasson suggests that Cody's Wild West enacted American national identity, and that it was Bill Cody's physical self, available in arenas everywhere, that enforced the terms of American manhood in his story of the West. Honor, justice, strength, and skill were displayed there where boys and young men could almost reach out and touch their hero. Advertising for Cody's colonization schemes played upon that subconscious attraction to the man himself. Bill Cody is here, they seemed to say: would it not be a good idea to be where he is? Consequently, there was what advertising people call a "buzz" about Wyoming in those years that can be traced directly to Buffalo Bill.[6]

Cody once remarked to a friend, Clarence Rowley, that his winter visit to Cody tired him out. "Besides my own business I had so much to do for the town. Which they expect me to do, as I am heavily interrested there. And being the father of the town, when I am there they expect me to lead."[7] At the time he wrote these words, the town had in fact long since ceased to rely on him. George Beck was far more important to the growth of Cody in the first decade of the twentieth century, along with Jake Schwoob and some other early settlers who committed their lives to the place. But there were many dimensions to being "the father of the town." An aspect of the role that appealed to him was living the life of noblesse oblige. In the early days this meant actually holding court in the Irma, receiving settlers in and around Cody who were having a hard time, and dispensing charity like an English lord. He obviously felt personally engaged in the success of all who followed him there, and he acted on that feeling. The role that fell most comfortably on his shoulders, perhaps, and the one that led directly to his place in the town's self-conception, was that of the town cheerleader. From the earliest years his annual return to Cody was an occasion for a celebration. (His physical encounters with the town were conditioned, in large part, by his travel schedule with the Wild West show, which kept him on the road from March to November of nearly every year.)

After 1902 these parties were held at the Irma, hundreds were invited, and the drinking often went on all night long. The newspapers lovingly reported on these affairs; it is as if the heartbeat of Cody was most evident when the Colonel and his friends came together to celebrate.[8]

The town went all out for the 1905 celebration, which came at the end of a two-year sojourn of the show in Europe. The newspaper promoted the evening with a large picture of Buffalo Bill on the front page, accompanied by a more than ordinarily sycophantic oration by Cody's friend, D. Frank Powell, also known as "White Beaver." "He comes," wrote Powell, "and over saddle horn, in deepest thought doth bend—no thoughts of honor won abroad; not pride for social recognition won which most men crave and is in profusion his—but of the past he thinks, and of the future waking dreams has he."[9] All the music, speeches, and dancing were arranged for the night of December 1, but the train broke down and Buffalo Bill did not arrive in town until the next morning. Never mind; they had their party without him, and trooped to the train the next day to welcome him home. The newspaper editor thought Cody "looks younger and is more active and alert than when he came home three years ago."[10]

Within a few years, the annual party for Buffalo Bill grew apart from the occasion of his return. In 1911, the reception was held in March, and in 1912 it was in January. Although he had always enjoyed playing the role of the "far-gazer," the one who saw the bountiful future of the Big Horn Basin, as he grew older futurity became more and more the principal theme of the annual gathering. In 1911, he urged his fellow townsmen to get together to put in the kind of water and sewer systems he thought the town needed to grow, and he promised to expand the Irma if they did. The 1912 dinner, as already seen, was an evening given over to pounding the Reclamation Service, but he also took the occasion to campaign for game law reform and automobiles in Yellowstone. Even while taking on public issues of importance, he took care not to lose his character as the town's biggest booster. He was optimistic about things working out in Cody and in the West generally. "Little Willie is getting a bit aged and gray, but with all that I feel as happy and optimistic as I always have and I am going to keep feeling that way as long as I possibly can and I want my friends in Cody to do the same."[11]

He still felt an obligation to work for civic benefit where he felt he had particular opportunity. People in town often expressed unhappiness with what they saw as the Burlington Railroad's tepid support for tourism over their new road to Yellowstone. Late in 1914, Buffalo Bill called a public meeting before leaving for parts east, with the intent of stimulating the formation of a transportation company that could handle unlimited tourist travel. With that kind of assurance, he expected to be able to use his personal influence to convince the railroad to "boost for the Cody way."[12] But his engagement in these civic affairs after 1910 nevertheless demanded far less of him than was true of earlier years. Beneath the surface of his confession to Rowley we may detect a hint of his own need to be needed by his town, which by 1912 was doing a reasonable job of running itself.

Indeed, in the years following the arrival of the railroad, Cody had prospered. Surely fewer than 500 in 1900, the population of the town more than doubled, to 1,220, by 1905. There was an entire generation of men younger than the Old Scout moving into positions of influence in the town, men like William L. Simpson, attorney, newspaperman, and general gadfly; Jake Schwoob, owner of the Cody Trading Company; and banker H. R. Weston. Although it lost population at the 1910 and 1915 censuses, Cody was by a wide margin the largest town in the northern Big Horn Basin in 1915.[13] Buffalo Bill had made possible much of that growth by his investment in the town, which one newspaper estimated in 1903 at $216,500.[14] The years of the Colonel's investment were pretty much over by that time, but he had cemented for himself a place in the life of the town that no one could challenge.

Nor did death displace him in the hearts of his townsmen. It could be argued that, through the agency of the Cody Club, which spread his picture all over town in everything they published and across the country in their advertising, he was more present in death than he had been in life. In 1932, for instance, Cody boosters put on a banquet at the Medinah Athletic Club in Chicago on Buffalo Bill's birthday, with speakers on the life of Buffalo Bill and motion pictures of the Cody Country. The program for the banquet featured a picture of the Colonel on the cover, of course, with Horatio's paean to Hamlet (unattributed) beneath it. In the hands of these latter-day boosters, Bill Cody's identity was bound up here with the country, and if "Nature might stand up and say to the World, 'There was a Man,'" people would naturally think the country itself was similarly beyond compare. It was perfectly appropriate that this man who had made a fortune by creating himself as a symbol of what he thought the West had been should be repackaged for commercial purposes in this way. In the promotional literature of the Cody Club and the Burlington Railroad, the land from Cody to Yellowstone lost its original identity and became "Buffalo Bill Country." He had made and spent a fortune, and now others would do the same in his name.[15] There can be little doubt that he would have enjoyed this kind of memorial. Having spent most of his life moving between East and West, and working for years to bring wealthy, famous, and powerful men from the East to the Basin, Bill Cody in spirit blessed the creation of a town and an industry that worked tirelessly to promote themselves in his image.

He might have learned, by the end of his days, that fame and publicity could be double-edged weapons. As perhaps the most famous man in America, the first genuine celebrity Wyoming had ever known, Cody found himself paradoxically in an environment that proved exceptionally difficult for him to manipulate to his advantage. The people with whom he was yoked in building the Cody Canal and subsequent enterprises fell easily into the habit of deferring to him. As he did not possess to any great extent the faculty of self-criticism, he found himself time and again propelled forward by his own energy, blindness, or willfulness into situations from which it was difficult or impossible to recover. It would have been helpful if Elwood Mead, for instance, had been less dazzled by the man and more able to exercise some restraint on the overweening ambitions revealed in Cody's irrigation and other development schemes. Among his partners in the Shoshone Irrigation Company only Nate Salsbury would contradict or criticize him, and Cody had had years to learn how to discount Salsbury's advice. George Beck, important as he was to the canal and to the town, nearly always gave way to Cody, and was frequently complicit in crazy behavior like the Wallenberg contract. The result was the chaos we now know to be the real history of the settlement project at Cody.

It has long been known that Buffalo Bill got along well with his sisters and fought almost constantly with his wife. Personal matters like this fall outside the scope of this book for the most part, but where they help us to get a clearer view of the man we should pay attention. He seems to have felt responsible for his sisters. He employed them and their families in several of his Wyoming ventures. Ed Goodman, the son of his sister Julia, was the first postmaster at Cody, and Julia herself was the first manager of the Irma Hotel. Cody's correspondence with Julia

A late portrait of Buffalo Bill, this genial countenance graced the cover of the brochure advertising the TE as a dude ranch, and also appeared in his 1915 "Hotels in the Rockies" brochure. Courtesy of Buffalo Bill Historical Center, Cody, Wyo.; P.6.145.

reveals a close and loving connection. His care for Julia extended even to the language he used in his letters to her: although he never demonstrated the slightest Christian piety in any other work or writing, these letters are filled with it, almost certainly because he knew it was so important to her.[16] His sister Helen and her husband, Duluth publisher Hugh Wetmore, provided the presses for the first *Cody Enterprise*. His sister May took up land next to his ranch, which he then incorporated into the TE. May moved to Cody in 1903, married Louis Decker, and managed the Irma after Julia moved away. The strength of Bill Cody's feeling as a family man was evidenced in many ways through his Wyoming work.[17]

Certainly the most dramatic Cody family experience during his Wyoming years was the 1905 divorce trial, in which Bill attempted to put away Louisa, his wife of nearly forty years. This episode was widely covered in the state and national press, and has since been retold in detail by historians.[18] Cody made his home in Wyoming, and Lulu, as she was familiarly known, lived in North Platte, Nebraska. Cody initiated the action in Wyoming. Wyoming's divorce law may have seemed more accommodating to him, as it allowed incompatibility as a ground for divorce, but Cody may well have had other reasons for choosing that time and place to pursue the issue. As Wyoming's celebrity capitalist, his experience of dealing with the officers of the state might well have led him to expect that he would get his way in any proceeding held in Wyoming. Cody charged that Louisa had made his life in North Platte intolerable by refusing to allow his friends into their home there, and that she had attempted to poison him. It was not a strong case; the poison allegations, while sensational, were not at all difficult to defend against. Louisa's attorneys managed to make Cody's own womanizing and drinking into central issues, and they succeeded in preventing the divorce. If the Colonel did choose to initiate the suit in Wyoming in expectation of a friendly hearing, he judged the situation poorly. His celebrity could not carry him any father in a courtroom than in a business negotiation.

Cody's decades of experience with advertising and its effects some-times led him into a confusion between the world as it was and the world as he wanted it to be. He would tell a direct lie if it served his purpose, but in general, for most of his life, he behaved as if truth were an inconvenience or an irrelevance. As he grew older, the tending of his personal myth obviously took precedence over considerations of fact or fiction. The extravagant, even impossible, plans he publicly proclaimed— leading the automobiles into Yellowstone, leading the largest hunt ever undertaken—were not so much lies as gestures toward the idea of "Buffalo Bill" that he must have felt fading within himself. Their implausibility was a small weight in the balance against the possibility of recharging his diminishing personhood.

In common with many promoters, he came to believe that if he said a thing often enough it would become true. He continued to pronounce the Cody Canal a success until he simply had to walk away from it. This inability to recognize contradictory evidence might, perversely, also have led to good outcomes. Some of his partners and other interested parties, like the Burlington people, saw little prospect for success at Cody. All the evidence they saw was available to Buffalo Bill, but he ignored it and bulled ahead, and in the end got his town on its feet. Still, he never got out of the habit of announcing grand schemes that never came off, or deceiving himself that a bad investment was about to turn good. He did more than enough in his life in Wyoming to earn himself a large place in its history. Only the contrast with the self-advertised Buffalo Bill can make the life of the real Bill Cody seem something of a disappointment.

The American, as personified in the hero of the Wild West, was a self-reliant individual, capable of overcoming all manner of difficulties through skill or—if necessary—by force, and withal honest and cheerful. This vision was the core of the myth of the West, the reason why many people came to consider the story of Euro-American conquest of the West the true creation story of America. This was the kind of person Americans wanted to be. The myth, which blended seamlessly with Buffalo Bill's idea of his own history and the history of the westward movement in America, obscured more history than it revealed. Most critically, the emphasis on the struggle of the individual to overcome obstacles thrown up by the environment, whether natural or human, served to direct the attention of Americans away from the role played in the settling of the West by cooperative or corporate entities. Yet it was precisely during the lifetime of Buffalo Bill's Wild West show that the process of incorporation began to take hold in America, changing American culture in ways that contradicted that mythical construction at every turn.[19]

Alan Trachtenberg has explored in cultural terms what he calls "the incorporation of America." Although it came about as the limited liability corporation charged into dominance in American business after the Civil War, Trachtenberg's view of incorporation extends well beyond the confines of business practice. He means to direct our attention to "the emergence of a changed, more tightly structured society with new hierarchies of control, and also changed conceptions of that society, of America itself."[20] Not only business corporations but government, both state and federal, played crucial roles in the emergence of this newly organized society. In this view, the work of the young Buffalo Bill hunting for the railroads (where he earned his name) and scouting for the army was an essential part of the incorporation process, clearing the land of animals and people that would not be part of a newly organized America. And it does not end there. The Wild West show itself was a corporation, jointly owned by Cody and Salsbury. The Shoshone Irrigation Company, the Cody Military College, Cody's Wyoming Coal Company, were also corporations founded by Buffalo Bill for the purpose of doing business. His voting preference, stated most forcefully in the 1896 election, was for the corporate business ticket of William McKinley.

In retrospect, it seems clear that the man who was the very image of the free individual on the open plain, the man with his gun against the world, was in many ways the bearer of the spirit of incorporation when he entered Wyoming in 1895. Certainly the Populists saw him in that light. He did what he could to fasten corporate control on the resources of the Big Horn Basin. He worked to bring in the Burlington Railroad, probably the most efficient agent of incorporation that corner of the West had seen. He opened the way (albeit unwittingly and actively pushed by the Burlington) for the federal government to establish control of the water of the Shoshone. Submitting his rifle, the symbol of frontier independence, to the control of the state, he led the way to the commodification of wildlife and the spread of the control of the state over the terms upon which man would meet the wilderness. Finally, he led in the creation of a tourist economy that domesticated what had been wild and made it accessible—while still mildly thrilling—to those who entered into it as consumers.

Famed as an Indian fighter, willing to do his part in the Ghost Dance troubles of 1890, Buffalo Bill also conducted himself with friendship and even honor to many of the Indians who worked for him and hunted with him and attended his festivals. He was widely recognized as a "friend of the Indian," as by Rodman Wanamaker at the famous 1909 banquet honoring Cody and announcing Wanamaker's intention to build a great Indian statue in New York Harbor. Cody devoted several pages of his final autobiography, *The Great West That Was*, to pleading the case for Indians as good citizens of the new America. But even this can be seen as a move in the incorporation game. Trachtenberg notes that "a fabric of fantasy, nostalgia, and idealization appeared toward the end of the nineteenth century as a kind of shroud for 'the Vanishing American.'"[21] Fantasy and nostalgia were Cody's stock in trade, whether he was on stage, in the arena, or in print. He may unwittingly have served the process of incorporation best when he sugar-coated it with his fantasies of the freedom of the frontier individual. Surely Joy Kasson was on the mark when she emphasized how Indians at the Wild West—she could have said the same thing about Indians at the Park County Fair in Cody in 1913—were colorful and safe while seeming to connect visitors to a mythical past.

Bill Cody was not always comfortable with the world as it changed around him. He tried to take the lead in incorporating the Big Horn Basin, but he was not very efficient as an incorporator. None of the corporations he presided over there could be said to have succeeded. His true imagination remained rooted in his youth: "the old free mountain life for me," he wrote to his painter friend, R. Farrington Elwell, when under stress on the road.[22] He never figured out how to deal with the federal government, as it changed in response to the general wave of incorporation around the turn of the century. He became bitter about what he perceived as his mistreatment at the hands of the Reclamation Service. We might say he was enthusiastic about the incorporation process when he was doing it, but rather less so when it was being done to him. In this, he was no different than anyone else, but, of course, Buffalo Bill Cody was different from everyone else. His agonies were played out, as his triumphs had been, in public.

We may take his life in Wyoming as an example of the conflicted state of many Americans at the turn of the twentieth century, being pulled (and occasionally pushing) into a corporate civilization at a dizzying rate, resisting when he felt the process rubbing his skin raw, crying out when he found his way blocked, finally settling for what space he could find in the tightly organized world of the twentieth century. Bill Cody may have embodied not only the fantasies of the western past, but also the contradictions and conflict attendant upon such massive social and cultural change. The town and the state he left behind are still caught up in the myriad contradictions Cody encompassed, perhaps because he succeeded so well at advancing the course of incorporation while masking it with his own life. Nothing was as common in the pages of the *Enterprise* in those years as complaints about the Burlington Railroad and the federal

The old man in winter: the last photograph of Buffalo Bill at the TE, winter 1916. Courtesy of Buffalo Bill Historical Center, Cody, Wyo.; P.69.320.

government, major forces for incorporation that accompanied William Cody to the Big Horn Basin.

The concept of imposture, so central to Louis Warren's understanding of Cody's life and career in general, offers also a way to think, in particular, of his Wyoming experience. Warren focuses on Cody's use of his early days on the frontier to make his way in show business, offering a compelling case that "imposture" is the best way to see the career of Buffalo Bill. Warren shows how dubious the many claims made on behalf of Cody's frontier experience actually were. The frontier imposture relied upon experience in the distant West, which he then took east to audiences eager for some contact with that part of American national life, audiences willing to believe virtually anything told to them by a man whose self-presentation was as artful as Buffalo Bill's was.

Naturally, as Cody succeeded in building a fortune from playing that role, he sought out and enjoyed the company of men of great wealth and power. When he returned west, in 1893, he presented himself as a man of power and wealth in his own right. No longer simply the man of the frontier, he now rubbed elbows with corporation presidents. In Wyoming, Cody may be said to have developed what we might call a "capitalist imposture," a confidently asserted claim to great scope and ability in the corporate world. As with the frontier imposture, the capitalist imposture relied upon the distance between East and West, and the exaggerated respect afforded wealthy easterners once they crossed the Missouri River. (Cody would have understood that intuitively, as he had felt that way toward wealthy eastern hunters when he first met them as a young guide.) Of course, the frontier imposture did not ever break down; Cody himself spent considerable time near the end of his life reinforcing it for posterity and profit. He was not as fortunate in his capitalist imposture. There were no obvious checks to his frontier self-presentation, but the ledger-book world of corporate activity is structured to expose and punish impostors.

William Cody left a mixed inheritance for the land and people of the Big Horn Basin. His biggest impact, of course, was on the town of Cody and the river valleys to the west. The townspeople bought in wholeheartedly to their founder's frontier imposture. Buffalo Bill was the first thing they had to sell, and they sold him aggressively. Cody men led the way in establishing "Good Roads" associations to get people to Cody and dude ranchers' associations to take care of them. The town was not completely an Old West theme park, what with oil refineries, sulphur mines, and gypsum products sustaining something like an industrial work force, but tourism was its major source of identity and revenue, and that depended upon the William Cody heritage as much as on the beautiful natural setting. The Buffalo Bill who was celebrated in Cody throughout the twentieth century was the man of the Old West and the Wild West. The Bill Cody who came to Wyoming to build big cities and thousands of farms, to say nothing of his other schemes, was allowed to recede almost to the vanishing point.

Cody embraced its role as a cowboy town through the annual Cody Stampede and the summer-long Cody Nite Rodeo, a more or less continuous Wild West entertainment for tourists staying in the thousands of beds provided for them. Bars, supper clubs, and (for at least half of the century) brothels gave the town a flavor that was marketable far and wide as quintessentially western. In the second half of the century more sedate entertainments entered the mix, as the Buffalo Bill Historical Center, art galleries, and related activities moved to the fore, branding

Cody as a New West center. William Cody's Wild West inheritance proved bankable for his town right on through the century, but it was his particular determination to bring the East to Cody that finally enabled Cody to become more than just another rodeo town.[23]

The BBHC is not simply a local organization. The Whitney Gallery of Western Art, the Plains Indian Museum, and the Winchester Firearms Museum quickly earned national respect in their fields, as the new Draper Museum of Natural History promises to do. Additionally, the Board of Trustees of the BBHC contains a great many men and women who represent corporate achievement and wealth from all over the nation. They may own homes or even ranches in the river valleys west of town, but they represent the kind of metropolitan connection that Bill Cody himself set out to create. The first of this long stream of well-heeled easterners to "acquire" Cody was William Robertson Coe, whose bequest enabled the founding of the BBHC. In the second half of the century, a great deal of the board's important business was conducted at Peter Kriendler's "21" Club in New York City. As a result of this connection of people and money, Cody is a far different town from any other in the Big Horn Basin.[24]

The other Big Horn Basin towns in which William Cody had an interest grew in quite other directions. Ralston has scratched out a tenuous existence, a wide spot in the road with a gas station, a bar, and very few people. Garland, more substantial than Ralston at the beginning of the century, was by the end nothing more than a secondary road junction. Powell, the town Cody tried to stop, grew and prospered throughout the century, one of only two reasonably successful Reclamation-founded towns in the West. Although close to Cody in population for most of the century, it was and is a far different town. A square mile of undifferentiated farmland straddling the canal and the railroad, it was functional and little more. Powell was dry by choice before Prohibition and not very wet after it. People in Powell who wanted a little excitement would go over to Cody. Steadfastly middle-class, built first of all to serve the farmers, then enriched in the middle of the century by a very productive oil field north of town, there was nothing cosmopolitan at all about Powell. It seems safe to say that neither Garland nor Ralston would have developed as Powell did if Bill Cody and the Lincoln Land Company had been successful in stopping the Reclamation Service from building Powell. The fact that Cody already had ownership interest in both those towns shaped Powell as a bastion of middle-class respectability. Bill Cody did not like the Reclamation Service and Carolyn Lockhart, Cody's self-proclaimed spiritual heiress, penned in her diary: "I don't like Powellites."[25]

Powell is a monument to William Cody's capitalist imposture, as Cody is to his frontier imposture. If he had been the kind of man who could pull together great capital in the pursuit of major social and economic objectives, the Reclamation Service never would have got a start on the Shoshone Project, and Powell would never have been built. But even if he had been successful enough as a capitalist to have got a start, it is extremely doubtful he would have built as well as the government did. The records of large Carey Act projects in Wyoming present a picture of unrelieved failure. As he never got his plan going, the Reclamation Service had a clear field in which to work. The men of the USRS were able to design literally a model project: centered around a government town, watering ultimately 93,000 acres entirely by gravity flow from the big Shoshone Dam, the Shoshone Project was recreated to scale for the Department of Interior exhibit at the Pan-Pacific Exhibition in San Francisco in 1915.[26] The Project suffered the full range of problems that beset federal reclamation in the early twentieth century, but there can be no doubt that, socially and agriculturally, the Big Horn Basin has been better served by this federal project than it would have been by anything Cody could have built.

It would not do to end this study emphasizing the negative elements of William Cody's life in Wyoming. There is some kind of achievement in a century of the celebration of one's name, which is the most obvious mark of his life in the Big Horn Basin. It is important to note that this success was the result of work undertaken mostly on his own in developing the elements of a tourist economy along the Shoshone River; it was not a matter of a corporate initiative at all. It is true that tourism could not have succeeded without the Burlington Railroad, but we now know that the railroad people did what they did for their own good reasons. The tourist work that Cody and others did owed a great deal to the Wild West show experience. That hunting big game formed an important element of the tourist economy around Cody reached back even further than the Wild West, to his days as a scout and guide for the Fifth Cavalry. In the terms we are using here, these initiatives depended essentially on his frontier imposture. Cody's continued importance in the tourist economy of his namesake town, represented most solidly in the Buffalo Bill Historical Center, simply ignores the failure of his capitalist imposture; it depends entirely on the success of the other one.

We cannot ever entirely separate his Wyoming life and work from his life and work on the national scene. Just as he remained a popular, even beloved figure across the nation, so the people in his hometown continued to love him. And even in the ledger book of his life, the debts that wore him down at the end were not primarily the result of failed enterprises in the Big Horn Basin. (To be fair, we should note that the money to buy and build in Wyoming did not come from profits earned in the Basin, either.) He left something for Louisa to live on there, the TE and the Irma Hotel, both of which she sold soon after he died. The grand vision he set out for Mike Russell in 1895 never materialized, as we know, and he was denied even the opportunity to stretch out under a tree with Mike and swap lies. But his failures were for the most part entombed with him on Lookout Mountain near Denver, and his accomplishments, real and imagined, told and retold until the picture of him that hangs throughout the Big Horn Basin today is unmistakably the benign, fatherly figure everyone loved. If this is an imposture, we can almost hear him say, make the most of it.

Abbreviations

AHC	American Heritage Center, University of Wyoming, Laramie.
BBHC	McCracken Library, Buffalo Bill Historical Center, Cody, Wyo.
BBL	Buffalo Bill Letters to George T. Beck, 1895–1910. Collection no. 9972, American Heritage Center, University of Wyoming, Laramie.
BBMG	Buffalo Bill Museum and Grave Archive, Lookout Mountain, Golden, Col.
BP	George T. Beck Papers. Collection no. 59, American Heritage Center, University of Wyoming, Laramie.
BFP	Beck Family Papers. Collection no. 10386, American Heritage Center, University of Wyoming, Laramie.
CB&Q	Records of the Chicago, Burlington, and Quincy Railroads, Newberry Library, Chicago.
CCF	Central Classified File of the correspondence of the Secretary of the Interior, RG 48, NA.
GCWSE	General Correspondence of the Wyoming State Engineer, Wyoming State Archives, Cheyenne.
LBSE	Letterpress Book of the State Engineer, Wyoming State Archives, Cheyenne.
LC	Library of Congress, Washington, D.C.
NA	National Archives, Washington, D.C.

NSHS   Nebraska State Historical Society, Lincoln.

PCHSA   Park County Historical Society Archives, Cody, Wyo.

RG 48   Record Group 48, Department of Interior, National
          Archives, Washington, D.C.

RG 115   Record Group 115, Records of the Bureau of Reclama-
          tion, Rocky Mountain Branch of the National Archives,
          Denver, Col.

USRS   United States Reclamation Service

WFC   William Frederick Cody

WFCC   William F. Cody Collection, MS 6, McCracken Library,
          Buffalo Bill Historical Center, Cody.

WSA   Wyoming State Archives, Cheyenne, Wyo.

Notes

INTRODUCTION

1. Fernand Braudel, *The Mediterranean and the Mediterranean World in the Age of Philip II,* trans. Sian Reynolds (1972), 17 (Preface to the first edition).

2. Kasson, *Buffalo Bill's Wild West,* 1–63. See also Warren's treatment of Cody's relationship with the frontier army, *Buffalo Bill's America,* 82–149.

3. Yost, *Buffalo Bill,* 255–60. The nature of private enterprise irrigation development in the West has been explored by Pisani, *To Reclaim a Divided West; Water,* esp. 104–108.

4. The frontier imposture, as Warren sees it, was an exploration of the boundary between fact and fiction undertaken by such men as Wild Bill Hickock to create a public space where they could perform and turn a profit from their experience as scouts, gunfighters, hunters, or whatever image they could sell to an eager public. The question of whether they ever actually did the deeds for which they claimed credit was left conveniently up in the air. See *Buffalo Bill's America,* 73–79. William Cody's particular imposture involved ostentatious claims to authenticity, which a man like Hickock would have avoided.

CHAPTER ONE: COMING INTO THE BASIN

1. King, *History of Wildlife,* 9–14.

2. See Harris, *John Colter.*

3. See Lowe, *Bridger Trail.*

4. Schuchert and LeVene, *O. C. Marsh,* esp. pp. 103, 129. There are some notes from Cody to Marsh in 1873 and 1874 in Marsh's correspondence; see Othniel C. Marsh Papers, microfilm reel no. 3, Manuscripts and Archives, Yale University Library; Russell, *Lives and Legends,* 166–68. The newspaper interview was with the *Big Horn County Rustler,* Jan. 21, 1910; reprinted in the *Cody Enterprise,* Feb. 20, 1946. Unfortunately, a recent author has reiterated this ancient error regarding Cody's entry into the Basin; see Milton L. Woods, *Big Horn Basin,* 200. Woods gives the year as 1871, repeating Cody's own confusion in his 1879 autobiography, *Life of Hon. William F. Cody* (1879; repr., University of Nebraska Press, 1978),

278. Cody recalls clearly in his 1879 book that he spent only one day with Marsh, and while he declared himself impressed with the professor's theories, there is no specific reference to the Basin in that book.

5. Wetmore, *Last of the Great Scouts*, 253–55; Russell, *Lives and Legends,* 279–80.

6. Mills, *Report of the Big Horn Expedition.*

7. Walter and Code, "Elwood Mead," 1611–18. Donald J. Pisani accepted the 1888 date from the obituary in his short account of the activities of the Shoshone Land and Irrigation Company in *To Reclaim a Divided West,* 254–59.

8. Russell, *Lives and Legends,* 236–51 and 420–30; Yost, *Buffalo Bill,* 162–260; *Historic Sheridan Inn* publications, Sheridan, Wyo. Woods, *Big Horn Basin,* 201, apparently following Yost, states that Cody was the "moving force" behind the construction of the Sheridan Inn.

9. McLaird, "Ranching in the Big Horns," 157–85. See also Beck's draft autobiography in BP, box 7.

10. Wasden, *From Beaver to Oil,* 161–63. See also his unpublished manuscript, dated 1975, "The Beginning of the Cody Canal and Townsite," BBHC.

11. Yost, *Buffalo Bill,* 213. Woods repeats this questionable observation (of Mrs. Beck visiting in North Platte) in *Big Horn Basin,* 200 (without attribution), and concludes categorically that this was the beginning of the Cody-Beck association.

12. David J. Wasden, "Cody Canal," 2–5, BBHC. McLaird, "Building the Town of Cody," 73–105, dates the trip as 1893, following Beck's memoir, but it appears that this is an instance of Beck's faulty recall three decades after the fact.

13. Betty Beck Roberson and Jane Beck Johnson, "Beckoning Frontiers," unpublished memoir of their father, George T. Beck, Beck Collection, PCHSA. The draft is in Beck's voice and is virtually identical to his draft autobiography in BP, box 7, AHC.

14. Yost, *Buffalo Bill,* 258–59.

15. The report is dated Aug. 18, 1894. A copy of it may be found in BP, box 20, folder 3. There is one biography of Mead, Kluger's, *Turning on Water with a Shovel.* The book is not comprehensive, offering very little insight into this stage of Mead's career.

16. "Shoshone Irrigation Project Water Rights; Brief History of Project Permits," in Shoshone Irrigation District Archives, Powell, Wyo.

17. Mead, "Report on the South Side Canal," BP, box 20, folder 3. Mead refers here to a company that is not yet incorporated, knowing that Beck and Alger planned to put one together. The Carey Act is discussed in Lee, *Reclaiming the American West;* Dunbar, *Forging New Rights;* and Pisani, *To Reclaim A Divided West.*

18. *First Biennial Report,* 20.

19. *Second Biennial Report,* 164–65. Mead used both names in the second report, but subsequent reports used only Shoshone. Hiram Chittenden to Mead, Oct. 28, 1896, Nov. 2, 22, 1896, Jan. 22, 30, 1897; Frank Mondell to Mead, Dec. 23, 1897—all in GCWSE, 1890–1902. Briefly, in 1897, at the instance of Major Chittenden, Mead seemed inclined to have the river renamed "Colter River," in honor of the first U.S. citizen to travel up it, but too much was invested by then in "Shoshone"; Chittenden to Mead, Jan. 23 and 30, 1897, and Mead to Gov. W. A. Richards, Feb. 1, 1897, GCWSE, 1890–1902. Ultimately, at Chittenden's suggestion, the name was changed by statute on Feb. 14, 1901: *Session Laws of the State of Wyoming passed by the Sixth State Legislature* (1901), 38. Chittenden himself subsequently filed the name change with the U.S. Board on Geographic Names: U.S. Board on Geographic Names files, Reston, Va., card 686.2, Shoshone River.

20. Wasden, "Cody Canal," 13–14; Mead to W. E. Hymer, Mar. 25, 1895, GCWSE, 1890–1902, WSA; Mead to Alger, July 23, 1895, and Mead to George Holdrege, Aug. 1, 1895,

LBSE; *First Annual Report of the State Board of Land Commissioners* (1896), 5–10. Water permits in Wyoming were issued in terms of cubic feet per second (cfs) of constant flow, employing the calculation that one cfs provided water sufficient to irrigate seventy acres of land.

21. "Beckoning Frontiers," Part IV, 11–13, Beck Collection, PCHSA.

22. Cody to Mead, Mar. 22, 1895, GCWSE, 1902–1913. The surviving correspondence from Cody to Mead is all filed in this series, even if by date it should have been filed in the 1890–1902 series. Cody's trip into the Basin with Beck is described in "Beckoning Frontiers," 10–17.

23. WFC to Mike Russell, July 13, 1895, W. F. Cody (Buffalo Bill) Papers, box 1, folder 5, Beinecke Library, Yale University.

CHAPTER TWO: "CHRISTOPHER COLUMBUS" DIGS A DITCH

1. Salsbury to Beck, Oct. 30, 1902, BP, box 2, folder 12. See also Russell, *Lives and Legends*, 298–304.

2. WFC to Mead, Mar. 22, 1895, GCWSE, 1902–1913.

3. Wasden, "Cody Canal," 14–17. It is important to note here the the approval by the State Land Board amounted simply to a request to the General Land Office to segregate the designated land under the terms of the Carey Act. There remained a considerable amount of bureaucratic labor before the project was finally and fully approved. See *First Annual Report of the State Board of Land Commissioners* (1896), 5–7.

4. Assistant state engineer C. M. Gilcrest to Mead, Apr. 15, 1895, LBSE.

5. WFC to Beck, May 12, [1895], from Scranton, Pa., BBL, box 1, folder 1. Cody's reference to "either side of the river," indicating a vision of his project rather larger than the one they had a permit to build, is explained below.

6. WFC to Beck, June 26, 1895, from Newport; see also WFC to Beck, June 14, 1895, from Boston—both in BBL, box 1, folder 1. In September, Alger had hopes of bringing in some Standard Oil men, which would have guaranteed the entire project; Alger to Mead, Sept. 11, 1895, GCWSE, 1890–1902.

7. WFC to Beck, July 2, 1895, from Lowell, Mass., BBL, box 1, folder 1.

8. WFC to Mead, Aug. 9, [1895], GCWSE, 1902–1913.

9. WFC to Beck, August 13, 1895, BBL, box 1, folder 1.

10. Ibid., Sept. 29, 1895.

11. Ibid., Oct. 4, 1895.

12. Beck to Mead, Oct. 21, 1895, GCWSE, 1890–1902.

13. Francis E. Warren to Elwood Mead, Oct. 3, 1895, Francis E. Warren Papers, Series I: General Correspondence (microfilm), AHC.

14. WFC to Beck, Oct. 6, 1895, BBL, box 1, folder 1. Buffalo Bill's sister, Helen Cody Wetmore, was married to a man whom Cody set up in the newspaper business in Duluth, Minn.; Russell, *Lives and Legends*, 279–80.

15. WFC to Beck, Oct. 16, 1895, BBL, box 1, folder 1.

16. Ibid., Oct. 19, 1895.

17. Ibid., Oct. 21, 1895. Beck described the working conditions to Elwood Mead in an undated letter, probably Nov. 1895, in GCWSE, 1890–1902.

18. WFC to Beck, Oct. 21, [1895], BP, box 1, folder 10.

19. Ibid., Oct. 27, 1895, BBL, box 1, folder 1.

20. Contract agreements among Beck, Cody, Bleistein, and John Davies concerning two mining claims, Nov. 30, 1895, in BP, [box 1, folder 10], copy in Beck Collection, PCHSA;

Rumsey to Beck, Dec. 9, 1895, BFP, box 1, folder 4; Beck to Mead, [Nov.? 1895], GCWSE, 1890–1902.

21. Mead to Alger, Nov. 23, 1895, LBSE; "Report on the South Side Canal," 10–11, BP, box 20, folder 3.

22. WFC to Beck, Oct. 4, 1895, BBL, box 1, folder 1. Foote's letter to Secretary Smith is in Records of the General Land Office, Carey Act Cases 1895–1917, box 6, E. 962, RG 49, NA. For Wyoming populism, see Gould, *Wyoming;* Carroll, "Robert Foote," 9–23, may also be of interest.

23. WFC to Beck, Oct. 6, 1895, BBL, box 1, folder 1.

24. Mead to WFC, Oct. 11, 1895, LBSE; *First Annual Report of the State Board of Land Commissioners,* 6. Warren's role in the politics of development is brought out by Lilley and Gould, "Western Irrigation Movement," in Gressley, *American West,* 57–76. Idaho Carey Act applications in the first year were also all rejected at the U.S. Land Office; see Williams, *Carey Act in Idaho,* (1970).

25. Mead to WFC, Oct. 11, 1895, LBSE.

26. Ibid., Sept. 13, 1895. The headgate, shown in Fig. 1, was placed on the river where water was diverted into the canal, to control the flow into the ditch.

27. WFC to Mead, Sept. 18, 1895, GCWSE, 1902–1913.

28. Ibid., Oct. 25, [1895].

29. Mead to WFC, Nov. 4, 1895, LBSE.

30. WFC to Beck, Dec. 13, 1895, BP, box 1, folder 10; Yost, *Buffalo Bill,* 266. A scraper was a horse-drawn blade that moved dirt.

31. LBSE, Oct. 24, 1895 to Jan. 30, 1896, 235–41.

32. Ibid.

33. WFC to Beck, telegram from New York, Jan. 24, 1896, BFP, box 1, folder 5.

34. Ibid., second telegram from New York.

35. W. M. Gilcrest, asst. state engineer, to Editor, *Big Horn County Rustler,* Feb. 14, 1896, GCWSE, 1890–1902; WFC to Gilcrest, Jan. 15, 1896, GCWSE, 1902–1913; Alger to Beck, Dec. 2, 1895, and Mondell to Beck, Dec. 24, 1895, BFP, box 1, folder 4.

36. WFC to Mead, March 11, 1896, GCWSE, 1902–1913.

37. Mead to WFC, March 12, 1896, LBSE.

38. Mead to Warren, March 13, 1896, LBSE.

39. WFC to Beck, March 26, [1896], BBL, box 1, folder 1; the letter is filed with 1895 correspondence, but was obviously written in 1896.

40. Mead to WFC, March 14, 1896, LBSE.

41. WFC to Beck, June 3, 14, 26, and July 2, 24, 27, 1895, BBL. box 1, folder 1. However, Cody still thought as late as April 1896 that Paxton could be persuaded to come in. WFC to Beck, telegram, April 11, 1896, BFP, box 1, folder 6.

42. WFC to Beck, telegram, June 8, 1895, and Salsbury to Alger, July 26, 1895, BFP, box 1, folder 4.

43. H. C. Alger to Mead, Sept. 11, 1895, GCWSE, 1890–1902.

44. WFC to Beck, Sept. 15, 1895, BBL, box 1, folder 1; Wasden, "Cody Canal," 20–21.

45. Hymer to Beck, May 6, Alger to Beck, July 21, and Higbie to Beck, Aug. 5, 1895, BFP, box 1, folder 4.

46. WFC to Beck, telegram Aug. 28 and Sept 10, 1895, BFP, box 1, folder 4; ibid., Sept. 15 and Sept 23, 1895, BBL, box 1, folder 1; Mead to W. E. Hymer, Mar. 25, 1895, LBSE; Rumsey to Beck, Dec. 9, 1895, BFP, box 1, folder 4, and Jan. 24, 1896, BFP, box 1, folder 5.

Cody had obviously hoped to bring more prospective investors along on that hunting trip; see WFC to Beck, Oct. 16, [1895], BBL, box 1, folder 1.

47. WFC to Beck, Mar. 26, [1896], BBL, box 1, folder 1.

48. Black America was a show Cody and Salsbury put together on the model of the Wild West, intended as an "Exhibition of Negro Life and Character." It opened in Brooklyn in 1895 but closed after a run of only a few weeks. It cost the two of them well over $100,000. Warren, *Buffalo Bill's America*, 434–37.

49. WFC to Beck, telegram from Buffalo, N.Y., Apr. 6, 1896, BFP, box 1, folder 6. Copies of the contracts may be found in Public Lands Records, Applications for entry, Box 1, WSA. See also Salsbury to Beck, Mar. 25, 1896, and J. A. Van Orsdel to Beck, Mar. 28, 1896, BFP, box 1, folder 5.

50. WFC to Beck, March 10, 1896, BBL, box 1, folder 2.

51. Ibid., March 26, 1896.

52. Salsbury's observations on Cody's managerial abilities were expressed in an unpublished manuscript he wrote around 1900, when he was in a fit of pique with his star. See "Cody, Manager," box 2, folder 64, Nathan Salsbury Papers, YCAL MSS 17, Beinecke Library, Yale University.

53. WFC to Mead, March 28, 1896, GCWSE, 1902–1913; Mead to WFC, March 26, 1896, LBSE.

54. Salsbury to Beck, March 11, 1896, BFP, box 1, folder 5.

55. Ibid., April 2, 1896, BFP, box 1, folder 6.

56. WFC to Mead, March 28, 1896, GCWSE, 1902–1913.

57. Mead to Edward Gillette, April 16, 1896, LBSE.

58. Mead to Beck, March 19, 1896, LBSE.

59. WFC to Beck, April 3, 1896, BBL, box 1, folder 2.

60. Ibid., Apr. 13, 1896.

61. Ibid., Apr. 28, 1896.

62. Alger to Beck, May 13, 1896, BFP, box 1, folder 7.

63. WFC to Beck, May 8 and 13, 1896, BBL, box 1, folder 2. "Red Bluffs" was a troublesome patch of land on the canal line; see Chapter 3.

64. WFC to Beck, May 17, 1896, BBL, box 1, folder 2.

65. Ibid., May 25, 1896.

66. Rumsey to Beck, April 16, 1896, BFP, box 1, folder 6. In a postscript Rumsey advised Beck to destroy this letter, perhaps because he felt he had been too candid in reference to Cody.

67. Ibid., April 30, 1896.

68. Salsbury to WFC, May 1, 1896, BFP, box 1, folder 7.

69. Ibid. Salsbury sent a carbon copy of this letter to Beck, so he would know how they wanted things done, and perhaps also for a kind of personal reassurance.

70. Alger to Beck, May 21 and 22, Rumsey to Beck, May 21, 1896, BFP, box 1, folder 7.

71. WFC to Beck, May 29, 1896, BBL, box 1, folder 2. By the date of this letter, there, in fact, had been no land sold under the canal.

72. WFC to Beck, [June 1896], BBL, box 1, folder 14.

73. "Cody, Manager," Salsbury MSS, box 2, folder 64, YCAL MSS 17, Beinecke Library.

74. Wasden, "Cody Canal," 25; Report of Geo. T. Beck to the Board of Directors for 1896, BP, box 20, folder 5; Daisy Sorrenson to Beck (in Chicago), June 1, 1896, BP, box 1, folder 12; Elwood Mead to Edward Gillette in Sheridan, June 22, 1896, GCWSE.

75. WFC to Beck, July 5, 1896, BBL, box 1, folder 2. It is clear from an exchange between Nate Salsbury and the Colonel that the agent of disruption and disinformation was Cody's ranch manager, W. O. "Okie" Snyder; see Nathan Salsbury Papers, box 1, folder 12, YCAL MSS 17, Beinecke Library.

76. WFC to Beck, July 5, 1896, BBL, box 1, folder 2.

77. Ibid., Aug 1, 1896; Mead to Edward Gillette, June 22, 1896, LBSE.

78. WFC to Beck, Aug. 14, 1896, BBL, box 1, folder 2.

79. Ibid., Aug. 17, 1896. The Democrats, led by William Jennings Bryan, campaigned in 1896 for the free coinage of silver. Warren is of the opinion that Cody wore his politics lightly, that he would have been equally happy with a Bryan victory in 1896. My reading of his words and actions in Wyoming leads me to conclude that, at least, from 1896 onward he was steadfastly Republican. Warren's statement (*Buffalo Bill's America*, 265) that Cody helped to organize the Democratic Party in his new town is based on a reading of the evidence that I do not share.

80. Salsbury to Beck, July 30, and Aug. 14, 1896, BFP, box 1, folder 8.

81. "Resources of the Shoshone Irrigation Company," no author, no date (but later than July 16, 1896), BP, box 20.

82. Gerrans, Rumsey, and Bleistein to Beck, June 11, 1896, BP, box 1, folder 12.

83. WFC to Beck, July 7 and Aug 1, 1896, BBL, box 1, folder 2.

84. Beck to Alger, July 28, 1896, Shoshone Irrigation Co. (SIC) Letterpress Book, BP, box 25.

85. Beck to Salsbury, Aug. 7, and Beck to Alger, Aug. 26, 1896, SIC Letterpress Book, BP, box 25; WFC to Beck, Sept. 16, 1896, BBL, box 1, folder 2. A fuller account of the county seat fight follows in Chapter 3.

86. WFC to Beck, Aug. 23, 1896, BP, box 1, folder 12; Beck to WFC, Aug. 26 and Aug. 29, 1896, SIC Letterpress Book, BP, box 25; Alger to Beck, Sept. 21, 1896, BFP, box 1, folder 8.

87. Salsbury to Beck, Aug. 14, 1896, BFP, box 1, folder 8.

88. Salsbury to WFC, Sept. 14, 1896, BFP, box 1, folder 8.

89. WFC to Beck, Aug. 14, 17, 23, and 31, 1896, BBL, box 1, folder 2; Beck to WFC, Aug. 23, 26, 31, and Sept. 4, 1896, SIC Letterpress Book, BP, box 25.

90. Report of George Beck, mgr. of the Shoshone Irrigation Co., [Dec.] 1896, BP, box 20, folder 5.

91. WFC to Beck, Apr. 3, 6, 28, May 7 and 13, Sept. 3, 1896, BBL, box 1, folder 2; Records of Shoshone Land and Irrigation Co, 1896, BP, box 20, folder 5.

92. Nov. 24, 1896, Statement of Account of WFC with Shoshone Irrigation Co., BP, box 20, folder 5.

93. Report from Hayden to Beck, Oct. 29, 1896, BP, box 20, folder 5.

CHAPTER THREE: A TOWN IN THE WILDERNESS

1. Russell, *Lives and Legends*, 84–85; Yost, *Buffalo Bill*, 13–15.

2. A copy of the original plat is published in Cook et al., *Buffalo Bill's Town*, 48.

3. Mead to H. C. Alger, Nov. 1, 1895, GCWSE, 1890–1902; WFC to Beck, May 12, July 2, and July 24, 1895, BBL, box 1, folder 1; Wyoming State Engineer, Water permit applications, no. 1207. Some authors have speculated that Hymer was an agent of the Lincoln Land Co., the development arm of the Burlington Railroad; see Haglund, "Buffalo Bill Cody Country," 41–43. This tale derives from C. E. Hayden's memoir (see below), which confuses

Hymer with Albert Heimer of Red Lodge. W. E. Hymer was from Holdrege, Nebraska, and although he could certainly have had dealing with the Burlington there, the Lincoln Land Co. had no business in the Cody area for another five years.

4. WFC to Beck, Sept. 15, 1895, BBL, box 1, folder 1.

5. Ibid., Sept. 25, 1895. Such things as saloon license fees were never under the control of the Shoshone Irrigation Company, and the people of Cody who actually made these decisions were never in favor of exclusionary license fees.

6. WFC to Beck, Oct. 6, 1895, BBL, box 1, folder 1.

7. Salsbury to Beck, Oct. 2, 1895, BFP, box 1, folder 4.

8. Ibid.

9. WFC to Beck, Oct. 21, 1895, BP, box 1, folder 10.

10. WFC to Beck, Oct. 27, 1895, BBL, box 1, folder 1.

11. Cook et al., *Buffalo Bill's Town*, 48.

12. "Beckoning Frontiers," Part IV, 17.

13. Ibid., 18.

14. Memoirs of Charles E. Hayden, holograph MS, PCHSA. Marquette was the little village at the meeting of the North and South Forks of the Shoshone that served as Company headquarters until the founding of Cody.

15. Cook et al., *Buffalo Bill's Town*, 52.

16. Hayden, MS memoir, PCHSA; Mondell to Beck, May 20, 1896, BFP. box 1, folder 7. Hayden's account directly contradicts Beck's. I choose to follow Hayden's recollection because it is much less self-serving than Beck's and the consultation it describes is free of the high-handed individual determination for which Beck takes credit. Although he seems masterful in his memoir, Beck was careful, even deferential in his dealings with Buffalo Bill, especially in these early days.

17. WFC to Beck, Aug 1, 1896, BBL, box 1, folder 2.

18. Ibid., from LaCrosse, Wisc., Sept. 7, [1896].

19. Hayden Memoir, PCHSA.

20. Beck to WFC, Oct. 16, 1896, SIC Letterpress Book, BP, box 25; "Beckoning Frontiers," part IV, 18; *Shoshone Valley News*, Dec. 3, 1896, PCHSA.

21. Mead to Horace Alger, Nov. 23, 1895, LBSE; [D. H. Elliott], land commissioner, to Salsbury, Jan. 28, 1897, BP, box 1, folder 14; Beck to WFC, Sept. 1, 1897, SIC Letterpress Book, BP, box 25; Minutes of Directors meeting, Shoshone Irrigation Co., Feb. 9, 1897, BP, box 20, folder 6. The north-to-south distribution of the names of the directors on Cody's city streets follows the order in which these four took up their quarter-sections, with room for Bleistein and Alger to fit in along the way.

22. Report to the Directors of the Shoshone Irrigation Co., Dec. 1896, BP, box 20, folder 5.

23. *Shoshone Valley News* may be seen in the PCHSA; Beck to Salsbury, Oct. 2, 1896, SIC Letterpress Book, BP, box 25; Minutes of Board of Directors meeting, Feb. 9, 1897, BP, box 20, folder 7; Beck to Salsbury, Apr. 26, 1897, SIC Letterpress Book, BP, box 25.

24. WFC to Beck, Aug. 11 and Aug. 14, 1896, BBL, box 1, folder 2.

25. Ibid., Aug. 31, 1896.

26. WFC to Beck, Sept. 19 [1896], BBL, box 1, folder 2; Beck to WFC, Sept. 11, 1896, to Salsbury, Sept. 16, 1896, and to Bleistein, same date, SIC Letterpress Book, BP, box 25.

27. WFC to Beck, Sept. 20, 1896, BBL, box 1, folder 2.

28. Ibid., Oct 8, [1896]; Beck to WFC, Sept 11, 1896, SIC Letterpress Book, BP, box 25.

29. Salsbury to Beck, Oct. 8, 1896, BFP, box 1, folder 8.

30. Beck to WFC, Oct. 10, 1896, SIC Letterpress Book, BP, box 25. The political development of Big Horn County is described in detail in Wasden, *From Beaver to Oil,* 59–67. We should note in passing that the town that was chosen as county seat, Basin City, was nearly as new and as small as Cody, though less isolated. Wasden raises the possibility that Basin people encouraged Beck to get into this contest simply to draw strength away from Otto, the only established town in the new county.

31. WFC to Beck, Sept. 3, 1896, BBL, box 1, folder 2. "Irma" was the name of a small village near the head of the Canal, built to provide a center for the first settlers on the project. See Chapter 4.

32. Beck to WFC, Sept. 11, 1896, SIC Letterpress Book, BP, box 25.

33. "Notes of Mr. Beck" for weeks ending Apr. 17 and 24, 1897, BP, box 20, folder 6; Charles Hayden, "History of the Big Horn Basin," Hayden scrapbook no. 1, p. 5, PCHSA.

34. "Notes of Mr. Beck" for weeks ending May 1, 15, and 22, 1897, BP, box 20, folder 6.

35. Ibid. for weeks ending Apr. 10, 17, and 24, May 22 and 29, 1897, BP, box 20, folder 6. The story of the Nagel colony follows in Chapter 4.

36. Ibid. for weeks ending Apr. 24, May 1 and 29, June 5, and Aug. 7, 1897, and "Engineer's report" for week ending May 29, 1897, BP, box 20, folder 6.

37. "Notes of Mr. Beck" for weeks ending June 26 and Aug. 7, 1897, undated [Aug. 1897], Oct. 23, and Nov. 13, 1897, BP, box 20, folder 6.

38. Ibid. for weeks ending Apr. 10 and Nov. 20, 1897, BP, box 20, folder 6.

39. Ibid. for week beginning July 12, 1897, BP, box 20, folder 6. Mondell's role in the development of the valley will be discussed more fully below, in Chapter 10. See also my article, "Buffalo Bill Cody and Wyoming Water Politics": 433–51.

40. "Notes of Mr. Beck," Oct. 30, Nov. 6, and Nov. 20, 1897, BP, box 20, folder 6.

41. Ibid., Nov. 6 and 13, 1897, BP, box 20, folder 6.

42. Ibid., Jan. 5, 1898, BP, box 20, folder 7.

43. Minutes of the meeting of the Board of Directors, undated [Mar. 12, 1898], BP, box 20, folder 7; Salsbury to Beck, May 3, 1898, BP, box 1, folder 20; "Notes of Mr. Beck," Apr. 20, 1898, BP, box 20, folder 7.

44. WFC to Mead, Dec. 29, 1897, GCWSE, 1902–1913. The Fort mentioned here was Fort Russell, predecessor of today's Fort Warren, on the edge of Cheyenne.

45. WFC to Mead, Jan. 24, 1898, GCWSE, 1902–1913.

46. "Notes of Mr. Beck," Apr. 1, 1898, BP, box 20, folder 7; WFC to Beck, Mar. 12, 1898, BP, box 1, folder 19; Beck to Salsbury, May 13, 1898, BP, box 20, folder 7; WFC to Beck, May 20, [1898], BP, box 2, folder 2, [letter is misdated 1899 and filed with that year's correspondence, but clearly was written in 1898]; Gerrans to Beck, July 15, 1898, BP, box 1, folder 21.

47. WFC to Beck, July 9, 1898, from Erie, Pa., BBL, box 1, folder 4.

48. Ibid., July 19, 1898.

49. Salsbury to Beck, Apr. 23, 1899, BFP, box 1, folder 9.

50. "Notes of Mr. Beck," Jan. 5, Mar. 16, Apr. 1 and 20, 1898, BP, box 20, folder 7; Rumsey to Beck, Mar. 1, 1898, and Gerrans to Beck, Mar. 21, 1898, BP, box 1, folder 19; WFC to Beck, June 4 and 24, 1898, BBL, box 1, folder 4. See McLaird, "Building the Town of Cody," 73–105.

51. No census was recorded for Cody in 1900, so we cannot know for certain. Thermopolis, the largest town in the Basin for the next twenty years, had only 299 people in 1900. Wyoming Department of Administration and Information, Economic Analysis Division website, http://eadiv.wy.us/demog_data/cntycity_hist.htm.

52. Cook et al., *Buffalo Bill's Town,* 50–51; "Beckoning Frontiers," Book IV, 42.

CHAPTER FOUR: SETTLING THE LAND

1. It is clear from Don Pisani's analysis of the Carey Act that the settlement problem was common wherever the Act was applied. As he put it, "The most obvious question about the Carey Act—how it could manage to lure farmers west in the midst of a depression—was never asked." See Pisani, *To Reclaim a Divided West,* 254.

2. WFC to Beck, Oct. 19, 1895, BBL, box 1, folder 1.

3. WFC to Mead, Mar. 26, 1896, GCWSE, 1902–1913.

4. WFC to Beck, Apr. 6 and 13, 1896, BBL, box 1, folder 2.

5. Ibid., Apr. 13, 1896.

6. Salsbury to Beck, Apr. 2, 1896, and WFC to Beck, telegram, from Buffalo, Apr. 6, 1896, BFP, box 1, folder 6.

7. Nagle to Beck, telegram, Apr. 8, 1896, BFP, box 1, folder 6.

8. Nagle to Beck, Mar. 7 and 16, and Apr. 3, 1896, BP, box 1, folder 11.

9. WFC to Beck, telegrams, Apr. 10, 11, and 12, 1896, BFP, box 1, folder 6.

10. Ibid., telegram, Apr. 14, 1896.

11. WFC to Beck in Chicago, telegram, Apr. 14, 1896, BFP, box 1, folder 6.

12. Ibid., Apr. 15, 1896 (two telegrams).

13. WFC to Beck, Apr. 13, 1896, BBL, box 1, folder 2; Authorization and order of Shoshone Land and Irrigation Co, Apr. 18, 1896, BP, box 1, folder 12; WFC to Beck, telegram, Apr. 19, 1896, and Nagle to Beck, telegram, Apr. 21, 1896, BFP, box 1, folder 6.

14. Wasden, "Cody Canal," 38; "Beckoning Frontiers," part IV, 41.

15. WFC to Beck, Oct. 6, 1895, BBL, box 1, folder 1; WFC to Beck, Apr. 6, 1896, and n.d. [June, 1896], BBL, box 1, folder 2; Nagle to Beck, Mar. 7, 1896, and Nagle to Cody, Mar. 16, 1896, BP, box 1, folder 11; WFC to Mead, Mar. 26, 1896, GCWSE, 1902–1913.

16. Mead to WFC, Mar. 26, 1896, LBSE.

17. Mead to Beck, Mar. 19, 1896, LBSE.

18. Public Land Records, Certificates of Entry, Box 1, WSA.

19. WFC to Beck, July 7, 1896, BBL, box 1, folder 2.

20. Ibid., July 5, 1896.

21. State Board of Land Commissioners to Beck, July 22, 1896, BP, box 1, folder 12; Beck's Report to Shoshone Irr. Co, 1896, BP, box 20, folder 5; WFC to Mead, Jan. 8, 1897, GCWSE 1902–1913.

22. Charles Hayden, "History of the Big Horn Basin," Hayden scrapbook no. 1, p. 5, PCHSA; "Notes of Mr. Beck, Oct. 23, 1897, BP, box 20, folder 6. The irony of this position might be appreciated by reading David Murdoch's attribution to Buffalo Bill of the central role in preparing the public to accept cowboys as frontier heroes; see Murdoch, *The American West* (2000).

23. WFC to Beck, Aug. 17, 1896, BBL, box 1, folder 2; Grouard to Beck, July 12, 1896, BP, box 1, folder 12; Beck to Salsbury, Aug. 7, 1896, SIC Letterpress Book, BP, box 25.

24. Beck to WFC, Aug. 23, 1896, SIC Letterpress Book, BP, box 25; WFC to Beck, Aug. 23, 1896, BP, box 1, folder 12.

25. Salsbury to Beck, Apr. 27, 1896, BFP, box 1, folder 6.

26. Minutes of the Arid Land Board, Aug. 10, 1896, Public Lands Records, WSA; Report of George Beck to the Directors of the Shoshone Irrigation Co., [Dec.] 1896, BP, box 20, folder 5.

27. Wasden, "Cody Canal," 36–37; BP, box 1, folder 13; "Beckoning Frontiers," Part IV, 41.

28. Mead to Shoshone Irr. Co., Dec. 22, 1896, LBSE. Salsbury expressed his idea in a letter to George Beck, Mar. 11, 1896, BFP, box 1, folder 5.

29. WFC to Mead, Jan. 8, 1897, GCWSE, 1902–1913; Letterpress Book of the SIC Land Commissioner, passim, BP, box 25; Elliott to Beck, July 30, 1897, BP, box 1, folder 16. A copy of the brochure, as revised in 1898 by George Beck, is deposited in the Records of the General Land Office, RG 49, Unidentified Divisions, Carey Act cases, 1896–1917, E. 962, Box 3, NA. The 1895 brochure is in BP, box 20, folder 4.

30. "Homes in the Big Horn Basin," RG 49, Carey Act Cases, 1896–1917, E. 962, box 3, NA.

31. Richard White's deeply perceptive essay, "Frederick Jackson Turner and Buffalo Bill," published with a companion essay by Patricia Nelson Limerick in *Frontier in American Culture,* 7–65, shows how Cody's narrative of the frontier was built upon the rifle, even as he promoted irrigated farming.

32. Cody's correspondence with Elwood Mead contains references to these parties; see, *e.g.,* letter of Oct. 19, 1896, GCWSE, 1902–1913. Beck's memoir talks lovingly of the early hunts up the South Fork and names many of the famous men Cody brought to join them: Generals Nelson Miles and Leonard Wood, secretaries of War, Interior, and Navy, famous painters like Frederic Remington, etc.; "Beckoning Frontiers," IV, 62–69.

33. *Shoshone Valley News,* Nov. 26, 1896, PCHSA; WFCC, Series VI:A, Wild West Show Programs and Brochures, 1883–1901.

34. WFC to Mead, Jan. 8, 1897, GCWSE, 1902–1913; "Notes of Mr. Beck" for the week ending June 5, 1897, BP, box 20, folder 6.

35. "Notes of Mr. Beck" for weeks ending June 5 and June 19, 1897, BP, box 20, folder 6.

36. Beck's disenchantment with Elliott began even before May; see "Notes of Mr. Beck" for weeks ending April 24, May 1 and 22, BP, box 20, folder 6; Beck to Alger, May 14 and June 11, 1897, in SIC Letterpress Book, BP, box 25; "Notes of Mr. Beck" for week beginning July 12, 1897, BP, box 20, folder 6.

37. Minutes of a meeting of the Board of the Shoshone Irrigation Co., Feb. 9, 1897, BP, box 20, folder 6; D. H. Elliott to Nate Salsbury, Feb. 6, 1897, BP, box 1, folder 14; Letterpress Book of the SIC Land Commissioner, esp. letters of May 11, July 30, and Aug. 2, 1897, BP, box 25.

38. Elliott to Beck, July 8, 1897, and Elliott to WFC, July 21 and July 30, 1897, BP, box 1, folder 16; Elliott to WFC, July 8, 1897, and Elliott to Salsbury, June 26, 1897, Letterpress Book of the SIC Land Commissioner, BP, box 25; "Notes of Mr. Beck" for week beginning July 12, 1897, BP, box 20, folder 6; Elliott to Beck, Aug. 26, 1897, BP, box 1, folder 17. Unfortunately, none of the correspondence survives in the Papers of Eugene V. Debs, 1834–1945 (1983). The Social Democracy colonization scheme is discussed by Salvatore in *Eugene V. Debs,* 162–167.

39. Multiple letters between Elliott and his agents may be found in BP, box 1, folders 14–16. Elliott's letters to WFC (July 21) and Beck (July 30) detail some of the problems he encountered.

40. "Notes of Mr. Beck" for week ending June 11, 1897, BP, box 20, folder 6; Elliott to Beck, Aug. 26, 1897, BP, box 1, folder 17, and Beck to Company land agents, Sept. 1, 1897, folder 18.

41. "Notes of Mr. Beck" Saturday, July 31, 1897, BP, box 20, folder 6.

42. Elliott to WFC, Aug. 2, 1897, BP, box 1, folder 17.

43. WFC to Beck, Aug. 7, 1897, BP, box 1, folder 17. When Buffalo Bill was upset he tended to use a formal signature, as opposed to the familiar "Col." when feeling good.

44. First Assistant Postmaster General to Beck, Sept. 29, 1897, BP, box 1, folder 18; Minutes of the Arid Land Board, Mar. 2, Apr. 6, and Dec. 1, 1897, Public Lands Records, WSA.

45. "Notes of Mr. Beck," undated [Aug. and Sept. 1897], BP, box 20, folder 6.

46. Ibid., undated [Sept. 1897], Oct. 2, 1897, and Jan. 5, 1898.

47. Ibid., Oct. 2 and Oct. 9, 1897.

48. Ibid., Oct. 23, 1897.

49. Ibid., Nov. 7 and Nov. 13, 1897.

50. WFC to C. B. Jones, Apr. 9, 1898, BBL, box 1, folder 4.

51. Cf. Warren, *Buffalo Bill's America*, 417–53.

52. "Notes of Mr. Beck," Feb. 26, 1898, BP, box 20, folder 7.

53. Ibid.

54. Gilman to Beck, July 13, 1899, BFP, box 1, folder 9.

55. WFC to Russell, Dec. 27, 1899, WFCC, Series I: B, Box 1, folder 17.

56. Public Land Records, Applications for Entry, Box 1, WSA.

57. John Opie, *Law of the Land*, 63–69, offers a good recent discussion of homesteading. The locus classicus for such matters is still Gates, *Public Land Law Development*, 387–434; see also his "Homestead Act," in Ottoson, *Land Use Policy*, 28–46, reprinted in Gates, *Jeffersonian Dream*, 40–56.

58. Carey Act and Wyoming enabling legislation reprinted in Shoshone Irrigation Co. brochure, 1898; *Third Biennial Report of the State Engineer, 1895–1896* (1896), 17–27; Act of June 11, 1896, Sundry Civil Appropriations for the Department of Interior, 29 Stat. 434. Although the change in patenting procedure was authorized by Congress in 1896, regulations to implement it were completed only in 1898; Gov. W. A. Richards to Beck, Jan. 28, 1898, BP, box 1, folder 19.

59. Beck to Commissioner of the GLO, Sept. 1, 1897, BP, box 1, folder 18; Beck to Elwood Mead, Oct. 13, 189[8], GCWSE, 1890–1902; WFC to Mead, Sept. 11, 1898, GCWSE, 1902–1913; Mead to Gov. W. A. Richards, Oct. 18, 1898, and Mead to George Beck, Oct. 18, 1898, LBSE; Records of the General Land Office, RG 49, Unidentified Divisions, Carey Act Cases 1896–1917, E. 962, Box 3, NA.

60. Register and Receiver, U.S. Land Office, Lander, Wyo., to Commissioner, General Land Office, May 6, 1899, Carey Act Cases 1896–1917, Box 3, E. 962, RG 49, NA; Mead to WFC, May 10, 1899, LBSE.

61. Commissioner, GLO, to Register and Receiver, Lander Office, Dec. 28, 1900, Carey Act Cases 1896–1917, Box 3, E. 962, RG 49, NA; Beck's Report to Directors, Jan. 14, 1900, BP, box 20, folder 8.

62. Affidavit of Hudson W. Darrah, 18 Oct. 1899, Carey Act Cases 1896–1917, Box 3, E. 962, RG 49, NA.

63. U.S. Commissioner S. E. Stillwell to Register and Receiver, Lander, Wyo., July 31, 1900, and Binger Herman, Commissioner GLO, to Register and Receiver, Lander, Wyo., Dec. 28, 1900, in Carey Act Cases 1896–1917, Box 3, E. 962, RG 49.

64. Pisani, *To Reclaim a Divided West*, 261–63, explores a range of opposition to the Carey Act in Wyoming.

65. Daniel Belgrad has recently developed the idea of conflicting articulations of an "ideology of opportunity" in a compelling new look at the Johnson County War. Although

we are dealing with litigation instead of invasion in the Big Horn Basin, I think the analysis applies here. See Belgrad, "Johnson County War as Political Violence": 159–78.

CHAPTER FIVE: "I WISH TO GOD I HAD NEVER SEEN THE BASIN!"

1. "Beckoning Frontiers," IV, 28.
2. Ibid.
3. Phoebe A. Hearst to Beck, Mar. 5, 1898, BP, box 1, folder 19; Minutes of a meeting of the directors of the Shoshone Irrigation Co., Feb. 9, 1897, BP, box 20, folder 7.
4. "Notes of Mr. Beck," April, 1897, BP, box 20, folder 6; "Mr. Hayden's Report to Mr. Beck" for week ending Apr. 24, 1897, BP, box 20, folder 6; Minutes of the meeting of the Directors of the Shoshone Irrigation Co., Feb. 9, 1897, BP, box 20, folder 6.
5. Bleistein to Beck, Apr. 17, 1897, BP, box 1, folder 15.
6. Beck to Bleistein, Apr. 26, 1897, and Beck to Salsbury, Apr. 26, 1897, SIC Letterpress Book, BP, box 25.
7. Beck to Salsbury, Apr. 12, 1897, SIC Letterpress Book, BP, box 25.
8. "Notes of Mr. Beck," weeks ending May 8, 15, and 22, 1897, and "Report of Mr. Hayden," week ending May 15, 1897, BP, box 20, folder 6.
9. "Notes of Mr. Beck," weeks ending May 15, 22, 29, June 5 and 11, 1897, and "Engineer's Report," weeks ending May 29 and June 5, 1897, BP, box 20, folder 6. The work Mead was preparing was the first survey for the Cody-Salsbury Canal, the subject of Chapter 10.
10. "Engineer's Report" for the week ending June 12, 1897, and "Notes of Mr. Beck" for week ending June 26 and July 3, 1897, BP, box 20, folder 6.
11. "Notes of Mr. Beck" for week ending July 3, 1897, BP, box 20, folder 6.
12. "Engineer's Reports" for the weeks ending July 24 and 31, and Aug. 7, 1897, and "Notes of Mr. Beck" for week ending Aug. 7, subsequent undated reports for August and September, Oct. 2 and 23, 1897, BP, box 20, folder 6.
13. "Notes of Mr. Beck" for week ending July 10, 1897, and "Engineer's Reports" for the weeks ending July 24 and 31, 1897; "Notes of Mr. Beck" for Oct. 9, 1897, BP, box 20, folder 6.
14. "Notes of Mr. Beck" for the weeks ending July 10, 31, and Aug. 7, 1897, and "Engineer's Report" for weeks ending July 17, 24, and 31, 1897, BP, box 20, folder 6.
15. "Notes of Mr. Beck," Oct. 23, 1897, BP, box 20, folder 6.
16. "Notes of Mr. Beck," Feb. 16 and Mar. 14, 1898, BP, box 20, folder 7.
17. WFC to Beck, Mar. 12, 1898, BP, box 1, folder 19; Minutes of the meeting of the Directors of the Shoshone Irrigation Co., [Mar. 12, 1898], BP, box 20, folder 7; WFC to Mead, Sept. 2 and Oct. 7, 1896, GCWSE, 1902–13. Bronson Rumsey was also from Buffalo, but he, along with Beck and Alger, missed this meeting.
18. "Notes of Mr. Beck," Apr. 1, 1898, BP, box 20, folder 7.
19. WFC to Beck, Apr. 8, [1898], BP, box 2, folder 1.
20. Alger to Beck, Mar. 8, 1898, BP, box 1, folder 19.
21. Ibid.
22. Salsbury to Beck, May 3, 1898, BP, box 1, folder 20; Alger to Beck, Mar. 8, 1898, BP, box 1, folder 19; WFC to Beck, May 19, 1898, Alger to Beck, May 25, 1898, Rumsey to Beck, May 30, 1898, and Gerrans to Beck, July 15, 1898, BP, box 1, folder 20.
23. "Notes of Mr. Beck," May 2, 1898, BP, box 20, folder 7; Rumsey to Beck, Sept. 29, 1897, Gerrans to Beck, Oct. 1, 1897, BP, box 1, folder 18; Rumsey to Beck, May 30, 1898, BP, box 1, folder 20; "Notes of Mr. Beck," June 10, 1898, BP, box 20, folder 7.

24. WFC to Beck, May 19, 1898, BP, box 1, folder 20.

25. Beck to Salsbury, May 13, 1898, filed with Beck's Notes to Directors, BP, box 20, folder 7.

26. WFC to Beck, June 8, 1898, BP, box 1, folder 20; WFC to Beck, June 4, 1898, BBL, box 1, folder 4.

27. Minutes of the Director's Meeting, July 1, 1898, and Trial Balance, June 27, 1898, attached to minutes, BP, box 20, folder 7.

28. WFC to Beck, telegram, June 21, 1898, BP, box 1, folder 20; E. H. Clark to Beck, telegram, July 1, 1898, BP, box 1, folder 21.

29. "Notes of Mr. Beck," July 13, 1898, BP, box 20, folder 7.

30. WFC to Beck, July 20, 1898, BBL, box 1, folder 4.

31. "Notes of George T. Beck," Aug. 17, 1898, BP, box 20, folder 7.

32. Ibid.

33. Ibid.

34. WFC to Beck, Aug. 21, 1898, BP, box 1, folder 21.

35. Ibid., Sept. 18, 1898.

36. Ibid.

37. WFC to Beck, Oct. 9, 1898, BBL, box 1, folder 4. This closing reference to General Miles is a good instance of Cody's reflex name-dropping. It was unlikely in the extreme that the Commanding General of the Army would be able to "get away" for a hunt with his friends during the Spanish-American War!

38. Minutes [handwritten] of the meeting of the Board of Directors, undated [but clearly autumn 1898], BP, box 20, folder 7; Salsbury to Beck, Dec. 12, 1898, BP, box 1, folder 21.

39. Beck to Mead, Oct. 13, 1898, GCWSE, 1890–1902.

CHAPTER SIX: CORPORATIONS ALONG THE SHOSHONE

1. WFC to Elwood Mead, Feb. 28, 1899, GCWSE; Big Horn County District Court Civil Files, Cases 48 and 51, WSA; Beck's Report to Col. Cody and the Directors, Apr. 27, 1899, BP, box 20, folder 8.

2. WFC to Beck, Mar. 10, 1899, BBL, box 1, folder 5.

3. WFC to Beck, Mar. 9, 13, 17, and 24, 1899, BP, box 2, folder 1.

4. WFC to Beck, Apr. 15, 1899, BP, box 2, folder 1.

5. WFC to Beck, Apr. 23, 1899, BBL, box 1, folder 5.

6. Beck's report to directors, Apr. 27, 1899, BP, box 20, folder 8; WFC to Beck, Sept. 19, [1899], BBL, box 1, folder 5.

7. [Gerrans] to WFC, Mar. 14, 1899, BP, box 2, folder 1.

8. Salsbury to Beck, Apr. 5, 1899, BP, box 2, folder 1.

9. WFC to Beck, Mar. 24, 1899, BP, box 2, folder 1.

10. Salsbury to Beck, Apr. 23, 1899, BFP, box 1, folder 9.

11. WFC to Beck, June 28, 1899, BBL, box 1, folder 5.

12. WFC to Beck, July 5, 1899, BP, box 2, folder 1. See also letters of June 12 and June 24, same folder.

13. WFC to Beck, June 2, 1899, BBL, box 1, folder 5.

14. WFC to Beck, July 5, 1899, BP, box 2, folder 2.

15. WFC to Beck, July 18, 1899, BP, box 2, folder 2; WFC to Beck, Aug. 12 [1899], BBL, box 1, folder 5.

16. WFC to Beck, July 18, 1899, BBL, box 1, folder 5. See also WFC to Beck, June 12, 1899, BP, box 2, folder 2.

17. WFC to Beck, June 28, 1899, BBL, box 1, folder 5; Hinkle Smith to Beck, July 21, 1899, Arta Boal to Beck, June 14, 1899, and WFC to Beck, Aug. 24, 1899, BP, box 2, folder 2.

18. Peggy and Harold Samuels, *Frederic Remington*, 292. These authors also offer a brief account of a visit to Wyoming in 1897, but it is filled with factual errors, and—as no other mention of it survives—I am inclined to believe they have somehow conflated it with the 1899 visit. Remington published an account of riding Pryor Gap with Cheyenne scouts out of Fort Keogh on the Yellowstone River, titled "Artist Wanderings among the Cheyennes," in *Century*, August 1889. In his memoir, Beck recalled the visit as one during which Remington did "little or no work," but had a very good time in other ways; "Beckoning Frontiers," Book IV, 83. His 1908 visit produced some significant landscape work; see Hassrick and Webster, *Frederic Remington; a Catalogue Raisonne*, 825. An account of the party at Irma Lake is in Charles Hayden's unpublished memoir in PCHSA, 14–15.

19. WFC to Beck, Aug. 24, 1899, BP, box 2, folder 2. See also WFC to Beck, June 2 and 28, 1899, BBL, box 1, folder 5.

20. WFC to Beck, July 5, 1899, BP, box 2, folder 2.

21. Yost, *Buffalo Bill*, 292.

22. WFC to Beck, July 5 and 18, 1899, BP, box 2, folder 2.

23. Gillette, *Locating the Iron Trail*, 117–22.

24. WFC to Beck, July 18, 1899, BBL, box 1, folder 5.

25. W. S. Collins to Beck, July 30, 1899, and W. S. Metz to Beck, Aug. 10, 1899, BP, box 2, folder 2.

26. WFC to Beck, Aug 24, 1899, BP, box 2, folder 2.

27. Ibid., Sept. 20, 1899.

28. Ibid., Oct. 9, [1899].

29. Ibid., Oct. 11 and 12, 1899.

30. Kingston to Beck, Oct. 17, 1899, BP, box 2, folder 2.

31. WFC to Mike Russell, WFCC, series I:B, box 1, folder 17.

32. Beck's reports to the directors, Shoshone Irrigation Co., Jan. 14 and Mar. 6, 1900, in BP, box 20, folder 8. The matter may be seen from the Mormon side in a series of letters from Kingston to the Governor of Wyoming, Dec. 30, 1899, Feb. 1, 1900, and Mar. 30, 1900, Correspondence of Governor DeForest Richards, Box 7, WSA.

33. Welch, *History of the Big Horn Basin*, 54. See also Lindsay, *Big Horn Basin*.

34. See Chapter 10.

35. Welch, *Big Horn Basin*, 58–60. The exchange between Salsbury and Cody has been variously attributed. It could not have happened in Welch's presence; he might well have heard the tale in later years from Buffalo Bill or another party. It is unmistakably clear from Welch's account that the Mormons considered themselves to be friends with Buffalo Bill, and there is no record of any payment for the relinquishment.

36. Rumsey to [?] in Burlington, May 9, 1900, BP, box 2, folder 3; Beck's report to the Directors, June 1, 1900, BP, box 20, folder 8.

37. Commissioner of General Land Office to Register and Receiver, Lander, Wyo., July 19, 1905, file no. 74.0299, BBMG.

38. Van Orsdel to Beck, Feb. 24, 1900, BP, box 2, folder 3.

39. WFC to Hinkle, Mar. 1, 1900, WFCC, series I:B, box 1, folder 15.

40. WFC to Van Orsdel, June 25, 1900, BP, box 2, folder 3.

41. Van Orsdel to Beck, Feb. 24, 1900, BP, box 2, folder 3; Beck's report to Directors, June 1, 1900, BP, box 20, folder 8; Commissioner, General Land Office, to Register and Receiver, Lander, July 19, 1905, file no. 74.0299, BBMG. A few years later, in 1904, Darrah purchased from the Shoshone Irrigation Co. a water right for 160 acres adjoining his coal land for one dollar. It is impossible to know if this was part of a deal worked out in 1901; Entry no. 291, Applications for Entry, Public Land Records, WSA.

42. Burdick to WFC, July 11, 1900, BP, box 2, folder 4.

43. WFC to Beck, June 20 and June 25, 1900, BP, Box 2, folder 3.

44. WFC to Beck, July 17, 1900, BP, Box 2, folder 4.

45. Beck report to Directors, Aug. 1, 1900, BP, box 20, folder 8. See Chapter 4 for discussion of the land patent protest.

46. WFC to Beck, Mar. 1, 1900, BP, box 2, folder 3.

47. Ibid., Mar. 5, [1900].

48. Ibid., Mar. 13, 1900.

49. Beck to the Board of Directors, Mar. 6, 1900, BP, box 20, folder 8.

50. WFC to Beck, Mar. 31, 1900; Salsbury to Beck, Apr. 3 and June 14, 1900, BP, box 2, folder 3; WFC to Beck, July 6, 1900, BP, box 2, folder 4.

51. Burdick to WFC, Mar. 12, 1900; WFC to Beck, Mar. 13 and Mar. 31, 1900; Beck to WFC (telegram), Mar. 23, 1900, BP, box 2, folder 3; Burdick to WFC, July 11, 1900, BP, box 2, folder 4.

52. See Chapter 7.

53. WFC to Beck, Oct. 24, 1900, BBL, box 1 folder 6; Morrill to Beck, Dec. 1, 1900, and Dec. 3, 1900 (telegram), BP, box 2, folder 4.

54. WFC to Beck, July 24, 1900, BP, box 2, folder 4.

55. Salsbury to Beck, Oct. 20, 1900, BFP, box 1, folder 10.

56. WFC to Beck, Oct. 1, 1900, BP, box 2, folder 4; F. A. Nagle to Beck, Nov. 8, 1897, BP, box 1, folder 18, and May 20, 1898, BP, box 1, folder 20.

57. WFC to Beck, Oct. 23 and 24, 1900, BP, box 2, folder 4. See Chapter 9 for more on the coal company.

58. Shoshone Irrigation Co. Treasurer's trial balance, Dec. 22, 1900, BP, box 20, folder 8; Wallenberg to Beck, Feb. 12, 1901, BFP, box 1, folder 11.

CHAPTER SEVEN: THE BURLINGTON COMES TO CODY

1. Overton, *Burlington Route,* 227–35. See also Gillette's memoir, *Locating the Iron Trail,* and correspondence from R. J. McClure to C. E. Perkins, esp. Nov. 8, 1890, in CB&Q Records, 33 1890, 6.91: New Lines, general. Internal correspondence of the Burlington men refers familiarly to Beck and Horace Alger, the two Sheridan men among the Shoshone Irrigation Co. directors.

2. Interview with Arlan W. Coons printed in the *Greybull Standard and Tribune,* Mar. 21, 1946.

3. Overton, *Burlington Route,* 241.

4. Gillette to George Holdrege, undated [probably 1896], in Big Horn Basin [BHB] file, and McClure to Perkins, Jan. 23, 1894, New Lines-general file, CB&Q. Gillette's prediction with respect to the Crow Reservation came true in 1904; Hoxie, *Parading through History,* 177.

5. Calvert to Holdrege, Sept. 4, 1896, and Holdrege to C. E. Perkins, Oct. 19, 1896, BHB file, CB&Q; Beck to WFC, Aug. 19, 1896, SIC Letterpress Book, BP, box 25. The

"Timber Reserve" to which Calvert referred was the great tract of forest set aside by President Benjamin Harrison in 1891, as a buffer against development around Yellowstone Park. From those reserves grew the National Forest system.

6. Morrill to Perkins, Nov. 4, 1899, BHB file, CB&Q.

7. Ibid.

8. Ibid., Nov. 9, 1899.

9. Ibid.

10. Ibid., Nov. 22, 1899.

11. Perkins to Holdrege, Aug. 14, 1899; Holdrege to Perkins, Sept. 15 and 16, 1899, BHB file, CB&Q.

12. F. W. Hunnewell to Perkins, Oct. 8, 1899; Holdrege to Perkins, Nov. 17, 1899, Jan. 4, 1900, and Feb. 22, 1900; BHB file, CB&Q.

13. WFC to Beck, Mar. 1, 1900, BP, box 2, folder 3; see also WFC to Beck, Sept. 19, [1899], BBL, box 1 folder 5.

14. WFC to Manderson, Mar. 5, 1900, BHB file, CB&Q.

15. Manderson to Perkins, Mar. 8, 1900, BHB file, CB&Q.

16. WFC to C. E. Perkins, Apr. 2, 1900, and Perkins to WFC, Apr. 5, 1900, BHB file, CB&Q.

17. Perkins to Holdrege, Apr. 5, 1900, BHB file, CB&Q.

18. Beck's report to the Directors, Apr. 28, 1900, BP, box 20, folder 8.

19. WFC to Perkins, Apr. 30, 1900, BHB file, CB&Q.

20. Calvert to Holdrege, May 20, 1900; Holdrege to C. E. Perkins, May 21, 1900, in BHB file, CB&Q.

21. Perkins to Holdrege, Jan. 29, 1901, BHB file, CB&Q.

22. Calvert to Holdrege, Feb. 4, 1901, BHB file, CB&Q.

23. Ibid.

24. Holdrege to Perkins, Feb. 21, 1901, Perkins to Holdrege, Feb. 22, 1901, and CB&Q Board memo, Apr. 17, 1901, in BHB file, CB&Q.

25. This account relies on Russell, *Lives and Legends,* 84–85, and Warren, *Buffalo Bill's America,* 47–50. Russell does not query Cody's figures on the size of Rome, but Warren is more critical, as well as more comprehensive. There is no way that Rome could have boasted two hundred houses within a month of founding.

26. Salsbury to Beck, Apr. 3, 1900, BP, box 2, folder 3; Beck's report to Directors, June 1, 1900, BP, box 20, folder 8; Warren, *Buffalo Bill's America,* 486.

27. Beck's report to Directors, Aug. 1, 1900, BP, box 20, folder 8; Van Orsdel to WFC, telegram, June 18, 1900, and WFC to Beck, June 25, 1900, BP, box 2, folder 3; C. H. Morrill to Beck, July 11, 1900, BP, box 2, folder 4; Memorandum signed by Morrill and Beck, June 20, 1900, in Lincoln Land Co. records, Town Files: Cody, Wyo., NSHS.

28. Lincoln Land Co. records, Town Files: Cody, Wyo., esp. June 18, July 9 and 25, Aug. 29 and 30, 1901, NSHS. The Cody Trading Co. promised to pay the Lincoln Land Co. $300 if they kept the business part of town where it was; see Jacob Schwoob statement, BP, box 2, folder 6. The original plat of Cody may be seen on p. 52 of Cook et al., *Buffalo Bill's Town.* By comparison with the imposition of standard town plans along the railroad in South Dakota, this replatting was only a moderate interference with the founders' plans; see Nelson, *After the West Was Won,* 82–86.

29. WFC to Morrill, Aug. 8, 1902, Morrill to Sec. Minor, Aug. 11, 1902, and Receipt signed by WFC, Dec. 6, 1902, in Lincoln Land Co. records, Town Files: Cody, Wyo., NSHS.

30. BP, box 20, folders 8–10; Public Lands Records, Applications for Entry, Box 1, WSA; "Beckoning Frontiers," Part IV, p. 30; Statement of Shoshone Irrigation Co., Dec. 1, 1905, BP, box 21, folder 2.

31. Correspondence between Beck and Morrill, Oct. 1903, Lincoln Land Co. Records, Town Files, Cody, Wyo., NSHS.

32. Records of the Lincoln Land Company business in Cody are in BP, box 14, folder 2.

33. Lincoln Land Co. to Bronson Rumsey, Trustee, Jan. 11, 1929, forwarded to George Beck Apr. 11, 1929, BP, series III, subseries I (Business Records), box 14, folder 2 (Lincoln Land Company).

34. See Borne, *Dude Ranching*. Chapter 12 details the support of the railroads for this essential element of the western tourist industry.

35. Concerning the Burlington route, see "The Big Horn Basin, Wyoming," Chicago, [1902], Yale Collection of Western Americana, Beinecke Rare Book and Manuscript Library, Yale University.

CHAPTER EIGHT: THE DEMISE OF THE
SHOSHONE IRRIGATION COMPANY

1. Wallenberg to Beck, Mar. 14, 1901, BP, box 2, folder 5, and T. A. Griffin to Beck, Apr. 20, 1901, BP, box 2, folder 4.

2. WFC to Beck, Apr. 29, 1901, from Lynchburg, Va., BP, box 2, folder 5.

3. WFC to Beck, May 2, 1901, BP, box 2, folder 6. For the Military College, see Chapter 9.

4. Lincoln Land Co. to Beck, May 10 and 18, 1901, BP, box 2, folder 6.

5. Alger to Beck, June 27, 1901, and Rumsey to Beck, July 12, 1901, BFP, box 1, folder 11; Cody and Beck Bond in WFCC, Series I:A, box 2, folder 32.

6. Bond to Beck, Dec. 26, 1901, BP, box 2, folder 7; Land Commissioners to State Engineer, Oct. 31, 1901, GCWSE, 1890–1902.

7. Bond to Beck, Dec. 26, 1901, BP, box 2, folder 7.

8. Minutes of meeting of the Shoshone Irrigation Co. Board of Directors, Dec. 2, 1901, BP, box 20, folder 8; Bleistein to Kelsey, Dec. 24, 1901, and Kelsey to Bleistein, Dec. 30, 1901, BP, box 2, folder 7; Bond to Beck, Jan. 22, 1902, WFC to Beck, Jan. 26 and Feb. 9, 1902, and Salsbury to Beck, Feb. 11, 1902, BP, box 2, folder 8. The Cody-Salsbury project is the subject of Chapter 10.

9. Minutes of meeting of the Board of Directors of the Shoshone Irrigation Co., Mar. 31, 1902, BP, box 20, folder 8; H. M. Gerrans to Beck, Mar. 13, 1902, BFP, box 2, folder 1; WFC to C. L. Hinkle, Mar. 10 and May 28, 1902, WFCC, Series I:B, Box 1, folder 18. See also Cook, *Wiley's Dream of Empire*.

10. WFC to Beck, Apr. 26, 1902, BP, box 2, folder 9.

11. WFC to Fred Bond, June 30, 1902, GCWSE, 1902–13.

12. Bond to Beck, June 20, 1902, WFC to Beck, June 30, 1902, BP, box 2, folder 10; WFC to Beck, July 2 and Aug. 11, 1902, and Bond to Beck, July 12, 1902, BP, box 2, folder 11; Bleistein to Beck, June 8, 1902, BFP, box 2, folder 1.

13. WFC to Beck, Aug. 11, 1902, BP, box 2, folder 11.

14. WFC to Beck, Sept. 20, 1902, BP, box 6, folder 12.

15. WFC to Beck, July 8 and 25, Aug. 2, Sept. 12 and 22, 1902, BBL, box 1, folder 8; Report to the Directors of the Shoshone Irrigation Co, June 30, 1903, BP, box 20, folder 10.

16. Beck to Johnston, Sept. 5, 1903, Johnston to Governor Fenimore Chatterton, Oct. 21, 1903, and Johnston to Beck, Dec. 8, 1903, GCWSE, 1902–1913.

17. George Beck diary for 1904, BP, box 7.

18. Johnston to Chatterton, Oct. 21, 1903, GCWSE, 1902–1913.

19. Letter of certification of the Cody Canal, Nov. 23, 1904, Carey Act Records, Box 3, E. 962, RG 49, NA.

20. State Engineer's report to the Land Board, Oct. 31, 1905, copy filed with the complaint of Fred Houston against the Shoshone Irrigation Co., case file no. 768, Big Horn County District Court records, WSA.

21. Ibid.

22. Report of the Cody Canal Company [actually Shoshone Irrigation Co.] to the State Land Board, Dec. 8, 1904, and Dec. 20, 1905, BP, box 21, folder 1; Statement of Shoshone Irrigation Co., Dec. 1, 1905, BP, box 21, folder 2.

23. Case file no. 457, Big Horn County District Court Records, WSA.

24. Case files 457, 768, 764, Big Horn County District Court Records, WSA.

25. "Instructions to the Jury" in *McGhan v. Shoshone Irrigation Co.*, H. S. Ridgley Collection, Box 1, AHC. Ridgley was the attorney for the company. For the company position, see case file no. 457, Second Defense.

26. WFC to Beck, Aug. 10, 1908, BP, box 3, folder 6; Harry Weston to George Bleistein, Aug. 20, 1909, BP, box 3, folder 7; Bleistein to Beck, Apr. 29, 1916, WFCC, series I:A, box 2, folder 37. The affair of Gustav Wallenberg is discussed near the end of this chapter.

27. Agreement of 13 Apr. 1907 and agreement of 12 Oct. 1907, List of Lands patented to the state, and Attorney General to Commissioner of Public Lands, June 29, 1907, in Cody Canal records, Carey Act projects, box 3, Public Land Records, WSA.

28. *W. B. Ackles, et al, vs. Shoshone Irrigation Co., et al,* Records of Big Horn County District Court, file no. 670, WSA.

29. *Park County Enterprise,* July 13, 1912.

30. Salsbury to Beck, June 15, 1902, BFP, box 2, folder 1.

31. Wallenberg contract with Shoshone Irrigation Co., Jan. 18, 1902; Wallenberg to Beck, Jan. 24 and 29, 1902; BP, box 2, folder 8.

32. WFC to Beck, Feb. 1 and Feb. 2, 1902, BP, box 2, folder 8.

33. WFC to Beck, Apr. 26, 1902, BP, box 2, folder 9; Wallenberg to Beck, Mar. 14, 1902, BP, box 2, folder 9, and Thad Gregory to Wallenberg, June 8, 1902, BP, box 2, folder 10.

34. Wallenberg to Shoshone Irrigation Co., July 2, 1902, BP, box 2, folder 11; statement of land payments from Wallenberg to Beck, 1902–1903, BP, box 20, folder 10.

35. Beck report to Board of Shoshone Irrigation Co., handwritten, [fall, 1904], and Minutes of meeting of the Board, Shoshone Irrigation Co., Dec. 15, 1904, BP, box 21, folder 1; Charles Thornton to L. L. Babcock, Sept. 25, 1905, and H. M. Gerrans to Beck, Nov. 23, 1905, BP, box 21, folder 2; Wallenberg to Beck, July 3, 1905, and Wallenberg to WFC, Nov. 12, Nov. 15, and Dec. 11, 1907, WFCC, Series I:A, Box 2, folder 28; W. L. Walls to Fred Bentley, Nov. 24, 1907, BP, box 21, folder 4.

CHAPTER NINE: HAVING IT ALL

Epigraph: BFP, box 1, folder 5.

1. WFC to Beck, Apr. 19, 1901, BBL, box 1, folder 7; WFC to Curtis L. Hinkle, Apr. 15, 1901, WFCC, Series I:B, box 1, folder 16.

2. WFC to Hinkle, Apr. 15, 1901, WFCC, Series I:B, box 1, folder 16.

3. WFC to Beck, Apr. 19, 1901, BBL, box 1, folder 7.

4. Ibid.; WFC to Beck, May 2, 1901, BP, box 2, folder 6.

5. Elwood Mead to C. W. Burdick, Feb. 5, 1896, GCWSE, 1890–1902.

6. WFC to Hinkle, Apr. 27, 1901, WFCC, Series I:B, box 1, folder 16.

7. Ibid., May 17, 1901.

8. Ibid., June 4, 1901.

9. *Wyoming Stockgrower and Farmer*, Oct. 10, 1902.

10. Salsbury to WFC, Dec. 19, 1901, Nathan Salsbury Papers, YCAL MSS 17, Beinecke Library, Yale University. The Military College idea briefly resurfaced after Cody's death, when the newly formed Buffalo Bill Memorial Association floated it as an appropriate memorial; *Park County Enterprise*, Dec. 5, 1917.

11. WFC to DeForest Richards, May 22, 1901, WFCC, Series I: B, box 1, folder 16; form letter to officers and members, May 27, 1901, endorsed by WFC to J. H. Peake, editor of the *Cody Enterprise*, BP, box 2, folder 6.

12. WFC to Beck, May 22, 1901, BP, box 2, folder 6. Information on the National Elks Home may be found at www.elkshome.org/history.

13. WFC to Hinkle, May 14, 1902, WFCC, Series I:B, box 1, folder 18.

14. Draft certificate of incorporation, WFCC, series I:A, box 2, folder 29; Wyoming Secretary of State inactive corporation files, file no. 2410, WSA; George T. Beck file, PCHSA.

15. Beck to Rumsey, June 11, 1897, SIC Letterpress Book for 1897, BP, box 25; WFC last will and testament (dated 14 Feb 1906), WFCC, Series I:C, box 1, folder 11; Wyoming Secretary of State, inactive corporation files, files no. 2244 and no. 6053; Salsbury to Beck, Mar. 25, 1896, BFP, box 1, folder 5; Rumsey to Beck, Mar. 29, Apr. 7, and Apr. 12, 1897, BFP, box 1, folder 9.

16. Papers of George Ward Holdrege, Box 1, folder 9, NSHS; Edward Gillette to Beck, Oct. 18, 1901, BP, box 2, folder 7; Notes of Mr. Beck, July 11, 12, and 31, Aug. 7, and [Sept. n.d.], and Engineer's Report, July 17 and 24, 1897, BP, box 20, folder 6.

17. Morrill to Beck, July 30, 1901, BFP, box 1, folder 11.

18. Rumsey to Beck, Apr. 12, 1897, BFP, box 1, folder 9; Davis to Rumsey, Mar. 18, 1903, and Rumsey to Beck, Mar. 26, [1903], BFP, box 2, folder 3. It should be noted that none of the mining prospects discussed here ever led to a commercially producing mine. Surrounded by states with vast wealth in precious metals, Wyoming had to be content with coal and oil.

19. Wilbur Knight to Beck, July 9, 1902, BP, box 2, folder 11; C. H. Morrill to Beck, July 24, 1903, BP, box 2, folder 14; *Wyoming Stockgrower and Farmer*, Oct. 10, 1902, Aug. 11, 1903, Oct. 27, 1903; *Cody Enterprise*, Nov. 12, 1903; placer location certificates in the Beck collection, PCHSA; Rumsey to Beck, Mar. 23, [1903], and Bleistein to Beck, Mar. 24, 1903, BFP, box 2, folder 3.

20. Placer Mining Records, BP, box 11, folder 5.

21. Beck to N. M. Kaufman, July 21, 1909, BP, box 3, folder 7; *Park County Enterprise*, Nov. 23, 1910.

22. WFC to Beck, Oct. 22 and Nov. 1, [1909], BP, box 6, folder 12; *Park County Enterprise*, Apr. 20, 27, and Nov. 23, 1910; File no. 11125, Wyoming Secretary of State inactive corporation files, WSA; Cody's Shoshone Oil Co. stock certificate dated Feb. 4, 1910, WFCC, series I:C, box 1, folder 27; Beck's Oil Co. stock in Beck collection, PCHSA; C. H. Morrill to Beck, Jan. 31, 1910, and H. M. Gerrans to Beck, Feb. 8, 1910, BP, box 3, folder 9.

23. WFC to E. E. Arbuckle, June 16 [1915], WFCC, Series I:B, box 2 folder 10.

24. WFC to Frank and Nellie Cody, [March 1915], William C. Garlow Collection, AHC.

25. *Park County Enterprise*, Jan. 5, 1916.

26. WFC to Julia Goodman, Mar. 23, 1902, in *Letters from "Buffalo Bill,"* ed. Stella Foote, 49.

27. WFC to Julia Goodman, May 22, 1902, ibid., 50.

28. Towne's description of the hotel opening celebration is in his article, "Preacher's Son on the Loose with Buffalo Bill Cody" 40–55. See also Rust, *Historic Hotels,* and Russell, *Lives and Legends,* 427–29.

29. WFC to Julia Goodman, Mar. 28, 1903, *Letters from "Buffalo Bill,"* 54.

30. WFC to Julia Goodman, June 5, 1903, ibid., 56.

31. WFCC, series I:C, box 1, folder 28.

32. Minutes of the Town Council, vol. I, Cody, Wyo.

33. Russell, *Lives and Legends,* 427–29.

34. Correspondence between WFC and W. L. Walls, his attorney in Cody, Documents 74.0458–74.0464, 74.0469–74.0486, BBMG.

35. WFC to Fenimore Chatterton, June 12, 1903, Correspondence of Governor Fenimore Chatterton, box 2, WSA. A month later Cody reiterated his promise to the governor to make the *Enterprise* "a straight out and out Republican sheet; Correspondence of Gov. Chatterton, box 2, WSA.

36. Big Horn County Transcripts, Park County Clerk's Office, Book One, 632, and Book Two, 107; Commissioner, General Land Office, to Register and Receiver, Lander, July 19, 1905; WFC to W. L. Walls, Feb. 14 and 28, April 11 and 20, June 9, 1906, and June 5, 1907, and Walls to WFC, July 1, 1907, files no. 74.0299 through 74.0420, BBMG.

37. Prospectus for Cody's Wyoming Coal Company, WFCC, Series I:C, box 1, folder 23. See also certificate for one hundred shares in the company in box 1, folder 15.

38. WFC to W. A. Richards, Sept. 25, 1903, WFCC, Series I:B, box 1, folder 19.

39. Yost, *Buffalo Bill,* 346–48; W. Hudson Kensel, *Pahaska Tepee,* 24.

40. H. S. Ridgley Papers, collection no. 264, box 1, folder 2, AHC.

41. Assistant Commissioner, General Land Office, to Register and Receiver, Lander, Wyo., Apr. [9?], 1908, Serial Patent File, 1908–1951, box 9006, folder 283610, Records of the General Land Office, RG 49, NA.

42. All the documents referenced in this discussion may be found in the Serial Patent File, 1908–1951, box 9006, folder 283610, Records of the General Land Office, RG 49, NA.

43. Big Horn County Transcripts, Book One, 422, and Book Two, 454, Park County Clerk's office, Cody Wyo.

44. Minutes of the State Land Commission, 1896–1902, Mar. 15, 1897, WSA.

45. Minutes of the State Land Commission, 1896–1902, Mar. 16, 1897, WSA; Mead to Anderson, Mar. 1, 1897, and Mead to WFC, Mar. 9, 1897, LBSE. For what it is worth, the large lease granted to Carey was disallowed by the State Land Board under review; Minutes, Oct. 18, 1899.

46. Mead to Charles Gilchrest, June 23, 1897, and Mead to WFC, Nov. 3, 1897, LBSE.

47. A great deal of this land activity is recorded in Big Horn County transcripts, Books 1–3, Park County Clerk's office, Cody, Wyo. The 1911 tax rolls are on microfilm in the Park County Treasurer's office, Cody.

48. Applications for Entry, box 1, Public Lands Records, WSA; Johnston to Beck, Mar. 14 and 22, 1904, Beck to Johnston, Mar. 28, 1904, and Nov. 3, 1905, GCWSE, 1902–1913; F. A. Johnston to Beck, Aug. 18, 1903, BFP, box 2, folder 3; "Beckoning Frontiers," Book IV, 50–54.

49. Sulphur Placer records, BP, box 11, folder 5.

50. Russell Kimball to Beck, Feb. 9, 1911, same to WFC, George Bleistein, and Henry Gerrans, Feb. 13, 1911, BP, box 3, folder 10; Beck collection, PCHSA.

CHAPTER TEN: THE CODY-SALSBURY PROPOSITION

1. The dam, completed in 1910, was known as Shoshone Dam until 1946, the centennial of William F. Cody's birth, when it and the lake were renamed in his honor. Our traveler would have found a much larger lake, 650,000 acre-feet, if his trip had taken place after 1982, when twenty-five feet were added to the height of the dam.

2. George Beck's Notes on construction, June 5–14, 1897, BP, box 20, folder 6; Mead to WFC, Mar. 12, 1896, LBSE. Typical of the confusion among historians is the linkage of the Cody Canal to the Buffalo Bill Dam, as seen in Russell, *Lives and Legends,* 426, or in the brief account by Rosa and May in *Buffalo Bill and His Wild West,* 190–91.

3. WFC to Mead, Sept. 2, 1896, and Mar. 28, 1896, GCWSE, 1902–1913.

4. WFC to Mead, Oct. 7, 1896, GCWSE, 1902–1913.

5. Mead to Hymer, Feb. 19, 1897, LBSE.

6. WFC to Mead, Mar. 17, 1897, GCWSE, 1902–1913; WFC to Mead, Oct. 2, 1896, GCWSE, 1902–1913; Mead to WFC, Feb. 19, 1897, LBSE.

7. Mead to Warren, July 23, 1897, LBSE; Salsbury to Mead, Mar. 25, 1897, GCWSE, 1902–1913; Mead to John H. Renshawe, June 21, 1897, and Mead to Fred Bond, June 22, 1897, LBSE.

8. Warren to Mead, July 27, 1897, Francis E. Warren Papers, Series I (microfilm), AHC.

9. Anna Morley to WFC, Aug. 20, 1897, LBSE; John Whiting, "Water Right Studies of the Shoshone Irrigation Project in Wyoming," (1953), 57–58 (unpublished MS in Shoshone Irrigation District Archives, Powell, Wyo).

10. WFC to Mead, Dec. 29, 1897, GCWSE, 1902–1913; Whiting, "Water Right Studies," 57–58.

11. WFC to Mead, July 7, 1898, GCWSE, 1902–1913; also Jan. 24, Mar. 31, May 18, and June 10, 1898, GCWSE 1902–1913.

12. Mead to WFC, July 11, 1898, Mar. 1, Apr. 27, and May 10, 1899, LBSE; WFC to Mead, Feb. 28, May 15, 23, 30, 1899, GCWSE, 1902–1913; Whiting, "Water Right Studies," 60–64.

13. Mead to WFC, June 14, 1898, and Mar. 1, 1899, LBSE; Minutes of the Arid Lands Board, 1895–1953, Public Land Records, WSA; Commissioner of General Land Office to Governor of Wyoming, July 15, 1901, Correspondence of Governor DeForest Richards, box 9, WSA.

14. Welch, *History of the Big Horn Basin,* 58–60.

15. Charles Kingston to Governor Richards, Dec. 30, 1899; Abraham Woodruff to Governor Richards, Dec. 30, 1899, Feb. 19 and Mar. 16, 1900, Correspondence of Governor DeForest Richards, box 7; Gov. Richards to Woodruff, Mar. 26, 1900, Letterpress Book of Governor DeForest Richards, WSA. The actual Cody-Salsbury segregation south of the river was 9,440 acres.

16. Gov. Richards to WFC, Sept. 4, 1900, Letterpress Book of Governor DeForest Richards, WSA.

17. Richards to Woodruff, Sept. 14, 1900, Letterpress Book; L. E. Decker [WFC secretary] to Gov. Richards, Sept. 9, 1900, Correspondence of Governor DeForest Richards, box 5, WSA.

18. Richards to WFC, June 4, 1902, Letterpress Book; Kingston to Richards, Aug. 26, 1901, Correspondence of Governor DeForest Richards, box 5, WSA.

19. WFC to Holdrege, Sept. 17, 1902, RG 115, E. 3, Shoshone 958, box 912; Richards to WFC, June 21, 1902, Letterpress Book. Kelsey's survey, dated Sept. 20, 1901, may be seen in RG 115, Engineering and Research Center Project Reports, 1910–1955, box 782.

20. WFC to Hinkle, Mar. 10, 1902, WFCC, Series I:B, box 1, folder 18.

21. Ibid., Aug. 18, 1902.

22. WFC to Richards, Aug. 29, 1902, Correspondence of Gov. DeForest Richards, box 5, WSA.

23. WFC to Holdrege, Sept. 17, 1902, RG 115, E. 3, Shoshone 958, box 912.

24. Frank Kelsey, "Report on the Location and Estimated Cost of the Cody and Salsbury Canal," Sept. 20, 1901, in RG 115, Engineering and Research Center Project Reports, 1910–1955, box 782. It is important to note that none of the Cody-Salsbury Canal plans ever imagined a storage reservoir the likes of what the Reclamation Service constructed.

25. John Martin to WFC, Aug. 24, [1902], Correspondence of Governor DeForest Richards, Box 5, WSA. Charles Walcott's diary of the trip indicates that Holdrege himself was along; 1902 Diary, box 14, folder 2, Charles D. Walcott Collection, Archives and Special Collections, Smithsonian Institution. For an understanding of western water issues leading up to 1902, see Pisani, *To Reclaim a Divided West*. For the work of the USGS in that period, see Donald Worster's biography of John Wesley Powell, *A River Running West* (2001).

26. WFC to Richards, Aug. 29, 1902, Correspondence of Governor DeForest Richards, box 5, WSA.

27. Holdrege to Walcott, Sept. 22, 1902, RG 115, E. 3, Shoshone 958, box 912.

28. Indenture dated 12 Dec. 1902, filed in RG 115, E. 3, Shoshone 958, box 912; Walcott to Holdrege, Sept. 27, 1902, RG 115, E. 3, Shoshone 958, box 912.

29. Richards to Walcott, Jan. 24, 1903, Letterpress Book; Richards to Edward Gillette, CB&Q Superintendent, Jan. 5, 1903, Letterpress Book.

30. Warren to T. F. Burke, Feb. 4, 1903, Correspondence of Governor DeForest Richards, box 5, WSA.

31. Richards to Woodruff, June 14, 1901, Letterpress Book; Richards to Walcott, Feb. 9, 1903, Letterpress Book, and Feb. 24, 1903, RG 115, E. 3, box 912.

32. WFC to Richards, Mar. 9, 1903, Correspondence of Governor DeForest Richards, box 5, WSA; Richards to WFC, Feb. 24, 1903, Letterpress Book.

33. Walcott to Richards, Feb. 19, 1903, Correspondence of Governor DeForest Richards, box 7; Byron Sessions to Richards, Mar. 5, 1903, Correspondence, Box 8. A complete account of this entire affair may be found in Bonner, "Buffalo Bill Cody and Wyoming Water Politics": 433–51.

34. Chatterton to WFC, May 7, 1903, Letterpress Book of Governor DeForest Richards, WSA. (Chatterton's staff, apparently in the interests of holding down expenditures, continued to take letterpress impressions in Governor Richards's book until it was full.)

35. Chatterton to WFC, June 8, 1903, and Chatterton to Abraham Woodruff, May 8, 1903, Letterpress Book of Governor DeForest Richards, WSA.

36. Walcott to Chatterton, Oct. 21, 1903, Correspondence of Governor Fenimore Chatterton; Chatterton to Walcott, Nov. 6, 1903, Letterpress Book of Governor DeForest Richards.

37. Walcott to Secretary of Interior, Dec. 29, 1903, RG 115, E.3, Shoshone 958, Box 912; D. H. McFall in Cody to Chatterton, Feb. 10, 1904, Correspondence of Governor Fenimore Chatterton, box 2, WSA.

38. Chatterton to Walcott, Jan. 4, 1904, Letterpress Book of Gov. Fenimore Chatterton. Copies of the letter were sent to a large number of people, including the congressional delegation.

39. See, for example, Mondell to Chatterton, Jan. 10 and 22, 1904, Correspondence of Governor Fenimore Chatterton, WSA; Newell to Chatterton, Jan. 27, 1904, RG 115, E. 3, Shoshone 958, Box 912.

40. Holdrege to Newell, Jan. 4, 1904, RG 115, E. 3, Shoshone 958, box 912; Chatterton to Mondell, Jan. 14, 1904, Letterpress Book of Gov. Fenimore Chatterton, and Mondell to Chatterton, Jan. 22, 1904, Correspondence of Governor Fenimore Chatterton, WSA.

41. Chatterton to Holdrege, Feb. 8, 1904, Letterpress Book of Governor Fenimore Chatterton; *Laramie Republican*, Feb. 1, 1904. It eventually came out that the Oregon Basin papers were slow to clear the Land Office because Wyoming officials had failed to file complete entries.

42. Cody's decision to divorce his wife, Louisa, and the consequences of that ill-fated suit, are treated fully by Warren in *Buffalo Bill's America*, 498–519.

43. *Cody Enterprise*, Nov. 19 and 26, Dec. 3, 1903, Jan. 21 and 28, 1904; *Cheyenne Leader*, Dec. 8, 23, and 30, 1903, Jan. 16, 1904.

44. Cody's revised and simplified history of these complex negotiations included a vision of himself bowing to the wishes of the people of Cody and sending the willing investors back to England after a good hunt. See WFC to Secretary of the Interior James R. Garfield, July 27, 1908, and Jan. 29, 1909, RG 115, E. 3, box 899, folder 448-A1.

45. Holdrege to Chatterton, Feb. 11, 1904, Correspondence of Governor Fenimore Chatterton, box 2, WSA. Cody confided to a friend that Arta's death was "the worst sorrow of my life"; WFC to Irving R. Bacon, Feb. 21, 1904, Irving R. Bacon Artist File, BBHC.

46. WFC to Chatterton, Feb. 15, 1904, Correspondence of Governor Fenimore Chatterton, box 2, WSA; Russell, *Lives and Legends,* 431; Chatterton to WFC, Feb. 4, 1904, Chatterton to G. W. Holdrege, Feb. 8, 1904, and Chatterton to Charles Walcott, Feb. 10, 1904, Letterpress Book; Holdrege to Chatterton, Feb. 11, 1904, Correspondence of Governor Fenimore Chatterton, box 2, WSA.

47. Holdrege to Chatterton, Feb. 11, 1904, WFC to Chatterton, Feb. 15, 1904 (letter) and WFC to Chatterton, Feb. 15, 1904 (telegram), Manderson to Chatterton, Feb. 15, 1904 (telegram), Chatterton to Manderson (draft of telegram), Feb. 16, 1904, Tynan to Chatterton, Feb. 20, 1904 (telegram), Correspondence of Governor Fenimore Chatterton, box 2, WSA.

48. Manderson to Chatterton (telegram), Feb. 15, 1904, Correspondence of Governor Fenimore Chatterton, box 2, WSA.

49. Senator Warren summed up the proceedings in his acerbic way in a pair of confidential letters to W. E. Chaplin of Cheyenne, dated Feb. 20 and Mar. 13, 1904, in the Francis E. Warren Papers, microfilm box 29, AHC.

50. Chatterton to Welch, Jan. 2, 1904, Letterpress Book of Governor Fenimore Chatterton. The tract of land in question was often referred to as the Whistle Creek tract.

51. Extensive correspondence between state and federal officials on this settlement is to be found in RG 115, E. 3, Shoshone 958, box 912.

CHAPTER ELEVEN: "I KNOW THEE NOT, OLD MAN . . ."

1. Frank Kelsey, Report on the Cody and Salsbury Canal, RG 115, Engineering and Research Center Project Reports, 1910–1955, 520–SHO, box 782.

2. *Wyoming Stockgrower and Farmer*, Dec. 13, 1905.

3. Ibid., Sept. 13, 1906; WFC to Theodore Roosevelt, Feb. 25, 1908, RG 115, E. 3, box 888, folder 48.

4. WFC to Roosevelt, Feb. 25, 1908, RG 115, E. 3, box 888, folder 48.

5. F. H. Newell to William Loeb, Secretary to the President, March 5, 1908, RG 115, E. 3, box 888, folder 48.

6. See, for example, *Wyoming Stockgrower and Farmer*, Sept. 13, 1906, and July 23, 1908.

7. WFC to Theodore Roosevelt, Mar. 10, 1905, RG 115, E. 3, Box 899, folder 448-A1.

8. Ibid.

9. Newell to William Loeb, Secretary to the President, Mar. 18, 1905, RG 115, E. 3, Box 899, folder 448-A1; Roosevelt to WFC, Mar. 11, 1905, Papers of Theodore Roosevelt, Series 2, vol. 54, 323 (MF #337), LC.

10. Park County, Wyoming, Deed Records, Book 2, p. 69, Park County Clerk's Office, Cody; Collins Land Co. to Lincoln Land Co., Mar. 16, 1904, Town Files—Ralston, Lincoln Land Company Records, MS 3648, NSHS. Gates, *History of Public Land Law Development,* 570–71, explains lieu lands. Rumors about government plans were consolidated in an account published in the *Wyoming Stockgrower and Farmer,* July 12, 1905.

11. H. N. Savage to F. H. Newell, Sept. 16, 1905, RG 115, E. 3, box 898, folder 448-A.

12. Ibid.

13. Savage to Newell, Dec. 6, 1905, RG 115, E. 3, box 899, folder 448-A1. Cody's record of service to the government was, in fact, quite scanty. His Civil War military enlistment in the Seventh Kansas Volunteer Cavalry "was remarkable for its lack of distinction," and required only a few months of active service; Warren, *Buffalo Bill's America,* 38. As a scout with the cavalry during the Indian wars he was a well-paid private contractor.

14. Roosevelt to WFC, Feb. 16, 1906, Papers of Theodore Roosevelt, series 2, vol. 61, 281 (MF # 340), LC.

15. Mondell to Newell, Aug. 3, 1906, and July 19, 1906, RG 115, E. 3, box 899, folder 448-A1.

16. Newell to Mondell, Aug. 8, 1906, RG 115, E. 3, box 899, folder 448-A1.

17. WFC to Newell (from Milan), May 4, 1906, RG 115, E. 3, Shoshone 958A, box 912.

18. Newell to Savage, May 22, 1906, Savage to Newell, June 1, 1906, and Newell to WFC, June 19, 1906, RG 115, E. 3, Shoshone 958A, box 912.

19. WFC to Roosevelt, Aug. 16, 1906, RG 115, E. 3, Shoshone 958A, box 912.

20. Ibid.

21. Roosevelt to WFC, Aug. 27, 1906, Papers of Theodore Roosevelt, Series 2, vol. 66, 209 (MF # 342), LC.

22. Walcott to Roosevelt, Oct. 1, 1906, RG 115, E. 3, Shoshone 958A, box 912.

23. Savage to Newell, Feb. 5, 1907, C. H. Morrill to Savage, Feb. 2, 1907, and Acting Chief Engineer to Savage, Feb. 26, 1907, RG 115, E. 3, Shoshone 958A, box 912.

24. Walcott to Garfield, Sept. 13, 1907; WFC to Roosevelt, Aug. 2, 1907, RG 115, E. 3, box 899, folder 448-A1.

25. Acting Secretary of Interior to William Loeb, Aug. 9, 1907, RG 115, E. 3, box 899, folder 448-A1.

26. Secretary of Interior to Postmaster General, Oct. 3, 1907, and Secretary of Interior to Mondell, Dec. 5, 1907, RG 48, CCF 1907–1936, 8-3 Shoshone; E. P. Bracken, CB&Q Division Superintendent, to Savage, Nov. 6, 1907, RG 115, E. 3, Shoshone 271, box 1319.

27. WFC to C. H. Morrill, Jan. 7, 1908, and Report dated June 30, 1908, Town Files—Ralston, Lincoln Land Co. Records, NSHS.

28. Project Engineer Jeremiah Ahern to Savage, Feb. 4, 1908; Petition to Ahern to open Powell townsite, May 21, 1908; Savage to Newell, June 11, 1908; Newell to Savage, June 16, 1908; Warren to Newell, July 13, 1908—all in RG 115, E. 3, Box 899, folder 448-A1.

29. Garfield to WFC, Aug. 18, 1908, RG 48, CCF 1907–1936, 8-3 Shoshone; *Wyoming Stockgrower and Farmer,* July 23, 1908. Cody and W. L. Walls discussed plans for putting pressure on Garfield when he was in Cody to get him to move on the High Line; files 74.0434 and 74.0441, BBMG.

30. Acting director USGS to H. N. Savage, RG 115, E. 3, box 899, folder 448-A1.

31. WFC to Secretary Garfield, July 27, 1908, RG 115, E. 3, box 899, folder 448-A1.

32. Newell to Acting Director USRS, Aug. 16, 1908, and Savage to Director USRS, Aug. 29, 1908, RG 115, E. 3, box 899, folder 448-A1.

33. Mondell to Garfield, Nov. 15, 1908, RG 115, E. 3, box 899, folder 448-A1.

34. Garfield to Warren, Nov. 24, 1908, and Garfield to Mondell, Nov. 25, 1908, RG 48, CCF 1907–1936, 8-3 Shoshone.

35. Garfield to WFC, Jan. 22, 1909, RG 48, CCF 1907–1936, 8-3 Shoshone.

36. See Skowronek, *Building a New American State*.

37. W. A. Sickler, Shoshone Project Irrigation Manager, to Director, USRS, Nov. 30, 1908, RG 115, E. 3, box 899, folder 448-A1.

38. W. A. Deming to Secretary of Interior, Jan. 18, 1909, RG 115, E. 3, box 899, folder 448-A1.

39. Citizens Ticket Platform, May 8, 1909, PCHSA.

40. *Powell Tribune*, March 20, 1909.

41. Louis Warren, who says Cody stopped drinking in 1901, explores the chasm between drinkers and respectable family men as he explains the course of the sensational Cody divorce trial in 1904–1905. Although he also concludes that it was the people of the Shoshone Valley who dashed Cody's hopes for his townsites, he overlooks the similar role that the social divide over temperance played there. See *Buffalo Bill's America,* 506–509, 530–32. Engineers building the Shoshone Project had struggled for years to maintain a sober work force, against the machinations of saloon-keepers from Cody who set up tents near Reclamation camps in violation of Wyoming law. For the national context of the temperance struggle, see Lender and Martin, *Drinking in America*, esp. 109–32.

42. WFC to Garfield, Jan. 29, 1909, RG 115, E. 3, box 899, folder 448-A1.

43. WFC to Garfield, Feb. 13, 1909, RG 115, E. 3, box 899, folder 448-A1.

44. Garfield to WFC, Mar. 2, 1909, RG 48, CCF 1907–1936, 8-3 Shoshone.

45. Ballinger to WFC, Apr. 7, 1909; Petition to the Secretary of the Interior for the establishment of the town of Powell, Feb. 15, 1909—both in RG 48, CCF 1907–1936, 8-3 Shoshone.

46. W. L. Walls to Secretary of Interior, July 18, 1910; Frank Pierce, Acting Secretary of Interior to Walls, Aug. 6, 1910, and Sept. 7, 1910; Director of the USRS to the Secretary of the Interior, Oct. 11, 1909—all in RG 48, CCF 1907–1936, 8-3 Shoshone.

47. Secretary of Interior to Acting Secretary, Aug. 14, 1911, CCF 1907–1936, 8-3 Shoshone; *Park County Enterprise*, Sept. 30 and Oct. 14, 1911. The editorial was titled "Uncle Sam's Annual Gift."

48. Town of Cody petition to Secretary of Interior, April 1, 1912; WFC to Secretary of Interior, April 1, 1912; First Assistant Secretary to Mayor of Cody, June 3, 1912, CCF 1907–1936, 8-3 Shoshone. Cody's municipal water right from the Shoshone River was never at issue; the government could not charge for that. But if the town took the water from the reservoir, the 1906 federal law dictating the terms of sale of water to entities outside of Reclamation projects took precedence.

49. *Park County Enterprise*, Jan. 6 and Mar. 27, 1912, and Dec. 23, 1914.

CHAPTER TWELVE: NEW WORK FOR A NEW CENTURY

1. Warren, *Buffalo Bill's America*, 472ff.

2. *New York Tribune*, Dec. 14, 1903, and *New York Times*, Apr. 24, 1907.

3. Warren has a very interesting discussion of the "white Indian" tradition in American life and letters in *Buffalo Bill's America,* 125–49. Daniel J. Herman employs the term "American Native" for these same men, in *Hunting and the American Imagination* (2001), 159–87.

4. Woodbury, "History of Southern Utah and its National Parks": 189–93; Prentiss Ingraham, "In the Saddle with Buffalo Bill," *New York Banner Weekly*, Feb. 25, 1893. Woodbury sets the trip in 1891, but Ingraham, who was there, dates his letter Nov. 19, 1892. For Ingraham's relationship with Cody, see Russell, *Lives and Legends,* 268–73. The photographs may be seen at Document P2402, Latter-Day Saints Church Archives, Salt Lake City, Utah.

5. Russell, *Lives and Legends*, 169–84.

6. The Davies book, *Ten Days on the Plains*, was republished by Southern Methodist University Press in 1985, with an extensive introduction by Paul A. Hutton. Warren, *Buffalo Bill's America,* 140–49, discusses perceptively Cody's appropriation of the role of the "white Indian" and the way he turned it to his advantage as he merged guiding and life on the stage. He suggests, as does Hutton, that the 1871 hunt was a turning point in Cody's sense of his own life's possibilities.

7. WFC to Julia Goodman, July 18, 1894, in Foote, *Letters from "Buffalo Bill,"* 41–42. His big plans for that business in 1894 were spoiled by the railroad strike.

8. "Buffalo Bill," *Cosmopolitan*: 139–40. Joy Kasson seems unwilling to conclude that Cody actually wrote this, but the style of it seems to me unmistakably his; see Kasson, *Buffalo Bill's Wild West*, 230. Hutton regards it as a considerable improvement over his treatment of the hunt in his 1879 autobiography.

9. Herman, *Hunting and the American Imagination*, 218–53.

10. Ibid., 122–58.

11. Blair, *Wildlife Management in Wyoming,* 29–40.

12. Mead to Cody, Dec. 22, 1896, LBSE.

13. Cody to Mead, Jan. 8, 1897, GCWSE, 1902–1913.

14. Mead to Cody, Mar. 9, 1897, LBSE; Cody to Mead, Mar. 17, 1897, GCWSE, 1902–1913. Some New Yorkers who hoped to be part of the club wrote Mead demanding to know why Wyoming would not provide them the land. He offered in reply a patient rehearsal of Wyoming law and politics; see Mead to Philip M. Lydig, Apr. 5, 1897, LBSE.

15. A copy of the brochure is in Box 3, Entry 962, Carey Act Cases, 1896–1917, General Land Office Records, RG 49, NA.

16. See, for instance, *Wyoming Stockgrower and Farmer*, June 16, 1903. A. A. Anderson, of whom more below, strongly supported the idea of game preserves; see his memoir, *Experiences and Impressions,* 89–116.

17. *New York Tribune*, Jan. 18, 1901.

18. Chamberlin, Cook, and Monteith, *Cody Club,* 1–3; Nate Salsbury to George Beck, Oct. 9, 1900, WFCC, Series I:A, box 2, folder 32.

19. Cody "Preserving the Game": 1292–93. Wyoming's 1899 game law deputized licensed guides as assistant game wardens in an attempt to achieve enforcement of the game limits without incurring much in the way of expenses; see Blair, *Wildlife Management in Wyoming*, 36–37.

20. Cody, "Preserving the Game."

21. Governor Richards to Game Warden Albert Nelson, Aug. 14, 1901, Letterpress Book of Governor DeForest Richards, WSA.

22. Trefethen, *Crusade for Wildlife*, 122–23; John Reiger, *American Sportsmen*.

23. Warren, *The Hunter's Game*, 177. Jacoby, *Crimes against Nature,* offers cognate arguments to Warren's.

24. Governor DeForest Richards to State Game Warden Albert Nelson, Jan. 6, [1902], Letterpress Book of Governor DeForest Richards, WSA. There is significant correspondence between George Beck and the governor on the subject of game laws throughout these years; see, for instance, Beck to Governor Richards, Jan. 24, 1898, complaining about the marauding of one "Frenchy" Devoe, asking for game law enforcement, in BP, box 1, folder 19.

25. Herman, "Hunting Democracy": 23–33.

26. *Cody Enterprise,* Oct. 8, 1903.

27. Ibid., Oct. 22, 1903.

28. *Wyoming Stockgrower and Farmer*, Nov. 1, 1906; see also issue for Oct. 18, 1906, and Beck's account in "Beckoning Frontiers," Part IV, 74–77.

29. *New York Tribune*, Oct. 30, 1906.

30. Seton, *Biography of a Grizzly*; Wasner, *From Beaver to Oil*, 301–308; *Cody Enterprise*, May 1, 1915; William T. Hornaday Papers, MSS 2, Camp-Fire Club of America, box 1, folders 1–5, Wildlife Conservation Society Archives, New York Zoological Park, New York City.

31. Anderson, *Experiences and Impressions*, 98; historical roster of Camp Fire Club membership, provided by Shawn Orbanick, Greenwich, Conn., current club historian; Pratt to Hornaday, Aug. 31, Sept. 2, and Nov. 4, 1909, Hornaday Papers, box 1, general correspondence 1903–1910; *New York Times,* Jan. 9, 1910.

32. W. R. Coe to Mrs. Henry H. R. Coe, May 11, 1954, Coe Family Papers, box 22, folder 3, Planting Fields Foundation Archives, Planting Fields Arboretum State Historical Park, Oyster Bay, N.Y.; Camp Fire Club records, 1908, Hornaday Papers, box 2, folder 1; Coe Family Papers, box 22, folder 4.

33. The best record of the Coe family's charitable involvement with Cody is in Bartlett, *From Cody to the World*. Buffalo Bill's cultivation of a friendship with the Coe family around the time of the sale of the ranch is revealed in a series of letters from him to Coe in the W. F. Cody Papers, WA MSS S-197, folder 7, Beinecke Library, Yale University.

34. Russell, *Lives and Legends*, 452–56.

35. *Park County Enterprise*, Aug. 13 and 27, Sept. 6, 10, 13, 17, and 20, 1913; Day, "The Prince Who Would Be Mayor": 54–58, in WFCC, Series I:D, box 1, folder 8.

36. *Park County Enterprise,* Sept. 17, 1913.

37. *Park County Enterprise*, Oct. 1, 1913; Gates's visit to Wyoming ended in his own death, still shrouded in mystery, in his private car as the train prepared to depart; *Park County Enterprise*, Oct. 29, 1913; Day, "The Prince Who Would Be Mayor": 57–58. A set of six photographs of the meeting of Buffalo Bill, Plenty Coups, and the Prince of Monaco were published by Phillips in *The West,* 150–51.

38. *Wyoming Stockgrower and Farmer*, July 2, 1909.

39. *Park County Enterprise*, Jan. 13 and 27, Feb. 13, and Apr. 14, 1915.

40. W. R. Coe to Beck, Feb. 17, 1913, BP, box 4, folder 1.

41. A. A. Anderson to Beck, Feb. 11, 1913, BP, box 4, folder 1; Blair, *Wildlife Management in Wyoming*, 41–50. The new preserves near Cody were in Boulder Basin and Hoodoo Basin.

42. *Park County Enterprise*, Aug. 18 and 21, and Nov. 17, 1915.

43. *New York Times*, Sept. 1, 1912, and May 1, 1904; Notes of activities of Camp Fire Club members for 1908, box 2, folder 1, and general correspondence 1903–1910, box 1, William T. Hornaday Papers, Wildlife Conservation Society Archives; *Park County Enterprise*, Jan. 6, 1912; WFC to Larom and WFC to John Clark, Secretary of the Rocky Mountain Club, December 7, 1916, WFCC, Series I:B, box 2, folder 9. Information on the character

of the Rocky Mountain Club is scattered through the *New York Times*; see, for instance, Nov. 1, 1907, Dec. 28, 1913, Dec. 26, 1917.

44. Morrill, *The Morrills,* 99–100.

45. Russell, *Lives and Legends*, 427; Beck to WFC, Aug. 19, 1896, SIC Letterpress Book, 1896–97, BP, box 25.

46. Kensel, *Pahaska Tepee*, 11–15; "Beckoning Frontiers," Part IV, 57–58; Beecher, *Bishop of the Great Plains*, 123–24; *Cody Enterprise*, Feb. 6, 1901.

47. Warren, *Buffalo Bill's America*, 494–519; Yost, *Buffalo Bill,* 314–36.

48. *Cody Enterprise*, Oct. 1, 1903; Assistant Secretary of the Interior to Commissioner of General Land Office, March 10, 1904, Microfilm 620, roll 295, Records of the Land and Railroads Division, Letters Sent 1849–1904, RG 48; Secretary of the Interior to Commissioner of General Land Office, Oct. 31, 1904, MF 620, roll 304, ibid. An existing but undeveloped permit for the Wapiti site secured by two early pioneers from Marquette, J. D. Start and W. T. Borron, was canceled to make way for Cody.

49. Register of Letters Received, Patents and Miscellaneous Division, Department of the Interior, 1904, RG 48.

50. J. Barton Key to WFC, Dec. 31, 1903, WFCC, Series I:B, box 2, folder 28; Kensel, *Pahaska Tepee*, 17–27.

51. Kensel, *Pahaska Tepee*, 17–41. Figure 21 shows one of Cody's White Steamers with a full load of hunters in front of the Irma Hotel.

52. WFC to Clarence [Buell], Oct. 21, [1913?], WFCC, Series I:B, box 1, folder 3.

53. Russell, *Lives and Legends*, 451; *Park County Enterprise*, Mar. 24, 1915.

54. *Park County Enterprise,* June 16, 1915.

55. "An Ideal Outing at Buffalo Bill's Hotels in the Rockies," WFCC, Series I:D, box 2, folder 5.

56. WFCC, Series I: D, box 1, folder 18.

57. The classic treatment of eastern men's fascination with the West is White, *Eastern Establishment and the Western Experience*. A recent study by Murdoch, *American West,* covers some of the same ground in an interesting way. A good discussion of scouting and the frontier is that of MacDonald, *Sons of the Empire*. Dan Beard testified in his autobiography, *Hardly a Man Is Now Alive*, 354–55, that Cody was with him in the founding of the Sons of Daniel Boone, a precursor to the Boy Scouts. Deloria devotes a chapter of *Playing Indian* (95–127) to explorations of the scouting and camping movements.

58. Kasson, *Buffalo Bill's Wild West*, 266–67, explores connections among Cody, Baden-Powell, and the founders of the Boy Scouts of America. Deloria, 107–114, explores the tensions between Beard and Seton on the use of Indian imagery and woodcraft in American scouting; clearly Cody was closer to Beard than to Seton, more the pioneer than the Indian, as the curriculum of his Cavalry School suggests.

59. *Park County Enterprise*, Dec. 29, 1915.

60. WFC to "Buck" [identified as Arbuckle from other correspondence], n.p., n.d., WFCC, Series I:B, box 1, folder 3.

61. WFCC, Series I:D, box 2, folder 5.

62. Charles Wayland Towne, "A Wild West Show Every Day" and "Swapping Yarns with Buffalo Bill," *Boston Evening Transcript*, Jan. 8, 1916. See also Towne's "Preacher's Son on the Loose with Buffalo Bill Cody," 40–55.

63. *Northern Wyoming Herald*, Aug. 8 and 22, 1917. See Roundy, "Origins and Early Development of Dude Ranching." Cf. Rothman, *Devil's Bargains,* 10–28.

CONCLUSION

1. Warren, *Buffalo Bill's America*, 546–49. The quoted description is from William Shakespeare, *King Lear*, Act III, scene iv.

2. Salsbury MSS, Beinecke Library, box 2, folder 64.

3. Warren, *Buffalo Bill's America*, 495–98; "Beckoning Frontiers," passim.

4. Beecher, *Bishop of the Great Plains*, 116.

5. The 1915 population of the town was 1,035, about 200 fewer than in 1905 when the work force for the Shoshone Dam construction inflated the numbers. See Secretary of State, Census of Wyoming, WSA. Cody was the second largest town in the Basin in 1915.

6. Kasson, *Buffalo Bill's Wild West*, 266–68.

7. WFC to Rowley, Apr. 5, 1912, WFCC, Series I:B, box 2, folder 17.

8. Cody's charitable activities are described in Hook, "Seven Months in Cody, Wyoming," 10–11.

9. *Wyoming Stockgrower and Farmer*, Nov. 29, 1905; the quoted passage is only a small part of a very long panegyric, all of the same tone.

10. Ibid., Dec. 6, 1905.

11. *Park County Enterprise*, Jan. 6, 1912, Mar. 11, 1911.

12. Ibid., Dec. 9, 1914.

13. State of Wyoming, Secretary of State, Census of Wyoming, 1905, 1910, 1915, WSA.

14. *Wyoming Stockgrower and Farmer*, Nov. 3, 1903. It should probably go without saying that no one can have any idea how accurate this estimate might be. It uses the figure of $60,000, for instance, for the Irma Hotel; Cody usually claimed he spent $80,000 on the Irma. Of course, we have also seen how unreliable his own estimates could be.

15. Chamberlin, Cook, and Monteith, *Cody Club*, 40–58; Program for Dinner and Dance in celebration of the Birthday of Colonel William F. Cody, Feb. 26, 1932, Medinah Athletic Club, Chicago, in William F. Cody biographical files, folder 8, AHC.

16. Most of his letters to Julia are printed in Foote's *Letters from "Buffalo Bill."*

17. Russell, *Lives and Legends*, 426–29.

18. Yost, *Buffalo Bill*, 314–36; Warren, *Buffalo Bill's America*, 498–519.

19. An effective statement of the conflict between the myth of the individual and the historical reality of western America may be found in Limerick's *Legacy of Conquest* (1986).

20. Trachtenberg, *Incorporation of America*, 3–4.

21. Ibid., 37; Krupicka, "Cody and Wanamaker."

22. WFC to Elwell, July 29, 1907, WFCC, Series I:B, box 2, folder 2.

23. See the new book by Liza Nicholas, *Becoming Western*, 33–113, for an interesting set of observations on Buffalo Bill and his legacy in Cody in the twentieth century.

24. Bartlett, *From Cody to the World*, 93–145.

25. Manuscript diary of Carolyn Lockhart, Jan. 2, 1920, box 1, Accession no. 177, AHC. The other successful Reclamation town is Rupert, Idaho.

26. *Reclamation Record*, June 1915, 257–58. For Carey Act projects in Wyoming, see Bonner, "Elwood Mead, Buffalo Bill Cody, and the Carey Act in Wyoming."

Bibliography

ARCHIVAL MATERIALS

Buffalo Bill Historical Center, Cody, Wyo. McCracken Library. Irving R. Bacon Artist File.
———. William F. Cody Collection.
———. William C. Garlow Collection.
Buffalo Bill Museum and Grave, Golden, Col. Archives.
Camp Fire Club of America, Greenwich, Conn. Membership roster.
Cody, Wyo., City Hall. Minutes of the Town Council.
Denver Public Library, Denver, Col. Western History Manuscript Collection. William F. Cody Papers, CMSS-M688.
Latter-Day Saints Church Archives, Salt Lake City, Utah.
Library of Congress, Washington, D.C. Papers of Theodore Roosevelt.
National Archives, Washington, D.C. Records of the Department of Interior, RG 48.
———. Records of the General Land Office, RG 49.
National Archives, Rocky Mountain Branch, Denver, Col. Records of the Bureau of Reclamation, RG 115.
Nebraska State Historical Society, Lincoln. Records of the Lincoln Land Company.
———. Papers of George Ward Holdrege.
Newberry Library, Chicago. Records of the Chicago, Burlington, and Quincy Railroad.
New York Zoological Park, New York City. Wildlife Conservation Society Archives. William T. Hornaday Papers, MSS 2.
Papers of Eugene V. Debs, 1834–1945. University Microfilms, 1983.
Park County Clerk's Office, Cody, Wyo. Big Horn County Transcripts.
———. Deed Records.
Park County Treasurer's Office, Cody, Wyo. 1911 county tax rolls.
Park County Historical Society Archives, Cody, Wyo. George T. Beck Collection.
———. Charles E. Hayden Collection.
Planting Fields Arboretum State Historical Park, Oyster Bay, N.Y. Planting Fields Foundation Archives. Coe Family Papers.

Smithsonian Institution, Washington, D.C. Archives and Special Collections. Charles D. Walcott Collection.

University of Wyoming, Laramie. American Heritage Center. George T. Beck Papers, Accession no. 59.

————. Beck Family Papers, Accession no. 10386.

————. Buffalo Bill Letters to George T. Beck, Accession no. 9972.

————. Caroline Lockhart Papers, Accession no. 177.

————. H. S. Ridgley Papers, Accession no. 264.

————. Francis E. Warren Papers, Accession no. 13.

United States Board on Geographic Names files, Reston, Va.

Wyoming State Archives, Cheyenne. Big Horn County District Court Civil Files.

————. Letterpress Books of the Wyoming State Engineer (microfilm).

————. Letterpress Books of Governor DeForest Richards.

————. Letterpress Books of Governor Fenimore Chatterton.

————. General Correspondence of the Wyoming State Engineer, 1890–1902 (microfilm).

————. General Correspondence of the Wyoming State Engineer, 1902–1913 (microfilm).

————. General Correspondence of Governor DeForest Richards.

————. General Correspondence of Governor Fenimore Chatterton.

————. Public Lands Records. Applications for Entry.

————. Public Lands Records. Minutes of the Arid Lands Board.

————. Public Lands Records. Minutes of the State Land Commission.

————. Secretary of State Records. Census of Wyoming.

————. Secretary of State Records. Inactive Corporation Files.

Wyoming State Engineer. Water Permit Applications.

Yale University, New Haven, Conn. Beinecke Rare Books and Manuscripts Library. Yale Collection of Western Americana. W. F. Cody (Buffalo Bill) Papers, MSS WA MSS S-197.

————. Nathan Salsbury Papers, YCAL MSS 17.

Yale University, New Haven. Sterling Library Manuscripts and Archives. Othniel C. Marsh Papers.

GOVERNMENT PUBLICATIONS

Mills, Captain Anson, Third Cavalry. *Report of the Big Horn Expedition, August 15 to September 30, 1874.* Independence Rock, Wyoming Territory, 1874.

Session Laws of the State of Wyoming passed by the Sixth State Legislature. Laramie, 1901.

United States Congress. 29 Stat. 434. Sundry Civil Appropriations for the Department of Interior. Act of June 11, 1896.

Williams, Mikel. *The History of Development and Current Status of the Carey Act in Idaho.* Idaho Department of Reclamation, 1970.

Wyoming State Board of Land Commissioners. *First Annual Report.* Cheyenne, 1896.

Wyoming State Engineer. *First Biennial Report of the State Engineer to the Governor of Wyoming.* Cheyenne, 1892.

————. *Second Biennial Report of the State Engineer to the Governor of Wyoming.* Cheyenne, 1895.

————. *Third Biennial Report of the State Engineer, 1895–1896.* Cheyenne, 1896.

NEWSPAPERS

Boston Evening Transcript, 1916.

Cody Enterprise, 1903–1910, 1946, 1969.

Cheyenne Leader, 1904.
Greybull Standard and Tribune, 1946.
Laramie Republican, 1904.
New York Banner Weekly, 1893.
New York Times, 1897, 1904, 1907, 1912, 1913, 1917.
New York Tribune, 1901, 1903, 1906.
Omaha World-Herald, 1911.
Northern Wyoming Herald, 1917.
Park County Enterprise, 1910–1921.
Powell Tribune, 1909.
Shoshone Valley News, 1896.
Wyoming Stockgrower and Farmer, 1902-1911.

BOOKS AND ARTICLES

Anderson, A[rchibald] A. *Experiences and Impressions: The Autobiography of Colonel A. A. Anderson*. New York: Macmillan, 1933.

Bartlett, Richard A. *From Cody to the World: The First Seventy-Five Years of the Buffalo Bill Memorial Association*. Cody, Wyo.: Buffalo Bill Historical Center, 1992.

Beard, Daniel Carter. *Hardly a Man Is Now Alive; The Autobiography of Dan Beard*. New York: Doubleday, Doran and Co., 1939.

Beecher, George Allen. *A Bishop of the Great Plains*. Philadelphia: Church Historical Society, 1950.

Belgrad, Daniel. "'Power's Larger Meaning': The Johnson County War as Political Violence in an Environmental Context." *Western Historical Quarterly* 33, 2 (2002): 159–77.

Blackstone, Sarah J. *The Business of Being Buffalo Bill: Selected Letters of William F. Cody, 1879–1917*. New York: Praeger, 1988.

Blair, Neal. *The History of Wildlife Management in Wyoming*. Cheyenne: Wyoming Game and Fish Department, 1987.

Bonner, Robert E. "Buffalo Bill Cody and Wyoming Water Politics." *Western Historical Quarterly* 33, 4 (2002): 433–51.

———. "Elwood Mead, Buffalo Bill Cody, and the Carey Act in Wyoming." *Montana: The Magazine of Western History* 55, 1 (2005): 36–51.

Borne, Lawrence R. *Dude Ranching: A Complete History*. Albuquerque: University of New Mexico Press, 1983.

———. *Welcome to My West: I. H. Larom: Dude Rancher, Conservationist, Collector*. Cody, Wyo.: Buffalo Bill Historical Center, 1982.

"Buffalo Bill." "Famous Hunting Parties of the Plains." *The Cosmopolitan* 17, 2 (June 1894): 131–43.

Carroll, Murray L. "Robert Foote: A Forgotten Wyoming Pioneer." *Annals of Wyoming* 74, 1 (2002), 9–23.

Chamberlin, Agnes, Jeannie Cook, and Joanita Monteith. *The Cody Club, 1900–1999*. Cody, Wyo.: Yellowstone Printing, 1999.

Cody, William F. *The Life of Hon. William F. Cody, known as Buffalo Bill*. Hartford: Frank E. Bliss, 1879; reprinted University of Nebraska Press, 1978.

Cody, W[illia]m F. (Buffalo Bill). "Preserving the Game." *The Independent* 53 (June 6, 1901): 1292–93.

Cook, Jeannie. *Wiley's Dream of Empire*. Cody, Wyo.: Yellowstone Printing Co., 1990.

Cook, Jeannie, Lynn Johnson Houze; Bob Edgar, and Paul Fees. *Buffalo Bill's Town in the Rockies: A Pictorial History of Cody, Wyoming*. Virginia Beach, Va: Donning Company, 1996.

Davies, Henry. *Ten Days on the Plains*. Dallas: Southern Methodist University Press, 1985. (Reprint of 1872 private publication.)

Day, Helene R. "The Prince Who Would Be Mayor: Albert of Monaco Hunts with Buffalo Bill." *American West* (Jan-Feb. 1985): 54–58.

Deloria, Philip J. *Playing Indian*. New Haven: Yale University Press, 1998.

Dunbar, Robert G. *Forging New Rights in Western Waters*. Lincoln: University of Nebraska Press, 1983.

Foote, Stella A., ed. *Letters from "Buffalo Bill."* Billings Mont.: Foote Publishing Co., 1954.

Frankfurt, Harry G. *On Bullshit*. Princeton: Princeton University Press, 2005.

Gates, Paul W. *History of Public Land Law Development*. Washington, D.C.: Public Land Law Review Commission, 1968.

———. "The Homestead Act: Free Land Policy in Operation, 1862–1935." In H.W. Ottoson, ed., *Land Use Policy and Problems in the United States*. Lincoln: University of Nebraska Press, 1963.

———. *The Jeffersonian Dream: Studies in the History of American Land Policy and Development*. Ed. Allan G. and Margaret B. Bogue. Albuquerque: University of New Mexico Press, 1996.

Gillette, Edward. *Locating the Iron Trail*. Boston: Christopher Publishing House, 1925.

Gould, Lewis. *Wyoming: A Political History, 1868–1896*. New Haven: Yale University Press, 1968.

Haglund, Kristine. "Buffalo Bill Cody Country." *The Westerner's Brand Book* 32, 6 (1975).

Harris, Burton. *John Colter: His Years in the Rockies*. New York: Charles Scribner's Sons, 1952; reprinted University of Nebraska Press, 1993.

Hassrick, Peter, and Melissa Webster. *Frederic Remington: A Catalogue Raisonné of Paintings, Watercolors and Drawings*. Cody, Wyo.: Buffalo Bill Historical Center, 1996.

Herman, Daniel J. *Hunting and the American Imagination*. Washington, D.C.: Smithsonian Institution Press, 2001.

Herman, Daniel J. "Hunting Democracy." *Montana: The Magazine of Western History* 55, 3 (2005): 22–33.

Hook, James W. "Seven Months in Cody, Wyoming, 1905–1906." *Annals of Wyoming* 26, 1 (1954): 3–24.

Hoxie, Fred. *Parading through History: The Making of the Crow Indian Nation in America, 1805–1935*. Cambridge: Cambridge University Press, 1995.

Jacoby, Karl. *Crimes against Nature: Squatters, Poachers, Thieves, and the Hidden History of American Conservation*. Berkeley: University of California Press, 2001.

Kasson, Joy S. *Buffalo Bill's Wild West: Celebrity, Memory, and Popular History*. New York: Hill and Wang, 2000.

Kensel, W. Hudson. *Pahaska Tepee: Buffalo Bill's Old Hunting Lodge and Hotel, a History, 1901–1946*. Cody, Wyo.: Buffalo Bill Historical Center, 1987.

King, Calvin L. *History of Wildlife in the Big Horn Basin of Wyoming*. Cheyenne: Pioneer Printing Co., n.d.

Kluger, James R. *Turning On Water with a Shovel: The Career of Elwood Mead*. Albuquerque: University of New Mexico Press, 1992.

Krupicka, Katrina. "Cody and Wanamaker: The Foundation of American Indian Citizenship." *Points West* (Winter 2003): 24–29.

Lee, Lawrence B. *Reclaiming the American West: An Historiography and Guide*. Santa Barbara: ABC-Clio, 1980.

Lender, Mark, and James Martin. *Drinking in America: A History*. New York: Free Press, 1982.

Lilley, William, and Lewis Gould. "The Western Irrigation Movement, 1879–1902." In Gene Gressley, ed., *The American West: a Reorientation*. Laramie: University of Wyoming Publications, 1966: 57–76.

Limerick, Patricia Nelson. *The Legacy of Conquest: The Unbroken Past of the American West*. New York: W. W. Norton, 1987.

Lindsay, Charles. *The Big Horn Basin*. Lincoln: University of Nebraska Press, 1932.

Lowe, James A. *The Bridger Trail*. Spokane: Arthur H. Clark Co., 1999.

MacDonald, Robert H. *Sons of the Empire: The Frontier and the Boy Scout Movement, 1880–1918*. Toronto: University of Toronto Press, 1993.

McLaird, James D. "Ranching in the Big Horns: George T. Beck, 1856–1894." *Annals of Wyoming* 39, 2 (1967): 157–85.

———. "Building the Town of Cody: George T. Beck, 1894–1943." *Annals of Wyoming* 40, 1 (1968): 73–105.

Morrill, Charles Henry. *The Morrills and Reminiscences*. Chicago and Lincoln: University Publishing Co., [1917].

Moses, Lester George. *Wild West Shows and the Images of American Indians, 1883–1933*. Albuquerque: University of New Mexico Press, 1996.

Murdoch, David Hamilton. *The American West: The Invention of a Myth*. Reno: University of Nevada Press, 2000.

Nelson, Paula M. *After the West Was Won: Homesteaders and Town-Builders in Western South Dakota, 1900–1917*. Iowa City: University of Iowa Press, 1986.

Nicholas, Liza J. *Becoming Western: Stories of Culture and Identity in the Cowboy State*. Lincoln: University of Nebraska Press, 2006.

Opie, John. *The Law of the Land*. Lincoln: University of Nebraska Press, 1994.

Overton, Richard C. *Burlington Route; A History of the Burlington Lines*. New York: Alfred A. Knopf, 1965.

Phillips, David R. *The West: An American Experience*. Chicago: Henry Regnery Co., 1973.

Pisani, Donald J. *To Reclaim a Divided West: Water, Law, and Public Policy, 1848–1902*. Albuquerque: University of New Mexico Press, 1992.

———. *Water and American Government: The Reclamation Bureau, National Water Policy, and the West, 1902–1935*. Berkeley: University of California Press, 2002.

Reiger, John. *American Sportsmen and the Origins of Conservation*. New York: Winchester Press, 1975.

Remington, Frederic. "Artist Wanderings among the Cheyennes." *Century* (Aug. 1889).

Rothman, Hal K. *Devil's Bargains: Tourism in the Twentieth-Century American West*. Lawrence: University Press of Kansas, 1998.

Rosa, Joseph G., and Robin May. *Buffalo Bill and His Wild West: A Pictorial Biography*. Lawrence: University Press of Kansas, 1989.

Roundy, Charles G. "The Origins and Early Development of Dude Ranching in Wyoming." *Annals of Wyoming*, vol. 45, no. 1 (Spring 1973): 5–25.

Runte, Alfred. *National Parks: The American Experience*. Lincoln: University of Nebraska Press, 1979.

Russell, Don. *The Lives and Legends of Buffalo Bill*. Norman: University of Oklahoma Press, 1960.

Rust, Mary J. M. *Historic Hotels of the Rocky Mountains*. Niwot, Col.: Roberts Rinehart, 1997.

Salvatore, Nick. *Eugene V. Debs: Citizen and Socialist*. Urbana: University of Illinois Press, 1982.

Samuels, Peggy, and Harold Samuels. *Frederic Remington*. Austin: University of Texas Press, 1982.

Schuchert, Charles, and Clara Mae LeVene. *O. C. Marsh, Pioneer in Paleontology*. New Haven: Yale University Press, 1940.

Seton, Ernest Thompson. *The Biography of a Grizzly*. New York: The Century Co., 1899.

Skowronek, Stephen. *Building a New American State: The Expansion of National Administrative Capacities, 1877–1920*. New York: Cambridge University Press, 1982.

Towne, Charles W. "A Preacher's Son on the Loose with Buffalo Bill Cody." *Montana: The Magazine of Western History* 18, 4 (1968): 40–55.

Trachtenberg, Alan. *The Incorporation of America: Culture and Society in the Gilded Age*. New York: Hill and Wang, 1982.

Trefethen, James B. *Crusade for Wildlife: Highlights in Conservation Progress*. New York: Boone and Crockett Club, 1961.

Van West, Carroll. *Capitalism on the Frontier: Billings and the Yellowstone Valley in the Nineteenth Century*. Lincoln: University of Nebraska Press, 1993.

Walter, R. F., and W. H. Code. "Elwood Mead." *Transactions of the American Society of Civil Engineers*, 102 (1937).

Warren, Louis S. *Buffalo Bill's America: William Cody and the Wild West Show*. New York: Alfred A. Knopf, 2005.

———. *The Hunter's Game: Poachers and Conservationists in Twentieth-Century America*. New Haven: Yale University Press, 1997.

Wasden, David J. *From Beaver to Oil: A Century in the Development of Wyoming's Big Horn Basin*. Cheyenne: Pioneer Printing, 1973.

Welch, Charles. *History of the Big Horn Basin*. Salt Lake City: Deseret News Publication, 1940.

Wetmore, Helen Cody. *The Last of the Great Scouts*. New York: Grosset and Dunlap, 1899.

White, G. Edward. *The Eastern Establishment and the Western Experience: The West of Frederic Remington, Theodore Roosevelt, and Owen Wister*. New Haven: Yale University Press, 1968.

White, Richard. "Frederick Jackson Turner and Buffalo Bill." In *The Frontier in American Culture*, ed. James R. Grossman. Berkeley: University of California Press, 1994: 7–65.

Winchester, Juti. "Work and More Work: A Seasonal Look at Buffalo Bill." *Points West Online* (Winter 2002).

Woodbury, Angus M. "History of Southern Utah and Its National Parks; Kaibab and North Rim." *Utah Historical Quarterly* (July–October 1944): 189–94.

Woods, Milton L. *Wyoming's Big Horn Basin: A Late Frontier*. Spokane: Arthur H. Clark, 1997.

Worster, Donald. *A River Running West: The Life of John Wesley Powell*. New York: Oxford University Press, 2001.

Yost, Nellie Snyder. *Buffalo Bill: His Family, Friends, Fame, Failures, and Fortunes*. Chicago: Swallow Press, 1979.

UNPUBLISHED WORKS

Historic Sheridan Inn advertisements, Sheridan Inn, Sheridan, Wyo.

Roberson, Betty Beck, and Jane Beck Johnson. "Beckoning Frontiers; A Footnote to American History." Deposited in the George Beck Collection, Park County Historical Society Archives, Cody, Wyo.

Wasden, David J. "The Beginning of the Cody Canal and Townsite." Deposited in the McCracken Library, Buffalo Bill Historical Center, Cody, Wyo.

Whiting, John. "Water Right Studies of the Shoshone Irrigation Project in Wyoming." U.S. Department of Interior, Bureau of Reclamation, 1953. Deposited in the Shoshone Irrigation District Archives, Powell, Wyo.

Index

of federal government, 217–21, 224; and
Indians, 239, 264–65; and Mormon
colonists, 116–19, 189–91; and the myth
of the West, 263–67; partner in Cody-
Salsbury Canal, 96–97, 117–18, 144,
184–89, 192, 194–202, 205, 209, 215–17;
patron of state officials, 91, 119–20, 128,
146, 149, 158–60, 162, 172, 185, 187,
190–91, 196, 229; politics, 42, 83, 147,
170, 178, 278n79; president of Shoshone
Irrigation Co., 41–42, 44, 46, 48, 64, 66,
69–89, 93–97, 100–115, 119–22, 124–25,
143–48, 150, 152–56; president of
Shoshone Land and Irrigation Co., 10,
13–16, 18, 20–40; public relations of,
200–201, 225–28, 231, 234, 237–38,
241–43, 246–47, 250–52, 257, 262–63,
265–66; rancher, 14, 15, 27, 95–96, 108,
112, 145, 174–79, 221–22, 237; relations
with USRS, 206–215, 217, 219, 221,
223–24, 265, 269; town father, 62–63,
108, 113, 124, 141, 223, 257–59, 263,
269–70; town founder, 49, 50, 52–60, 62,
64–67, 136; "white Indian," 141, 226–28,
234, 242, 252, 298n3, 298n6; and
Wyoming history, 256–57, 265–70; and
Wyoming tourism, 169–70, 174, 227,
239, 242–47, 250–53
Cody Canal, 14, 18, 24, 27, 29–30, 37, 48,
78–79, 145, 182, 184–85, 196, 202, 208,
216, 221, 233, 242, 250, 255–56, 260,
263; construction through 1896, 16, 30,
37, 40, 45; construction after 1896, 94,
96–101, 104–105, 109, 142–44, 146–47,
154; environmental problems, 41, 47,
93–98, 104–106, 111, 151; inadequacies,
130, 143–44, 147–49, 151, 156; inspec-
tions, 122–23, 143–44, 147–49; settlement, 25, 29, 35, 45, 75–82, 83–85,
86–88, 89, 138, 149, 154–55
Cody Canal Association, 151–53, 221
Cody Club, 124, 142, 207, 231–32, 259–60
Cody Enterprise [known as *Park County
Enterprise* after February, 1910], 114,

154, 165–67, 170–72, 201, 218, 222–23,
239, 250–51, 265
Cody Military College, 142, 157–62, 231,
247, 264
Cody-Salsbury Canal, 117, 133, 144, 160,
187–88; also known as "North side project," 96–97, 184, 187; conflict between
Wyoming and federal government,
197–201; construction and financing
difficulties, 190–96, 206, 212; relinquishment to State of Wyoming, 194–201,
223; transfer of water right to United
States, 202–203, 205, 211, 217; water
rights, 62, 184, 186–87, 193, 195, 200
Cody Trading Co., 109, 115, 259, 288n28
Cody, Wyo., 9, 44, 49, 197–98, 200–203,
206, 209–10, 215, 236, 256–58, 263;
advertising, 77, 79–81, 87, 140, 146,
159, 167, 225–26, 235, 238, 240, 252,
259–60; after arrival of railroad,
142, 259; Episcopal church, 67; first
founding ("Cody City"), 50, 52–55,
61; parks, 54, 60–61, 86–87; permanent
founding, 53–55, 279n21; Prince
Albert visit, 237–38; pro-saloon town,
218, 267, 279n5, 297n41; sale of the
townsite, 123, 136–37, 139–40, 142;
schools, 62, 66–67, 86–87, 100; sewerage, 169, 258; tourism, 243–46,
252–53, 259–60, 267–70; water supply,
59–60, 67, 95–97, 100, 105, 110–11,
135, 192, 222–23, 258
Coe, William Robertson, 236, 240; philanthropy, 237, 268
Colorado Springs, Colo., 52, 162
Corbett, Wyo., 135–36, 210
Cosmopolitan, 227, 230
Crow Indians, 5, 6, 49, 114, 128–29, 158,
237–38
Cunningham, Dennis, 13, 31, 70, 72

Darlington, Frank, 98–99, 163–64
Darrah, Hudson W., 106, 125, 287n41;
conflict with Shoshone Irrigation Co.